SELECTED PROSE

CHARLES LAMB, essayist, poet and letter writer, was born in the Inner Temple, London, in 1775. He was educated on a scholarship at Christ's Hospital, and there became friendly with Coleridge. In 1789 he started work as a clerk, first with a city merchant, then in 1791 at the South Sea House, and finally in 1792 with the accountant's office of the East India Company, where he remained until his retirement in March 1825. Lamb's personal life was a tragic one: in 1796 his sister, Mary, in a mad seizure stabbed their mother to death. Thereafter Lamb agreed to take responsibility for Mary, who relapsed for brief periods into bouts of madness.

Lamb's literary career began as a writer of poetry, and in 1794 he and Coleridge wrote sonnets for the *Morning Post*, and Lamb also had four sonnets in Coleridge's volume *Poems on Various Subjects* (1796) and more poems in the second edition (1797). He also wrote some plays which were notably unsuccessful; a romance, *Rosamund Gray* (1798), and, with his sister, various works for children, the *Tales from Shakespeare* (1807) being the most popular. His first work of criticism was *Specimens of the English Dramatic Poets Who Lived about the Time of Shakespeare* (1808), which, together with other important works of that time, stimulated the growing interest in the old English dramatic authors. In August 1820 he started contributing essays signed 'Elia' to the *London Magazine*, and in 1823 they were collected as *Essays of Elia*; another volume, *The Last Essays of Elia*, was published in 1833. Some of the best of Lamb's writing is to be found in his *Letters* (2 vols., 1848). Lamb's retirement from his 'official confinement' with the East India Company brought at first a sense of relief, then a gradual decline. During the later years of his life he and Mary (who died in 1847) moved to Enfield, where, missing the city and his friends, Lamb led a rather aimless and miserable life. He died in 1834.

·

ADAM PHILLIPS is an English child psychotherapist working in New York.

CHARLES LAMB

Selected Prose

EDITED BY ADAM PHILLIPS

PENGUIN BOOKS

Penguin Books Ltd, Harmondsworth, Middlesex, England
Viking Penguin Inc., 40 West 23rd Street, New York, New York 10010, U.S.A.
Penguin Books Australia Ltd, Ringwood, Victoria, Australia
Penguin Books Canada Ltd, 2801 John Street, Markham, Ontario, Canada L3R 1B4
Penguin Books (N.Z.) Ltd, 182–190 Wairau Road, Auckland 10, New Zealand

This edition first published 1985

For permission to reprint Charles Lamb's letters, thanks are due to the following:
Dent/Methuen, for material from *The Letters of Charles Lamb*,
edited by E. V. Lucas (1935); Cornell University Press, for material from
The Letters of Charles and Mary Anne Lamb, edited by E. W. Marrs (1975).
Charles Lamb's unpublished review of the first volume of Hazlitt's *Table Talk*
is reproduced by permission of the Henry W. and Albert A. Berg Collection
(Manuscript no. 220284B), the New York Public Library, Astor, Lenox
and Tilden Foundations.

Made and printed in Great Britain by
Richard Clay (The Chaucer Press) Ltd,
Bungay, Suffolk
Typeset in Monophoto Bembo

CONTENTS

ESSAYS AND SKETCHES (1821–7)   213

LETTERS   263

NOTE ON THE TEXT

The texts used in this selection are from:

Lucas, E. V. (ed.), *The Letters of Charles Lamb: To Which are Added Those of his Sister, Mary Lamb*, 3 vols., Dent and Methuen, 1935

Lucas, E. V. (ed.), *The Works of Charles and Mary Lamb*, 7 vols., Methuen, 1903–5

Macdonald, W. (ed.), *The Works of Charles Lamb*, 12 vols., Dent, 1903

Marrs, W., Jr (ed.), *The Letters of Charles and Mary Lamb*, Cornell University Press, 1975– (3 volumes published so far, covering the years from 1796 to 1817)

ACKNOWLEDGEMENT

I would like to thank the following people for their help:
Hugh Haughton, Jane Brodie, Simon Wood, James Harpur, Dom Hendricks
and Clive Panto.

INTRODUCTION

'Poor Lamb! Poor England, when such a despicable abortion is named genius!' Carlyle wrote in his diary after visiting Lamb in 1831. As a writer of appealing and slightly eccentric 'occasional' essays, Lamb endeared himself to late-Victorian and Edwardian readers. Although in his last years Lamb was by all accounts a sad caricature of the legend he was to inherit after his death, Carlyle was virtually unique for being quite uncharmed by him, distrusting the way he talked:

All must be packed up into epigrammatic contrasts, startling exaggerations, claptraps that will get a plaudit from the galleries! I have heard a hundred anecdotes about William Hazlitt for example; yet cannot by ever so much cross-questioning even form to myself the smallest notion of how it really stood with him. Wearisome, inexpressibly wearisome to me is that sort of clatter; it is not walking (to the end of time you would never advance, for these persons indeed have no whither); it is not bounding and frisking in graceful, natural joy; it is dancing – a St Vitus's dance . . . Charles Lamb I sincerely believe to be in some considerable degree insane . . . he is witty by denying truisms and abjuring good manners . . . Besides, he is now a confirmed, shameless drunkard.

Carlyle's contempt for Lamb is more finely perceptive than the generosity of some of his friends. The sense that there was, perhaps, something compulsively evasive about Lamb that was also indicative of a new, modern kind of sensibility goes some way to countering the legend that has exempted him from intelligent consideration. Writing to Marianne Hunt in 1823 Mary Shelley reports

a good saying of Lamb's: talking of someone he said, 'Now some men who are very veracious are called matter-of-fact men; but such an one I should call a matter-of-lie man.'

Writing his greatest essays under the enigmatic name of Elia, Lamb inherited the tradition of the eighteenth-century periodical essay of Addison, Steele and Johnson. Johnson, Lamb wrote, 'deals out opinion, which he would have you take for argument; and is perpetually ob-truding his own particular views of life for universal truths'. In his unpublished review of Hazlitt's *Table-Talk*, Lamb described the new essay in which particular views of life 'obtruded' only if they were represented as universal truths. It had required the invention of a fictitious persona, Steele's Isaac Bickerstaff, to allow 'still further licence in the delivery of . . . peculiar humours and opinions'. This 'further licence' characterized the *Essays of Elia*, with their variety, their wish to improvise and not to improve, and their flair for ordinary life, full of his 'peculiar humours and opinions'. Elia treated serious subjects, like the theories of history in 'A Dissertation upon Roast Pig', in a beguiling, apparently ingenuous way. In 'Grace before Meat', or 'A Bachelor's Complaint', he examined the arbitrary power of conventional views and manners with a disarming casualness, telling stories and alluding to bits and pieces of literature. The essays, like the letters, revealed not only Lamb's idiosyncratic reading but a vigorous moral intelligence that was always whimsically understated. His art made light of things. The invention of Elia released Lamb from the constraints of argument and universal truth, but it made the identity of Elia himself perplexing.

In what was to be a life of passionate and dutiful commitment there was the pleasure of being elusive. In 1796, at the age of twenty-one, Lamb returned home from work to find that his sister, Mary, had stabbed their mother to death. Ten years his senior, she had been nursing both their aged parents for some time, and the signs of strain were such that on the morning before the murder, Lamb had tried and failed to get a Dr Pitcairn to see Mary. As the *Morning Chronicle* reported, 'for a few days prior to this the family had observed some symptoms of insanity in her'. If the tragedy had occurred only three years later, under a new Act of Parliament Mary would have been imprisoned for life. As it was, in a characteristic reaction, and against the wishes of their elder brother, John, Lamb determined that she should not be sent away. Despite the coroner's verdict of lunacy, Lamb got permission from the parish authorities to take responsibility for her for the rest of his life. Nearly every year, from 1797 to Lamb's death in 1834, Mary relapsed for brief periods, sometimes months; during those years, as a consequence of her madness, they had to move house nearly a dozen times (see, for example, Letter 12).

Lamb started work in the South Sea Company in 1791, almost immediately after leaving school, and his devotion to Mary led him to work for thirty-three years of his adult life as a clerk in the East India Company. Unlike the friends for which he has become famous – Hazlitt, Wordsworth and Coleridge – all Lamb's working life was taken up by his routine employment; and all his writing, apart from the letters, was done after hours. It was the tragedy and duty of his life, with the apparently innocent charm of his writings, that gave Lamb what Roy Park has called 'the status of cultural teddy-bear in the Victorian Establishment'.

It is striking that the two stark facts of Lamb's life, Mary's madness and the actual nature of his work, are not documented in any detail, either by his contemporaries or by later writers. From early in the nineteenth century there was increasing interest in the lives and personalities of artists and a new market for biography. When Lewes and Talfourd, his first biographers, revealed after Mary's death in 1847 the actual harshness of Lamb's life, the legend was set. The *Life* tended to sentimentalize both his heroic oddness and his writings, isolating Lamb's domestic concerns from the rest of his life and the period in which he lived – a time of almost revolutionary social and political unrest in England. Lamb nearly always wrote for liberal, reformist editors and publishers. But there was now good reason why there appeared to be in Lamb's writings what Orwell describes in a different context as 'no attention to the urgent problems of the moment, above all no politics in the narrower sense'. Even when Lamb was attacked as an 'Anarchist', with Coleridge, Southey and Lloyd (by the magazine the *Anti-Jacobin*, in 1797), Lloyd wrote in Lamb's defence that he was 'a man too much occupied with real and painful duties – duties of high personal self-denial – to trouble himself about speculative matters'.

Lamb wrote finely of the risk that we might 'sink the existence of vice and misery in our speculations'; but there seemed a determination on the part of his admirers, however patronizing or implausible, that Lamb should be exempted from his time. On the one hand there were the horrors of his ordinary life, his sister's madness and the monotonous strain of his work; on the other there was his amusing, sometimes nostalgic charm as an essayist and exemplary friend, for whom the collecting and reading of literature was a relief from the reality of his circumstances. He became the man who, as Wilde said, 'had, undoubtedly, great sorrows, or motives for sorrow, but ... could console himself at a moment's notice for the real tragedies of life by reading any one of the Elizabethan tragedies, provided it was in a folio edition'. He was an embodiment of a Victorian ideal of heroic renunciation. Having read one of Lamb's letters, Thackeray is reported to have pressed it to his forehead with the words, 'Saint Charles!' Whether Lamb was silly or saintly, he was popular not as a writer but as the character suggested by his writings and reinvented within a coercive mythology of the writer as benign eccentric.

*

Lamb was born in the Temple in London in 1775. His paternal grandfather had been a cobbler, but his descendants on both sides seem to have been mostly servants or agricultural labourers. His father, John Lamb, had come to London from Lincoln as a young man, having been a footman in Bath. He became a waiter at the barristers' dinners in the Inner Temple Hall, and then worked for over fifty years as a general assistant to the barrister Samuel Salt, who became a Whig member of parliament. It was through Salt that Lamb was sponsored for a place at Christ's Hospital School, where he met Coleridge and made, at least in retrospect, a distinctive impression. His friend Valentine Le Grice wrote:

> I never heard his name mentioned without the addition of Charles, although as there was no other boy of the name of Lamb, the addition was unnecessary; but there was an implied kindness in it, and it was a proof that his gentle manners excited that kindness.

'Gentle' was a word that a number of people were drawn to use about Lamb, and to which he took exception when Coleridge referred to him as 'gentle-hearted Charles' in his poem 'This Lime-Tree Bower My Prison' ('the meaning of gentle is equivocal at best, and almost always means poor-spirited', as Lamb wrote back to him – see Letters 14 and 16). Since oratory was a crucial part of the entrance examinations, Lamb's stutter, coupled with his lack of finances, prevented him going up to university after school. Had he gone there, Wordsworth wrote, 'he would have probably been preserved from the indulgences of social humours and fancies which were often injurious to himself, and causes of severe regret to his friends'.

The accounts of Lamb by his contemporaries, from his schooldays onwards, stress three particular things about him: his great kindness, his lack of affectation and his considerable peculiarity, usually associated with his eccentric humour ('His jokes would be the sharpest thing in the world,' wrote Hazlitt, 'but that they are blunted by his good nature. He wants malice – which is a pity'). Lamb's infamous good nature, and the conviviality he writes about so brilliantly, created its own kind of demand on him. Every so often in the letters, the great pleasure he takes in his friends is interrupted by a feeling of harassment and a need for privacy. In 1806 he was driven to take a room to write in 'to avoid my nocturnal – alias *knock-eternal* – visitors'. One of the first writers to celebrate the anonymity of the city, Lamb also wrote of the intrusiveness of commercial city life which brought with it new needs for privacy and new anxieties about that privacy. Some of Lamb's less well-known essays (Edax, Hospita) glimpse at the rituals of genteel privacy with a fascination and sense of the bizarre that anticipate Dickens.

Keats complains of having been 'devastated and excruciated' by Lamb's 'bad and repeated puns', but after his death his friends insisted on the uniqueness of his humour which, as Proctor wrote in the *Athenaeum* in 1835, 'was not affected. It was a style, – a habit.' It was distinctive of Lamb's character. 'He could not enter a room without a joke,' George Dyer wrote, 'and he may be said to have almost conversed in extemporaneous humour.' For most of his life people seem to have enjoyed Lamb (see Appendix One), though there was clearly something unsettling about his love of the excessive and the inappropriate. An article in the *British Quarterly Review* for May 1848 told of

a whimsical recklessness which would occasionally beset him. To give an instance: he dined one day at the house of a friend of ours, and on entering the drawing-room after dinner, saw a gentleman standing in the middle of the room, whose bent shoulders, in school-boy leap-frog phrase, 'made a back'; the temptation was too great for Lamb, he placed his hands on the unconscious victim and flew over his head, to the astonished indignation of many and amusement of the few.

De Quincey writes of an evening in which Lamb fell asleep in his company:

On awaking from his brief slumber, Lamb sat for some time in profound silence, and then with most startling rapidity, sang out – 'Diddle, diddle, dumpkins'; not looking at me, but as if soliloquizing. For five minutes he relapsed into the same deep silence; from which again he started up into the same abrupt utterance of – Diddle, diddle, dumpkins. I could not help laughing aloud at the extreme energy of this sudden communication, contrasted with the deep silence that went before and followed. Lamb smilingly begged to know what I was laughing at, and with a look of as much surprise as if it were I that had done something unaccountable, and not himself.

Lamb's relish for punning suggests that there was something calculated about his absurd impulsiveness. He was also committed, by inclination, to a belief that being ridiculous was a form of intelligence. His 'love of Fools' has a subtlety beyond mere self-justification. He wrote in 'All Fools' Day':

I had more yearnings towards that simple architect, that built his house upon the sand, than I entertained for his more cautious neighbour ... I venerate an honest obliquity of understanding. The more laughable blunders a man shall commit in your company, the more tests he giveth you, that he will not betray or overreach you.

It is perhaps not extraordinary that a man who felt himself to be so appropriated, by his sister, by his work, by his friends, should come to love the inappropriate.

The combination of Lamb's stutter and his temperament gave this same abrupt, impromptu quality to his conversation. Elia often addresses the reader directly in the essays, and it is as though the reader is being talked to, but in a leisurely way. In company Lamb always talked in bursts. Coleridge, writing to Godwin, said that Lamb's taste

acts so as to appear like the unmechanic simplicity of an Instinct – in brief he is worth an hundred men of mere Talents. Conversation with the latter tribe is like the use of leaden bells – one warms by exercise – Lamb every now & then eradiates, & the beam, tho' single and fine as a hair, yet is rich with colours, & I both see & feel it.

Lamb's conversation was neither relentless nor rehearsed but almost inspired. Thomas Wainewright, a fellow contributor to the *London Magazine*, noticed that there was also something tricky and divisive about his conversation:

. . . if another began . . . he was liable to interrupt – or rather append, in a mode difficult to define, whether as misapprehensive or mischievous.

It sometimes seemed as though Lamb feared not being misunderstood. He certainly found the pressure of seriousness unbearable. 'It was at Godwin's that I met him, with Holcroft and Coleridge,' wrote Hazlitt, 'where they were disputing fiercely which was the best – Man as he was, or man as he is to be. "Give me," says Lamb, "man as he is not to be."'

Lamb himself spent some time in a madhouse in 1795, three years after starting at the East India House. Few details about this are known, apart from Lamb's own account in a letter and a revealing piece by his schoolfriend Le Grice (see Letter 1, note 4). The relative secrecy surrounding his sister's madness probably reflects how disreputable it seemed and how frightening it was. We get a glimpse in the letters of Lamb needing to get a strait-jacket for Mary when she breaks down on a journey, but he writes more often of how abject and lonely he feels when she is ill and has to go away. He occasionally writes about madness but shows no special interest in recording the details of Mary's condition. Proctor's *Memoir of Lamb*, published in 1866, provides the most vivid account of the kind of vigilance that was required of Lamb:

If any exciting talk occurred he had to dismiss his friend, with a whisper. If any stupor, or extraordinary silence was observed, then he had to rouse her instantly. He has been seen to take the kettle from the fire and place it for a moment on her head-dress to startle her into recollection. He lived in a state of constant anxiety . . .

Lamb, once he was at home, had to be consistently attentive to her mood, organizing their life together in a way that would protect her from too much excitement. It is possible that protecting her was a way of protecting himself from other things, and that the image of Lamb's devoted service to his sister overlooks the mutuality of need in their relationship. They certainly complemented each other in ways that Mary, at least, could allow herself to question. She once wrote:

I know my dismal faces have been almost as great a drawback upon Charles's comfort, as his feverish, teazing ways have been upon mine. Our love for each other has been the torment of our lives hitherto.

Lamb's only proposal of marriage, to the actress Fanny Kelly in 1819, was turned down (though he may not have known this) because of her fear of the madness in the family.

When his friend Proctor got married in 1824, Lamb wrote to him about his work:

I am married myself – to a severe step-wife, who keeps me, not at bed and board, but at desk and board, and is jealous of my morning aberrations. I cannot slip out to congratulate kinder unions. It is well she leaves me alone o' nights – the damn'd Day-hag *business*. She is even peeping over me to see I am writing no Love Letters. I come, my dear – where is the Indigo Sale Book?

Lamb's good-natured resentment about his working life prompted some of his finest inventiveness.

His attentiveness to Mary's mood at home was matched by the meticulousness of his accounting work for the East India Company. 'The Honourable East India Company', as it was then known, exploited its employees almost as much as its empire. During the period of Lamb's employment (1792–1825) it was a vastly influential trading company. Lamb's department audited the accounts of the indigo, tea, drugs and other commodities that poured into their warehouses to be sold off at auctions. Having met Lamb for the first time at his work, De Quincey gave one of the few descriptions of Lamb's office:

I was shown into a small room, or else a small section of a large one . . . in which was a very lofty writing desk, separated by a still higher railing from that part of the floor on which . . . the laity . . . were allowed to approach the clerus or clerkly rulers of the room. Within the railing sat, to the best of my re-membrance, six quill-driving gentlemen ... they were all too profoundly immersed in their oriental studies to have any sense of my presence.

De Quincey conveys a sense of the reverential hierarchy, the atmosphere of close concentration. For thirty-three years Lamb was immersed in his 'oriental studies'. He was increasingly obsessed, as the letters show, by the cost to his health, the lack of time to himself and his temperamental unsuitability for the over-careful, exacting work of accounting. In his office he had a copy of *Booth's Tables of Simple Interest*, a standard work on the subject, on the inside cover of which he wrote mock reviews of the book, including: 'This is a Book of great interest, but does not much engage our sympathy.' Sympathy was to be one of those words which Lamb would, in Coleridge's term, 'desynonymise'.

Though most of Lamb's published writing is more or less obliquely about coercion, the kind of essays he wrote (apart from 'The Good Clerk, A Character') tend to preclude direct engagement with the world of his work. He was writing, as he said, for 'the most untheorizing reader', and never made grandiose claims for the significance of his writings. He insisted that his real 'Works' could be found on the shelves of East India House: 'More MSS. in folio than ever Aquinas left, and full as useful!' Retirement through ill-health in 1825 from his 'official confinement', his '33 years' slavery', brought immense relief at first, then a gradual decline. The essays 'The Superannuated Man' and 'The Convalescent' were written at about this time. The nine and a half years of his retirement are a miserable record of Mary's frequent bouts of madness and Lamb's aimlessness. After moving out of London with Mary towards the end of his life, to Enfield, he missed 'the fresher air of the metropolis', the inverted pastoral of the city that he had been inventing over the years. Fonder, as he said, 'of Men sects than of insects', he needed his friends and his occupation.

'No good criticism of Lamb, strictly speaking, can ever be written,' Swinburne wrote in 1886, 'because nobody can do justice to his work who does not love it too well to feel himself capable of giving judgement on it.' This most damning of judgements speaks of the curious power of Lamb's writing, which, together with certain compelling details of Lamb's personal life, has thwarted any kind of critical reading of his work. It is part of Elia's complicity with the reader to disarm criticism. The assumption is not that his work wouldn't bear scrutiny, but that somehow one wouldn't want to scrutinize it. An unassertive writer, unallied to any obvious vested interests, Lamb has always satisfied his readers. Leigh Hunt, reviewing Lamb's first collected works of 1818, broached the problem only to go on to suggest its peculiar accomplishment:

> There is a spirit in Mr Lamb's productions which is in itself so anti-critical, and tends so much to reconcile us to all that is in the world, that the effect is almost neutralizing to everything but complacency and a quiet admiration . . . the author's genius [is] in fact of an anti-critical nature (his very criticism chiefly tending to overthrow the critical spirit . . .).

Hunt begins with the conviction that there is something smug about Lamb's acceptance of things as they are, but then feels, in a way that he can't quite formulate, that there is actually something rather undermining about Lamb's anti-critical criticism. It was the critical spirit, as one of the spirits of the age, that Lamb wrote against so inoffensively. And it is an appropriate irony that in the *Essays of Elia* he would turn his distrust of the definitive, imposing view into an aesthetic that would be virtually unacknowledged.

Having begun as a poet in Coleridge's company in the 1790s, Lamb went on in his spare time to write plays (which were notably unsuccessful); *Rosamund Gray*, a romance (1798) and, with his sister, various works for children: the *Tales from Shakespeare* (1807), in which Lamb 'did the tragedies', have been the most consistently popular of all his works. Unlike his contemporaries Coleridge, Hazlitt and Hunt, he never wrote from economic necessity, and what he did write was at the request of editors and friends. Lamb took a long time to find the style and form for his preoccupations, writing his first Essay of Elia for the *London Magazine* when he was forty-five. His talent, though, can be discerned earlier in the letters, with their particular inventive enthusiasm, and the echoes of his favourite authors – Sir Thomas Browne, Burton, Sterne, Shakespeare, and the lesser-known Elizabethan dramatists that Lamb made popular. ('The beauty of the world of words in that age,' he wrote, 'was in their being less definite than they are now, fixed and petrified.') Lamb's early 'imitations' of Robert Burton (1802) provide a preface in miniature to his later work, by imagining his critics who

> will blame, hiss, reprehende in many things, cry down altogether, my collections for crude, inept, putid . . . verbose, incrudite, and not sufficiently abounding in authorities *dogmata* sentences, of learneder writers which have been before me . . . judge of my labours to be nothing else than a messe of opinions.

With a sure sense of himself as 'nothing else than a messe of opinions',

Lamb turned the private, rambling, 'wit-melancholy' of the letters into the public form of the conversational essay that was personal, but not intimate; seemingly casual, but shrewdly mannered and allusive. With Elia, Lamb found a way of organizing with apparent ease the wonderfully coherent and lively prose of his best letters. His description of Captain Burney's household conveys Lamb's genial idea of order:

> a visiting place where every guest is so perfectly at his ease . . . where harmony is so strangely the result of confusion. Everybody is at cross-purposes, yet the effect is so much better than uniformity . . . the most perfect *concordia discors* you shall meet with.

Wary of an urbane wit, or a visionary confidence, it was part of Elia's persona to be self-possessed but often at cross-purposes with himself and other people.

In Lamb's letters there is an extraordinary responsiveness both to his own experience and to the presence of his individual correspondents. His early critical essays are preoccupied with the markedly unreceptive character of the contemporary audience for the arts. He puts this down to 'that accursed critical faculty, which, making a man the judge of his own pleasures, too often constitutes him the executioner of his own and others'. It is not the suspension of disbelief that Lamb is advocating, but of disapproval. What he observes of the audience in the boxes at the theatre is a new detachment:

> I see such frigid indifference, such unconcerned spectatorship, such impenetrability to pleasure or its contrary, such being in the house and yet not of it, certainly they come far nearer the nature of the Gods . . .

Elia would claim, nearly ten years later, that he could 'look with no indifferent eye upon things or persons', that he regarded indifference as a pretension.

Lamb's indignation about privileged attitudes is convincingly argued in the remarkable essays on Hogarth and Shakespeare that he was writing at the same time as some of the theatre criticism for which he became well known among contemporary actors and critics. The standards of taste imposed by the Academy consigned Hogarth to the status of a 'mere comic painter'. But Lamb identified their 'extreme narrowness of system alone', their 'rage for classification', as an organized denial of the conditions of the life of the time. It not only pre-empted any response to the pictures, it also numbed perception of life itself. As Lamb says, comparing Poussin's 'Plague at Athens' with Hogarth's 'Gin Lane', 'Disease, and Death, and bewildering Terror, in Athenian garments are endurable', whereas Hogarth is dismissed for his vulgar contemporary subject-matter. Hogarth was an important artist for Lamb because his prints 'prevent that disgust at common life ... which an unrestricted passion for ideal forms and beauties is in danger of producing'. Throughout his writing Lamb protected an idea of ordinariness, of common life, that was not merely drab, and which prompted Hazlitt's superbly simple compliment in *The Spirit of the Age* that 'his love of the actual does not proceed from a want of taste for the ideal'.

Hogarth gave Lamb the opportunity to elaborate what was to become an important idea for him: that great art was unfinished in the sense that it relied on the imaginative involvement of the audience to complete it. It was not something that by virtue of its perfection diminished its audience. It was not an idol but an invitation. He valued

imaginary work, where the spectator must meet the artist in his conceptions half-way; and it is peculiar to the confidence of high genius alone to trust so much to spectators or readers. Lesser artists show everything distinct and full, as they require an object to be made out to themselves before they can comprehend it.

In his best criticism Lamb insisted that although art employed artifice it should do so in order to suggest rather than to instruct. When we see Shakespeare's tragedies performed, the characters and scenes become visually distinct. This pre-empts the kind of imaginative involvement we feel when we read the plays. Lamb does not say that the plays cannot be performed, but that performance is a different kind of experience, one that too easily accommodates the intensity of feeling. There is something coercive in the very vividness of the acted play that can inure us to feeling by simplifying the complexities of character into definite people. 'How cruelly this operates upon the mind,' Lamb wrote, 'to have its free conceptions thus cramped and pressed down to the measure of a strait-lacing actuality.' There were the beginnings here, as in the other early pieces, of an aesthetic that was evolving out of Lamb's experience of the pressures of a 'strait-lacing actuality' and that would find its final, unfinished form in his greatest essay, 'Imperfect Sympathies'.

Though Lamb wrote very little in the years between these early essays and the great period of the *Essays of Elia* (1820–26), he must have acquired a considerable but mixed reputation by the time the *London Magazine* began on 1 January 1820. After the painter Haydon had recommended Lamb as a possible contributor, the editor, John Scott, wrote to Baldwin, the owner of the new magazine:

I should be very glad to have Mr Lamb as an auxiliary – but I have no real means of procuring him: and indeed I believe he is what is called a very idle man, – who hates trouble and above all a regular occupation.

Despite Scott's reservations, Lamb's contributions were secured and he was paid double the rate of the other contributors. Publishing what became Hazlitt's *Table-Talk*, De Quincey's *Confessions of an English Opium Eater*, as well as Lamb's *Essays of Elia*, the *London* was an influential literary success; but with a circulation of about 1,600 a month, far less than *Blackwoods* (its Tory rival in Edinburgh), it was not financially viable enough to last longer than a few years.

Scott's prospectus, and choice of contributor, pitched the new magazine as one in which he was 'not, on the whole, sorry, that our authors have rather suggested systems than engaged in them'. The writers for which the magazine became famous wrote idiosyncratic, often explicitly autobiographical pieces about a wide range of subjects. The titles of Hazlitt's essays – 'On Going a Journey', 'On the Ignorance of the Learned', 'On the Pleasures of Painting', 'On Living to Oneself', 'On the Fear of Death' – are all suggestive of general, unspecialized middle-class interests. Lamb's titles are more specific and often more quirky. Less intent than Hazlitt, more casual in his distractions and less fierce about his prejudices, Elia appeared as the most accessible and charmingly humorous of the London essayists. 'Who does not eulogize his writing,' his editor wrote, 'for displaying a spirit of deep and warm humanity, enlivened by a vein of poignant wit, – not caustic, yet searching.' Not everyone was pleased. The one hostile review of the first *Essays of Elia* in the *Monthly Magazine* complained of a 'disagreeable quaintness and affectation', a 'ridiculous puerility'. Others were more puzzled by Lamb's wit, what the *Monthly Review* called a 'rich but peculiar fund of drollery'. Trying to define this odd humour, the reviewer wrote of Lamb's 'original humour; – a sort of simple shrewdness and caustic irony, such as we have occasionally known to baffle, in the shape of a simple witness, some keen-set and veteran practitioner of the law'. It was a large part of Lamb's subtlety, in his life as in his writing, to charm people and yet in some way to unsettle their response to him. Like the simple witness, he loved to baffle people, especially people with any kind of militant intent or conviction.

Above all, the essays of Elia aroused interest without being divisively controversial. Unlike the essays of Hunt or Hazlitt, they rarely referred to contemporary events. They were original but harmless, excluding, as Marilyn Butler has written,

both the old Neo-classical posture of addressing the world in generalities in order to change it, and the modern Coleridgean posture of the literary man as sage, as extraordinary. Lamb's ordinariness made him in the 1820s ... his variant of the man of letters was the figure with which the middle-class readership could empathize.

It was precisely the ease with which this middle-class readership could empathize with Elia that made him so easy to dismiss ('The unthinking man in the street,' Denys Thompson pointed out contemptuously, 'shares a number of Lamb's tastes and interests – drink, gastronomy and smoking'). When Lamb created Elia as pen-name (or pun-name), he found the stamp of a recognizable but elusive character. Though he loved the essays of Plutarch and Montaigne because they 'imparted their own personal peculiarities to their themes', Lamb's essays expressed the personal peculiarities of a fictitious character. There was a certain cunning in his comment that 'the more my character becomes known, the less my veracity will come to be suspected'.

With the essay 'Imperfect Sympathies', however, Lamb found an implicit rationale for the character of his work in the description of a certain kind of temperament. Though couched in terms of the traditional distrust between Englishmen and Scotsmen, it is a vital document in the tradition (which includes Hazlitt and Keats) of benign scepticism about the mind's finalities; a spirit of inquiry that can trust its pleasure in the anomalous and the unfinished:

The owners of the sort of faculties I allude to, have minds rather suggestive, than comprehensive. They have no pretences to much clearness or precision in their ideas, or in their manner of expressing them ... Hints and glimpses, germs and crude essays at a system, is the utmost they pretend to ... They will throw out a random word in or out of season, and be content to let it pass for what it is worth ... They delight to impart their defective discoveries as they arise, without waiting for their full development.

It was most important to Lamb that people could be fools without being made fools of. Averse to knowingness and dogmatic assertion, dispirited by the way the decided view stifles the imagination, Lamb provides a celebration of the ordinary mind as reliably tentative, a new self-mocking egotism of whims and guesses, committed to a 'messe of opinions' rather than great explanations; an absolute belief, as he once wrote, that 'it is good to love the unknown'.

*

Although he warned Bernard Barton to be 'careless about the whimsies of such a half-baked notionalist' as himself (Letter 53), Lamb's letters and essays tend to have certain insistent preoccupations. There is an often erotic interest in food, and a fascination with the compulsive and the bizarre in people which demonstrates his love of individuality. There is a profound moral curiosity about generosity and indebtedness; about what people give to each other, and how gifts – whether of books, food or thoughts – can become thefts. Above all, there is a disarming robust and self-amused uncertainty about things.

His contemporary readers and acquaintances were never quite sure whether Lamb was evasive or not. De Quincey noted his 'propensity to mystify a stranger', but added that 'the very foundation of Lamb's peculiar character was laid in his absolute abhorrence of all affectation'. It is a compelling and curiously modern combination of qualities and is reflected in his writing. It was only at the end of his life that Lamb was described by his friends as mad. There is an evocative entry in Crabb Robinson's diary for 28 May 1832:

> I was reading Boccaccio when Lamb was again at my door. He however did not stay, but I made a cup of coffee for him. He had slept at Talfourd's again with his clothes on. Yet in the midst of this half crazy irregularity he was so full of sensibility that speaking of his sister he had tears in his eyes. He talked about his favourite poems with his usual warmth, praising Andrew Marvell extravagantly.

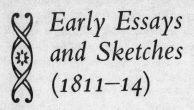

Early Essays and Sketches (1811–14)

ON THE GENIUS AND CHARACTER
OF HOGARTH

WITH SOME REMARKS ON A PASSAGE IN THE WRITINGS
OF THE LATE MR BARRY

ONE of the earliest and noblest enjoyments I had when a boy was in the contemplation of those capital prints by Hogarth, the *Harlot's* and *Rake's Progresses*, which, along with some others, hung upon the walls of a great hall in an old-fashioned house[1] in —shire, and seemed the solitary tenants (with myself) of that antiquated and life-deserted apartment.

Recollection of the manner in which those prints used to affect me, has often made me wonder, when I have heard Hogarth described as a mere comic painter, as one of those whose chief ambition was to *raise a laugh*. To deny that there are throughout the prints which I have mentioned circumstances introduced of a laughable tendency, would be to run counter to the common notions of mankind; but to suppose that in their *ruling character* they appeal chiefly to the risible faculty, and not first and foremost to the very heart of man, its best and most serious feelings, would be to mistake no less grossly their aim and purpose. A set of severer Satires (for they are not so much Comedies, which they have been likened to, as they are strong and masculine Satires) less mingled with any thing of mere fun, were never written upon paper, or graven upon copper. They resemble Juvenal, or the satiric touches in *Timon of Athens*.

I was pleased with the reply of a gentleman, who being asked which book he esteemed most in his library, answered, – 'Shakspeare:' being asked which he esteemed next best, replied, – 'Hogarth.' His graphic representations are indeed books: they have the teeming, fruitful, suggestive meaning of *words*. Other pictures we look at, – his prints we read.

In pursuance of this parallel, I have sometimes entertained myself with comparing the *Timon of Athens* of Shakspeare (which I have just mentioned) and Hogarth's *Rake's Progress* together. The story, the moral, in both is nearly the same. The wild course of riot and extravagance, ending in the one with driving the Prodigal from the society

of men into the solitude of the deserts, and in the other with conducting the Rake through his several stages of dissipation into the
still more complete desolations of the mad-house, in the play and in
the picture are described with almost equal force and nature. The
levee of the Rake, which forms the subject of the second plate in the
series, is almost a transcript of Timon's levee in the opening scene of
that play. We find a dedicating poet, and other similar characters, in
both.

The concluding scene in the *Rake's Progress* is perhaps superior to
the last scenes of *Timon*. If we seek for something of kindred excellence in poetry, it must be in the scenes of Lear's beginning madness,
where the King and the Fool and the Tom-o'-Bedlam conspire to
produce such a medley of mirth checked by misery, and misery
rebuked by mirth; where the society of those 'strange bed-fellows'
which misfortunes have brought Lear acquainted with, so finely sets
forth the destitute state of the monarch, while the lunatic bans of the
one, and the disjointed sayings and wild but pregnant allusions of the
other, so wonderfully sympathize with that confusion, which they
seem to assist in the production of, in the senses of that 'child-changed
father.'

In the scene in Bedlam, which terminates the *Rake's Progress*, we find
the same assortment of the ludicrous with the terrible. Here is desperate
madness, the overturning of originally strong thinking faculties, at
which we shudder, as we contemplate the duration and pressure of
affliction which it must have asked to destroy such a building; – and
here is the gradual hurtless lapse into idiocy, of faculties, which at their
best of times never having been strong, we look upon the consummation
of their decay with no more pity than is consistent with a smile. The
mad taylor, the poor driveller that has gone out of his wits (and truly he
appears to have had no great journey to go to get past their confines) for
the love of *Charming Betty Careless*, – these half-laughable, scarce-pitiable
objects take off from the horror which the principal figure would of
itself raise, at the same time that they assist the feeling of the scene by
contributing to the general notion of its subject: –

> Madness, thou chaos of the brain,
> What art, that pleasure giv'st, and pain?
> Tyranny of Fancy's reign!
> Mechanic Fancy, that can build
> Vast labyrinths and mazes wild,

> With rule disjointed, shapeless measure,
> Fill'd with horror, fill'd with pleasure!
> Shapes of horror, that would even
> Cast doubts of mercy upon Heaven.
> Shapes of pleasure, that, but seen,
> Would split the shaking sides of Spleen.*

Is it carrying the spirit of comparison to excess to remark, that in the poor kneeling weeping female, who accompanies her seducer in his sad decay, there is something analogous to Kent, or Caius, as he delights rather to be called, in *Lear*, – the noblest pattern of virtue which even Shakspeare has conceived, – who follows his royal master in banishment, that had pronounced *his* banishment, and forgetful at once of his wrongs and dignities, taking on himself the disguise of a menial, retains his fidelity to the figure, his loyalty to the carcass, the shadow, the shell and empty husk of Lear?

In the perusal of a book, or of a picture, much of the impression which we receive depends upon the habit of mind which we bring with us to such perusal. The same circumstance may make one person laugh, which shall render another very serious; or in the same person the first impression may be corrected by after-thought. The misemployed incongruous characters at the *Harlot's Funeral*, on a superficial inspection, provoke to laughter; but when we have sacrificed the first emotion to levity, a very different frame of mind succeeds, or the painter has lost half his purpose. I never look at that wonderful assemblage of depraved beings, who, without a grain of reverence or pity in their perverted minds, are performing the sacred exteriors of duty to the relics of their departed partner in folly, but I am as much moved to sympathy from the very want of it in them, as I should be by the finest representation of a virtuous death-bed surrounded by real mourners, pious children, weeping friends, – perhaps more by the very contrast. What reflexions does it not awake, of the dreadful heartless state in which the creature (a female too) must have lived, who in death wants the accompaniment of one genuine tear. That wretch who is removing the lid of the coffin to gaze upon the corpse with a face which indicates a perfect negation of all goodness or womanhood – the hypocrite parson and his demure partner – all the fiendish group – to a thoughtful mind present a moral emblem more affecting than if the poor friendless carcass had been depicted as thrown out to the woods, where

* Lines inscribed under the plate.

wolves had assisted at its obsequies, itself furnishing forth its own funeral banquet.

It is easy to laugh at such incongruities as are met together in this picture, – incongruous objects being of the very essence of laughter, – but surely the laugh is far different in its kind from that thoughtless species to which we are moved by mere farce and grotesque. We laugh when Ferdinand Count Fathom,[2] at the first sight of the white cliffs of Britain, feels his heart yearn with filial fondness towards the land of his progenitors, which he is coming to fleece and plunder, – we smile at the exquisite irony of the passage, – but if we are not led on by such passages to some more salutary feeling than laughter, we are very negligent perusers of them in book or picture.

It is the fashion with those who cry up the great Historical School in this country, at the head of which Sir Joshua Reynolds is placed, to exclude Hogarth from that school, as an artist of an inferior and vulgar class. Those persons seem to me to confound the painting of subjects in common or vulgar life with the being a vulgar artist. The quantity of thought which Hogarth crowds into every picture would alone *unvulgarize* every subject which he might choose. Let us take the lowest of his subjects, the print called *Gin Lane*. Here is plenty of poverty and low stuff to disgust upon a superficial view; and accordingly, a cold spectator feels himself immediately disgusted and repelled. I have seen many turn away from it, not being able to bear it. The same persons would perhaps have looked with great complacency upon Poussin's celebrated picture of the *Plague at Athens.** Disease and Death and bewildering Terror, in *Athenian garments* are endurable, and come, as the delicate critics express it, within the 'limits of pleasurable sensation.' But the scenes of their own St Giles's, delineated by their own countryman, are too shocking to think of. Yet if we could abstract our minds from the fascinating colours of the picture, and forget the coarse execution (in some respects) of the print, intended as it was to be a cheap plate, accessible to the poorer sort of people, for whose instruction it was done, I think we could have no hesitation in conferring the palm of superior genius upon Hogarth, comparing this work of his with Poussin's picture. There is more of imagination in it – that power which draws all things to one, – which makes things animate and inanimate, beings with their attributes, subjects and their accessaries, take one colour, and serve to one effect. Every thing in the print, to use a vulgar

* At the late Mr Hope's, in Cavendish Square.

expression, *tells*. Every part is full of 'strange images of death.' It is perfectly amazing and astounding to look at. Not only the two prominent figures, the woman and the half-dead man, which are as terrible as any thing which Michael Angelo ever drew, but every thing else in the print contributes to bewilder and stupefy, – the very houses, as I heard a friend of mine express it, tumbling all about in various directions, seem drunk – seem absolutely reeling from the effect of that diabolical spirit of phrenzy which goes forth over the whole composition. – To show the poetical and almost prophetical conception in the artist, one little circumstance may serve. Not content with the dying and dead figures, which he has strewed in profusion over the proper scene of the action, he shows you what (of a kindred nature) is passing beyond it. Close by the shell, in which, by direction of the parish beadle, a man is depositing his wife, is an old wall, which, partaking of the universal decay around it, is tumbling to pieces. Through a gap in this wall are seen three figures, which appear to make a part in some funeral procession which is passing by on the other side of the wall, out of the sphere of the composition. This extending of the interest beyond the bounds of the subject could only have been conceived by a great genius. Shakspeare, in his description of the painting of the Trojan War, in his *Tarquin and Lucrece*, has introduced a similar device, where the painter made a part stand for the whole: –

> For much imaginary work was there,
> Conceit deceitful, so compact, so kind,
> That for Achilles' image stood his spear,
> Grip'd in an armed hand; himself behind
> Was left unseen, save to the eye of mind:
> A hand, a foot, a face, a leg, a head,
> Stood for the whole to be imagined.

This he well calls *imaginary work*, where the spectator must meet the artist in his conceptions half way; and it is peculiar to the confidence of high genius alone to trust so much to spectators or readers. Lesser artists shew every thing distinct and full, as they require an object to be made out to themselves before they can comprehend it.

When I think of the power displayed in this (I will not hesitate to say) sublime print, it seems to me the extreme narrowness of system alone, and of that rage for classification, by which, in matters of taste at least, we are perpetually perplexing instead of arranging our ideas, that would make us concede to the work of Poussin above-mentioned, and deny to this of Hogarth, the name of a grand serious composition.

We are for ever deceiving ourselves with names and theories. We call one man a great historical painter, because he has taken for his subjects kings or great men, or transactions over which time has thrown a grandeur. We term another the painter of common life, and set him down in our minds for an artist of an inferior class, without reflecting whether the quantity of thought shewn by the latter may not much more than level the distinction which their mere choice of subjects may seem to place between them; or whether, in fact, from that very common life a great artist may not extract as deep an interest as another man from that which we are pleased to call history.

I entertain the highest respect for the talents and virtues of Reynolds, but I do not like that his reputation should overshadow and stifle the merits of such a man as Hogarth, nor that to mere names and classifications we should be content to sacrifice one of the greatest ornaments of England.

I would ask the most enthusiastic admirer of Reynolds, whether in the countenances of his *Staring* and *Grinning Despair*, which he has given us for the faces of Ugolino and dying Beaufort, there be any thing comparable to the expression which Hogarth has put into the face of his broken-down rake in the last plate but one of the *Rake's Progress*,* where a letter from the manager is brought to him to say that his play 'will not do'? Here all is easy, natural, undistorted, but withal what a mass of woe is here accumulated! – the long history of a mis-spent life is compressed into the countenance as plainly as the series of plates before had told it; here is no attempt at Gorgonian looks which are to freeze the beholder, no grinning at the antique bed-posts, no face-making, or consciousness of the presence of spectators in or out of the picture, but grief kept to a man's self, a face retiring from notice with the shame which great anguish sometimes brings with it, – a final leave taken of hope, – the coming on of vacancy and stupefaction, – a beginning alienation of mind looking like tranquillity. Here is matter for the mind of the beholder to feed on for the hour together, – matter to feed and fertilize the mind. It is too real to admit one thought about the power of the artist who did

---

* The first perhaps in all Hogarth for serious expression. That which comes next to it, I think, is the jaded morning countenance of the debauchée in the second plate of the *Marriage Alamode*, which lectures on the vanity of pleasure as audibly as any thing in Ecclesiastes.

it. – When we compare the expression in subjects which so fairly admit of comparison, and find the superiority so clearly to remain with Hogarth, shall the mere contemptible difference of the scene of it being laid in the one case in our Fleet or King's Bench Prison, and in the other in the State Prison of Pisa, or the bed-room of a cardinal, – or that the subject of the one has never been authenticated, and the other is matter of history, – so weigh down the real points of the comparison, as to induce us to rank the artist who has chosen the one scene or subject (though confessedly inferior in that which constitutes the soul of his art) in a class from which we exclude the better genius (who has happened to make choice of the other) with something like disgrace?*

The *Boys under Demoniacal Possession* of Raphael and Dominichino, by what law of classification are we bound to assign them to belong to the great style in painting, and to degrade into an inferior class the Rake of Hogarth when he is the Madman in the Bedlam scene? I am sure he is far more impressive than either. It is a face which no one that has seen can easily forget. There is the stretch of human suffering to the utmost endurance, severe bodily pain brought on by strong mental agony, the frightful obstinate laugh of madness, – yet all so unforced and natural, that those who never were witness to madness in real life, think they see nothing but what is familiar to them in this face. Here are no tricks of distortion, nothing but the natural face of agony. This is high tragic painting, and we might as well deny to Shakspeare the honours of a great tragedian, because he has interwoven scenes of mirth with the serious business of his plays, as refuse to Hogarth the same praise for the two concluding scenes of the *Rake's Progress*, because of the Comic

* Sir Joshua Reynolds, somewhere in his lectures,[3] speaks of the *presumption* of Hogarth in attempting the grand style in painting, by which he means his choice of certain Scripture subjects. Hogarth's excursions into Holy Land were not very numerous, but what he has left us in this kind have at least this merit, that they have expression of *some sort or other* in them, – the *Child Moses before Pharaoh's Daughter*, for instance: which is more than can be said of Sir Joshua Reynolds' *Repose in Egypt*, printed for Macklin's Bible, where for a Madonna he has substituted a sleepy, insensible, unmotherly girl, one so little worthy to have been selected as the Mother of the Saviour, that she seems to have neither heart nor feeling to entitle her to become a mother at all. But indeed the race of Virgin Mary painters seems to have been cut up, root and branch, at the Reformation. Our artists are too good Protestants to give life to that admirable commixture of maternal tenderness with reverential awe and wonder approaching to worship, with which the Virgin Mothers of L. da Vinci and Raphael (themselves by their divine countenances inviting men to worship) contemplate the union of the two natures in the person of their Heaven-born Infant.

Lunatics* which he has thrown into the one, or the Alchymist that he has introduced in the other, who is paddling in the coals of his furnace, keeping alive the flames of vain hope within the very walls of the prison to which the vanity has conducted him, which have taught the darker lesson of extinguished hope to the desponding figure who is the principal person of the scene.

It is the force of these kindly admixtures, which assimilates the scenes of Hogarth and of Shakspeare to the drama of real life, where no such thing as pure tragedy is to be found; but merriment and infelicity, ponderous crime and feather-light vanity, like twi-formed births, disagreeing complexions of one inter-texture, perpetually unite to shew forth motley spectacles to the world. Then it is that the poet or painter shows his art, when in the selection of these comic adjuncts he chooses such circumstances as shall relieve, contrast with, or fall into, without forming a violent opposition to, his principal object. Who sees not that the Grave-digger in *Hamlet*, the Fool in *Lear*, have a kind of correspondency to, and fall in with, the subjects which they seem to interrupt, while the comic stuff in *Venice Preserved*, and the doggrel nonsense of the Cook and his poisoning associates in the *Rollo* of Beaumont and Fletcher, are pure, irrelevant, impertinent discords, – as bad as the quarrelling dog and cat under the table of the *Lord and the Disciples at Emmaus* of Titian?

Not to tire the reader with perpetual reference to prints which he may not be fortunate enough to possess, it may be sufficient to remark, that the same tragic cast of expression and incident, blended in some instances with a greater alloy of comedy, characterizes his other great work, the *Marriage Alamode*, as well as those less elaborate exertions of his genius, the prints called *Industry* and *Idleness*, the *Distrest Poet*, &c. forming, with the *Harlot's* and *Rake's Progresses*, the most considerable if not the largest class of his productions, – enough surely to rescue Hogarth from the imputation of being a mere buffoon, or one whose general aim was only to *shake the sides*.

---

* There are of madmen, as there are of tame,
  All humour'd not alike. We have here some
  So apish and fantastic, play with a feather;
  And though 'twould grieve a soul to see God's image
  So blemish'd and defac'd, yet do they act
  Such antick and such pretty lunacies,
  That, spite of sorrow, they will make you smile.
  Others again we have, like angry lions,
  Fierce as wild bulls, untameable as flies.

            Honest Whore.[4]

There remains a very numerous class of his performances, the object of which must be confessed to be principally comic. But in all of them will be found something to distinguish them from the droll productions of Bunbury[5] and others. They have this difference, that we do not merely laugh at, we are led into long trains of reflection by them. In this respect they resemble the characters of Chaucer's *Pilgrims*, which have strokes of humour in them enough to designate them for the most part as comic, but our strongest feeling still is wonder at the comprehensiveness of genius which could crowd, as poet and painter have done, into one small canvas so many diverse yet co-operating materials.

The faces of Hogarth have not a mere momentary interest, as in caricatures, or those grotesque physiognomies which we sometimes catch a glance of in the street, and, struck with their whimsicality, wish for a pencil and the power to sketch them down; and forget them again as rapidly, – but they are permanent abiding ideas. Not the sports of nature, but her necessary eternal classes. We feel that we cannot part with any of them, lest a link should be broken.

It is worthy of observation, that he has seldom drawn a mean or insignificant countenance.* Hogarth's mind was eminently reflective; and, as it has been well observed of Shakspeare, that he has transfused his own poetical character into the persons of his drama (they are all more or less *poets*,) Hogarth has impressed a *thinking character* upon the persons of his canvas. This remark must not be taken universally. The exquisite idiotism of the little gentleman in the bag and sword beating his drum in the print of the *Enraged Musician*, would of itself rise up against so sweeping an assertion. But I think it will be found to be true of the generality of his countenances. The knife-grinder and Jew flute-player in the plate just mentioned, may serve as instances instead of a thousand. They have intense thinking faces, though the purpose to which they are subservient by no means required it; but indeed it seems as if it was painful to Hogarth to contemplate mere vacancy or insignificance.

This reflection of the artist's own intellect from the faces of his characters, is one reason why the works of Hogarth, so much more than those of any other artist, are objects of meditation. Our intellectual

* If there are any of that description, they are in his *Strolling Players*, a print which has been cried up by Lord Orford as the richest of his productions, and it may be, for what I know, in the mere lumber, the properties, and dead furniture of the scene, but in living character and expression it is (for Hogarth) lamentably poor and wanting; it is perhaps the only one of his performances at which we have a right to feel disgusted.

natures love the mirror which gives them back their own likenesses. The mental eye will not bend long with delight upon vacancy.

Another line of eternal separation between Hogarth and the common painters of droll or burlesque subjects, with whom he is often confounded, is the sense of beauty, which in the most unpromising subjects seems never wholly to have deserted him. 'Hogarth himself,' says Mr Coleridge,* from whom I have borrowed this observation, speaking of a scene which took place at Ratzeburg, 'never drew a more ludicrous distortion, both of attitude and physiognomy, than this effect occasioned: nor was there wanting beside it one of those beautiful female faces which the same Hogarth, *in whom the satirist never extinguished that love of beauty which belonged to him as a poet,* so often and so gladly introduces as the central figure in a crowd of humorous deformities, which figure (such is the power of true genius) neither acts nor is meant to act as a contrast; but diffuses through all, and over each of the group, a spirit of reconciliation and human kindness; and even when the attention is no longer consciously directed to the cause of this feeling, still blends its tenderness with our laughter: and *thus prevents the instructive merriment at the whims of nature, or the foibles or humours of our fellow-men, from degenerating into the heart-poison of contempt or hatred.*' To the beautiful females in Hogarth, which Mr C. has pointed out, might be added, the frequent introduction of children (which Hogarth seems to have taken a particular delight in) into his pieces. They have a singular effect in giving tranquillity and a portion of their own innocence to the subject. The baby riding in its mother's lap in the *March to Finchley,* (its careless innocent face placed directly behind the intriguing time-furrowed countenance of the treason–plotting French priest) perfectly sobers the whole of that tumultuous scene. The boy mourner winding up his top with so much unpretending insensibility in the plate of the *Harlot's Funeral,* (the only thing in that assembly that is not a hypocrite) quiets and soothes the mind that has been disturbed at the sight of so much depraved man and woman kind.

I had written thus far, when I met with a passage in the writings of the late Mr Barry,[6] which, as it falls in with the *vulgar notion* respecting Hogarth, which this Essay has been employed in combating, I shall take the liberty to transcribe, with such remarks as may suggest themselves to me in the transcription; referring the reader for a full answer to that which has gone before.

* *The Friend,* No. XVI.

Notwithstanding Hogarth's merit does undoubtedly entitle him to an honourable place among the artists, and that his little compositions, considered as so many dramatic representations, abounding with humour, character, and extensive observations on the various incidents of low, faulty, and vicious life, are very ingeniously brought together, and frequently tell their own story with more facility than is often found in many of the elevated and more noble inventions of Rafaelle, and other great men; yet it must be honestly confessed, that in what is called knowledge of the figure, foreigners have justly observed, that Hogarth is often so raw and unformed, as hardly to deserve the name of an artist. But this capital defect is not often perceivable, as examples of the naked and of elevated nature but rarely occur in his subjects, which are for the most part filled with characters, that in their nature tend to deformity; besides, his figures are small, and the jonctures, and other difficulties of drawing that might occur in their limbs, are artfully concealed with their clothes, rags, &c. But what would atone for all his defects, even if they were twice told, is his admirable fund of invention, ever inexhaustible in its resources; and his satyr, which is always sharp and pertinent, and often highly moral, was (except in a few instances, where he weakly and meanly suffered his integrity to give way to his envy) seldom or never employed in a dishonest or unmanly way. Hogarth has been often imitated in his satirical vein, sometimes in his humorous; but very few have attempted to rival him in his moral walk. The line of art pursued by my very ingenious predecessor and brother academician, Mr Penny, is quite distinct from that of Hogarth, and is of a much more delicate and superior relish; he attempts the heart, and reaches it, whilst Hogarth's general aim is only to shake the sides; in other respects no comparison can be thought of, as Mr Penny has all that knowledge of the figure and academical skill, which the other wanted. As to Mr Bunbury, who had so happily succeeded in the vein of humour and caricatura, he has for some time past altogether relinquished it, for the more amiable pursuit of beautiful nature: this, indeed, is not to be wondered at, when we recollect that he has, in Mrs Bunbury, so admirable an exemplar of the most finished grace and beauty continually at his elbow. But (to say all that occurs to me on this subject) perhaps it may be reasonably doubted, whether the being much conversant with Hogarth's method of exposing meanness, deformity, and vice, in many of his works, is not rather a dangerous, or, at least, a worthless pursuit; which, if it does not find a false relish and a love of and search after satyr and buffoonery in the spectator, is at least not unlikely to give him one. Life is short; and the little leisure of it is much better laid out upon that species of art which is employed about the amiable and the admirable, as it is more likely to be attended with better and nobler consequences to ourselves. These two pursuits in art may be compared with two sets of people with whom we might associate: if we give ourselves up to the Foots, the Kenricks,[7] &c. we shall be continually busied and paddling in whatever is ridiculous, faulty, and vicious in life; whereas there are those to be found with whom we should be in the constant pursuit and study of all that gives a value and a dignity to human nature. [Account of a Series of Pictures in the Great Room of the Society of Arts, Manufactures, and Commerce, at the Adelphi, by James Barry, R.A., Professor of Painting to the Royal Academy; reprinted in the last quarto edition of his works.]

'– It must be honestly confessed, that in what is called knowledge of the figure, foreigners have justly observed,' &c.

It is a secret well known to the professors of the art and mystery of criticism, to insist upon what they do not find in a man's works, and to pass over in silence what they do. That Hogarth did not draw the naked figure so well as Michael Angelo might be allowed, especially as 'examples of the naked,' as Mr Barry acknowledges, 'rarely (he might almost have said never) occur in his subjects;' and that his figures under their draperies do not discover all the fine graces of an Antinous or an Apollo, may be conceded likewise; perhaps it was more suitable to his purpose to represent the average forms of mankind in the mediocrity (as Mr Burke [8] expresses it) of the age in which he lived: but that his figures in general, and in his best subjects, are so glaringly incorrect as is here insinuated, I dare trust my own eye so far as positively to deny the fact. And there is one part of the figure in which Hogarth is allowed to have excelled, which these foreigners seem to have overlooked, or perhaps calculating from its proportion to the whole (a seventh or an eighth, I forget which) deemed it of trifling importance; I mean the human face; a small part, reckoning by geographical inches, in the map of man's body, but here it is that the painter of expression must condense the wonders of his skill, even at the expense of neglecting the 'jonctures and other difficulties of drawing in the limbs,' which it must be a cold eye that in the interest so strongly demanded by Hogarth's countenances has leisure to survey and censure.

'The line of art pursued by my very ingenious predecessor and brother academician, Mr Penny.'

The first impression caused in me by reading this passage, was an eager desire to know who this Mr Penny was. This great surpasser of Hogarth in the 'delicacy of his relish,' and the 'line which he pursued,' where is he, what are his works, what has he to shew? In vain I tried to recollect, till by happily putting the question to a friend who is more conversant in the works of the illustrious obscure than myself, I learnt that he was the painter of a *Death of Wolfe* which missed the prize the year that the celebrated picture of West on the same subject obtained it; that he also made a picture of the *Marquis of Granby relieving a Sick Soldier*; moreover, that he was the inventor of two pictures of *Suspended and Restored Animation*, which I now remember to have seen in the Exhibition some years since, and the prints from which are still extant in good men's houses. This then, I suppose, is the line of subjects in which Mr Penny was so much superior to Hogarth. I confess I am not of that opinion. The relieving of poverty by the purse, and the restoring of a young man to his parents by using the methods prescribed by the Humane Society, are doubtless very amiable subjects, pretty things to teach the first rudiments of humanity; they amount to about as much instruction as the stories of good boys that give away their custards to poor beggar-boys in children's books. But, good God! is this *milk for babes* to be set up in opposition to Hogarth's moral scenes, his *strong meat for men?* As well might we prefer the fulsome verses upon their own goodness, to which the gentlemen of the Literary Fund annually sit still with such shameless patience to listen, to the satires of Juvenal and Persius; because the former are full of tender images of Worth relieved by Charity, and Charity stretching out her hand to rescue sinking Genius, and the theme of the latter is men's crimes and follies with their black consequences — forgetful meanwhile of those strains of moral pathos, those sublime heart-touches, which these poets (in *them* chiefly showing themselves poets) are perpetually darting across the otherwise appalling gloom of their subject — consolatory remembrancers, when their pictures of guilty mankind have made us even to despair for our species, that there is such a thing as virtue and moral dignity in the world, that her unquenchable spark is not utterly out — refreshing admonitions, to which we turn for shelter from the too great heat and asperity of the general satire.

And is there nothing analogous to this in Hogarth? nothing which 'attempts and reaches the heart?' — no aim beyond that of 'shaking the sides?' — If the kneeling ministering female in the last scene of the *Rake's Progress*, the Bedlam scene, of which I have spoken before, and have dared almost to parallel it with the most absolute idea of Virtue which Shakspeare has left us, be not enough to disprove the assertion; if the sad endings of the Harlot and the Rake, the passionate heart-bleeding en-treaties for forgiveness which the adulterous wife is pouring forth to her assassinated and dying lord in the last scene but one of the *Marriage Alamode*, — if these be not things to touch the heart, and dispose the mind to a meditative tenderness: is there nothing sweetly conciliatory in the mild, patient face and gesture with which the wife seems to allay and ventilate the feverish irritated feelings of her poor poverty-distracted mate (the true copy of the *genus irritabile*) in the print of the *Distrest Poet?* or if an image of maternal love be required, where shall we find a sublimer view of it than in that aged woman in *Industry and Idleness* (plate V.) who is clinging with the fondness of hope not quite extinguished to her brutal vice-hardened child, whom she is accompanying to the ship which is to bear him away from his native soil, of which he has been adjudged unworthy: in whose shocking face every trace of the human countenance seems obliterated, and a brute beast's to be left instead, shocking and repulsive to all but her who watched over it in his cradle before it was so sadly altered, and feels it must belong to her while a pulse by the vindictive laws of his country shall be suffered to continue to beat in it. Compared with such things, what is Mr Penny's 'knowledge of the figure and academical skill which Hogarth wanted?'

With respect to what follows concerning another gentleman, with the congratulations to him on his escape out of the regions of 'humour and caricatura,' in which it appears he was in danger of travelling side by side with Hogarth, I can only congratulate my country, that Mrs Hogarth knew *her* province better than, by disturbing her husband at his pallet, to divert him from that universality of subject, which has stamped him perhaps, next to Shakspeare, the most inventive genius which this island has produced, into the 'amiable pursuit of beautiful nature,' *i.e.* copying ad infinitum the individual charms and graces of Mrs H—.

'Hogarth's method of exposing meanness, deformity, and vice, paddling in whatever is ridiculous, faulty, and vicious.'

A person unacquainted with the works thus stigmatised would be apt to imagine, that in Hogarth there was nothing else to be found but subjects of the coarsest and most repulsive nature. That his imagination was naturally unsweet, and that he delighted in raking into every species of moral filth. That he preyed upon sore places only, and took a pleasure in exposing the unsound and rotten parts of human nature; – whereas, with the exception of some of the plates of the *Harlot's Progress*, which are harder in their character than any of the rest of his productions, (the *Stages of Cruelty* I omit as mere worthless caricaturas, foreign to his general habits, the offspring of his fancy in some wayward humour), there is scarce one of his pieces where vice is most strongly satirised, in which some figure is not introduced upon which the moral eye may rest satisfied; a face that indicates goodness, or perhaps mere good hum-

ouredness and carelessness of mind (negation of evil) only, yet enough
to give a relaxation to the frowning brow of satire, and keep the general
air from tainting. Take the mild, supplicating posture of patient Poverty
in the poor woman that is persuading the pawnbroker to accept her
clothes in pledge, in the plate of *Gin Lane*, for an instance. A little does
it, a little of the *good* nature overpowers a world of *bad*. One cordial
honest laugh of a Tom Jones absolutely clears the atmosphere that was
reeking with the black putrifying breathings of a hypocrite Blifil.[9] One
homely expostulating shrug from Strap, warms the whole air which the
suggestions of a gentlemanly ingratitude from his friend Random[10]
had begun to freeze. One 'Lord bless us!' of Parson Adams[11] upon the
wickedness of the times, exorcises and purges off the mass of iniquity
which the world-knowledge of even a Fielding could cull out and rake
together. But of the severer class of Hogarth's performances, enough, I
trust, has been said to shew that they do not merely shock and repulse;
that there is in them the 'scorn of vice' and the 'pity' too; something to
touch the heart, and keep alive the sense of moral beauty; the 'lacrymæ
rerum,' and the sorrowing by which the heart is made better. If they be
bad things, then is satire and tragedy a bad thing; let us proclaim at once
an age of gold, and sink the existence of vice and misery in our speculations; let us

    – wink, and shut our apprehensions up
    From common sense of what men were and are:

let us *make believe* with the children, that every body is good and happy;
and, with Dr Swift, write panegyrics upon the world.

    But that larger half of Hogarth's works which were painted more for
entertainment than instruction (though such was the suggestiveness of
his mind, that there is always something to be learnt from them), his
humorous scenes, – are they such as merely to disgust and set us against
our species?

    The confident assertions of such a man as I consider the late Mr Barry
to have been, have that weight of authority in them which staggers, at
first hearing, even a long preconceived opinion. When I read his pathetic
admonition concerning the shortness of life, and how much better the
little leisure of it were laid out upon 'that species of art which is employed
about the amiable and the admirable;' and Hogarth's 'method' proscribed as a 'dangerous or worthless pursuit,' I began to think there was
something in it; that I might have been indulging all my life a passion
for the works of this artist, to the utter prejudice of my taste and moral

sense; but my first convictions gradually returned, a world of good-natured English faces came up one by one to my recollection, and a glance at the matchless *Election Entertainment*, which I have the happiness to have hanging up in my parlour, subverted Mr Barry's whole theory in an instant.

In that inimitable print, (which in my judgment as far exceeds the more known and celebrated *March to Finchley*, as the best comedy exceeds the best farce that ever was written,) let a person look till he be saturated, and when he has done wondering at the inventiveness of genius which could bring so many characters (more than thirty distinct classes of face) into a room and set them down at table together, or otherwise dispose them about, in so natural a manner, engage them in so many easy sets and occupations, yet all partaking of the spirit of the occasion which brought them together, so that we feel that nothing but an election time could have assembled them; having no central figure or principal group, (for the hero of the piece, the Candidate, is properly set aside in the levelling indistinction of the day, one must look for him to find him) nothing to detain the eye from passing from part to part, where every part is alike instinct with life, – for here are no furniture-faces, – no figures brought in to fill up the scene like stage choruses, but all dramatis personæ: when he shall have done wondering at all these faces so strongly charactered, yet finished with the accuracy of the finest miniature; when he shall have done admiring the numberless appendages of the scene, those gratuitous doles which rich genius flings into the heap when it has already done enough, the over-measure which it delights in giving, as if it felt its stores were exhaustless; the dumb rhetoric of the scenery – for tables, and chairs, and joint-stools in Hogarth, are living and significant things; the witticisms that are expressed by words, (all artists but Hogarth have failed when they have endeavoured to combine two mediums of expression, and have introduced words into their pictures), and the unwritten numberless little allusive pleasantries that are scattered about; the work that is going on in the scene, and beyond it, as is made visible to the 'eye of mind,' by the mob which chokes up the doorway, and the sword that has forced an entrance before its master; when he shall have sufficiently admired this wealth of genius, let him fairly say what is the *result* left on his mind. Is it an impression of the vileness and worthlessness of his species? or is it not the general feeling which remains, after the individual faces have ceased to act sensibly on his mind, a *kindly one in favour of his species?* was not the general air of the scene wholesome? did it do the heart hurt to be among it? Something of a riotous spirit to be sure is there, some worldly-mindedness in some of the faces, a Doddingtonian smoothness which does not promise any superfluous degree of sincerity in the fine gentleman who has been the occasion of calling so much good company together: but is not the general cast of expression in the faces, of the good sort? do they not seem cut out of the *good old rock*, substantial English honesty? Would one fear treachery among characters of their expression? or shall we call their honest mirth and seldom-returning relaxation by the hard names of vice and profligacy? That poor country fellow, that is grasping his staff (which, from that difficulty of feeling themselves at home which poor men experience at a feast, he has never parted with since he came into the room), and is enjoying with a relish that seems to fit all the capacities of his soul the slender joke, which that facetious wag his neighbour is practising upon the gouty gentleman, whose eyes the effort to suppress pain has made as round as rings – does it shock the 'dignity of human nature' to look at that man, and to sympathise with him in the seldom-heard joke which has unbent his care-worn, hard-working visage, and drawn iron smiles from it? or with that full-hearted cobbler, who is honouring with the grasp of an honest fist the unused palm of that annoyed patrician, whom the licence of the time has seated next him.

I can see nothing 'dangerous' in the contemplation of such scenes as this, or the *Enraged Musician*, or the *Southwark Fair*, or twenty other pleasant prints which come crowding in upon my recollection, in which the restless activities, the diversified bents and humours, the blameless peculiarities of men, as they deserve to be called, rather than their 'vices and follies,' are held up in a laughable point of view. All laughter is not of a dangerous or soul-hardening tendency. There is the petrifying sneer of a demon which excludes and kills Love, and there is the cordial laughter of a man which implies and cherishes it. What heart was ever made the worse by joining in a hearty laugh at the simplicities of Sir Hugh Evans or Parson Adams, where a sense of the ridiculous mutually kindles and is kindled by a perception of the amiable? That tumultuous harmony of singers that are roaring out the words, 'The world shall bow to the Assyrian throne,' from the opera of *Judith*, in the third plate of the series called the *Four Groups of Heads*; which the quick eye of Hogarth must have struck off in the very infancy of the rage for sacred oratorios in this country, while 'Music yet was young;' when we have done smiling at the deafening distortions, which these tearers of devotion to rags and tatters, these takers of Heaven by storm, in their boisterous mimicry of the occupation of angels, are making, – what unkindly impression is left behind, or what more of harsh or contemptuous feeling, than when we quietly leave Uncle Toby and Mr Shandy [12] riding their hobby-horses about the room? The conceited, long-backed Sign-painter, that with all the self-applause of a Raphael or Corregio (the twist of body which his conceit has thrown him into has something of the Corregiesque in it) is contemplating the picture of a bottle which he is drawing from an actual bottle that hangs beside him, in the print of *Beer Street*, – while we smile at the enormity of the self-delusion, can we help loving the good humour and self-complacency of the fellow? Would we willingly wake him from his dream?

I say not that all the ridiculous subjects of Hogarth have necessarily something in them to make us like them; some are indifferent to us, some in their natures repulsive, and only made interesting by the wonderful skill and truth to nature in the painter; but I contend that there is in most of them that sprinkling of the better nature, which, like holy water, chases away and disperses the contagion of the bad. They have this in them besides, that they bring us acquainted with the every-day human face, – they give us skill to detect those gradations of sense and virtue (which escape the careless or fastidious observer) in the countenances of the world about us; and prevent that disgust at common life, that *tædium quotidianarum formarum*,[13] which an unrestricted passion for ideal forms and beauties is in danger of producing. In this, as in many other things, they are analogous to the best novels of Smollett or Fielding.

(*Reflector*, No. III, 1811)

ON THE TRAGEDIES
OF SHAKSPEARE

CONSIDERED WITH REFERENCE TO THEIR FITNESS
FOR STAGE REPRESENTATION

TAKING a turn the other day in the Abbey, I was struck with the affected attitude of a figure, which I do not remember to have seen before, and which upon examination proved to be a whole-length of the celebrated Mr Garrick. Though I would not go so far with some good catholics abroad as to shut players altogether out of consecrated ground, yet I own I was not a little scandalized at the introduction of theatrical airs and gestures into a place set apart to remind us of the saddest realities. Going nearer, I found inscribed under this harlequin figure the following lines: —

> To paint fair Nature, by divine command
> Her magic pencil in his glowing hand,
> A Shakspeare rose; then, to expand his fame
> Wide o'er this breathing world, a Garrick came.
> Though sunk in death the forms the Poet drew,
> The Actor's genius bade them breathe anew;
> Though, like the bard himself, in night they lay,
> Immortal Garrick call'd them back to day:
> And till Eternity with pow'r sublime
> Shall mark the mortal hour of hoary Time,
> Shakspeare and Garrick, like twin-stars shall shine,
> And earth irradiate with a beam divine.

It would be an insult to my readers' understandings to attempt any thing like a criticism on this farrago of false thoughts and nonsense. But the reflection it led me into was a kind of wonder, how, from the days of the actor here celebrated to our own, it should have been the fashion to compliment every performer in his turn, that has had the luck to please the town in any of the great characters of Shakspeare, with the notion of possessing a *mind congenial with the poet's:* how people should come thus unaccountably to confound the power of originating poetical images and conceptions with the faculty of being able to read or recite the same when put into words;* or what connection that absolute mastery over the heart and soul of man, which a great dramatic poet possesses, has with those low tricks upon the eye and ear, which a player by observing a few general effects, which some common passion, as grief, anger, &c. usually has upon the gestures and exterior, can so easily compass. To know the internal workings and movements of a great mind, of an Othello or a Hamlet for instance, the *when* and the *why* and the *how far* they should be moved; to what pitch a passion is becoming; to give the reins and to pull in the curb exactly at the moment when the drawing in or the slackening is most graceful; seems to demand a reach of intellect of a vastly different extent from that which is employed upon the bare imitation of the signs of these passions in the countenance or gesture, which signs are usually observed to be most lively and emphatic in the weaker sort of minds, and which signs can, after all, but indicate some passion, as I said before, – anger, or grief, generally; but of the motives and grounds of the passion, wherein it differs from the same passion in low and vulgar natures, of these the actor can give no more idea by his face or gesture than the eye (without a metaphor) can speak, or the muscles utter intelligible sounds. But such is the instantaneous nature of the impressions which we take in at the eye and ear at a play-house, compared with the slow apprehension oftentimes of the understanding in reading, that we are apt not only to sink the play-writer in the consideration which we pay to the actor, but even to identify in our minds, in a perverse manner, the actor with the character which he represents. It is difficult for a frequent play-goer to disembarrass the idea of Hamlet from the person and voice of Mr K.[1] We speak of Lady Macbeth, while we are in reality thinking of Mrs S.[2] Nor is this confusion incidental alone to unlettered persons, who, not possessing the advantage of reading, are necessarily dependent upon the stage-player for all the pleasure which they can receive from the drama, and to whom the very idea of *what an author is* cannot be made comprehensible without some pain and perplexity of mind: the error is one from which persons otherwise not meanly lettered, find it almost impossible to extricate themselves.

---

* It is observable that we fall into this confusion only in *dramatic* recitations. We never dream that the gentleman who reads Lucretius in public with great applause is therefore a great poet and philosopher; nor do we find that Tom Davies, the bookseller, who is recorded to have recited the Paradise Lost better than any man in England in his day (though I cannot help thinking there must be some mistake in this tradition), was therefore, by his intimate friends, set upon a level with Milton.

Never let me be so ungrateful as to forget the very high degree of satisfaction which I received some years back from seeing for the first time a tragedy of Shakspeare performed, in which those two great performers sustained the principal parts. It seemed to embody and realize conceptions which had hitherto assumed no distinct shape. But dearly do we pay all our life after for this juvenile pleasure, this sense of distinctness. When the novelty is past, we find to our cost that instead of realizing an idea, we have only materialized and brought down a fine vision to the standard of flesh and blood. We have let go a dream, in quest of an unattainable substance.

How cruelly this operates upon the mind, to have its free conceptions thus cramped and pressed down to the measure of a strait-lacing actuality, may be judged from that delightful sensation of freshness, with which we turn to those plays of Shakspeare which have escaped being performed, and to those passages in the acting plays of the same writer which have happily been left out in the performance. How far the very custom of hearing any thing *spouted*, withers and blows upon a fine passage, may be seen in those speeches from Henry the Fifth, &c. which are current in the mouths of school-boys, from their being to be found in *Enfield Speakers*, and such kind of books. I confess myself utterly unable to appreciate that celebrated soliloquy in Hamlet, beginning 'To be, or not to be,' or to tell whether it be good, bad, or indifferent, it has been so handled and pawed about by declamatory boys and men, and torn so inhumanly from its living place and principle of continuity in the play, till it is become to me a perfect dead member.

It may seem a paradox, but I cannot help being of opinion that the plays of Shakspeare are less calculated for performance on a stage than those of almost any other dramatist whatever. Their distinguishing excellence is a reason that they should be so. There is so much in them, which comes not under the province of acting, with which eye, and tone, and gesture, have nothing to do.

The glory of the scenic art is to personate passion, and the turns of passion; and the more coarse and palpable the passion is, the more hold upon the eyes and ears of the spectators the performer obviously possesses. For this reason, scolding scenes, scenes where two persons talk themselves into a fit of fury, and then in a surprising manner talk themselves out of it again, have always been the most popular upon our stage. And the reason is plain, because the spectators are here most palpably appealed to, they are the proper judges in this war of words, they are the legitimate ring that should be formed round such 'intellectual prize-fighters.' Talking is the direct object of the imitation here. But in all the best dramas, and in Shakspeare above all, how obvious it is, that the form of *speaking*, whether it be in soliloquy or dialogue, is only a medium, and often a highly artificial one, for putting the reader or spectator into possession of that knowledge of the inner structure and workings of mind in a character, which he could otherwise never have arrived at *in that form of composition* by any gift short of intuition. We do here as we do with novels written in the *epistolary form*. How many improprieties, perfect solecisms in letter-writing, do we put up with in *Clarissa* and other books, for the sake of the delight which that form upon the whole gives us.

But the practice of stage representation reduces every thing to a controversy of elocution. Every character, from the boisterous blasphemings of Bajazet to the shrinking timidity of womanhood, must play the orator. The love-dialogues of Romeo and Juliet, those silver-sweet sounds of lovers' tongues by night; the more intimate and sacred sweetness of nuptial colloquy between an Othello or a Posthumus with their married wives; all those delicacies which are so delightful in the reading, as when we read of those youthful dalliances in Paradise –

> – As beseem'd
> Fair couple link'd in happy nuptial league,
> Alone;

by the inherent fault of stage representation, how are these things sullied and turned from their very nature by being exposed to a large assembly; when such speeches as Imogen addresses to her lord, come drawling out of the mouth of a hired actress, whose courtship, though nominally addressed to the personated Posthumus, is manifestly aimed at the spectators, who are to judge of her endearments and her returns of love.

The character of Hamlet is perhaps that by which, since the days of Betterton, a succession of popular performers have had the greatest ambition to distinguish themselves. The length of the part may be one of their reasons. But for the character itself, we find it in a play, and therefore we judge it a fit subject of dramatic representation. The play itself abounds in maxims and reflexions beyond any other, and therefore we consider it as a proper vehicle for conveying moral instruction. But Hamlet himself – what does he suffer meanwhile by being dragged forth as a public schoolmaster, to give lectures to the crowd! Why, nine parts in ten of what Hamlet does, are transactions between himself and his moral sense, they are the effusions of his solitary musings, which he retires to holes and corners and the most sequestered parts of the palace to pour forth; or rather, they are the silent meditations with which his bosom is bursting, reduced to *words* for the sake of the reader, who must else remain ignorant of what is passing there. These profound sorrows, these light-and-noise-abhorring ruminations, which the tongue scarce dares utter to deaf walls and chambers, how can they be represented by a gesticulating actor, who comes and mouths them out before an audience, making four hundred people his confidants at once. I say not that it is the fault of the actor so to do; he must pronounce them *ore rotundo*, he must accompany them with his eye; he must insinuate them into his auditory by some trick of eye, tone, or gesture, or he fails. *He must be thinking all the while of his appearance, because he knows that all the while the spectators are judging of it.* And this is the way to represent the shy, negligent, retiring Hamlet.

It is true that there is no other mode of conveying a vast quantity of thought and feeling to a great portion of the audience, who otherwise would never earn it for themselves by reading; and the intellectual acquisition gained this way may, for aught I know, be inestimable; but I am not arguing that Hamlet should not be acted, but how much Hamlet is made another thing by being acted. I have heard much of the wonders which Garrick performed in this part; but as I never saw him, I must have leave to doubt whether the representation of such a character came within the province of his art. Those who tell me of him, speak of his eye, of the magic of his eye, and of his commanding voice: physical properties, vastly desirable in an actor, and without which he can never insinuate meaning into an auditory, – but what have they to do with Hamlet? what have they to do with intellect? In fact, the things aimed at in theatrical representation, are to arrest the spectator's eye upon the form and the gesture, and so to gain a more favourable hearing to what is spoken: it is not what the character is, but how he looks; not what he says, but how he speaks it. I see no reason to think that if the play of Hamlet were written over again by some such writer as Banks or Lillo,[3] retaining the process of the story, but totally omitting all the poetry of it, all the divine features of Shakspeare, his stupendous intellect; and only taking care to give us enough of passionate dialogue, which neither Banks nor Lillo was never at a loss to furnish; I see not how the effect could be much different upon an audience, nor how the actor has it in his power to represent Shakspeare to us differently from his representation of Banks or Lillo. Hamlet would still be a youthful accomplished prince, and must be gracefully personated; he might be puzzled in his mind, wavering in his conduct, seemingly, – cruel to Ophelia; he might see a ghost, and start at it, and address it kindly when he found it to be his father; all this in the poorest and most homely language of the servilest creeper after nature that ever consulted the palate of an audience; without troubling Shakspeare for the matter: and I see not but there would be room for all the power which an actor has, to display itself. All the passions and changes of passion might remain: for those are much less difficult to write or act than is thought, it is a trick easy to be attained, it is but rising or falling a note or two in the voice, a whisper with a significant foreboding look to announce its approach, and so contagious the counterfeit appearance of any emotion is, that let the words be what they will, the look and tone shall carry it off and make it pass for deep skill in the passions.

It is common for people to talk of Shakspeare's plays being *so natural*; that every body can understand him. They are natural indeed, they are grounded deep in nature, so deep that the depth of them lies out of the reach of most of us. You shall hear the same persons say that George Barnwell is very natural, and Othello is very natural, that they are both very deep; and to them they are the same kind of thing. At the one they sit and shed tears, because a good sort of young man is tempted by a naughty woman to commit a *trifling peccadillo*, the murder of an uncle or so,* that is all, and so comes to an untimely end, which is *so moving;* and at the other, because a blackamoor in a fit of jealousy kills his innocent white wife: and the odds are that ninety-nine out of a hundred would willingly behold the same catastrophe happen to both the heroes, and have thought the rope more due to Othello than to Barnwell. For of the texture of Othello's mind, the inward construction marvellously laid open with all its strengths and weaknesses, its heroic confidences and its human misgivings, its agonies of hate springing from the depths of love, they see no more

* If this note could hope to meet the eye of any of the Managers, I would intreat and beg of them, in the name of both the Galleries, that this insult upon the morality of the common people of London should cease to be eternally repeated in the holiday weeks. Why are the 'Prentices of this famous and well-governed city, instead of an amusement, to be treated over and over again with a nauseous sermon of George Barnwell? Why *at the end of their vistoes* are we to place the *gallows?* Were I an uncle, I should not much like a nephew of mine to have such an example placed before his eyes. It is really making uncle-murder too trivial to exhibit it as done upon such slight motives; – it is attributing too much to such characters as Millwood: – it is putting things into the heads of good young men, which they would never otherwise have dreamed of. Uncles that think any thing of their lives, should fairly petition the Chamberlain against it.

than the spectators at a cheaper rate, who pay their pennies a-piece to look through the man's telescope in Leicester-fields, see into the inward plot and topography of the moon. Some dim thing or other they see, they see an actor personating a passion, of grief, or anger, for instance, and they recognize it as a copy of the usual external effects of such passions; or at least as being true to *that symbol of the emotion which passes current at the theatre for it*, for it is often no more than that: but of the grounds of the passion, its correspondence to a great or heroic nature, which is the only worthy object of tragedy, – that common auditors know any thing of this, or can have any such notions dinned into them by the mere strength of an actor's lungs, – that apprehensions foreign to them should be thus infused into them by storm, I can neither believe, nor understand how it can be possible.

We talk of Shakspeare's admirable observation of life, when we should feel, that not from a petty inquisition into those cheap and every-day characters which surrounded him, as they surround us, but from his own mind, which was, to borrow a phrase of Ben Jonson's, the very 'sphere of humanity,' he fetched those images of virtue and of knowledge, of which every one of us recognizing a part, think we comprehend in our natures the whole; and oftentimes mistake the powers which he positively creates in us, for nothing more than indigenous faculties of our own minds, which only waited the application of corresponding virtues in him to return a full and clear echo of the same.

To return to Hamlet. – Among the distinguishing features of that wonderful character, one of the most interesting (yet painful) is that soreness of mind which makes him treat the intrusions of Polonius with harshness, and that asperity which he puts on in his interviews with Ophelia. These tokens of an unhinged mind (if they be not mixed in the latter case with a profound artifice of love, to alienate Ophelia by affected discourtesies, so to prepare her mind for the breaking off of that loving intercourse, which can no longer find a place amidst business so serious as that which he has to do) are parts of his character, which to reconcile with our admiration of Hamlet, the most patient consideration of his situation is no more than necessary; they are what we *forgive afterwards*, and explain by the whole of his character, but *at the time* they are harsh and unpleasant. Yet such is the actor's necessity of giving strong blows to the audience, that I have never seen a player in this character, who did not exaggerate and strain to the utmost these ambiguous features, – these temporary deformities in the character.

They make him express a vulgar scorn at Polonius which utterly
degrades his gentility, and which no explanation can render palateable;
they make him show contempt, and curl up the nose at Ophelia's father,
– contempt in its very grossest and most hateful form; but they get
applause by it: it is natural, people say; that is, the words are scornful,
and the actor expresses scorn, and that they can judge of: but why so
much scorn, and of that sort, they never think of asking.

So to Ophelia. – All the Hamlets that I have ever seen, rant and rave
at her as if she had committed some great crime, and the audience are
highly pleased, because the words of the part are satirical, and they are
enforced by the strongest expression of satirical indignation of which
the face and voice are capable. But then, whether Hamlet is likely to
have put on such brutal appearances to a lady whom he loved so dearly,
is never thought on. The truth is, that in all such deep affections as had
subsisted between Hamlet and Ophelia, there is a stock of *supererogatory
love*, (if I may venture to use the expression) which in any great grief of
heart, especially where that which preys upon the mind cannot be
communicated, confers a kind of indulgence upon the grieved party to
express itself, even to its heart's dearest object, in the language of a
temporary alienation; but it is not alienation, it is a distraction purely,
and so it always makes itself to be felt by that object: it is not anger, but
grief assuming the appearance of anger, – love awkwardly counterfeiting
hate, as sweet countenances when they try to frown: but such sternness
and fierce disgust as Hamlet is made to shew, is no counterfeit, but the
real face of absolute aversion, – of irreconcileable alienation. It may be
said he puts on the madman; but then he should only so far put on this
counterfeit lunacy as his own real distraction will give him leave; that is,
incompletely, imperfectly; not in that confirmed, practised way, like a
master of his art, or as Dame Quickly would say, 'like one of those
harlotry players.'

I mean no disrespect to any actor, but the sort of pleasure which
Shakspeare's plays give in the acting seems to me not at all to differ
from that which the audience receive from those of other writers; and,
they being in themselves essentially so different from all others, I must conclude
that there is something in the nature of acting which levels all distinctions.
And in fact, who does not speak indifferently of the Gamester and of
Macbeth as fine stage performances, and praise the Mrs Beverley in the
same way as the Lady Macbeth of Mrs S.? Belvidera, and Calista, and
Isabella, and Euphrasia, are they less liked than Imogen, or than Juliet,
or than Desdemona? Are they not spoken of and remembered in the

same way? Is not the female performer as great (as they call it) in one as in the other? Did not Garrick shine, and was he not ambitious of shining in every drawling tragedy that his wretched day produced, – the productions of the Hills and the Murphys and the Browns, – and shall he have that honour to dwell in our minds for ever as an inseparable concomitant with Shakspeare? A kindred mind! O who can read that affecting sonnet of Shakspeare which alludes to his profession as a player: –

> Oh for my sake do you with Fortune chide,
> The guilty goddess of my harmless deeds,
> That did not better for my life provide
> Than public means which public custom breeds –
> Thence comes it that my name receives a brand;
> And almost thence my nature is subdued
> To what it works in, like the dyer's hand –

Or that other confession: –

> Alas! 'tis true, I have gone here and there,
> And made myself a motly to thy view,
> Gor'd mine own thoughts, sold cheap what is most dear –

Who can read these instances of jealous self-watchfulness in our sweet Shakspeare, and dream of any congeniality between him and one that, by every tradition of him, appears to have been as mere a player as ever existed; to have had his mind tainted with the lowest players' vices, – envy and jealousy, and miserable cravings after applause; one who in the exercise of his profession was jealous even of the women-performers that stood in his way; a manager full of managerial tricks and stratagems and finesse: that any resemblance should be dreamed of between him and Shakspeare, – Shakspeare who, in the plenitude and consciousness of his own powers, could with that noble modesty, which we can neither imitate nor appreciate, express himself thus of his own sense of his own defects: –

> Wishing me like to one more rich in hope,
> Featur'd like him, like him with friends possest;
> Desiring *this man's art, and that man's scope.*

I am almost disposed to deny to Garrick the merit of being an admirer of Shakspeare. A true lover of his excellences he certainly was not; for would any true lover of them have admitted into his matchless scenes such ribald trash as Tate and Cibber,[4] and the rest of them, that

> With their darkness durst affront his light,

have foisted into the acting plays of Shakspeare? I believe it impossible that he could have had a proper reverence for Shakspeare, and have condescended to go through that interpolated scene in Richard the Third, in which Richard tries to break his wife's heart by telling her he loves another woman, and says, 'if she survives this she is immortal.' Yet I doubt not he delivered this vulgar stuff with as much anxiety of emphasis as any of the genuine parts: and for acting, it is as well calculated as any. But we have seen the part of Richard lately produce great fame to an actor by his manner of playing it, and it lets us into the secret of acting, and of popular judgments of Shakspeare derived from acting. Not one of the spectators who have witnessed Mr C.'s exertions in that part,[5] but has come away with a proper conviction that Richard is a very wicked man, and kills little children in their beds, with something like the pleasure which the giants and ogres in children's books are represented to have taken in that practice; moreover, that he is very close and shrewd and devilish cunning, for you could see that by his eye.

But is in fact this the impression we have in reading the Richard of Shakspeare? Do we feel any thing like disgust, as we do at that butcher-like representation of him that passes for him on the stage? A horror at his crimes blends with the effect that we feel, but how is it qualified, how is it carried off, by the rich intellect which he displays, his resources, his wit, his buoyant spirits, his vast knowledge and insight into characters, the poetry of his part, – not an atom of all which is made perceivable in Mr C.'s way of acting it. Nothing but his crimes, his actions, is visible; they are prominent and staring. The murderer stands out, but where is the lofty genius, the man of vast capacity, – the profound, the witty, accomplished Richard?

The truth is, the Characters of Shakspeare are so much the objects of meditation rather than of interest or curiosity as to their actions, that while we are reading any of his great criminal characters, – Macbeth, Richard, even Iago, – we think not so much of the crimes which they commit, as of the ambition, the aspiring spirit, the intellectual activity, which prompts them to overleap these moral fences. Barnwell is a wretched murderer; there is a certain fitness between his neck and the rope; he is the legitimate heir to the gallows; nobody who thinks at all can think of any alleviating circumstances in his case to make him a fit object of mercy. Or to take an instance from the higher tragedy, what else but a mere assassin is Glenalvon?[6] Do we think of any thing but of the crime which he commits, and the rack which he deserves? That is all which we really think about him. Whereas in corresponding characters in Shakspeare so little do the actions comparatively affect us, that while the impulses, the inner mind in all its perverted greatness, solely seems real and is exclusively attended to, the crime is comparatively nothing. But when we see these things represented, the acts which they do are comparatively everything, their impulses nothing. The state of sublime emotion into which we are elevated by those images of night and horror which Macbeth is made to utter, that solemn prelude with which he entertains the time till the bell shall strike which is to call him to murder Duncan, – when we no longer read it in a book, when we have given up that vantage-ground of abstraction which reading possesses over seeing, and come to see a man in his bodily shape before our eyes actually preparing to commit a murder, if the acting be true and impressive, as I have witnessed it in Mr K.'s performance of that part, the painful anxiety about the act, the natural longing to prevent it while it yet seems unperpetrated, the too close pressing semblance of reality, give a pain and an uneasiness which totally destroy all the delight which the words in the book convey, where the deed doing never presses upon us with the painful sense of presence: it rather seems to belong to history, – to something past and inevitable, if it has any thing to do with time at all. The sublime images, the poetry alone, is that which is present to our minds in the reading.

So to see Lear acted, – to see an old man tottering about the stage with a walking-stick, turned out of doors by his daughters in a rainy night, has nothing in it but what is painful and disgusting. We want to take him into shelter and relieve him. That is all the feeling which the acting of Lear ever produced in me. But the Lear of Shakspeare cannot be acted. The contemptible machinery by which they mimic the storm which he goes out in, is not more inadequate to represent the horrors of the real elements, than any actor can be to represent Lear: they might more easily propose to personate the Satan of Milton upon a stage, or one of Michael Angelo's terrible figures. The greatness of Lear is not in corporal dimension, but in intellectual: the explosions of his passion are terrible as a volcano; they are storms turning up and disclosing to the bottom that sea, his mind, with all its vast riches. It is his mind which is laid bare. This case of flesh and blood seems too insignificant to be thought on; even as he himself neglects it. On the stage we see nothing but corporal infirmities and weakness, the impotence of rage: while we read it, we see not Lear, but we are Lear, – we are in his mind, we are sustained by a grandeur which baffles the malice of daughters and storms; in the aberrations of his reason, we discover a mighty irregular power of reasoning, immethodized from the ordinary purposes of life, but exerting its powers, as the wind bloweth where it listeth, at will upon the corruptions and abuses of mankind. What have looks, or tones, to do with that sublime identification of his age with that of the *heavens themselves*, when in his reproaches to them for conniving at the injustice of his children, he reminds them that 'they themselves are old'? What gesture shall we appropriate to this? What has the voice or the eye to do with such things? But the play is beyond all art, as the tamperings with it shew: it is too hard and stony; it must have love-scenes, and a happy ending. It is not enough that Cordelia is a daughter, she must shine as a lover too. Tate has put his hook in the nostrils of this Leviathan, for Garrick and his followers, the showmen of the scene, to draw the mighty beast about more easily. A happy ending! – as if the living martyrdom that Lear had gone through, – the flaying of his feelings alive, did not make a fair dismissal from the stage of life the only decorous thing for him. If he is to live and be happy after, if he could sustain this world's burden after, why all this pudder and preparation, – why torment us with all this unnecessary sympathy? As if the childish pleasure of getting his gilt robes and sceptre again could tempt him to act over again his misused station, – as if at his years and with his experience, any thing was left but to die.

Lear is essentially impossible to be represented on a stage. But how many dramatic personages are there in Shakspeare, which though more tractable and feasible (if I may so speak) than Lear, yet from some circumstance, some adjunct to their character, are improper to be shewn to our bodily eye. Othello for instance. Nothing can be more soothing, more flattering to the nobler parts of our natures, than to read of a young Venetian lady of the highest extraction, through the force of love and from a sense of merit in him whom she loved, laying aside every consideration of kindred, and country, and colour, and wedding with a *coal-black Moor* – (for such he is represented, in the imperfect state of knowledge respecting foreign countries in those days, compared with our own, or in compliance with popular notions, though the Moors are now well enough known to be by many shades less unworthy of a white woman's fancy) – it is the perfect triumph of virtue over accidents, of the imagination over the senses. She sees Othello's colour in his mind. But upon the stage, when the imagination is no longer the ruling faculty, but we are left to our poor unassisted senses, I appeal to every one that has seen Othello played, whether he did not, on the contrary, sink Othello's mind in his colour; whether he did not find something extremely revolting in the courtship and wedded caresses of Othello and Desdemona; and whether the actual sight of the thing did not over-weigh all that beautiful compromise which we make in reading. And the reason it should do so is obvious, because there is just so much reality presented to our senses as to give a perception of disagreement, with not enough of belief in the internal motives, – all that which is unseen, – to overpower and reconcile the first and obvious prejudices.* What we see upon a stage is body and bodily action; what we are conscious of in reading is almost exclusively the mind, and its move-ments: and this I think may sufficiently account for the very different sort of delight with which the same play so often affects us in the reading and the seeing.

It requires little reflection to perceive, that if those characters in Shakspeare which are within the precincts of nature, have yet something in them which appeals too exclusively to the imagination, to admit of their being made objects to the senses without suffering a change and a diminution, – that still stronger the objection must lie against representing another line of characters, which Shakspeare has introduced to give a wildness and a supernatural elevation to his scenes, as if to remove them still farther from that assimilation to common life in which their ex-cellence is vulgarly supposed to consist. When we read the incantations of those terrible beings the Witches in Macbeth, though some of the ingredients of their hellish composition savour of the grotesque, yet is the effect upon us other than the most serious and appalling that can be imagined? Do we not feel spell-bound as Macbeth was? Can any mirth accompany a sense of their presence? We might as well laugh under a

---

* The error of supposing that because Othello's colour does not offend us in the reading, it should also not offend us in the seeing, is just such a fallacy as supposing that an Adam and Eve in a picture shall affect us just as they do in the poem. But in the poem we for a while have Paradisaical senses given us, which vanish when we see a man and his wife without clothes in the picture. The painters themselves feel this, as is apparent by the awkward shifts they have recourse to, to make them look not quite naked; by a sort of prophetic anachronism, antedating the invention of fig-leaves. So in the reading of the play, we see with Desdemona's eyes; in the seeing of it, we are forced to look with our own.

consciousness of the principle of Evil himself being truly and really present with us. But attempt to bring these things on to a stage, and you turn them instantly into so many old women, that men and children are to laugh at. Contrary to the old saying, that 'seeing is believing,' the sight actually destroys the faith; and the mirth in which we indulge at their expense, when we see these creatures upon a stage, seems to be a sort of indemnification which we make to ourselves for the terror which they put us in when reading made them an object of belief, − when we surrendered up our reason to the poet, as children to their nurses and their elders; and we laugh at our fears, as children who thought they saw something in the dark, triumph when the bringing in of a candle discovers the vanity of their fears. For this exposure of supernatural agents upon a stage is truly bringing in a candle to expose their own delusiveness. It is the solitary taper and the book that generates a faith in these terrors: a ghost by chandelier light,[7] and in good company, deceives no spectators, − a ghost that can be measured by the eye, and his human dimensions made out at leisure. The sight of a well-lighted house, and a well-dressed audience, shall arm the most nervous child against any apprehensions: as Tom Brown says of the inpenetrable skin of Achilles with his inpenetrable armour over it, 'Bully Dawson would have fought the devil with such advantages.'

Much has been said, and deservedly, in reprobation of the vile mixture which Dryden has thrown into the Tempest: doubtless without some such vicious alloy, the impure ears of that age would never have sate out to hear so much innocence of love as is contained in the sweet courtship of Ferdinand and Miranda. But is the Tempest of Shakspeare at all a fit subject for stage representation? It is one thing to read of an enchanter, and to believe the wondrous tale while we are reading it; but to have a conjuror brought before us in his conjuring-gown, with his spirits about him, which none but himself and some hundred of favoured spectators before the curtain are supposed to see, involves such a quantity of the *hateful incredible*, that all our reverence for the author cannot hinder us from perceiving such gross attempts upon the senses to be in the highest degree childish and inefficient. Spirits and fairies cannot be represented; they cannot even be painted, − they can only be believed. But the elaborate and anxious provision of scenery, which the luxury of the age demands, in these cases works a quite contrary effect to what is intended. That which in comedy, or plays of familiar life, adds so much to the life of the imitation, in plays which appeal to the higher faculties, positively destroys the illusion which it is introduced to aid. A parlour or a drawing-room, – a library opening into a garden, – a garden with an alcove in it, – a street, or the piazza of Covent Garden, does well enough in a scene; we are content to give as much credit to it as it demands; or rather, we think little about it, – it is little more than reading at the top of a page, 'Scene, a Garden;' we do not imagine ourselves there, but we readily admit the imitation of familiar objects. But to think by the help of painted trees and caverns, which we know to be painted, to transport our minds to Prospero, and his island and his lonely cell;* or by the aid of a fiddle dexterously thrown in, in an interval of speaking, to make us believe that we hear those supernatural noises of which the isle was full: – the Orrery Lecturer at the Hay-market [8] might as well hope, by his musical glasses cleverly stationed out of sight behind his apparatus, to make us believe that we do indeed hear the chrystal spheres ring out that chime, which if it were to inwrap our fancy long, Milton thinks,

> Time would run back and fetch the age of gold,
> And speckled vanity
> Would sicken soon and die,
> And leprous Sin would melt from earthly mould;
> Yea Hell itself would pass away,
> And leave its dolorous mansions to the peering day.

The Garden of Eden, with our first parents in it, is not more impossible to be shewn on a stage, than the Enchanted Isle, with its no less interesting and innocent first settlers.

The subject of Scenery is closely connected with that of the Dresses, which are so anxiously attended to on our stage. I remember the last time I saw Macbeth played, the discrepancy I felt at the changes of garment which he varied, – the shiftings and re-shiftings, like a Romish priest at mass. The luxury of stage-improvements, and the importunity of the public eye, require this. The coronation robe of the Scottish monarch was fairly a counterpart to that which our King wears when he goes to the Parliament-house, – just so full and cumbersome, and set out with ermine and pearls. And if things must be represented, I see not what to find fault with in this. But in reading, what robe are we conscious of? Some dim images of royalty – a crown and sceptre – may

---

* It will be said these things are done in pictures. But pictures and scenes are very different things. Painting is a world of itself, but in scene-painting there is the attempt to deceive; and there is the discordancy, never to be got over, between painted scenes and real people.

float before our eyes, but who shall describe the fashion of it? Do we see in our mind's eye what Webb[9] or any other robe-maker could pattern? This is the inevitable consequence of imitating every thing, to make all things natural. Whereas the reading of a tragedy is a fine abstraction. It presents to the fancy just so much of external appearances as to make us feel that we are among flesh and blood, while by far the greater and better part of our imagination is employed upon the thoughts and internal machinery of the character. But in acting, scenery, dress, the most contemptible things, call upon us to judge of their naturalness.

Perhaps it would be no bad similitude, to liken the pleasure which we take in seeing one of these fine plays acted, compared with that quiet delight which we find in the reading of it, to the different feelings with which a reviewer, and a man that is not a reviewer, reads a fine poem. The accursed critical habit, – the being called upon to judge and pronounce, must make it quite a different thing to the former. In seeing these plays acted, we are affected just as judges. When Hamlet compares the two pictures of Gertrude's first and second husband, who wants to see the pictures? But in the acting, a miniature must be lugged out; which we know not to be the picture, but only to show how finely a miniature may be represented. This showing of every thing, levels all things: it makes tricks, bows, and curtesies, of importance. Mrs S. never got more fame by any thing than by the manner in which she dismisses the guests in the banquet-scene in Macbeth: it is as much remembered as any of her thrilling tones or impressive looks. But does such a trifle as this enter into the imaginations of the readers of that wild and wonderful scene? Does not the mind dismiss the feasters as rapidly as it can? Does it care about the gracefulness of doing it? But by acting, and judging of acting, all these non-essentials are raised into an importance, injurious to the main interest of the play.

I have confined my observations to the tragic parts of Shakspeare. It would be no very difficult task to extend the enquiry to his comedies; and to show why Falstaff, Shallow, Sir Hugh Evans, and the rest, are equally incompatible with stage representation. The length to which this Essay has run will make it, I am afraid, sufficiently distasteful to the Amateurs of the Theatre, without going any deeper into the subject at present.

EDAX ON APPETITE

MR REFLECTOR, — I am going to lay before you a case of the most iniquitous persecution that ever poor devil suffered.

You must know, then, that I have been visited with a calamity ever since my birth. How shall I mention it without offending delicacy? Yet out it must. My sufferings, then, have all arisen from a most inordinate appetite —

Not for wealth, not for vast possessions, — then might I have hoped to find a cure in some of those precepts of philosophers or poets, — those *verba et voces* which Horace speaks of:

> quibus hunc lenire dolorem
> Possis, et magnam morbi deponere partem;[2]

not for glory, not for fame, not for applause, — for against this disease, too, he tells us there are certain *piacula*,[3] or, as Pope has chosen to render it,

> rhymes, which fresh and fresh applied,
> Will cure the arrant'st puppy of his pride;

nor yet for pleasure, properly so called: the strict and virtuous lessons which I received in early life from the best of parents, — a pious clergyman of the Church of England, now no more, — I trust have rendered me sufficiently secure on that side: —

No, Sir, for none of these things; but an appetite, in its coarsest and least metaphorical sense, — an appetite for *food*.

The exorbitances of my arrow-root and pappish days I cannot go back far enough to remember, only I have been told, that my mother's constitution not admitting of my being nursed at home, the woman who had the care of me for that purpose used to make most extravagant demands for my pretended excesses in that kind; which my parents, rather than believe any thing unpleasant of me, chose to impute to the known covetousness and mercenary disposition of that sort of people.

This blindness continued on their part after I was sent for home, up to the period when it was thought proper, on account of my advanced age, that I should mix with other boys more unreservedly than I had hitherto done. I was according sent to boarding-school.

Here the melancholy truth became too apparent to be disguised. The prying republic of which a great school consists, soon found me out: there was no shifting the blame any longer upon other people's shoulders, – no good-natured maid to take upon herself the enormities of which I stood accused in the article of bread and butter, besides the crying sin of stolen ends of puddings, and cold pies strangely missing. The truth was but too manifest in my looks, – in the evident signs of inanition which I exhibited after the fullest meals, in spite of the double allowance which my master was privately instructed by my kind parents to give me. The sense of the ridiculous, which is but too much alive in grown persons, is tenfold more active and alert in boys. Once detected, I was the constant butt of their arrows, – the mark against which every puny leveller directed his little shaft of scorn. The very Graduses and Thesauruses were raked for phrases to pelt me with by the tiny pedants. Ventri natus, – Venti deditus, – Vesana gula, – Escarum gurges, – Dapibus indulgens, – Non dans fræna gulæ, – Sectans lautæ fercula mensæ,[4] resounded wheresoever I past. I led a weary life, suffering the penalties of guilt for that which was no crime, but only following the blameless dictates of nature. The remembrance of those childish reproaches haunts me yet oftentimes in my dreams. My school-days come again, and the horror I used to feel, when in some silent corner retired from the notice of my unfeeling playfellows, I have sat to mumble the solitary slice of ginger-bread allotted me by the bounty of considerate friends, and have ached at heart because I could not spare a portion of it, as I saw other boys do, to some favourite boy; – for if I know my own heart, I was never selfish, – never possessed a luxury which I did not hasten to communicate to others; but my food, alas! was none; it was an indispensable necessary; I could as soon have spared the blood in my veins, as have parted that with my companions.

Well, no one stage of suffering lasts for ever: we should grow reconciled to it at length, I suppose, if it did. The miseries of my school-days had their end; I was once more restored to the paternal dwelling. The affectionate solicitude of my parents was directed to the good-natured purpose of concealing even from myself the infirmity which haunted me. I was continually told that I was growing, and the appetite I displayed was humanely represented as being nothing more than a symptom and an effect of that. I used even to be complimented upon it. But this temporary fiction could not endure above a year or two. I ceased to grow, but alas! I did not cease my demands for alimentary sustenance.

Those times are long since past, and with them have ceased to exist the fond concealment, – the indulgent blindness, – the delicate over-looking, – the compassionate fiction. I and my infirmity are left exposed and bare to the broad, unwinking eye of the world, which nothing can elude. My meals are scanned, my mouthfuls weighed in a balance: that which appetite demands, is set down to the account of gluttony, – a sin which my whole soul abhors, nay, which Nature herself has put it out of my power to commit. I am constitutionally disenabled from that vice; for how can he be guilty of excess, who never can get enough? Let them cease, then, to watch my plate; and leave off their ungracious comparisons of it to the seven baskets of fragments, and the super-naturally-replenished cup of old Baucis;[5] and be thankful that their more phlegmatic stomachs, not their virtue, have saved them from the like reproaches. I do not see that any of them desist from eating till the holy rage of hunger, as some one calls it, is supplied. Alas! I am doomed to stop short of that continence.

What am I to do? I am by disposition inclined to conviviality and the social meal. I am no gourmand: I require no dainties: I should despise the board of Heliogabalus,[6] except for its long sitting. Those vivacious, long-continued meals of the latter Romans, indeed I justly envy; but the kind of fare which the Curii and Dentati[7] put up with, I could be content with. Dentatus I have been called, among other unsavoury jests. Double-meal is another name which my acquaintance have palmed upon me, for an innocent piece of policy which I put in practice for some time without being found out; which was, – going the round of my friends, beginning with the most primitive feeders among them, who take their dinner about one o'clock, and so successively dropping in upon the next and the next, till by the time I got among my more fashionable intimates, whose hour was six or seven, I have nearly made up the body of a just and complete meal (as I reckon it), without taking more than one dinner (as they account of dinners) at one person's house. Since I have been found out, I endeavour to make up by a damper, as I call it, at home, before I go out. But alas! with me, increase of appetite truly grows by what it feeds on. What is peculiarly offensive to me at those dinner-parties is, the senseless custom of cheese, and the dessert afterwards. I have a rational antipathy to the former; and for fruit, and

those other vain vegetable substitutes for meat, (meat, the only legitimate aliment for human creatures since the flood, as I take it to be
deduced from that permission, or ordinance rather, given to Noah and
his descendants), I hold them in perfect contempt. Hay for horses. I
remember a pretty apologue, which Mandeville tells very much to this
purpose in his Fable of the Bees:[8] – He brings in a Lion arguing with a
Merchant, who had ventured to expostulate with this king of beasts
upon his violent methods of feeding. The Lion thus retorts: – 'Savage I
am; but no creature can be called cruel but what either by malice or
insensibility extinguishes his natural pity. The Lion was born without
compassion; we follow the instinct of our nature; the gods have appointed us to live upon the waste and spoil of other animals, and as long
as we can meet with dead ones, we never hunt after the living; 'tis only
man, mischievous man, that can make death a sport. Nature taught
your stomach to crave nothing but vegetables. – (Under favour of the
Lion, if he meant to assert this universally of mankind, it is not true.
However, what he says presently is very sensible.) – Your violent
fondness to change, and greater eagerness after novelties, have prompted
you to the destruction of animals without justice or necessity. The Lion
has a ferment within him, that consumes the toughest skin and hardest
bones, as well as the flesh of all animals without exception. Your
squeamish stomach, in which the digestive heat is weak and inconsiderable, won't so much as admit of the most tender parts of them,
unless above half the concoction has been performed by artificial fire
before-hand; and yet what animal have you spared, to satisfy the caprices
of a languid appetite? Languid I say; for what is man's hunger if
compared with the Lion's? Yours, when it is at the worst, makes you
faint; mine makes me mad: oft have I tried with roots and herbs to allay
the violence of it, but in vain; nothing but large quantities of flesh can
any ways appease it.' – Allowing for the Lion not having a prophetic
instinct to take in every lusus naturæ[9] that was possible of the human
appetite, he was, generally speaking, in the right; and the Merchant was
so impressed with his argument that, we are told, he replied not, but
fainted away. O, Mr Reflector, that I were not obliged to add, that the
creature who thus argues was but a type of me! Miserable man! *I am that
Lion.* 'Oft have I tried with roots and herbs to allay that violence, but in
vain; nothing but – '

Those tales which are renewed as often as the editors of papers want
to fill up a space in their unfeeling columns, of great eaters, – people
that devour whole geese and legs of mutton *for wagers*, are sometimes

attempted to be drawn to a parallel with my case. This wilful confounding of motives and circumstances, which make all the difference of moral or immoral in actions, just suits the sort of talent which some of my acquaintance pride themselves upon. *Wagers!* – I thank heaven, I was never mercenary, nor could consent to prostitute a gift (though but a left-handed one) of nature, to the enlarging of my worldly substance; prudent as the necessities, which that fatal gift has involved me in, might have made such a prostitution to appear in the eyes of an indelicate world.

Rather let me say, that to the satisfaction of that talent which was given me, I have been content to sacrifice no common expectations; for such I had from an old lady, a near relation of our family, in whose good graces I had the fortune to stand, till one fatal evening –. You have seen, Mr Reflector, if you have ever passed your time much in country towns, the kind of suppers which elderly ladies in those places have lying in petto [10] in an adjoining parlour, next to that where they are entertaining their periodically-invited coevals with cards and muffins. The cloth is usually spread some half-hour before the final rubber is decided, whence they adjourn to sup upon what may emphatically be called *nothing*. A sliver of ham, purposely contrived to be transparent to show the china-dish through it, neighbouring a slip of invisible brawn, which abuts upon something they call a tartlet, as that is bravely supported by an atom of marmalade, flanked in its turn by a grain of potted beef, with a power of such dishlings, *minims of hospitality*, spread in defiance of human nature, or rather with an utter ignorance of what it demands. Being engaged at one of these card-parties, I was obliged to go a little before *supper-time* (as they facetiously called the point of time in which they are taking these shadowy refections), and the old lady, with a sort of fear shining through the smile of courteous hospitality that beamed in her countenance, begged me to step into the next room and take something before I went out in the cold, – a proposal which lay not in my nature to deny. Indignant at the airy prospect I saw before me, I set to, and in a trice despatched the whole meal intended for eleven persons, – fish, flesh, fowl, pastry, – to the sprigs of garnishing parsley, and the last fearful custard that quaked upon the board. I need not describe the consternation, when in due time the dowagers adjourned from their cards. Where was the supper? – and the servants' answer, Mr —— had eat it all. – That freak, however, jested me out of a good three hundred pounds a year, which I afterwards was informed for a certainty the old lady meant to leave me. I mention it not in illustration of the unhappy faculty which I am possessed of; for any unlucky wag of a school-boy, with a tolerable appetite, could have done as much without feeling any hurt after it, – only that you may judge whether I am a man likely to set my talent to sale, or to require the pitiful stimulus of a wager.

I have read in Pliny, or in some author of that stamp, of a reptile in Africa, whose venom is of that hot, destructive quality, that wheresoever it fastens its tooth, the whole substance of the animal that has been bitten in a few seconds is reduced to dust, crumbles away, and absolutely disappears: it is called from this quality, the Annihilator. Why am I forced to seek, in all the most prodigious and portentous facts of Natural History, for creatures typical of myself. *I am that snake, that Annihilator:* 'wherever I fasten, in a few seconds –.'

O happy sick men, that are groaning under the want of that very thing, the excess of which is my torment! O fortunate, too fortunate, if you knew your happiness, invalids! What would I not give to exchange this fierce concoctive and digestive heat, – this rabid fury which vexes me, which tears and torments me, – for your quiet, mortified, hermit-like, subdued, and sanctified stomachs, – your cool, chastened inclinations, and coy desires for food!

To what unhappy figuration of the parts intestine I owe this unnatural craving, I must leave to the anatomists and the physicians to determine: they, like the rest of the world, have doubtless their eye upon me; and as I have been cut up alive by the sarcasms of my friends, so I shudder when I contemplate the probability that this animal frame, when its restless appetites shall have ceased their importunity, may be cut up also (horrible suggestion!) to determine in what system of solids or fluids this original sin of my constitution lay lurking. What work will they make with their acids and alkalines, their serums and coagulums, effervescences, viscous matter, bile, chyle, and acrimonious juices, to explain that cause which Nature, who willed the effect to punish me for my sins, may no less have determined to keep in the dark from them, to punish them for their presumption.

You may ask, Mr Reflector, to what purpose is my appeal to you; what can you do for me? Alas! I know too well that my case is out of the reach of advice, – out of the reach of consolation. But it is some relief to the wounded heart to impart its tale of misery; and some of my acquaintance, who may read my case in your pages under a borrowed name, may be induced to give it a more humane consideration than I could ever yet obtain from them under my own. Make them, if possible, to *reflect*, that an original peculiarity of constitution is no crime; that not that which goes into the mouth desecrates a man, but that which comes out of it, – such as sarcasm, bitter jests, mocks and taunts, and ill-natured observations; and let them consider, if there be such things (which we have all heard of) as Pious Treachery, Innocent Adultery, &c., whether there may not be also such a thing as Innocent Gluttony.

I shall only subscribe myself,
Your afflicted servant,
EDAX.

(*Reflector*, No. IV, 1811)

HOSPITA ON THE IMMODERATE INDULGENCE OF THE PLEASURES OF THE PALATE

MR REFLECTOR, – My husband and I are fond of company, and being in easy circumstances, we are seldom without a party to dinner two or three days in a week. The utmost cordiality has hitherto prevailed at our meetings; but there is a young gentleman, a near relation of my husband's, that has lately come among us, whose preposterous behaviour bids fair, if not timely checked, to disturb our tranquillity. He is too great a favourite with my husband in other respects, for me to remonstrate with him in any other than this distant way. A letter printed in your publication may catch his eye; for he is a great reader, and makes a point of seeing all the new things that come out. Indeed, he is by no means deficient in understanding. My husband says that he has a good deal of wit; but for my part I cannot say I am any judge of that, having seldom observed him open his mouth except for purposes very foreign to conversation. In short, Sir, this young gentleman's failing is, an immoderate indulgence of his palate. The first time he dined with us, he thought it necessary to extenuate the length of time he kept the dinner on the table, by declaring that he had taken a very long walk in the morning, and came in fasting; but as that excuse could not serve above once or twice at most, he has latterly dropped the mask altogether, and chosen to appear in his own proper colours without reserve or apology.

You cannot imagine how unpleasant his conduct has become. His way of staring at the dishes as they are brought in, has absolutely something immodest in it: it is like the stare of an impudent man of fashion at a fine woman, when she first comes into a room. I am positively in pain for the dishes, and cannot help thinking they have consciousness, and will be put out of countenance, he treats them so like what they are not.

Then again he makes no scruple of keeping a joint of meat on the table, after the cheese and fruit are brought in, till he has what he calls *done with it*. Now how awkward this looks, where there are ladies, you may judge, Mr Reflector, – how it disturbs the order and comfort of a meal. And yet I always make a point of helping him first, contrary to all good manners, – before any of my female friends are helped, – that he may avoid this very error. I wish he would eat before he comes out.

What makes his proceedings more particularly offensive at our house is, that my husband, though out of common politeness he is obliged to set dishes of animal food before his visitors, yet himself and his whole family (myself included) feed entirely on vegetables. We have a theory, that animal food is neither wholesome nor natural to man; and even vegetables we refuse to eat until they have undergone the operation of fire, in consideration of those numberless little living creatures which the glass helps us to detect in every fibre of the plant or root before it be dressed. On the same theory we boil our water, which is our only drink, before we suffer it to come to table. Our children are perfect little Pythagoreans: it would do you good to see them, in their nursery, stuffing their dried fruits, figs, raisins, and *milk*, which is the only approach to animal food which is allowed. They have no notion how the substance of a creature that ever had life can become food for another creature. A beef-steak is an absurdity to them; a mutton-chop, a solecism in terms; a cutlet, a word absolutely without any meaning; a butcher is nonsense, except so far as it is taken for a man who delights in blood, or a hero. In this happy state of innocence we have kept their minds, not allowing them to go into the kitchen, or to hear of any preparations for the dressing of animal food, or even to know that such things are practised. But as a state of ignorance is incompatible with a certain age; and as my eldest girl, who is ten years old next Midsummer, must shortly be introduced into the world and sit at table with us, where she will see some things which will shock all her received notions, I have been endeavouring by little and little to break her mind, and prepare it for the disagreeable impressions which must be forced upon it. The first hint I gave her upon the subject, I could see her recoil from it with the same horror with which we listen to a tale of Anthropophagism;[1] but she has gradually grown more reconciled to it in some measure, from my telling her that it was the custom of the world, – to which, however senseless, we must submit so far as we could do it with innocence, not to give offence; and she has shown so much strength of mind on other occasions, which I have no doubt is owing to the calmness and serenity superinduced by her diet, that I am in good hopes, when the proper season for her *début* arrives, she may be brought to endure the sight of a roasted chicken or a dish of sweetbreads, for the first time, without fainting. Such being the nature of our little household, you may guess what inroads into the economy of it, – what revolutions and turnings of things upside down, the example of such a feeder as Mr — is calculated to produce.

I wonder at a time like the present, when the scarcity of every kind of food is so painfully acknowledged, that *shame* has no effect upon him. Can he have read Mr Malthus's Thoughts on the Ratio of Food to Population?[2] Can he think it reasonable that one man should consume the sustenance of many?

The young gentleman has an agreeable air and person, such as are not unlikely to recommend him on the score of matrimony. But his fortune is not over large; and what prudent young woman would think of embarking hers with a man who would bring three or four mouths (or what is equivalent to them) into a family? She might as reasonably choose a widower in the same circumstances with three or four children.

I cannot think who he takes after. His father and mother, by all accounts, were very moderate eaters; only I have heard that the latter swallowed her victuals very fast, and the former had a tedious custom of sitting long at his meals. Perhaps he takes after both.

I wish you would turn this in your thoughts, Mr Reflector, and give us your ideas on the subject of excessive eating, and, particularly, of animal food.

HOSPITA.

(*Reflector*, No. IV, 1811)

THE GOOD CLERK,
A CHARACTER

WITH SOME ACCOUNT OF 'THE COMPLETE
ENGLISH TRADESMAN'

THE GOOD CLERK. – He writeth a fair and swift hand, and is compe-
tently versed in the Four First Rules of Arithmetic, in the Rule of Three
(which is sometimes called the Golden Rule) and in Practice. We
mention these things, that we may leave no room for cavillers to say,
that any thing essential hath been omitted in our definition; else, to
speak the truth, these are but ordinary accomplishments, and such as
every under-strapper at a desk is commonly furnished with. The character we treat of soareth higher.

He is clean and neat in his person; not from a vain-glorious desire of
setting himself forth to advantage in the eyes of the other sex (with
which vanity too many of our young sparks now-a-days are infected)
but to do credit (as we say) to the office. For this reason he evermore
taketh care that his desk or his books receive no soil; the which things he
is commmonly as solicitous to have fair and unblemished, as the owner
of a fine horse is to have him appear in good keep.

He riseth early in the morning; not because early rising conduceth to
health (though he doth not altogether despise that consideration) but
chiefly to the intent that he may be first at the desk. There is his post,
there he delighteth to be, unless when his meals, or necessity, calleth
him away; which time he alway esteemeth as lost, and maketh as short
as possible.

He is temperate in eating and drinking, that he may preserve a clear
head and steady hand for his master's service. He is also partly induced
to this observation of the rules of temperance by his respect for religion
and the laws of his country; which things (it may once for all be noted)
do add special assistances to his actions, but do not and cannot furnish
the main spring or motive thereto. His first ambition (as appeareth all
along) is to be a good Clerk; his next a good Christian, a good Patriot,
&c.

Correspondent to this, he keepeth himself honest, not for fear of the
laws, but because he hath observed how unseemly an article it maketh

in the Day Book or Ledger, when a sum is set down lost or missing; it being his pride to make these books to agree, and to tally, the one side with the other, with a sort of architectural symmetry and correspondence.

He marrieth, or marrieth not, as best suiteth with his employer's views. Some merchants do the rather desire to have married men in their Counting Houses, because they think the married state a pledge for their servants' integrity, and an incitement to them to be industrious; and it was an observation of a late Lord Mayor of London, that the sons of Clerks do generally prove Clerks themselves, and that Merchants encouraging persons in their employ to marry, and to have families, was the best method of securing a breed of sober, industrious young men attached to the mercantile interest. Be this as it may, such a character as we have been describing, will wait till the pleasure of his employer is known on this point; and regulateth his desires by the custom of the house or firm to which he belongeth.

He avoideth profane oaths and jesting, as so much time lost from his employ; what spare time he hath for conversation, which in a Counting House such as we have been supposing can be but small, he spendeth in putting seasonable questions to such of his fellows (and sometimes *respectfully* to the master himself) who can give him information respecting the price and quality of goods, the state of exchange, or the latest improvements in book-keeping; thus making the motion of his lips, as well as of his fingers, subservient to his master's interest. Not that he refuseth a brisk saying, or a cheerful sally of wit, when it comes unforced, is free of offence, and hath a convenient brevity. For this reason, he hath commonly some such phrase as this in his mouth: –

> It's a slovenly look
> To blot your book.

Or,

> Red ink for ornament, black for use,
> The best of things are open to abuse.

So upon the eve of any great holyday, of which he keepeth one or two at least every year, he will merrily say, in the hearing of a confidential friend, but to none other, –

> All work and no play
> Makes Jack a dull boy.

Or,

A bow always bent must crack at last.

But then this must always be understood to be spoken confidentially, and, as we say, *under the rose.*

Lastly, his dress is plain, without singularity; with no other ornament than the quill, which is the badge of his function, stuck under the dexter ear,[1] and this rather for convenience of having it at hand, when he hath been called away from his desk, and expecteth to resume his seat there again shortly, than from any delight which he taketh in foppery or ostentation. The colour of his clothes is generally noted to be black rather than brown, brown rather than blue or green. His whole deportment is staid, modest, and civil. His motto is Regularity. –

This Character was sketched, in an interval of business, to divert some of the melancholy hours of a Counting House. It is so little a creature of fancy, that it is scarce any thing more than a recollection of some of those frugal and economical maxims which, about the beginning of the last century, (England's meanest period) were endeavoured to be inculcated and instilled into the breasts of the London Apprentices,* by a class of instructors who might not inaptly be termed *The Masters of Mean Morals.* The astonishing narrowness and illiberality of the lessons contained in some of those books is inconceivable by those whose studies have not led them that way, and would almost induce one to subscribe to the hard censure which Drayton[3] has passed upon the mercantile spirit: –

> The gripple merchant, born to be the curse
> Of this brave Isle.

I have now lying before me that curious book by Daniel Defoe, 'The Complete English Tradesman.'[4] The pompous detail, the studied analysis of every little mean art, every sneaking address, every trick and subterfuge (short of larceny) that is necessary to the tradesman's occupation, with the hundreds of anecdotes, dialogues (in Defoe's liveliest manner) interspersed, all tending to the same amiable purpose, namely, the sacrificing of every honest emotion of the soul to what he calls the main chance, – if you read it in an *ironical sense*, and as a piece of *covered satire*, – make it one of the most amusing books which Defoe ever writ, as much so as any of his best novels. It is difficult to say what his

---

* This term designated a larger class of young men than that to which it is now confined; it took in the articled Clerks of Merchants and Bankers, the George Barnwells of the day.[2]

intention was in writing it. It is almost impossible to suppose him in earnest. Yet such is the bent of the book to narrow and to degrade the heart, that if such maxims were as catching and infectious as those of a licentious cast, which happily is not the case, had I been living at that time, I certainly should have recommended to the Grand Jury of Middlesex, who presented The Fable of the Bees,[5] to have presented this book of Defoe's in preference, as of a far more vile and debasing tendency. I will give one specimen of his advice to the young tradesman on the *Government of his Temper*. 'The retail tradesman in especial, and even every tradesman in his station, must furnish himself with a competent stock of patience; I mean that sort of patience which is needful to bear with all sorts of impertinence, and the most provoking curiosity that it is impossible to imagine the buyers, even the worst of them, are or can be guilty of. *A tradesman behind his counter must have no flesh and blood about him, no passions, no resentment;* he must never be angry, no not so much as seem to be so, if a customer tumbles him five hundred pounds worth of goods, and scarce bids money for any thing; nay, though they really come to his shop with no intent to buy, as many do, only to see what is to be sold, and though he knows they cannot be better pleased, than they are, at some other shop where they intend to buy, 'tis all one, the tradesman must take it, he must place it to the account of his calling, that *'tis his business to be ill used, and resent nothing;* and so must answer as obligingly to those that give him an hour or two's trouble and buy nothing, as he does to those who in half the time lay out ten or twenty pounds. The case is plain, and if some do give him trouble and do not buy, others make amends and do buy; and as for the trouble, 'tis the business of the shop.' Here follows a most admirable story of a mercer who, by his indefatigable meanness and more than Socratic patience under affronts, overcame and reconciled a lady, who upon the report of another lady that he had behaved saucily to some third lady, had determined to shun his shop, but by the over-persuasions of a fourth lady was induced to go to it; which she does, declaring before hand that she will buy nothing, but give him all the trouble she can. Her attack and his defence, her insolence and his persevering patience, are described in colours worthy of a Mandeville; but it is too long to recite. 'The short inference from this long discourse' (says he) 'is this, that here you see, and I could give you many examples like this, how and in what manner a shop-keeper is to behave himself in the way of his business; what impertinences, what taunts, flouts, and ridiculous things, he must bear in his trade, and must not show the least return, or the least signal of disgust: he must have no passions, no fire in his temper; he must be all soft and smooth; nay, if his real temper be naturally fiery and hot, he must shew none of it in his shop; he must be a perfect *complete hypocrite* if he will be a *complete tradesman*.'* It is true, natural tempers are not to be always counterfeited; the man cannot easily be a lamb in his shop, and a lion in himself; but let it be easy or hard, it must be done, and is done: there are men who have by custom and usage brought themselves to it, that nothing could be meeker and milder than they, when behind the counter, and yet nothing be more furious and raging in every other part of life; nay the provocations they have met with in their shops have so irritated their rage, that they would go up stairs from their shop, and fall into frenzies, and a kind of madness, and beat their heads against the wall, and perhaps mischief themselves, if not prevented, till the violence of it had gotten vent, and the passions abate and cool. I heard once of a shop-keeper that behaved himself thus to such an extreme, that when he was provoked by the impertinence of the customers, beyond what his temper could bear, he would go up stairs and beat his wife, kick his children about like dogs, and be as furious for two or three minutes as a man chained down in Bedlam; and again, when that heat was over, would sit down, and cry faster than the children he had abused; and after the fit, he would go down into the shop again, and be as humble, courteous, and as calm as any man whatever; so absolute a government of his passions had he in the shop and so little out of it; in the shop, a soulless animal that would resent nothing; and in the family a madman: in the shop, meek like a lamb; but in the family, outrageous, like a Lybian lion. The sum of the matter is, it is necessary for a tradesman to subject himself by all the ways possible, to his business; *his customers are to be his idols: so far as he may worship idols by allowance, he is to bow down to them, and worship them;* at least, he is not in any way to displease them, or shew any disgust or distaste whatsoever they may say or do; the bottom of all is, that he is intending to get money by them, and it is not for him that gets money to offer the least inconvenience to them by whom he gets it; he is to consider that, as Solomon says,[6] 'the borrower is servant to the lender, so the seller is servant to the buyer.' — What he says on the head of *Pleasures and Recreations* is not less amusing: — 'The tradesman's pleasure should be in his business; his companions should be his books, (he means

---

* As no qualification accompanies this maxim, it must be understood as the genuine sentiment of the author!

his Ledger, Wastebook, &c.) and if he has a family, he makes *his excursions up stairs and no further:* – none of my cautions aim at restraining a tradesman from diverting himself, as we call it, with his fire-side, or keeping company with his wife and children.' – Liberal allowance; nay, almost licentious and criminal indulgence! – but it is time to dismiss this *Philosopher of Meanness.* More of this stuff would illiberalize the pages of the *Reflector.* Was the man in earnest, when he could bring such powers of description, and all the charms of natural eloquence, in commendation of the meanest, vilest, wretchedest degradations of the human character? – Or did he not rather laugh in his sleeve at the doctrines which he inculcated, and retorting upon the grave citizens of London their own arts, palm upon them a sample of disguised Satire under the name of wholesome Instruction?

(*Reflector*, No. IV, 1811)

WORDSWORTH'S 'EXCURSION'

(A REVIEW)

THE volume before us, as we learn from the Preface, is 'a detached portion of an unfinished poem, containing views of man, nature, and society;' to be called the Recluse,[1] as having for its principal subject the 'sensations and opinions of a poet living in retirement;' and to be preceded by a 'record in verse of the origin and progress of the author's own powers, with reference to the fitness which they may be supposed to have conferred for the task.' To the completion of this plan we look forward with a confidence which the execution of the finished part is well calculated to inspire. – Meanwhile, in what is before us there is an ample matter for entertainment: for the 'Excursion' is not a branch (as might have been suspected) prematurely plucked from the parent tree to gratify an overhasty appetite for applause; but is, in itself, a complete and legitimate production.

It opens with the meeting of the poet with an aged man whom he had known from his schooldays; in plain words, a Scottish pedlar; a man who, though of low origin, had received good learning and impressions of the strictest piety from his stepfather, a minister and village schoolmaster. Among the hills of Athol, the child is described to have become familiar with the appearances of nature in his occupation as a feeder of sheep; and from her silent influences to have derived a character, meditative, tender, and poetical. With an imagination and feelings thus nourished – his intellect not unaided by books, but those, few, and chiefly of a religious cast – the necessity of seeking a maintenance in riper years, had induced him to make choice of a profession, the *appellation* for which has been gradually declining into contempt, but which formerly designated a class of men, who, journeying in country places, when roads presented less facilities for travelling, and the intercourse between towns and villages was unfrequent and hazardous, became a sort of link of neighbourhood to distant habitations; resembling, in some small measure, in the effects of their periodical returns, the caravan which Thompson so

feelingly describes[2] as blessing the cheerless Siberian in its annual
visitation, with 'news of human kind.'

In the solitude incident to this rambling life, power had been given
him to keep alive that devotedness to nature which he had imbibed in
his childhood, together with the opportunity of gaining such notices of
persons and things from his intercourse with society, as qualified him to
become a 'teacher of moral wisdom.' With this man, then, in a hale old
age, released from the burthen of his occupation, yet retaining much of
its active habits, the poet meets, and is by him introduced to a second
character – a sceptic – one who had been partially roused from an
overwhelming desolation, brought upon him by the loss of wife and
children, by the powerful incitement of hope which the French Revolution in its commencement put forth, but who, disgusted with the
failure of all its promises, had fallen back into a laxity of faith and
conduct which induced at length a total despondence as to the dignity
and final destination of his species. In the language of the poet, he

> – broke faith with those whom he had laid
> In earth's dark chambers.

Yet he describes himself as subject to compunctious visitations from
that silent quarter.

> – Feebly must they have felt,
> Who, in old time, attired with snakes and whips
> The vengeful Furies. Beautiful regards
> Were turned on me – the face of her I loved;
> The wife and mother; pitifully fixing
> Tender reproaches, insupportable! – p. 153.

The conversations with this person, in which the Wanderer asserts
the consolatory side of the question against the darker views of human
life maintained by his friend, and finally calls to his assistance the experience of a village priest, the third, or rather fourth interlocutor, (for
the poet himself is one,) form the groundwork of the 'Excursion.'

It will be seen by this sketch that the poem is of a didactic nature, and
not a fable or story; yet it is not wanting in stories of the most interesting
kind, – such as the lovers of Cowper and Goldsmith will recognize as
something familiar and congenial to them. We might instance the
Ruined Cottage, and the Solitary's own story, in the first half of the
work; and the second half, as being almost a continued cluster of narration. But the prevailing charm of the poem is, perhaps, that, conver-

sational as it is in its plan, the dialogue throughout is carried on in the very heart of the most romantic scenery which the poet's native hills could supply; and which, by the perpetual references made to it either in the way of illustration or for variety and pleasurable description's sake, is brought before us as we read. We breathe in the fresh air, as we do while reading Walton's Complete Angler;[3] only the country about us is as much bolder than Walton's, as the thoughts and speculations, which form the matter of the poem, exceed the trifling pastime and low-pitched conversation of his humble fishermen. We give the description of the 'two huge peaks,' which from some other vale peered into that in which the Solitary is entertaining the poet and his companion. 'Those,' says their host,

>   – if here you dwelt, would be
> Your prized companions. Many are the notes
> Which in his tuneful course the wind draws forth
> From rocks, woods, caverns, heaths, and dashing shores;
> And well those lofty brethren bear their part
> In the wild concert: chiefly when the storm
> Rides high; then all the upper air they fill
> With roaring sound, that ceases not to flow,
> Like smoke, along the level of the blast
> In mighty current; theirs, too, is the song
> Of stream and headlong flood that seldom fails;
> And in the grim and breathless hour of noon,
> Methinks that I have heard them echo back
> The thunder's greeting: nor have Nature's laws
> Left them ungifted with a power to yield
> Music of finer frame; a harmony,
> So do I call it, though it be the hand
> Of silence, though there be no voice; the clouds,
> The mist, the shadows, light of golden suns,
> Motions of moonlight, all come thither – touch,
> And have an answer – thither come, and shape
> A language not unwelcome to sick hearts,
> And idle spirits: there the sun himself
> At the calm close of summer's longest day
> Rests his substantial orb; – between those heights,
> And on the top of either pinnacle,
> More keenly than elsewhere in night's blue vault,

> Sparkle the stars as of their station proud.
> Thoughts are not busier in the mind of man,
> Than the mute agent stirring there: — alone
> Here do I sit and watch. — p. 84.

To a mind constituted like that of Mr Wordsworth, the stream, the torrent, and the stirring leaf — seem not merely to suggest associations of deity, but to be a kind of speaking communication with it. He walks through every forest, as through some Dodona;[4] and every bird that flits among the leaves, like that miraculous one* in Tasso, but in language more intelligent, reveals to him far higher love-lays. In his poetry nothing in Nature is dead. Motion is synonymous with life. 'Beside yon spring,' says the Wanderer, speaking of a deserted well, from which, in former times, a poor woman, who died heart-broken, had been used to dispense refreshment to the thirsty traveller,

> — beside yon spring I stood,
> And eyed its waters, till we seem'd to feel
> One sadness, they and I. For them a bond
> Of brotherhood is broken: time has been
> When every day the touch of human hand
> Dislodged the natural sleep that binds them up
> In mortal stillness. — p. 27.

To such a mind, we say — call it strength or weakness — if weakness, assuredly a fortunate one — the visible and audible things of creation present, not dim symbols, or curious emblems, which they have done at all times to those who have been gifted with the poetical faculty; but revelations and quick insights into the life within us, the pledge of immortality: —

> — the whispering air
> Sends inspiration from her shadowy heights,
> And blind recesses of the cavern'd rocks:
> The little rills, and waters numberless,
> Inaudible by day-light.

*With party-coloured plumes, and purple bill,
A wondrous bird among the rest there flew,
That in plain speech sung love-lays loud and shrill;
Her leden was like human language true;
So much she talk'd, and with such wit and skill,
That strange it seemèd how much good she knew.

Fairfax's Translation.[5]

'I have seen,' the poet says, and the illustration is an happy one:

> — I have seen
> A curious child, applying to his ear
> The convolutions of a smooth-lipp'd shell,
> To which, in silence hush'd, his very soul
> Listen'd intensely, and his countenance soon
> Brighten'd with joy; for murmurings from within
> Were heard — sonorous cadences! whereby,
> To his belief, the monitor express'd
> Mysterious union with its native sea.
> Even such a shell the universe itself
> Is to the ear of faith; and doth impart
> Authentic tidings of invisible things:
> Of ebb and flow, and ever-during power;
> And central peace subsisting at the heart
> Of endless agitation. — p. 191.

Sometimes this harmony is imaged to us by an echo; and in one instance, it is with such transcendent beauty set forth by a shadow and its corresponding substance, that it would be a sin to cheat our readers at once of so happy an illustration of the poet's system, and so fair a proof of his descriptive powers.

> Thus having reach'd a bridge that over-arch'd
> The hasty rivulet where it lay becalmed
> In a deep pool, by happy chance we saw
> A two-fold image; on a grassy bank
> A snow-white ram, and in the chrystal flood
> Another and the same! most beautiful,
> On the green turf with his imperial front,
> Shaggy and bold, and wreathed horns superb,
> The breathing creature stood; as beautiful,
> Beneath him, show'd his shadowy counterpart.
> Each had his glowing mountains, each his sky,
> And each seem'd centre of his own fair world;
> Antipodes unconscious of each other,
> Yet, in partition, with their several spheres,
> Blended in perfect stillness, to our sight! — p. 407.

Combinations, it is confessed, 'like those reflected in that quiet pool,' cannot be lasting: it is enough for the purpose of the poet, if they are felt. – They are at least his system; and his readers, if they reject them for their creed, may receive them merely as poetry. In him, *faith*, in friendly alliance and conjuction with the religion of his country, appears to have grown up, fostered by meditation and lonely communions with Nature – an internal principle of lofty consciousness, which stamps upon his opinions and sentiments (we were almost going to say) the character of an expanded and generous Quakerism.

From such a creed we should expect unusual results; and, when applied to the purposes of consolation, more touching considerations than from the mouth of common teachers. The first speculation of this sort perhaps in the poem before us, is the notion of the thoughts which may sustain the spirit, while they crush the frame of the sufferer, who from loss of objects of love by death, is commonly supposed to pine away under a broken heart.

> – If there be, whose tender frames have drooped
> Even to the dust, apparently, through weight
> Of anguish unrelieved, and lack of power
> An agonising spirit to transmute,
> Infer not hence a hope from those withheld
> When wanted most; a confidence impaired
> So pitiably, that, having ceased to see
> With bodily eyes, they are borne down by love
> Of what is lost, and perish through regret.
> Oh! no, full oft the *innocent sufferer sees*
> *Too clearly; feels too vividly; and longs*
> *To realize the vision with intense*
> *And over constant yearning;* – there, there lies
> The excess, by which the balance is destroy'd.
> Too, too contracted are these walls of flesh,
> This vital warmth too cold, these visual orbs,
> Though inconceivably endowed, too dim
> For any passion of the soul that leads
> To extasy; and, all the crooked paths
> Of time and change disdaining, takes its course
> Along the line of limitless desires. – p. 148.

With the same modifying and incorporating power, he tells us, –

> Within the soul a faculty abides

That with interpositions, which would hide
And darken, so can deal, that they become
Contingencies of pomp; and serve to exalt
Her native brightness. As the ample moon,
In the deep stillness of a summer eve,
Rising behind a thick and lofty grove,
Burns like an unconsuming fire of light,
In the green trees; and, kindling on all sides
Their leafy umbrage, turns the dusky veil
Into a substance glorious as her own,
Yea, with her own incorporated, by power
Capacious and serene. Like power abides
In man's celestial spirit; Virtue thus
Sets forth and magnifies herself; thus feeds
A calm, a beautiful, and silent fire,
From the incumbrances of mortal life,
From error, disappointment, nay, from guilt;
And sometimes, so relenting justice wills,
From palpable oppressions of despair. – p. 188.

This is high poetry; though (as we have ventured to lay the basis of
the author's sentiments in a sort of liberal Quakerism) from some parts
of it, others may, with more plausibility, object to the appearance of a
kind of Natural Methodism: we could have wished therefore that the
tale of Margaret had been postponed, till the reader had been strength-
ened by some previous acquaintance with the author's theory, and not
placed in the front of the poem, with a kind of ominous aspect, beautifully tender as it is. It is a tale of a cottage, and its female tenant,
gradually decaying together, while she expected the return of one whom
poverty and not unkindness had driven from her arms. We trust ourselves only with the conclusion –

– nine tedious years
From their first separation, nine long years,
She lingered in unquiet widowhood,
A wife and widow. I have heard, my friend,
That in yon arbour oftentimes she sate
Alone, through half the vacant Sabbath day;
And, if a dog pass'd by, she still would quit
The shade and look abroad. On this old bench
For hours she sate; and evermore her eye

> Was busy in the distance, shaping things
> That made her heart beat quick. You see that path;
> There to and fro she paced through many a day
> Of the warm summer, from a belt of hemp
> That girt her waist, spinning the long-drawn thread
> With backward steps. Yet ever as there pass'd
> A man whose garments shew'd the soldier's red,*
> The little child who sate to turn the wheel
> Ceased from his task; and she with faultering voice
> Made many a fond inquiry; and when they,
> Whose presence gave no comfort were gone by,
> Her heart was still more sad. And by yon gate,
> That bars the traveller's road, she often stood,
> And, when a stranger horseman came, the latch
> Would lift, and in his face look wistfully;
> Most happy, if from aught discovered there
> Of tender feeling, she might dare repeat
> The same sad question. Meanwhile her poor hut
> Sank to decay: for *he* was gone, whose hand,
> At the first nipping of October frost,
> Closed up each chink, and with fresh bands of straw
> Checquered the green-grown thatch. And so she lived
> Through the long winter, reckless and alone;
> Until her house by frost, and thaw, and rain
> Was sapp'd; and, while she slept, the nightly damps
> Did chill her breast; and in the stormy day
> Her tatter'd clothes were ruffled by the wind,
> Even at the side of her own fire. Yet still
> She loved this wretched spot, nor would for worlds
> Have parted hence: and still that length of road,
> And this rude bench, one torturing hope endeared,
> Fast rooted at her heart: and here, my friend,
> In sickness she remained; and here she died,
> Last human tenant of these ruin'd walls! – p. 46.

The fourth book, entitled 'Despondency Corrected,' we consider as the most valuable portion of the poem. For moral grandeur; for wide scope of thought and a long train of lofty imagery; for tender personal

---

* Her husband had enlisted for a soldier.

appeals; and a *versification* which we feel we ought to notice, but feel it also so involved in the poetry, that we can hardly mention it as a distinct excellence; it stands without competition among our didactic and descriptive verse. The general tendency of the argument (which we might almost affirm to be the leading moral of the poem) is to abate the pride of the calculating *understanding*, and to reinstate the *imagination* and the *affections* in those seats from which modern philosophy has laboured but too successfully to expel them.

'Life's autumn past,' says the grey-haired Wanderer,

> – I stand on winter's verge,
> And daily lose what I desire to keep;
> Yet rather would I instantly decline
> To the traditionary sympathies
> Of a most rustic ignorance, and take
> A fearful apprehension from the owl
> Or death-watch – and as readily rejoice
> If two auspicious magpies crossed my way –
> This rather would I do than see and hear
> The repetitions wearisome of sense,
> Where soul is dead and feeling hath no place. – p. 168.

In the same spirit, those illusions of the imaginative faculty to which the peasantry in solitary districts are peculiarly subject, are represented as the kindly ministers of *conscience:*

> – with whose service charged
> They come and go, appear and disappear;
> Diverting evil purposes, remorse
> Awakening, chastening an intemperate grief,
> Or pride of heart abating.

Reverting to the more distant ages of the world, the operation of that same faculty in producing the several fictions of Chaldean, Persian, and Grecian idolatry, is described with such seductive power, that the Solitary, in good earnest, seems alarmed at the tendency of his own argument. – Notwithstanding his fears, however, there is one thought so uncommonly fine, relative to the spirituality which lay hid beneath the gross material forms of Greek worship, in metal or stone, that we cannot resist the allurement of transcribing it –

> – Triumphant o'er this pompous show

Of art, this palpable array of sense,
On every side encountered; in despite
Of the gross fictions chanted in the streets
By wandering rhapsodists; and in contempt
Of doubt and bold denials hourly urged
Amid the wrangling schools – a SPIRIT hung,
Beautiful Region! o'er thy towns and farms,
Statues and temples, and memorial tombs;
And emanations were perceived; and acts
Of immortality, in Nature's course,
Exemplified by mysteries, that were felt
As bonds, on grave Philosopher imposed
And armed Warrior; and in every grove
A gay or pensive tenderness prevailed,
When piety more awful had relaxed.
    '*Take, running river, take these locks of mine –*'
Thus would the votary say – '*this severed hair,*
My vow fulfilling, do I here present,
Thankful for my beloved child's return,
Thy banks, Cephisus, he again hath trod,
Thy murmurs heard; and drunk the chrystal lymph
With which thou dost refresh the thirsty lip,
And moisten all day long these flowery fields.'
And doubtless, sometimes, when the hair was shed
Upon the flowing stream, a thought arose
Of Life continuous, Being unimpair'd;
That hath been, is, and where it was and is
There shall be; seen, and heard, and felt and known,
And recognized – existence unexposed
To the blind walk of mortal accident;
From diminution safe and weakening age;
While man grows old, and dwindles and decays;
And countless generations of mankind
Depart, and leave no vestige where they trod. – p. 174.

In discourse like this the first day passes away. – The second (for this almost dramatic poem takes up the action of two summer days) is varied by the introduction of the village priest; to whom the Wanderer resigns the office of chief speaker, which had been yielded to his age and experience on the first. The conference is begun at the gate of the church-yard; and after some natural speculations concerning death and immortality – and the custom of funereal and sepulchral observances, as deduced from a feeling of immortality – certain doubts are proposed respecting the quantity of moral worth existing in the world, and in that mountainous district in particular. In the resolution of these doubts, the priest enters upon a most affecting and singular strain of narration, derived from the graves around him. Pointing to hillock after hillock, he gives short histories of their tenants, disclosing their humble virtues, and touching with tender hand upon their frailties.

Nothing can be conceived finer than the manner of introducing these tales. With heaven above his head, and the mouldering turf at his feet – standing betwixt life and death – he seems to maintain that spiritual relation which he bore to his living flock, in its undiminished strength, even with their ashes; and to be in his proper cure, or diocese, among the dead.

We might extract powerful instances of pathos from these tales – the story of Ellen in particular – but their force is in combination, and in the circumstances under which they are introduced. The traditionary anecdote of the Jacobite and Hanoverian, as less liable to suffer by transplanting, and as affording an instance of that finer species of humour, that thoughtful playfulness in which the author more nearly perhaps than in any other quality resembles Cowper, we shall lay (at least a part of it) before our readers. It is the story of a whig who, having wasted a large estate in election contests, retired 'beneath a borrowed name' to a small town among these northern mountains, when a Caledonian laird, a follower of the house of Stuart, who had fled his country after the overthrow at Culloden, returning with the return of lenient times, had also fixed his residence.

>   – Here, then, they met,
> Those doughty champions; flaming Jacobite,
> And sullen Hanoverian! you might think
> That losses and vexations, less severe
> Than those which they had severally sustained,
> Would have inclined each to abate his zeal
> For his ungrateful cause; no, – I have heard
> My reverend father tell that, mid the calm
> Of that small town encountering thus, they filled
> Daily its bowling-green with harmless strife,
> Plagued with uncharitable thoughts the church,
> And vex'd the market-place! But in the breasts

Of these opponents gradually was wrought,
With little change of general sentiment,
Such change towards each other, that their days
By choice were spent in constant fellowship;
And, if at times they fretted with the yoke,
Those very bickerings made them love it more.
    A favourite boundary to their lengthen'd walks
This church-yard was. And, whether they had come
Treading their path in sympathy, and linked
In social converse, or by some short space
Discreetly parted to preserve the peace,
One spirit seldom failed to extend its sway
Over both minds, when they awhile had mark'd
The visible quiet of this holy ground
And breathed its soothing air. –

There live who yet remember to have seen
Their courtly figures – seated on a stump
Of an old yew, their favourite resting place.
But, as the remnant of the long-lived tree
Was disappearing by a swift decay,
They with joint care determined to erect
Upon its sight, a dial, which should stand,
For public use; and also might survive
As their own private monument; for this
Was the particular spot, in which they wished
(And heaven was pleased to accomplish their desire)
That, undivided, their remains should lie.
So, where the mouldered tree had stood, was raised
Yon structure, framing, with the ascent of steps
That to the decorated pillar lead,
A work of art, more sumptuous, as might seem,
Than suits this place; yet built in no proud scorn
Of rustic homeliness; they only aimed
To ensure for it respectful guardianship.
Around the margin of the plate, whereon
The shadow falls, to note the stealthy hours,
Winds an inscriptive legend. –
                    At these words
Thither we turned; and gathered, as we read,

The appropriate sense, in Latin numbers couched.
'Time flies; it is his melancholy task
To bring, and bear away, delusive hopes,
And re-produce the troubles he destroys.
But, while his business thus is occupied,
Discerning mortal! do thou serve the will
Of Time's eternal Master, and that peace,
Which the world wants, shall be for thee confirmed.'
                                              — pp. 270–3.

The causes which have prevented the poetry of Mr Wordsworth from attaining its full share of popularity are to be found in the boldness and originality of his genius. The times are past when a poet could securely follow the direction of his own mind into whatever tracts it might lead. A writer, who would be popular, must timidly coast the shore of prescribed sentiment and sympathy. He must have just as much more of the imaginative faculty than his readers, as will serve to keep their apprehensions from stagnating, but not so much as to alarm their jealousy. He must not think or feel too deeply.

If he has had the fortune to be bred in the midst of the most magnificent objects of creation, he must not have given away his heart to them; or if he have, he must conceal his love, or not carry his expressions of it beyond that point of rapture, which the occasional tourist thinks it not overstepping decorum to betray, or the limit which that gentlemanly spy upon Nature, the picturesque traveller, has vouchsafed to countenance. He must do this, or be content to be thought an enthusiast.

If from living among simple mountaineers, from a daily intercourse with them, not upon the footing of a patron, but in the character of an equal, he has detected, or imagines that he has detected, through the cloudy medium of their unlettered discourse, thoughts and apprehensions not vulgar; traits of patience and constancy, love unwearied, and heroic endurance, not unfit (as he may judge) to be made the subject of verse, he will be deemed a man of perverted genius by the philanthropist who, conceiving of the peasantry of his country only as objects of a pecuniary sympathy, starts at finding them elevated to a level of humanity with himself, having their own loves, enmities, cravings, aspirations, &c., as much beyond his faculty to believe, as his beneficence to supply.

If from a familiar observation of the ways of children, and much more from a retrospect of his own mind when a child, he has gathered more reverential notions of that state than fall to the lot of ordinary observers, and, escaping from the dissonant wranglings of men, has tuned his lyre, though but for occasional harmonies, to the milder utterance of that soft age, – his verses shall be censured as infantile by critics who confound poetry 'having children for its subject' with poetry that is 'childish,' and who, having themselves perhaps never been *children*, never having possessed the tenderness and docility of that age, know not what the soul of a child is – how apprehensive! how imaginative! how religious!

We have touched upon some of the causes which we conceive to have been unfriendly to the author's former poems. We think they do not apply in the same force to the one before us. There is in it more of uniform elevation, a wider scope of subject, less of manner, and it contains none of those starts and imperfect shapings which in some of this author's smaller pieces offended the weak, and gave scandal to the perverse. It must indeed be approached with seriousness. It has in it much of that quality which 'draws the devout, deterring the profane.' Those who hate the Paradise Lost will not love this poem. The steps of the great master are discernible in it; not in direct imitation or injurious parody, but in the following of the spirit, in free homage and generous subjection.

One objection it is impossible not to foresee. It will be asked, why put such eloquent discourse in the mouth of a pedlar? It might be answered that Mr Wordsworth's plan required a character in humble life to be the organ of his philosophy. It was in harmony with the system and scenery of his poem. We read Piers Plowman's Creed, and the lowness of the teacher seems to add a simple dignity to the doctrine. Besides, the poet has bestowed an unusual share of education upon him. Is it too much to suppose that the author, at some early period of his life, may himself have known such a person, a man endowed with sentiments above his situation, another Burns; and that the dignified strains which he has attributed to the Wanderer may be no more than recollections of his conversation, heightened only by the amplification natural to poetry, or the lustre which imagination flings back upon the objects and companions of our youth? After all, if there should be found readers willing to admire the poem, who yet feel scandalized at a *name*, we would advise them, wherever it occurs, to substitute silently the word *Palmer*, or *Pilgrim*, or any less offensive designation, which shall connect the notion of sobriety in heart and manners with the experience and privileges which a wayfaring life confers.

(*Quarterly Review*, October 1814)

 *From* Essays of Elia *(1823)*
and
Last Essays of Elia *(1833)*

THE TWO RACES OF MEN

THE human species, according to the best theory I can form of it, is composed of two distinct races, *the men who borrow*, and *the men who lend*. To these two original diversities may be reduced all those impertinent classifications of Gothic and Celtic tribes, white men, black men, red men. All the dwellers upon earth, 'Parthians, and Medes, and Elamites,' flock hither, and do naturally fall in with one or other of these primary distinctions. The infinite superiority of the former, which I choose to designate as the *great race*, is discernible in their figure, port, and a certain instinctive sovereignty. The latter are born degraded. 'He shall serve his brethren.' There is something in the air of one of this cast, lean and suspicious; contrasting with the open, trusting, generous manner of the other.

Observe who have been the greatest borrowers of all ages – Alcibiades – Falstaff – Sir Richard Steele – our late incomparable Brinsley [1] – what a family likeness in all four!

What a careless, even deportment hath your borrower! what rosy grills! what a beautiful reliance on Providence doth he manifest, – taking no more thought than lilies! What contempt for money – accounting it (yours and mine especially) no better than dross! What a liberal confounding of those pedantic distinctions of *meum* and *tuum!* [2] or rather, what a noble simplification of language (beyond Tooke), [3] resolving these supposed opposites into one clear, intelligible pronoun adjective! – What near approaches doth he make to the primitive *community*, – to the extent of one-half of the principle at least! –

He is the true taxer who 'calleth all the world up to be taxed'; and the distance is as vast between him and *one of us*, as subsisted betwixt the Augustan Majesty and the poorest obolary [4] Jew that paid it tribute-pittance at Jerusalem! – His exactions, too, have such a cheerful, voluntary air! So far removed from your sour parochial or state-gatherers, – those ink-horn varlets, who carry their want of welcome in their faces! He cometh to you with a smile, and troubleth you with no receipt; confining himself to no set season. Every day is his Candlemas, or his Feast of Holy Michael. He applieth the *lene tormentum* [5] of a pleasant look to your purse, – which to that gentle warmth expands her silken leaves, as naturally as the cloak of the traveller, for which sun and wind contended! He is the true Propontic which never ebbeth! The sea which taketh handsomely at each man's hand. In vain the victim, whom he delighteth to honour, struggles with destiny; he is in the net. Lend therefore cheerfully, O man ordained to lend — that thou lose not in the end, with thy worldly penny, the reversion promised. Combine not preposterously in thine own person the penalties of Lazarus and of Dives! — but, when thou seest the proper authority coming, meet it smilingly, as it were half-way. Come, a handsome sacrifice! See how light *he* makes of it! Strain not courtesies with a noble enemy.

Reflections like the foregoing were forced upon my mind by the death of my old friend,* Ralph Bigod, Esq., who departed this life on Wednesday evening; dying, as he had lived, without much trouble. He boasted himself a descendant from mighty ancestors of that name, who heretofore held ducal dignities in this realm. In his actions and sentiments he belied not the stock to which he pretended. Early in life he found himself invested with ample revenues; which, with that noble disinterestedness which I have noticed as inherent in men of the *great race*, he took almost immediate measures entirely to dissipate and bring to nothing: for there is something revolting in the idea of a king holding a private purse; and the thoughts of Bigod were all regal. Thus furnished, by the very act of disfurnishment; getting rid of the cumbersome luggage of riches, more apt (as one sings)

> To slacken virtue, and abate her edge,
> Than prompt her to do aught may merit praise,

he set forth, like some Alexander, upon his great enterprise, 'borrowing and to borrow!'

In his periegesis,[7] or triumphant progress throughout this island, it has been calculated that he laid a tithe part of the inhabitants under contribution. I reject this estimate as greatly exaggerated: — but having had the honour of accompanying my friend, divers times, in his perambulations about this vast city, I own I was greatly struck at first with the prodigious number of faces we met, who claimed a sort of respectful acquaintance with us. He was one day so obliging as to explain the phenomenon. It seems, these were his tributaries; feeders of his exchequer; gentlemen, his good friends (as he was pleased to express himself), to whom he had occasionally been beholden for a loan. Their

* John Fenwick, editor of the 'Albion.'[6]

multitudes did in no way disconcert him. He rather took a pride in numbering them; and, with Comus, seemed pleased to be 'stocked with so fair a herd.'

With such sources, it was a wonder how he contrived to keep his treasury always empty. He did it by force of an aphorism, which he had often in his mouth, that 'money kept longer than three days stinks.' So he made use of it while it was fresh. A good part he drank away (for he was an excellent toss-pot), some he gave away, the rest he threw away, literally tossing and hurling it violently from him – as boys do burrs, or as if it had been infectious, – into ponds, or ditches, or deep holes, – inscrutable cavities of the earth; – or he would bury it (where he would never seek it again) by a river's side under some bank, which (he would facetiously observe) paid no interest – but out away from him it must go peremptorily, as Hagar's offspring into the wilderness, while it was sweet. He never missed it. The streams were perennial which fed his fisc. When new supplies became necessary, the first person that had the felicity to fall in with him, friend or stranger, was sure to contribute to the deficiency. For Bigod had an *undeniable* way with him. He had a cheerful, open exterior, a quick jovial eye, a bald forehead, just touched with grey (*cana fides*).[8] He anticipated no excuse, and found none. And, waiving for a while my theory as to the *great race*, I would put it to the most untheorising reader, who may at times have disposable coin in his pocket, whether it is not more repugnant to the kindliness of his nature to refuse such a one as I am describing, than to say *no* to a poor petitionary rogue (your bastard borrower), who, by his mumping visnomy,[9] tells you, that he expects nothing better; and, therefore, whose preconceived notions and expectations you do in reality so much less shock in the refusal.

When I think of this man; his fiery glow of heart; his swell of feeling; how magnificent, how *ideal* he was; how great at the midnight hour; and when I compare with him the companions with whom I have associated since, I grudge the saving of a few idle ducats, and think that I am fallen into the society of *lenders*, and *little men*.

To one like Elia, whose treasures are rather cased in leather covers than closed in iron coffers, there is a class of alienators more formidable than that which I have touched upon; I mean your *borrowers of books* – those mutilators of collections, spoilers of the symmetry of shelves, and creators of odd volumes. There is Comberbatch,[10] matchless in his depredations!

That foul gap in the bottom shelf facing you, like a great eye-tooth knocked out – (you are now with me in my little back study in Bloomsbury, reader!) – with the huge Switzer-like tomes on each side (like the Guildhall giants, in their reformed posture, guardant of nothing) once held the tallest of my folios, *Opera Bonaventuræ*, choice and massy divinity, to which its two supporters (school divinity also, but of a lesser calibre, – Bellarmine, and Holy Thomas), showed but as dwarfs, – itself an Ascapart! – *that* Comberbatch abstracted upon the faith of a theory he holds, which is more easy, I confess, for me to suffer by than to refute, namely, that 'the title to property in a book (my Bonaventure, for instance), is in exact ratio to the claimant's powers of understanding and appreciating the same.' Should he go on acting upon this theory, which of our shelves is safe?

The slight vacuum in the left hand case – two shelves from the ceiling – scarcely distinguishable but by the quick eye of a loser – was whilom the commodious resting-place of Browne on Urn Burial. C. will hardly allege that he knows more about the treatise than I do, who introduced it to him, and was indeed the first (of the moderns) to discover its beauties – but so have I known a foolish lover to praise his mistress in the presence of a rival more qualified to carry her off than himself. – Just below, Dodsley's dramas want their fourth volume, where Vittoria Corombona is! The remainder nine are as distasteful as Priam's refuse sons, when the Fates *borrowed* Hector. Here stood the Anatomy of Melancholy, in sober state. – There loitered the Complete Angler; quiet as in life, by some stream side. – In yonder nook, John Buncle, a widower-volume, with 'eyes closed,' mourns his ravished mate.

One justice I must do my friend, that if he sometimes, like the sea, sweeps away a treasure, at another time, sea-like, he throws up as rich an equivalent to match it. I have a small under-collection of this nature (my friend's gatherings in his various calls), picked up, he had forgotten at what odd places, and deposited with as little memory at mine. I take in these orphans, the twice-deserted. These proselytes of the gate are welcome as the true Hebrews. There they stand in conjunction; natives, and naturalized. The latter seemed as little disposed to inquire out their true lineage as I am. – I charge no warehouse-room for these deodands,[11] nor shall ever put myself to the ungentlemanly trouble of advertising a sale of them to pay expenses.

To lose a volume to C. carries some sense and meaning in it. You are sure that he will make one hearty meal on your viands, if he can give no account of the platter after it. But what moved thee, wayward, spiteful K.,[12] to be so importunate to carry off with thee, in spite of tears and adjurations to thee to forbear, the Letters of that princely woman, the thrice noble Margaret Newcastle? – knowing at the time, and knowing that I knew also, thou most assuredly wouldst never turn over one leaf of the illustrious folio: – what but the mere spirit of contradiction, and childish love of getting the better of thy friend? – Then, worst cut of all! to transport it with thee to the Gallican land –

> Unworthy land to harbour such a sweetness,
> A virtue in which all ennobling thoughts dwelt,
> Pure thoughts, kind thoughts, high thoughts, her sex's wonder!

– hadst thou not thy play-books, and books of jests and fancies, about thee, to keep thee merry, even as thou keepest all companies with thy quips and mirthful tales? – Child of the Green-room, it was unkindly done of thee. Thy wife, too, that part-French, better-part-English-woman! – that *she* could fix upon no other treatise to bear away in kindly token of remembering us, than the works of Fulke Greville, Lord Brook – of which no Frenchman, nor woman of France, Italy, or England, was ever by nature constituted to comprehend a tittle! *Was there not Zimmerman on Solitude?*

Reader, if haply thou art blessed with a moderate collection, be shy of showing it; or if thy heart overfloweth to lend them, lend thy books; but let it be to such a one as S. T. C. – he will return them (generally anticipating the time appointed) with usury; enriched with annotations, tripling their value.[13] I have had experience. Many are these precious MSS. of his – (in *matter* oftentimes, and almost in *quantity* not infre-quently, vying with the originals) – in no very clerkly hand – legible in my Daniel; in old Burton; in Sir Thomas Browne; and those abstruser cogitations of the Greville, now, alas! wandering in Pagan lands – I counsel thee, shut not thy heart, nor thy library, against S. T. C.

(*London Magazine*, December 1820)

A QUAKERS' MEETING

Still-born Silence? thou that art
Flood-gate of the deeper heart!
Offspring of a heavenly kind!
Frost o' the mouth, and thaw o' the mind!
Secrecy's confidant, and he
Who makes religion mystery!
Admiration's speaking'st tongue!
Leave, thy desert shades among,
Reverend hermits' hallowed cells,
Where retired devotion dwells!
With thy enthusiasms come,
Seize our tongues, and strike us dumb!*

READER, would'st thou know what true peace and quiet mean: would'st thou find a refuge from the noises and clamours of the multitude; would'st thou enjoy at once solitude and society; would'st thou possess the depth of thine own spirit in stillness, without being shut out from the consolatory faces of thy species; would'st thou be alone, and yet accompanied; solitary, yet not desolate; singular, yet not without some to keep thee in countenance; – a unit in aggregate; a simple in composite: – come with me into a Quakers' Meeting.

Dost thou love silence deep as that 'before the winds were made'? go not out into the wilderness, descend not into the profundities of the earth; shut not up thy casements; nor pour wax into the little cells of thy ears, with little-faith'd self-mistrusting Ulysses. – Retire with me into a Quakers' Meeting.

For a man to refrain even from good words, and to hold his peace, it is commendable; but for a multitude, it is great mastery.

What is the stillness of the desert, compared with this place? what the uncommunicating muteness of fishes? – here the goddess reigns and revels. – 'Boreas, and Cesias, and Argestes loud,'[1] do not with their inter-confounding uproars more augment the brawl – nor the waves of the blown Baltic with their clubbed sounds – than their opposite (Silence

* From 'Poems of all sorts,' by Richard Fleckno, 1653.

her sacred self) is multiplied and rendered more intense by numbers, and by sympathy. She too hath her deeps, that call unto deeps. Negation itself hath a positive more or less; and closed eyes would seem to obscure the great obscurity of midnight.

There are wounds, which an imperfect solitude cannot heal. By imperfect I mean that which a man enjoyeth by himself. The perfect is that which he can sometimes attain in crowds, but nowhere so absolutely as in a Quakers' Meeting. – Those first hermits did certainly understand this principle, when they retired into Egyptian solitudes, not singly, but in shoals, to enjoy one another's want of conversation. The Carthusian is bound to his brethren by this agreeing spirit of incommunicativeness. In secular occasions, what so pleasant as to be reading a book through a long winter evening, with a friend sitting by – say, a wife – he, or she, too (if that be probable), reading another, without interruption, or oral communication? – can there be no sympathy without the gabble of words? – away with this inhuman, shy, single, shade-and-cavern-haunting solitariness. Give me, Master Zimmerman,[2] a sympathetic solitude.

To pace alone in the cloisters, or side aisles of some cathedral, time-stricken:

> Or under hanging mountains,
> Or by the fall of fountains;

is but a vulgar luxury, compared with that which those enjoy, who come together for the purposes of more complete, abstracted solitude. This is the loneliness 'to be felt.' – The Abbey Church of Westminster hath nothing so solemn, so spirit-soothing, as the naked walls and benches of a Quakers' Meeting. Here are no tombs, no inscriptions,

> – sands, ignoble things,
> Dropt from the ruined sides of kings –

but here is something, which throws Antiquity herself into the fore-ground – SILENCE – eldest of things – language of old Night – primitive Discourser – to which the insolent decays of mouldering grandeur have but arrived by a violent, and, as we may say, unnatural progression.

> How reverend is the view of these hushed heads,
> Looking tranquillity!

Nothing-plotting, nought-caballing, unmischievous synod! convocation without intrigue! parliament without debate! what a lesson dost thou read to Council, and to consistory! – if my pen treat of you lightly – as haply it will wander – yet my spirit hath gravely felt the wisdom of your custom, when, sitting among you in deepest peace, which some out-welling tears would rather confirm than disturb, I have reverted to the times of your beginnings, and the sowings of the seed by Fox and Dewesbury.[3] – I have witnessed that, which brought before my eyes your heroic tranquillity, inflexible to the rude jests and serious violences of the insolent soldiery, republican or royalist, sent to molest you – for ye sate betwixt the fires of two persecutions, the outcast and off-scowering of church and presbytery. – I have seen the reeling sea-ruffian, who had wandered into your receptacle, with the avowed intention of disturbing your quiet, from the very spirit of the place receive in a moment a new heart, and presently sit among ye as a lamb amidst lambs. And I remembered Penn before his accusers, and Fox in the bail-dock, where he was lifted up in spirit, as he tells us, and 'the Judge and the Jury became as dead men under his feet.'

Reader, if you are not acquainted with it, I would recommend to you, above all church-narratives, to read Sewel's History of the Quakers. It is in folio, and is the abstract of the journals of Fox, and the primitive Friends. It is far more edifying and affecting than anything you will read of Wesley and his colleagues. Here is nothing to stagger you, nothing to make you mistrust, no suspicion of alloy, no drop or dreg of the worldly or ambitious spirit. You will here read the true story of that much-injured, ridiculed man (who perhaps hath been a by-word in your mouth) – James Naylor: what dreadful sufferings, with what patience, he endured, even to the boring through of his tongue with red-hot irons, without a murmur; and with what strength of mind, when the delusion he had fallen into, which they stigmatized for blasphemy, had given way to clearer thoughts, he could renounce his error, in a strain of the beautifullest humility, yet keep his first grounds, and be a Quaker still! – so different from the practice of your common converts from enthusiasm, who, when they apostatise, *apostatise all*, and think they can never get far enough from the society of their former errors, even to the renunciation of some saving truths, with which they had been mingled, not implicated.

Get the Writings of John Woolman by heart; and love the early Quakers.

How far the followers of these good men in our days have kept to the primitive spirit, or in what proportion they have substituted formality for it, the Judge of Spirits can alone determine. I have seen faces in their assemblies, upon which the dove sate visibly brooding. Others again I have watched, when my thoughts should have been better engaged, in which I could possibly detect nothing but a blank inanity. But quiet was in all, and the disposition to unanimity, and the absence of the fierce controversial workings. – If the spiritual pretensions of the Quakers have abated, at least they make few pretences. Hypocrites they certainly are not, in their preaching. It is seldom indeed that you shall see one get up amongst them to hold forth. Only now and then a trembling female, generally *ancient,* voice is heard – you cannot guess from what part of the meeting it proceeds – with a low, buzzing, musical sound, laying out a few words which 'she thought might suit the condition of some present,' with a quaking diffidence, which leaves no possibility of supposing that any thing of female vanity was mixed up, where the tones were so full of tenderness, and a restraining modesty. – The men, for what I have observed, speak seldomer.

Once only, and it was some years ago, I witnessed a sample of the old Foxian orgasm. It was a man of giant stature, who, as Wordsworth phrases it, might have danced 'from head to foot equipt in iron mail.' His frame was of iron too. But *he* was malleable. I saw him shake all over with the spirit – I dare not say, of delusion. The strivings of the outer man were unutterable—he seemed not to speak, but to be spoken from. I saw the strong man bowed down, and his knees to fail – his joints all seemed loosening – it was a figure to set off against Paul Preaching – the words he uttered were few, and sound – he was evidently resisting his will – keeping down his own word-wisdom with more mighty effort, than the world's orators strain for theirs. 'He had been a WIT in his youth,' he told us, with expressions of a sober remorse. And it was not till long after the impression had begun to wear away, that I was enabled, with something like a smile, to recall the striking incongruity of the confession – understanding the term in its worldly acceptation – with the frame and physiognomy of the person before me. His brow would have scared away the Levites – the Jocos Risus-que [4] – faster than the Loves fled the face of Dis at Enna. By *wit*, even in his youth, I will be sworn he understood something far within the limits of an allowable liberty.

More frequently the Meeting is broken up without a word having been spoken. But the mind has been fed. You go away with a sermon, not made with hands. You have been in the milder caverns of Trophonius; [5] or as in some den, where that fiercest and savagest of all wild creatures, the TONGUE, that unruly member, has strangely lain tied up and captive. You have bathed with stillness. – O when the spirit is sore fretted, even tired to sickness of the janglings, and nonsense-noises of the world, what a balm and a solace it is, to go and seat yourself for a quiet half hour, upon some undisputed corner of a bench, among the gentle Quakers!

Their garb and stillness conjoined, present an uniformity, tranquil and herd-like – as in the pasture – 'forty feeding like one.' –

The very garments of a Quaker seem incapable of receiving a soil; and cleanliness in them to be something more than the absence of its contrary. Every Quakeress is a lily; and when they come up in bands to their Whitsun-conferences, whitening the easterly streets of the metropolis, from all parts of the United Kingdom, they show like troops of the Shining Ones.

(*London Magazine*, April 1821)

THE OLD AND THE NEW
SCHOOLMASTER

MY reading has been lamentably desultory and immethodical. Odd, out of the way, old English plays, and treatises, have supplied me with most of my notions, and ways of feeling. In every thing that relates to *science*, I am a whole Encyclopædia behind the rest of the world. I should have scarcely cut a figure among the franklins, or country gentlemen, in King John's days. I know less geography than a school-boy of six weeks' standing. To me a map of old Ortelius is as authentic as Arrowsmith.[1] I do not know whereabout Africa merges into Asia; whether Ethiopia lie in one or other of those great divisions; nor can form the remotest conjecture of the position of New South Wales, or Van Diemen's Land. Yet do I hold a correspondence with a very dear friend in the first-named of these two Terræ Incognitæ. I have no astronomy. I do not know where to look for the Bear, or Charles's Wain; the place of any star; or the name of any of them at sight. I guess at Venus only by her brightness — and if the sun on some portentous morn were to make his first appearance in the West, I verily believe, that, while all the world were gasping in apprehension about me, I alone should stand unterrified, from sheer incuriosity and want of observation. Of history and chronology I possess some vague points, such as one cannot help picking up in the course of miscellaneous study; but I never deliberately sat down to a chronicle, even of my own country. I have most dim apprehensions of the four great monarchies; and sometimes the Assyrian, sometimes the Persian, floats as *first* in my fancy. I make the wildest conjectures concerning Egypt, and her shepherd kings. My friend *M.*,[2] with great pains-taking, got me to think I understood the first proposition in Euclid, but gave me over in despair at the second. I am entirely unacquainted with the modern languages; and, like a better man than myself, have 'small Latin and less Greek.' I am a stranger to the shapes and texture of the commonest trees, herbs, flowers — not from the circumstance of my being town-born — for I should have brought the same inobservant spirit into the world with me, had I first seen it, 'on Devon's leafy shores,' — and am no less at a loss among purely town-objects, tools, engines, mechanic processes. —

Not that I affect ignorance – but my head has not many mansions, nor spacious; and I have been obliged to fill it with such cabinet curiosities as it can hold without aching. I sometimes wonder how I have passed my probation with so little discredit in the world, as I have done, upon so meagre a stock. But the fact is, a man may do very well with a very little knowledge, and scarce be found out, in mixed company; every body is so much more ready to produce his own, than to call for a display of your acquisitions. But in a *tête-à-tête* there is no shuffling. The truth will out. There is nothing which I dread so much, as the being left alone for a quarter of an hour with a sensible, well-informed man that does not know me. I lately got into a dilemma of this sort. –

In one of my daily jaunts between Bishopsgate and Shacklewell, the coach stopped to take up a staid-looking gentleman, about the wrong side of thirty, who was giving his parting directions (while the steps were adjusting), in a tone of mild authority, to a tall youth, who seemed to be neither his clerk, his son, nor his servant, but something partaking of all three. The youth was dismissed, and we drove on. As we were the sole passengers, he naturally enough addressed his conversation to me; and we discussed the merits of the fare; the civility and punctuality of the driver; the circumstance of an opposition coach having been lately set up, with the probabilities of its success – to all which I was enabled to return pretty satisfactory answers, having been drilled into this kind of etiquette by some years' daily practice of riding to and fro in the stage aforesaid – when he suddenly alarmed me by a startling question, whether I had seen the show of prize cattle that morning in Smithfield? Now as I had not seen it, and do not greatly care for such sort of exhibitions, I was obliged to return a cold negative. He seemed a little mortified, as well as astonished, at my declaration, as (it appeared) he was just come fresh from the sight, and doubtless had hoped to compare notes on the subject. However, he assured me that I had lost a fine treat, as it far exceeded the show of last year. We were now approaching Norton Falgate, when the sight of some shop-goods *ticketed* freshened him up into a dissertation upon the cheapness of cottons this spring. I was now a little in heart, as the nature of my morning avocations had brought me into some sort of familiarity with the raw material; and I was surprised to find how eloquent I was becoming on the state of the Indian market – when, presently, he dashed my incipient vanity to the earth at once, by inquiring whether I had ever made any calculation as to the value of the rental of all the retail shops in London. Had he asked of me, what song the Sirens sang, or what name Achilles assumed when he hid himself among women, I might, with Sir Thomas Browne, have hazarded a 'wide solution.'* My companion saw my embarrassment, and, the almshouses beyond Shoreditch just coming in view, with great good-nature and dexterity shifted his conversation to the subject of public charities; which led to the comparative merits of provision for the poor in past and present times, with observations on the old monastic institutions, and charitable orders; but, finding me rather dimly impressed with some glimmering notions from old poetic associations, than strongly fortified with any speculations reducible to calculation on the subject, he gave the matter up; and, the country beginning to open more and more upon us, as we approached the turnpike at Kingsland (the destined termination of his journey), he put a home thrust upon me, in the most unfortunate position he could have chosen, by advancing some queries relative to the North Pole Expedition. While I was muttering out something about the Panorama of those strange regions (which I had actually seen), by way of parrying the question, the coach stopping relieved me from any further apprehensions. My companion getting out, left me in the comfortable possession of my ignorance; and I heard him, as he went off, putting questions to an outside passenger, who had alighted with him, regarding an epidemic disorder, that had been rife about Dalston; and which, my friend assured him, had gone through five or six schools in the neighbourhood. The truth now flashed upon me, that my companion was a schoolmaster; and that the youth, whom he had parted from at our first acquaintance, must have been one of the bigger boys, or the usher. – He was evidently a kind-hearted man, who did not seem so much desirous of provoking discussion by the questions which he put, as of obtaining information at any rate. It did not appear that he took any interest, either, in such kind of inquiries, for their own sake; but that he was in some way bound to seek for knowledge. A greenish-coloured coat, which he had on, forbade me to surmise that he was a clergyman. The adventure gave birth to some reflections on the difference between persons of his profession in past and present times.

Rest to the souls of those fine old Pedagogues; the breed, long since extinct, of the Lilys, and the Linacres: [3] who believing that all learning was contained in the languages which they taught, and despising every other acquirement as superficial and useless, came to their task as to a sport! Passing from infancy to age, they dreamed away all their days as

* Urn Burial.

in a grammar-school. Revolving in a perpetual cycle of declensions, conjugations, syntaxes, and prosodies; renewing constantly the occupations which had charmed their studious childhood; rehearsing continually the part of the past; life must have slipped from them at last like one day. They were always in their first garden, reaping harvests of their golden time, among their *Flori-* and their *Spici-legia;* [4] in Arcadia still, but kings; the ferule of their sway not much harsher, but of like dignity with that mild sceptre attributed to king Basileus; the Greek and Latin, their stately Pamela and their Philoclea; with the occasional duncery of some untoward Tyro, serving for a refreshing interlude of a Mopsa, or a clown Damœtas!

With what a savour doth the Preface to Colet's, or (as it is sometimes called) Paul's 'Accidence,' set forth! 'To exhort every man to the learning of grammar, that intendeth to attain the understanding of the tongues, wherein is contained a great treasury of wisdom and knowledge, it would seem but vain and lost labour; for so much as it is known, that nothing can surely be ended, whose beginning is either feeble or faulty; and no building be perfect, whereas the foundation and ground work is ready to fall, and unable to uphold the burden of the frame.' How well doth this stately preamble (comparable to those which Milton commendeth as 'having been the usage to prefix to some solemn law, then first promulgated by Solon, or Lycurgus') correspond with and illustrate that pious zeal for conformity, expressed in a succeeding clause, which would fence about grammar-rules with the severity of faith-articles! – 'as for the diversity of grammars, it is well profitably taken away by the king's majesties wisdom, who foreseeing the inconvenience, and favourably providing the remedie, caused one kind of grammar by sundry learned men to be diligently drawn, and so to be set out, only everywhere to be taught for the use of learners, and for the hurt in changing of schoolmaisters.' What a *gusto* in that which follows: 'wherein it is profitable that he [the pupil] can orderly decline his noun and his verb.' *His* noun!

The fine dream is fading away fast; and the least concern of a teacher in the present day is to inculcate grammar-rules.

The modern schoolmaster is expected to know a little of every thing, because his pupil is required not to be entirely ignorant of anything. He must be superficially, if I may so say, omniscient. He is to know something of pneumatics; of chemistry; of whatever is curious, or proper to excite the attention of the youthful mind; an insight into mechanics is desirable, with a touch of statistics; the quality of soils, etc., botany, the constitution of his country, *cum multis aliis*.[5] You may get a notion of some part of his expected duties by consulting the famous Tractate on Education, addressed to Mr Hartlib.[6]

All these things – these, or the desire of them – he is expected to instil, not by set lessons from professors, which he may charge in the bill, but at school-intervals, as he walks the streets, or saunters through green fields (those natural instructors), with his pupils. The least part of what is expected from him, is to be done in school-hours. He must insinuate knowledge at the *mollia tempora fandi*.[7] He must seize every occasion – the season of the year – the time of the day – a passing cloud – a rainbow – a waggon of hay – a regiment of soldiers going by – to inculcate something useful. He can receive no pleasure from a casual glimpse of Nature, but must catch at it as an object of instruction. He must interpret beauty into the picturesque. He cannot relish a beggar-man, or a gipsy, for thinking of the suitable improvement. Nothing comes to him, not spoiled by the sophisticating medium of moral uses. The Universe – that Great Book, as it has been called – is to him indeed, to all intents and purposes, a book, out of which he is doomed to read tedious homilies to distasting schoolboys. – Vacations themselves are none to him, he is only rather worse off than before; for commonly he has some intrusive upper-boy fastened upon him at such high times; some cadet of a great family; some neglected lump of nobility, or gentry; that he must drag after him to the play, to the Panorama, to Mr Bartley's Orrery, to the Panopticon,[8] or into the country, to a friend's house, or his favourite watering-place. Wherever he goes, this uneasy shadow attends him. A boy is at his board, and in his path, and in all his movements. He is boy-rid, sick of perpetual boy.

Boys are capital fellows in their own way, among their mates; but they are unwholesome companions for grown people. The restraint is felt no less on the one side, than on the other. – Even a child, that 'plaything for an hour,' tires *always*. The noises of children, playing their own fancies – as I now hearken to them by fits, sporting on the green before my window, while I am engaged in these grave speculations at my neat suburban retreat at Shacklewell – by distance made more sweet – inexpressibly take from the labour of my task. It is like writing to music. They seem to modulate my periods. They ought at least to do so – for in the voice of that tender age there is a kind of poetry, far unlike the harsh prose-accents of man's conversation. – I should but spoil their sport, and diminish my own sympathy for them, by mingling in their pastime.

I would not be domesticated all my days with a person of very superior capacity to my own – not, if I know myself at all, from any considerations of jealousy or self-comparison, for the occasional communion with such minds has constituted the fortune and felicity of my life – but the habit of too constant intercourse with spirits above you, instead of raising you, keeps you down. Too frequent doses of original thinking from others, restrain what lesser portion of that faculty you may possess of your own. You get entangled in another man's mind, even as you lose yourself in another man's grounds. You are walking with a tall varlet, whose strides out-pace yours to lassitude. The constant operation of such potent agency would reduce me, I am convinced, to imbecility. You may derive thoughts from others; your way of thinking, the mould in which your thoughts are cast, must be your own. Intellect may be imparted, but not each man's intellectual frame. –

As little as I should wish to be always thus dragged upwards, as little (or rather still less) is it desirable to be stunted downwards by your associates. The trumpet does not more stun you by its loudness, than a whisper teases you by its provoking inaudibility.

Why are we never quite at our ease in the presence of a schoolmaster? – because we are conscious that he is not quite at his ease in ours. He is awkward, and out of place, in the society of his equals. He comes like Gulliver from among his little people, and he cannot fit the stature of his understanding to yours. He cannot meet you on the square. He wants a point given him, like an indifferent whist-player. He is so used to teaching, that he wants to be teaching *you*. One of these professors, upon my complaining that these little sketches of mine were any thing but methodical, and that I was unable to make them otherwise, kindly offered to instruct me in the method by which young gentlemen in *his* seminary were taught to compose English themes. – The jests of a schoolmaster are coarse, or thin. They do not *tell* out of school. He is under the restraint of a formal and didactive hypocrisy in company, as a clergyman is under a moral one. He can no more let his intellect loose in society, than the other can his inclinations. – He is forlorn among his co-evals; his juniors cannot be his friends.

'I take blame to myself,' said a sensible man of this profession, writing to a friend respecting a youth who had quitted his school abruptly, 'that your nephew was not more attached to me. But persons in my situation are more to be pitied, than can well be imagined. We are surrounded by young, and, consequently, ardently affectionate hearts, but *we* can never hope to share an atom of their affections. The relation of master and scholar forbids this. *How pleasing this must be to you, how I envy your feelings*, my friends will sometimes say to me, when they see young men, whom I have educated, return after some years' absence from school, their eyes shining with pleasure, while they shake hands with their old master, bringing a present of game to me, or a toy to my wife, and thanking me in the warmest terms for my care of their education. A holiday is begged for the boys; the house is a scene of happiness; I, only, am sad, at heart. – This fine-spirited and warm-hearted youth, who fancies he repays his master with gratitude for the care of his boyish years – this young man – in the eight long years I watched over him with a parent's anxiety, never could repay me with one look of genuine feeling. He was proud, when I praised; he was submissive, when I reproved him; but he did never *love* me – and what he now mistakes for gratitude and kindness for me, is but the pleasant sensation, which all persons feel at revisiting the scene of their boyish hopes and fears; and the seeing on equal terms the man they were accustomed to look up to with reverence. My wife too,' this interesting correspondent goes on to say, 'my once darling Anna, is the wife of a schoolmaster. – When I married her – knowing that the wife of a schoolmaster ought to be a busy notable creature, and fearing that my gentle Anna would ill supply the loss of my dear bustling mother, just then dead, who never sat still, was in every part of the house in a moment, and whom I was obliged sometimes to threaten to fasten down in a chair, to save her from fatiguing herself to death – I expressed my fears, that I was bringing her into a way of life unsuitable to her; and she, who loved me tenderly, promised for my sake to exert herself to perform the duties of her new situation. She promised, and she has kept her word. What wonders will not a woman's love perform? – My house is managed with a propriety and decorum, unknown in other schools; my boys are well fed, look healthy, and have every proper accommodation; and all this performed with a careful economy, that never descends to meanness. But I have lost my gentle, *helpless* Anna! – When we sit down to enjoy an hour of repose after the fatigue of the day, I am compelled to listen to what have been her useful (and they are really useful) employments through the day, and what she proposes for her tomorrow's task. Her heart and her features are changed by the duties of her situation. To the boys, she never appears other than the *master's wife*, and she looks up to me as the *boys' master;* to whom all show of love and affection would be highly improper, and unbecoming the dignity of her situation and mine. Yet *this* my gratitude forbids me to hint to her. For my sake she submitted to be this altered creature, and can I reproach her for it?' – For the communication of this letter, I am indebted to my cousin Bridget.

IMPERFECT SYMPATHIES[1]

> I am of a constitution so general, that it consorts and sympathiseth with all things; I have no antipathy, or rather idiosyncracy in anything. Those national repugnances do not touch me, nor do I behold with prejudice the French, Italian, Spaniard, or Dutch. – *Religio Medici.*

THAT the author of the Religio Medici,[2] mounted upon the airy stilts of abstraction, conversant about notional and conjectural essences; in whose categories of Being the possible took the upper hand of the actual; should have overlooked the impertinent individualities of such poor concretions as mankind, is not much to be admired. It is rather to be wondered at, that in the genus of animals he should have condescended to distinguish that species at all. For myself – earth-bound and fettered to the scene of my activities, –

> Standing on earth, not rapt above the sky,

I confess that I do feel the differences of mankind, national or individual, to an unhealthy excess. I can look with no indifferent eye upon things or persons. Whatever is, is to me a matter of taste or distaste; or when once it becomes indifferent, it begins to be disrelishing. I am, in plainer words, a bundle of prejudices – made up of likings and dislikings – the veriest thrall to sympathies, apathies, antipathies. In a certain sense, I hope it may be said of me that I am a lover of my species. I can feel for all indifferently, but I cannot feel towards all equally. The more purely-English word that expresses sympathy will better explain my meaning. I can be a friend to a worthy man, who upon another account cannot be my mate or *fellow*. I cannot *like* all people alike.*

* I would be understood as confining myself to the subject of *imperfect sympathies*. To nations or classes of men there can be no direct *antipathy*. There may be individuals born and constellated so opposite to another individual nature, that the same sphere cannot hold them. I have met with my moral antipodes, and can believe the story of two persons meeting (who never saw one another before in their lives) and instantly fighting.

> – We by proof find there should be
> 'Twixt man and man such an antipathy,

I have been trying all my life to like Scotchmen, and am obliged to desist from the experiment in despair. They cannot like me – and in truth, I never knew one of that nation who attempted to do it. There is something more plain and ingenuous in their mode of proceeding. We know one another at first sight. There is an order of imperfect intellects (under which mine must be content to rank) which in its constitution is essentially anti-Caledonian. The owners of the sort of faculties I allude to, have minds rather suggestive than comprehensive. They have no pretences to much clearness or precision in their ideas, or in their manner of expressing them. Their intellectual wardrobe (to confess fairly) has few whole pieces in it. They are content with fragments and scattered pieces of Truth. She presents no full front to them – a feature or side-face at the most. Hints and glimpses, germs and crude essays at a system, is the utmost they pretend to. They beat up a little game peradventure – and leave it to knottier heads, more robust constitutions, to run it down. The light that lights them is not steady and polar, but mutable and shifting; waxing, and again waning. Their conversation is accordingly. They will throw out a random word in or out of season, and be content to let it pass for what it is worth. They cannot speak always as if they were upon their oath – but must be understood, speaking or writing, with some abatement. They seldom wait to mature a proposition, but e'en bring it to market in the green ear. They delight to impart their defective discoveries as they arise, without waiting for their full development. They are no systematisers, and would but err more by attempting it. Their minds, as I said before, are suggestive merely. The brain of a true Caledonian (if I am not mistaken) is constituted upon quite a different plan. His Minerva is born in panoply. You are never admitted to see his ideas in their growth – if, indeed, they do grow, and

---

That though he can show no just reason why
For any former wrong or injury,
Can neither find a blemish in his fame,
Nor aught in face or feature justly blame,
Can challenge or accuse him of no evil,
Yet notwithstanding hates him as a devil.

The lines are from old Heywood's 'Hierarchie of Angels,' and he subjoins a curious story in confirmation, of a Spaniard who attempted to assassinate a King Ferdinand of Spain, and being put to the rack could give no other reason for the deed but an inveterate antipathy which he had taken to the first sight of the King.

– The cause which to that act compell'd him
Was, he ne'er loved him since he first beheld him.

are not rather put together upon principles of clockwork. You never catch his mind in an undress. He never hints or suggests any thing, but unlades his stock of ideas in perfect order and completeness. He brings his total wealth into company, and gravely unpacks it. His riches are always about him. He never stoops to catch a glittering something in your presence, to share it with you, before he quite knows whether it be true touch or not. You cannot cry *halves* to any thing that he finds. He does not find, but bring. You never witness his first apprehension of a thing. His understanding is always at its meridian – you never see the first dawn, the early streaks. – He has no falterings of self-suspicion. Surmises, guesses, misgivings, half-intuitions, semi-consciousnesses, partial illuminations, dim instincts, embryo conceptions, have no place in his brain, or vocabulary. The twilight of dubiety never falls upon him. Is he orthodox – he has no doubts. Is he an infidel – he has none either. Between the affirmative and the negative there is no border-land with him. You cannot hover with him upon the confines of truth, or wander in the maze of a probable argument. He always keeps the path. You cannot make excursions with him – for he sets you right. His taste never fluctuates. His morality never abates. He cannot compromise, or understand middle actions. There can be but a right and a wrong. His conversation is as a book. His affirmations have the sanctity of an oath. You must speak upon the square with him. He stops a metaphor like a suspected person in an enemy's country. 'A healthy book!' – said one of his countrymen to me, who had ventured to give that appellation to John Buncle,[3] – 'did I catch rightly what you said? I have heard of a man in health, and of a healthy state of body, but I do not see how that epithet can be properly applied to a book.' Above all, you must beware of indirect expressions before a Caledonian. Clap an extinguisher upon your irony, if you are unhappily blest with a vein of it. Remember you are upon your oath. I have a print of a graceful female after Leonardo da Vinci, which I was showing off to Mr —. After he had examined it minutely, I ventured to ask him how he liked MY BEAUTY (a foolish name it goes by among my friends) – when he very gravely assured me, that 'he had considerable respect for my character and talents' (so he was pleased to say), 'but had not given himself much thought about the degree of my personal pretensions.'[4] The misconception staggered me, but did not seem much to disconcert him. – Persons of this nation are particularly fond of affirming a truth – which nobody doubts. They do not so properly affirm, as annunciate it. They do indeed appear to have such a love of truth (as if, like virtue, it were valuable for itself) that all truth becomes equally valuable, whether the proposition that contains it be new or old, disputed, or such as is impossible to become a subject of disputation. I was present not long since at a party of North Britons, where a son of Burns was expected; and happened to drop a silly expression (in my South British way), that I wished it were the father instead of the son – when four of them started up at once to inform me, that 'that was impossible, because he was dead.' An impracticable wish, it seems, was more than they could conceive. Swift has hit off this part of their character, namely their love of truth, in his biting way, but with an illiberality that necessarily confines the passage to the margin.* The tediousness of these people is certainly provoking. I wonder if they ever tire one another! – In my early life I had a passionate fondness for the poetry of Burns. I have sometimes foolishly hoped to ingratiate myself with his countrymen by expressing it. But I have always found that a true Scot resents your admiration of his compatriot, even more than he would your contempt of him. The latter he imputes to your 'imperfect acquaintance with many of the words which he uses'; and the same objection makes it a presumption in you to suppose that you can admire him. – Thomson [5] they seem to have forgotten. Smollett they have neither forgotten nor forgiven, for his delineation of Rory [6] and his companion, upon their first introduction to our metropolis. – Speak of Smollett as a great genius, and they will retort upon you Hume's History compared with *his* Continuation of it. What if the historian had continued 'Humphrey Clinker'?

I have, in the abstract, no disrespect for Jews. They are a piece of stubborn antiquity, compared with which Stonehenge is in its nonage. They date beyond the pyramids. But I should not care to be in habits of familiar intercourse with any of that nation. I confess that I have not the nerves to enter their synagogues. Old prejudices cling about me. I cannot shake off the story of Hugh of Lincoln. [7] Centuries of injury, contempt, and hate, on the one side, – of cloaked revenge, dissimulation, and hate, on the other, between our and their fathers, must, and ought to affect the blood of the children. I cannot believe it can run clear and

---

* There are some people who think they sufficiently acquit themselves and entertain their company, with relating facts of no consequence, not at all out of the road of such common incidents as happen every day; and this I have observed more frequently among the Scots than any other nation, who are very careful not to omit the minutest circumstances of time or place; which kind of discourse, if it were not a little relieved by the uncouth terms and phrases, as well as accent and gesture peculiar to that country, would be hardly tolerable. – *Hints towards an Essay on Conversation.*

kindly yet; or that a few fine words, such as candour, liberality, the light of a nineteenth century, can close up the breaches of so deadly a disunion. A Hebrew is nowhere congenial to me. He is least distasteful on 'Change – for the mercantile spirit levels all distinctions, as all are beauties in the dark. I boldly confess that I do not relish the approximation of Jew and Christian, which has become so fashionable. The reciprocal endearments have, to me, something hypocritical and unnatural in them. I do not like to see the Church and Synagogue kissing and congeeing[8] in awkward postures of an affected civility. If *they* are converted, why do they not come over to us altogether? Why keep up a form of separation, when the life of it is fled? If they can sit with us at table, why do they keck[9] at our cookery? I do not understand these half convertites. Jews christianizing – Christians judaizing – puzzle me. I like fish or flesh. A moderate Jew is a more confounding piece of anomaly than a wet Quaker. The spirit of the synagogue is essentially *separative*. B—[10] would have been more in keeping if he had abided by the faith of his forefathers. There is a fine scorn in his face, which nature meant to be of – Christians. The Hebrew spirit is strong in him, in spite of his proselytism. He cannot conquer the Shibboleth. How it breaks out, when he sings, 'The Children of Israel passed through the Red Sea!' The auditors, for the moment, are as Egyptians to him, and he rides over our necks in triumph. There is no mistaking him. —B— has a strong expression of sense in his countenance, and it is confirmed by his singing. The foundation of his vocal excellence is sense. He sings with understanding, as Kemble[11] delivered dialogue. He would sing the Commandments, and give an appropriate character to each prohibition. His nation, in general, have not over-sensible countenances. How should they? – but you seldom see a silly expression among them. Gain, and the pursuit of gain, sharpen a man's visage. I never heard of an idiot being born among them. – Some admire the Jewish female physiognomy. I admire it – but with trembling. Jael had those full dark inscrutable eyes.

In the Negro countenance you will often meet with strong traits of benignity. I have felt yearnings of tenderness towards some of these faces – or rather masks – that have looked out kindly upon one in casual encounters in the streets and highways. I love what Fuller beautifully calls – these 'images of God cut in ebony.' But I should not like to associate with them, to share my meals and my good-nights with them – because they are black.

I love Quaker ways, and Quaker worship. I venerate the Quaker principles. It does me good for the rest of the day when I meet any of their people in my path. When I am ruffled or disturbed by any occurrence, the sight, or quiet voice of a Quaker, acts upon me as a ventilator, lightening the air, and taking off a load from the bosom. But I cannot like the Quakers (as Desdemona would say) 'to live with them.' I am all over sophisticated – with humours, fancies, craving hourly sympathy. I must have books, pictures, theatres, chit-chat, scandal, jokes, ambiguities, and a thousand whim-whams, which their simpler taste can do without. I should starve at their primitive banquet. My appetites are too high for the salads which (according to Evelyn) Eve dressed for the angel, my gusto too excited

To sit a guest with Daniel at his pulse.

The indirect answers which Quakers are often found to return to a question put to them may be explained, I think, without the vulgar assumption, that they are more given to evasion and equivocating than other people. They naturally look to their words more carefully, and are more cautious of committing themselves. They have a peculiar character to keep up on this head. They stand in a manner upon their veracity. A Quaker is by law exempted from taking an oath. The custom of resorting to an oath in extreme cases, sanctified as it is by all religious antiquity, is apt (it must be confessed) to introduce into the laxer sort of minds the notion of two kinds of truth – the one applicable to the solemn affairs of justice, and the other to the common proceedings of daily intercourse. As truth bound upon the conscience by an oath can be but truth, so in the common affirmations of the shop and the market-place a latitude is expected, and conceded, upon questions wanting this solemn covenant. Something less than truth satisfies. It is common to hear a person say, 'You do not expect me to speak as if I were upon my oath.' Hence a great deal of incorrectness and inadvertency, short of falsehood, creeps into ordinary conversation; and a kind of secondary or laic-truth is tolerated, where clergy-truth – oath-truth, by the nature of the circumstances, is not required. A Quaker knows none of this distinction. His simple affirmation being received, upon the most sacred occasions, without any further test, stamps a value upon the words which he is to use upon the most indifferent topics of life. He looks to them, naturally, with more severity. You can have of him no more than his word. He knows, if he is caught tripping in a casual expression, he forfeits, for himself, at least, his claim to the invidious exemption. He knows that his syllables are weighed – and how far a consciousness of this particular watchfulness, exerted against a person, has a tendency to produce indirect answers, and a diverting of the question by honest means, might be illustrated, and the practice justified, by a more sacred example than is proper to be adduced upon this occasion. The admirable presence of mind, which is notorious in Quakers upon all contingencies, might be traced to this imposed self-watchfulness – if it did not seem rather an humble and secular scion of that old stock of religious constancy, which never bent or faltered, in the Primitive Friends, or gave way to the winds of persecution, to the violence of judge or accuser, under trials and racking examinations. 'You will never be the wiser, if I sit here answering your questions till midnight,' said one of those upright Justicers to Penn,[12] who had been putting law-cases with a puzzling subtlety. 'Thereafter as the answers may be,' retorted the Quaker. The astonishing composure of this people is sometimes ludicrously displayed in lighter instances. – I was travelling in a stage coach with three male Quakers, buttoned up in the straitest non-conformity of their sect. We stopped to bait at Andover, where a meal, partly tea apparatus, partly supper, was set before us. My friends confined themselves to the tea-table. I in my way took supper. When the landlady brought in the bill, the eldest of my companions discovered that she had charged for both meals. This was resisted. Mine hostess was very clamorous and positive. Some mild arguments were used on the part of the Quakers, for which the heated mind of the good lady seemed by no means a fit recipient. The guard came in with his usual peremptory notice. The Quakers pulled out their money, and formally tendered it – so much for tea – I, in humble imitation, tendering mine – for the supper which I had taken. She would not relax in her demand. So they all three quietly put up their silver, as did myself, and marched out of the room, the eldest and gravest going first, with myself closing up the rear, who thought I could not do better than follow the example of such grave and warrantable personages. We got in. The steps went up. The coach drove off. The murmurs of mine hostess, not very indistinctly or ambiguously pronounced, became after a time inaudible – and now my conscience, which the whimsical scene had for a time suspended, beginning to give some twitches, I waited, in the hope that some justification would be offered by these serious persons for the seeming injustice of their conduct. To my great surprise, not a syllable was dropped on the subject. They sat as mute as at a meeting. At length the eldest of them broke silence, by inquiring of his next neighbour, 'Hast thee heard how indigos go at the India House?' and the question operated as a soporific on my moral feeling as far as Exeter.

(*London Magazine*, August 1821)

WITCHES, AND OTHER NIGHT-FEARS

WE are too hasty when we set down our ancestors in the gross for fools, for the monstrous inconsistencies (as they seem to us) involved in their creed of witchcraft. In the relations of this visible world we find them to have been as rational, and shrewd to detect an historic anomaly, as ourselves. But when once the invisible world was supposed to be opened, and the lawless agency of bad spirits assumed, what measures of probability, of decency, of fitness, or proportion – of that which distinguishes the likely from the palpable absurd – could they have to guide them in the rejection or admission of any particular testimony? – that maidens pined away, wasting inwardly as their waxen images consumed before a fire – that corn was lodged, and cattle lamed – that whirlwinds uptore in diabolic revelry the oaks of the forest – or that spits and kettles only danced a fearful-innocent vagary about some rustic's kitchen when no wind was stirring – were all equally probable where no law of agency was understood. That the prince of the powers of darkness, passing by the flower and pomp of the earth, should lay preposterous siege to the weak fantasy of indigent eld [1] – has neither likelihood nor unlikelihood *a priori* to us, who have no measure to guess at his policy, or standard to estimate what rate those anile souls may fetch in the devil's market. Nor, when the wicked are expressly symbolized by a goat, was it to be wondered at so much, that *he* should come sometimes in that body, and assert his metaphor. – That the intercourse was opened at all between both worlds was perhaps the mistake – but that once assumed, I see no reason for disbelieving one attested story of this nature more than another on the score of absurdity. There is no law to judge of the lawless, or canon by which a dream may be criticized.

I have sometimes thought that I could not have existed in the days of received witchcraft; that I could not have slept in a village where one of those reputed hags dwelt. Our ancestors were bolder or more obtuse. Amidst the universal belief that these wretches were in league with the author of all evil, holding hell tributary to their muttering, no simple Justice of the Peace seems to have scrupled issuing, or silly Headborough serving, a warrant upon them – as if they should subpœna Satan! –

Prospero in his boat, with his books and wand about him, suffers himself to be conveyed away at the mercy of his enemies to an unknown island. He might have raised a storm or two, we think, on the passage. His acquiescence is in exact analogy to the non-resistance of witches to the constituted powers. – What stops the Fiend in Spenser from tearing Guyon to pieces – or who had made it a condition of his prey, that Guyon must take assay of the glorious bait – we have no guess. We do not know the laws of that country.

From my childhood I was extremely inquisitive about witches and witch-stories. My maid, and more legendary aunt, supplied me with good store. But I shall mention the accident which directed my curiosity originally into this channel. In my father's book-closet, the History of the Bible, by Stackhouse, occupied a distinguished station. The pictures with which it abounds – one of the ark, in particular, and another of Solomon's temple, delineated with all the fidelity of ocular admeasurement, as if the artist had been upon the spot – attracted my childish attention. There was a picture, too, of the Witch raising up Samuel, which I wish that I had never seen.[2] We shall come to that hereafter. Stackhouse is in two huge tomes – and there was a pleasure in removing folios of that magnitude, which, with infinite straining, was as much as I could manage, from the situation which they occupied upon an upper shelf. I have not met with the work from that time to this, but I remember it consisted of Old Testament stories, orderly set down, with the *objection* appended to each story, and the *solution* of the objection regularly tacked to that. The *objection* was a summary of whatever difficulties had been opposed to the credibility of the history, by the shrewdness of ancient or modern infidelity, drawn up with an almost complimentary excess of candour. The *solution* was brief, modest, and satisfactory. The bane and antidote were both before you. To doubts so put, and so quashed, there seemed to be an end for ever. The dragon lay dead, for the foot of the veriest babe to trample on. But – like as was rather feared than realized from that slain monster in Spenser – from the womb of those crushed errors young dragonets would creep, exceeding the prowess of so tender a Saint George as myself to vanquish. The habit of expecting objections to every passage, set me upon starting more objections, for the glory of finding a solution of my own for them. I became staggered and perplexed, a sceptic in long coats. The pretty Bible stories which I had read, or heard read in church, lost their purity and sincerity of impression, and were turned into so many historic or chronologic theses to be defended against whatever impugners. I was not to disbelieve them, but – the next thing to that – I was to be quite sure that some one or other would or had disbelieved them. Next to making a child an infidel, is the letting him know that there are infidels at all. Credulity is the man's weakness, but the child's strength. O, how ugly sound scriptural doubts from the mouth of a babe and a suckling! – I should have lost myself in these mazes, and have pined away, I think, with such unfit sustenance as these husks afforded, but for a fortunate piece of ill-fortune, which about this time befel me. Turning over the picture of the ark with too much haste, I unhappily made a breach in its ingenious fabric – driving my inconsiderate fingers right through the two larger quadrupeds – the elephant, and the camel – that stare (as well they might) out of the two last windows next the steerage in that unique piece of naval architecture. Stackhouse was henceforth locked up, and became an interdicted treasure. With the book, the *objections* and *solutions* gradually cleared out of my head, and have seldom returned since in any force to trouble me. – But there was one impression which I had imbibed from Stackhouse, which no lock or bar could shut out, and which was destined to try my childish nerves rather more seriously. – That detestable picture!

I was dreadfully alive to nervous terrors. The night-time solitude, and the dark, were my hell. The sufferings I endured in this nature would justify the expression. I never laid my head on my pillow, I suppose, from the fourth to the seventh or eighth year of my life – so far as memory serves in things so long ago – without an assurance, which realized its own prophecy, of seeing some frightful spectre. Be old Stackhouse then acquitted in part, if I say, that to his picture of the Witch raising up Samuel – (O that old man covered with a mantle!) I owe – not my midnight terrors, the hell of my infancy – but the shape and manner of their visitation. It was he who dressed up for me a hag that nightly sate upon my pillow – a sure bedfellow, when my aunt or my maid was far from me. All day long, while the book was permitted me, I dreamed waking over his delineation, and at night (if I may use so bold an expression) awoke into sleep, and found the vision true. I durst not, even in the daylight, once enter the chamber where I slept, without my face turned to the window, aversely from the bed where my witch-ridden pillow was. – Parents do not know what they do when they leave tender babes alone to go to sleep in the dark. The feeling about for a friendly arm – the hoping for a familiar voice – when they wake screaming – and find none to soothe them – what a terrible shaking it is to their poor nerves! The keeping them up till midnight, through candle-light and the unwholesome hours, as they are called, – would, I am satisfied, in a medical point of view, prove the better caution. – That detestable picture, as I have said, gave the fashion to my dreams – if dreams they were – for the scene of them was invariably the room in which I lay. Had I never met with the picture, the fears would have come self-pictured in some shape or other –

> Headless bear, black man, or ape –

but, as it was, my imaginations took that form. – It is not book, or picture, or the stories of foolish servants, which create these terrors in children. They can at most but give them a direction. Dear little T. H.[3] who of all children has been brought up with the most scrupulous exclusion of every taint of superstition – who was never allowed to hear of goblin or apparition, or scarcely to be told of bad men, or to read or hear of any distressing story – finds all this world of fear, from which he has been so rigidly excluded *ab extra*, in his own 'thick-coming fancies'; and from his little midnight pillow, this nurse-child of optimism will start at shapes, unborrowed of tradition, in sweats to which the reveries of the cell-damned murderer are tranquillity.

Gorgons, and Hydras, and Chimæras dire – stories of Celæno and the Harpies – may reproduce themselves in the brain of superstition – but they were there before. They are transcripts, types – the archetypes are in us, and eternal. How else should the recital of that, which we know in a waking sense to be false, come to affect us at all? – or

> – Names, whose sense we see not,
> Fray us with things that be not?

Is it that we naturally conceive terror from such objects, considered in their capacity of being able to inflict upon us bodily injury? – O, least of all! These terrors are of older standing. They date beyond body – or, without the body, they would have been the same. All the cruel, tormenting, defined devils in Dante – tearing, mangling, choking, stifling, scorching demons – are they one half so fearful to the spirit of a man, as the simple idea of a spirit unembodied following him –

> Like one that on a lonesome road
> Doth walk in fear and dread,
> And having once turn'd round, walks on,
> And turns no more his head;

> Because he knows a frightful fiend
> Doth close behind him tread.*

That the kind of fear here treated of is purely spiritual — that it is strong in proportion as it is objectless upon earth — that it predominates in the period of sinless infancy — are difficulties, the solution of which might afford some probable insight into our ante-mundane condition, and a peep at least into the shadow-land of pre-existence.

My night-fancies have long ceased to be afflictive. I confess an occasional night-mare; but I do not, as in early youth, keep a stud of them. Fiendish faces, with the extinguished taper, will come and look at me; but I know them for mockeries, even while I cannot elude their presence, and I fight and grapple with them. For the credit of my imagination, I am almost ashamed to say how tame and prosaic my dreams are grown. They are never romantic, seldom even rural. They are of architecture and of buildings — cities abroad, which I have never seen, and hardly have hope to see. I have traversed, for the seeming length of a natural day, Rome, Amsterdam, Paris, Lisbon — their churches, palaces, squares, market-places, shops, suburbs, ruins, with an inexpressible sense of delight — a map-like distinctness of trace — and a daylight vividness of vision, that was all but being awake. — I have formerly travelled among the Westmoreland fells — my highest Alps, — but they are objects too mighty for the grasp of my dreaming recognition; and I have again and again awoke with ineffectual struggles of the inner eye, to make out a shape, in any way whatever, of Helvellyn. Methought I was in that country, but the mountains were gone. The poverty of my dreams mortifies me. There is Coleridge, at his will can conjure up icy domes, and pleasure-houses for Kubla Khan, and Abyssinian maids, and songs of Abara, and caverns,

> Where Alph, the sacred river, runs,

to solace his night solitudes — when I cannot muster a fiddle. Barry Cornwall has his tritons and his nereids gamboling before him in nocturnal visions, and proclaiming sons born to Neptune — when my stretch of imaginative activity can hardly, in the night season, raise up the ghost of a fish-wife. To set my failures in somewhat a mortifying light — it was after reading the noble Dream of this poet,[4] that my fancy ran strong upon these marine spectra; and the poor plastic power, such as it is, within me set to work, to humour my folly in a sort of dream that very night. Methought I was upon the ocean billows at some sea nuptials,

* Mr Coleridge's Ancient Mariner.

riding and mounted high, with the customary train sounding their conchs before me, (I myself, you may be sure, the *leading god,*) and jollily we went careering over the main, till just where Ino Leucothea [5] should have greeted me (I think it was Ino) with a white embrace, the billows gradually subsiding, fell from a sea-roughness to a sea-calm, and thence to a river-motion, and that river (as happens in the familiarization of dreams) was no other than the gentle Thames, which landed me, in the wafture of a placid wave or two, alone, safe and inglorious, somewhere at the foot of Lambeth palace.

The degree of the soul's creativeness in sleep might furnish no whimsical criterion of the quantum of poetical faculty resident in the same soul waking. An old gentleman, a friend of mine, and a humorist, used to carry this notion so far, that when he saw any stripling of his acquaintance ambitious of becoming a poet, his first question would be, – 'Young man, what sort of dreams have you?' I have so much faith in my old friend's theory, that when I feel that idle vein returning upon me, I presently subside into my proper element of prose, remembering those eluding nereids, and that inauspicious inland landing.

(*London Magazine*, October 1821)

GRACE BEFORE MEAT

THE custom of saying grace at meals had, probably, its origin in the early times of the world, and the hunter-state of man, when dinners were precarious things, and a full meal was something more than a common blessing; when a belly-full was a windfall, and looked like a special providence. In the shouts and triumphal songs with which, after a season of sharp abstinence, a lucky booty of deer's or goat's flesh would naturally be ushered home, existed, perhaps, the germ of the modern grace. It is not otherwise easy to be understood, why the blessing of food – the act of eating – should have had a particular expression of thanksgiving annexed to it, distinct from that implied and silent gratitude with which we are expected to enter upon the enjoyment of the many other various gifts and good things of existence.

I own that I am disposed to say grace upon twenty other occasions in the course of the day besides my dinner. I want a form for setting out upon a pleasant walk, for a moonlight ramble, for a friendly meeting, or a solved problem. Why have we none for books, those spiritual repasts – a grace before Milton – a grace before Shakspeare – a devotional exercise proper to be said before reading the Fairy Queen? – but, the received ritual having prescribed these forms to the solitary ceremony of manducation,[1] I shall confine my observations to the experience which I have had of the grace, properly so called; commending my new scheme for extension to a niche in the grand philosophical, poetical, and perchance in part heretical, liturgy, now compiling by my friend Homo Humanus, for the use of a certain snug congregation of Utopian Rabelæsian Christians, no matter where assembled.

The form then of the benediction before eating has its beauty at a poor man's table, or at the simple and unprovocative repasts of children. It is here that the grace becomes exceedingly graceful. The indigent man, who hardly knows whether he shall have a meal the next day or not, sits down to his fare with a present sense of the blessing, which can be but feebly acted by the rich, into whose minds the conception of wanting a dinner could never, but by some extreme theory, have entered. The proper end of food – the animal sustenance – is barely contemplated by them. The poor man's bread is his daily bread, literally his bread for the day. Their courses are perennial.

Again, the plainest diet seems the fittest to be preceded by the grace. That which is least stimulative to appetite, leaves the mind most free for foreign considerations. A man may feel thankful, heartily thankful, over a dish of plain mutton with turnips, and have leisure to reflect upon the ordinance and institution of eating; when he shall confess a perturbation of mind, inconsistent with the purposes of the grace, at the presence of venison or turtle. When I have sate (a *rarus hospes*) [2] at rich men's tables, with the savoury soup and messes steaming up the nostrils, and moistening the lips of the guests with desire and a distracted choice, I have felt the introduction of that ceremony to be unseasonable. With the ravenous orgasm upon you, it seems impertinent to interpose a religious sentiment. It is a confusion of purpose to mutter out praises from a mouth that waters. The heats of epicurism put out the gentle flame of devotion. The incense which rises round is pagan, and the belly-god intercepts it for his own. The very excess of the provision beyond the needs, takes away all sense of proportion between the end and means. The giver is veiled by his gifts. You are startled at the injustice of returning thanks – for what? – for having too much, while so many starve. It is to praise the Gods amiss.

I have observed this awkwardness felt, scarce consciously perhaps, by the good man who says the grace. I have seen it in clergymen and others – a sort of shame – a sense of the co-presence of circumstances which unhallow the blessing. After a devotional tone put on for a few seconds, how rapidly the speaker will fall into his common voice, helping himself or his neighbour, as if to get rid of some uneasy sensation of hypocrisy. Not that the good man was a hypocrite, or was not most conscientious in the discharge of the duty; but he felt in his inmost mind the incompatibility of the scene and the viands before him with the exercise of a calm and rational gratitude.

I hear somebody exclaim, – Would you have Christians sit down at table, like hogs to their troughs, without remembering the Giver? – no – I would have them sit down as Christians, remembering the Giver, and less like hogs. Or if their appetites must run riot, and they must pamper themselves with delicacies for which east and west are ransacked, I would have them postpone their benediction to a fitter season, when appetite is laid; when the still small voice can be heard, and the reason of the grace returns – with temperate diet and restricted dishes. Gluttony and surfeiting are no proper occasions for thanksgiving. When Jeshurun [3] waxed fat, we read that he kicked. Virgil knew the harpy-nature better, when he put into the mouth of Celæno any thing but a blessing. We may be gratefully sensible of the deliciousness of some kinds of food beyond others, though that is a meaner and inferior gratitude: but the proper object of the grace is sustenance, not relishes; daily bread, not delicacies; the means of life, and not the means of pampering the carcass. With what frame or composure, I wonder, can a city chaplain pronounce his benediction at some great Hall feast, when he knows that his last concluding pious word – and that, in all probability, the sacred name which he preaches – is but the signal for so many impatient harpies to commence their foul orgies, with as little sense of true thankfulness (which is temperance) as those Virgilian fowl! It is well if the good man himself does not feel his devotions a little clouded, those foggy sensuous steams mingling with and polluting the pure altar sacrifice.

The severest satire upon full tables and surfeits is the banquet which Satan, in the 'Paradise Regained,' provides for a temptation in the wilderness:

> A table richly spread in regal mode,
> With dishes piled, and meats of noblest sort
> And savour; beasts of chase, or fowl of game,
> In pastry built, or from the spit, or boiled,
> Gris-amber-steamed; all fish from sea or shore,
> Freshet or purling brook, for which was drained
> Pontus, and Lucrine bay, and Afric coast.

The Tempter, I warrant you, thought these cates would go down without the recommendatory preface of a benediction. They are like to be short graces where the devil plays the host. – I am afraid the poet wants his usual decorum in this place. Was he thinking of the old Roman luxury, or of a gaudy day at Cambridge? This was a temptation fitter for a Heliogabalus.[4] The whole banquet is too civic and culinary, and the accompaniments altogether a profanation of that deep, abstracted, holy scene. The mighty artillery of sauces, which the cook-fiend conjures up, is out of proportion to the simple wants and plain hunger of the guest. He that disturbed him in his dreams, from his dreams might have been taught better. To the temperate fantasies of the famished Son of God, what sort of feasts presented themselves? – He dreamed indeed,

> – As appetite is wont to dream,
> Of meats and drinks, nature's refreshment sweet.

But what meats? –

> Him thought, he by the brook of Cherith stood,
> And saw the ravens with their horny beaks
> Food to Elijah bringing, even and morn,
> Though ravenous, taught to abstain from what they brought;
> He saw the prophet also how he fled
> Into the desert, and how there he slept
> Under a juniper; then how awaked
> He found his supper on the coals prepared,
> And by the angel was bid rise and eat,
> And ate the second time after repose,
> The strength whereof sufficed him forty days:
> Sometimes, that with Elijah he partook,
> Or as a guest with Daniel at his pulse.

Nothing in Milton is finelier fancied than these temperate dreams of the divine Hungerer. To which of these two visionary banquets, think you, would the introduction of what is called the grace have been most fitting and pertinent?

Theoretically I am no enemy to graces; but practically I own that (before meat especially) they seem to involve something awkward and unseasonable. Our appetites, of one or another kind, are excellent spurs to our reason, which might otherwise but feebly set about the great ends of preserving and continuing the species. They are fit blessings to be contemplated at a distance with a becoming gratitude: but the moment of appetite (the judicious reader will apprehend me) is, perhaps, the least fit season for that exercise. The Quakers, who go about their business, of every description, with more calmness than we, have more title to the use of these benedictory prefaces. I have always admired their silent grace, and the more because I have observed their applications to the meat and drink following to be less passionate and sensual than ours. They are neither gluttons nor wine-bibbers as a people. They eat, as a horse bolts his chopt hay, with indifference, calmness, and cleanly circumstances. They neither grease nor slop themselves. When I see a citizen in his bib and tucker, I cannot imagine it a surplice.

I am no Quaker at my food. I confess I am not indifferent to the kinds of it. Those unctuous morsels of deer's flesh were not made to be received with dispassionate services. I hate a man who swallows it, affecting not to know what he is eating. I suspect his taste in higher matters. I shrink instinctively from one who professes to like minced veal. There is a physiognomical character in the tastes for food. C——[5] holds that a man cannot have a pure mind who refuses apple-dumplings. I am not certain but he is right. With the decay of my first innocence, I confess a less and less relish daily for these innocuous cates. The whole vegetable tribe have lost their gust with me. Only I stick to asparagus, which still seems to inspire gentle thoughts. I am impatient and querulous under culinary disappointments, as to come home at the dinner hour, for instance, expecting some savoury mess, and to find one quite tasteless and sapidless. Butter ill melted – that commonest of kitchen failures – puts me beside my tenour. – The author of the 'Rambler'[6] used to make inarticulate animal noises over a favourite food. Was this the music quite proper to be preceded by the grace? or would the pious man have done better to postpone his devotions to a season when the blessing might be contemplated with less perturbation? I quarrel with no man's tastes, nor would set my thin face against those excellent things, in their way, jollity and feasting. But as these exercises, however laudable, have little in them of grace or gracefulness, a man should be sure, before he ventures so to grace them, that while he is pretending his devotions otherwise, he is not secretly kissing his hand to some great fish – his Dagon[7] – with a special consecration of no ark but the fat tureen before him. Graces are the sweet preluding strains to the banquets of angels and children; to the roots and severer repasts of the Chartreuse; to the slender, but not slenderly acknowledged, refection of the poor and humble man: but at the heaped-up boards of the pampered and the luxurious they become of dissonant mood, less timed and tuned to the occasion, methinks, than the noise of those better befitting organs would be, which children hear tales of, at Hog's Norton. We sit too long at our meals, or are too curious in the study of them, or too disordered in our application to them, or engross too great a portion of these good things (which should be common) to our share, to be able with any grace to say grace. To be thankful for what we grasp exceeding our proportion is to add hypocrisy to injustice. A lurking sense of this truth is what makes the performance of this duty so cold and spiritless a service at most tables. In houses where the grace is as indispensable as the napkin, who has not seen that never settled question arise, as to *who shall say it;* while the good man of the house and the visitor clergyman, or some other guest belike of next authority from years or gravity, shall be bandying about the office between them as a matter of compliment, each of them not unwilling to shift the awkward burthen of an equivocal duty from his own shoulders?

I once drank tea in company with two Methodist divines of different persuasions, whom it was my fortune to introduce to each other for the first time that evening. Before the first cup was handed round, one of these reverend gentlemen put it to the other, with all due solemnity, whether he chose to *say any thing.* It seems it is the custom with some sectaries to put up a short prayer before this meal also. His reverend brother did not at first quite apprehend him, but upon an explanation, with little less importance he made answer, that it was not a custom known in his church: in which courteous evasion the other acquiescing for good manners' sake, or in compliance with a weak brother, the supplementary or tea-grace was waived altogether. With what spirit might not Lucian have painted two priests, of *his* religion, playing into each other's hands the compliment of performing or omitting a sacrifice, – the hungry God meantime, doubtful of his incense, with expectant nostrils hovering over the two flamens, and (as between two stools) going away in the end without his supper.

A short form upon these occasions is felt to want reverence; a long one, I am afraid, cannot escape the charge of impertinence. I do not quite approve of the epigrammatic conciseness with which that equivocal wag (but my pleasant school-fellow) C. V. L.,[8] when importuned for a grace, used to inquire, first slyly leering down the table, 'Is there no clergyman here?' significantly adding, 'thank G——.' Nor do I think our old form at school quite pertinent, where we were used to preface our bald bread and cheese suppers with a preamble, connecting with that humble blessing a recognition of benefits the most awful and overwhelming to the imagination which religion has to offer. *Non tunc illis erat locus.*[9] I remember we were put to it to reconcile the phrase 'good creatures,'[10] upon which the blessing rested, with the fare set before us, wilfully understanding that expression in a low and animal sense, – till some one recalled a legend, which told how in the golden days of Christ's, the young Hospitallers were wont to have smoking joints of roast meat upon their nightly boards, till some pious benefactor, commiserating the decencies, rather than the palates, of the children, commuted our flesh for garments, and gave us – *horresco referens*[11] – trowsers instead of mutton.

(*London Magazine*, November 1821)

MY FIRST PLAY

AT the north end of Cross Court there yet stands a portal, of some architectural pretensions, though reduced to humble use, serving at present for an entrance to a printing-office. This old door-way, if you are young, reader, you may not know was the identical pit entrance to Old Drury – Garrick's Drury [1] – all of it that is left. I never pass it without shaking some forty years from off my shoulders, recurring to the evening when I passed through it to see *my first play*. The afternoon had been wet, and the condition of our going (the elder folks and myself) was, that the rain should cease. With what a beating heart did I watch from the window the puddles, from the stillness of which I was taught to prognosticate the desired cessation! I seem to remember the last spurt, and the glee with which I ran to announce it.

We went with orders, which my godfather F. [2] had sent us. He kept the oil shop (now Davies's) at the corner of Featherstone Building, in Holborn. F. was a tall grave person, lofty in speech, and had pretensions above his rank. He associated in those days with John Palmer, the comedian, whose gait and bearing he seemed to copy; if John (which is quite as likely) did not rather borrow somewhat of his manner from my godfather. He was also known to, and visited by, Sheridan. It was to his house in Holborn that young Brinsley brought his first wife on her elopement with him from a boarding-school at Bath – the beautiful Maria Linley. My parents were present (over a quadrille table) when he arrived in the evening with his harmonious charge. – From either of these connexions it may be inferred that my godfather could command an order for the then Drury Lane theatre at pleasure – and, indeed, a pretty liberal issue of those cheap billets, in Brinsley's easy autograph, I have heard him say was the sole remuneration which he had received for many years' nightly illumination of the orchestra and various avenues of that theatre – and he was content it should be so. The honour of Sheridan's familiarity – or supposed familiarity – was better to my godfather than money.

F. was the most gentlemanly of oilmen: grandiloquent, yet courteous. His delivery of the commonest matters of fact was Ciceronian. He had two Latin words almost constantly in his mouth (how odd sounds Latin from an oilman's lips!), which my better knowledge since has enabled me to correct. In strict pronunciation they should have been sounded *vice versâ* – but in those young years they impressed me with more awe than they would now do, read aright from Seneca or Varro – in his own peculiar pronunciation monosyllabically elaborated, or Anglicized, into something like *verse verse*. By an imposing manner, and the help of those distorted syllables, he climbed (but that was little) to the highest parochial honours which St Andrew's has to bestow.

He is dead – and thus much I thought due to his memory, both for my first orders[3] (little wondrous talismans! – slight keys, and insignificant to outward sight, but opening to me more than Arabian paradises!) and moreover, that by his testamentary beneficence I came into possession of the only landed property which I could ever call my own – situate near the road-way village of pleasant Puckeridge, in Hertfordshire. When I journeyed down to take possession, and planted foot on my own ground, the stately habits of the donor descended upon me, and I strode (shall I confess the vanity?) with larger paces over my allotment of three-quarters of an acre, with its commodious mansion in the midst, with the feeling of an English freeholder that all betwixt sky and centre was my own. The estate has passed into more prudent hands, and nothing but an agrarian can restore it.

In those days were pit orders. Beshrew the uncomfortable manager who abolished them! – with one of these we went. I remember the waiting at the door – not that which is left – but between that and an inner door in shelter – O when shall I be such an expectant again! – with the cry of nonpareils, an indispensable play-house accompaniment in those days. As near as I can recollect, the fashionable pronunciation of the theatrical fruiteresses then was, 'Chase some oranges, chase some numparels, chase a bill of the play'; – chase *pro* chuse. But when we got in, and I beheld the green curtain that veiled a heaven to my imagination, which was soon to be disclosed — the breathless anticipations I endured! I had seen something like it in the plate prefixed to Troilus and Cressida, in Rowe's Shakspeare – the tent scene with Diomede – and a sight of that plate can always bring back in a measure the feeling of that evening. – The boxes at that time, full of well-dressed women of quality, projected over the pit; and the pilasters reaching down were adorned with a glistering substance (I know not what) under glass (as it seemed), resembling – a homely fancy – but I judged it to be sugar-candy – yet, to my raised imagination, divested of its homelier qualities, it appeared a glorified candy! – The orchestra lights at length arose, those 'fair Auroras!'

Once the bell sounded. It was to ring out yet once again – and, incapable of the anticipation, I reposed my shut eyes in a sort of resignation upon the maternal lap. It rang the second time. The curtain drew up – I was not past six years old – and the play was Artaxerxes! [4]

I had dabbled a little in the Universal History – the ancient part of it – and here was the court of Persia. I was being admitted to a sight of the past. I took no proper interest in the action going on, for I understood not its import – but I heard the word Darius, and I was in the midst of Daniel. All feeling was absorbed in vision. Gorgeous vests, gardens, palaces, princesses, passed before me. I knew not players. I was in Persepolis for the time; and the burning idol of their devotion almost converted me into a worshipper. I was awe-struck, and believed those significations to be something more than elemental fires. It was all enchantment and a dream. No such pleasure has since visited me but in dreams. – Harlequin's Invasion [5] followed; where, I remember, the transformation of the magistrates into reverend beldams seemed to me a piece of grave historic justice, and the tailor carrying his own head to be as sober a verity as the legend of St Denys.

The next play to which I was taken was the Lady of the Manor, of which, with the exception of some scenery, very faint traces are left in my memory. It was followed by a pantomime, called Lun's Ghost – a satiric touch, I apprehend, upon Rich, [6] not long since dead – but to my apprehension (too sincere for satire), Lun was as remote a piece of antiquity as Lud – the father of a line of Harlequins – transmitting his dagger of lath (the wooden sceptre) through countless ages. I saw the primeval Motley come from his silent tomb in a ghastly vest of white patchwork, like the apparition of a dead rainbow. So Harlequins (thought I) look when they are dead.

My third play followed in quick succession. It was the Way of the World. [7] I think I must have sat at it as grave as a judge; for, I remember, the hysteric affectations of good Lady Wishfort affected me like some solemn tragic passion. Robinson Crusoe followed; in which Crusoe, man Friday, and the parrot, were as good and authentic as in the story. – The clownery and pantaloonery of these pantomimes have clean passed out of my head. I believe, I no more laughed at them, than at the same age I should have been disposed to laugh at the grotesque Gothic heads (seeming to me then replete with devout meaning) that gape, and grin, in stone around the inside of the old Round Church (my church) of the Templars.

I saw these plays in the season 1781–2, when I was from six to seven

years old. After the intervention of six or seven other years (for at
school all play-going was inhibited) I again entered the doors of a
theatre. That old Artaxerxes evening had never done ringing in my
fancy. I expected the same feelings to come again with the same occasion.
But we differ from ourselves less at sixty and sixteen, than the latter
does from six. In that interval what had I not lost! At the first period I
knew nothing, understood nothing, discriminated nothing. I felt all,
loved all, wondered all –

> Was nourished, I could not tell how –

I had left the temple a devotee, and was returned a rationalist. The same
things were there materially; but the emblem, the reference, was gone!
– The green curtain was no longer a veil, drawn between two worlds,
the unfolding of which was to bring back past ages, to present 'a royal
ghost,' – but a certain quantity of green baize, which was to separate the
audience for a given time from certain of their fellow-men who were to
come forward and pretend those parts. The lights – the orchestra lights
– came up a clumsy machinery. The first ring, and the second ring, was
now but a trick of the prompter's bell – which had been, like the note of
the cuckoo, a phantom of a voice, no hand seen or guessed at which
ministered to its warning. The actors were men and women painted. I
thought the fault was in them; but it was in myself, and the alteration
which those many centuries – of six short twelvemonths – had wrought
in me. – Perhaps it was fortunate for me that the play of the evening
was but an indifferent comedy, as it gave me time to crop some unreasonable expectations, which might have interfered with the genuine
emotions with which I was soon after enabled to enter upon the first
appearance to me of Mrs Siddons in Isabella.[8] Comparison and re-
trospection soon yielded to the present attraction of the scene; and the
theatre became to me, upon a new stock, the most delightful of recreations.

(*London Magazine*, December 1821)

DISTANT CORRESPONDENTS

MY DEAR F. – When I think how welcome the sight of a letter from the world where you were born must be to you in that strange one to which you have been transplanted, I feel some compunctious visitings at my long silence. But, indeed, it is no easy effort to set about a correspondence at our distance. The weary world of waters between us oppresses the imagination. It is difficult to conceive how a scrawl of mine should ever stretch across it. It is a sort of presumption to expect that one's thoughts should live so far. It is like writing for posterity; and reminds me of one of Mrs Rowe's superscriptions, 'Alcander to Strephon, in the shades.' Cowley's Post-Angel is no more than would be expedient in such an intercourse. One drops a packet at Lombard Street, and in twenty-four hours a friend in Cumberland gets it as fresh as if it came in ice. It is only like whispering through a long trumpet. But suppose a tube let down from the moon, with yourself at one end, and *the man* at the other; it would be some balk to the spirit of conversation, if you knew that the dialogue exchanged with that interesting theosophist would take two or three revolutions of a higher luminary in its passage. Yet for aught I know, you may be some parasangs[2] nigher that primitive idea – Plato's man – than we in England here have the honour to reckon ourselves.

Epistolary matter usually compriseth three topics; news, sentiment, and puns. In the latter, I include all non-serious subjects; or subjects serious in themselves, but treated after my fashion, non-seriously. – And first, for news. In them the most desirable circumstance, I suppose, is that they shall be true. But what security can I have that what I now send you for truth shall not before you get it unaccountably turn into a lie? For instance, our mutual friend P. is at this present writing – *my Now* – in good health, and enjoys a fair share of worldly reputation. You are glad to hear it. This is natural and friendly. But at this present reading – *your Now* – he may possibly be in the Bench,[3] or going to be hanged, which in reason ought to abate something of your transport (*i.e.* at hearing he was well, &c.), or at least considerably to modify it. I am going to the play this evening, to have a laugh with Munden.[4] – You have no theatre, I think you told me, in your land of d—d realities. You naturally lick your lips, and envy me my felicity. Think but a moment, and you will correct the hateful emotion. Why, it is Sunday morning with you, and 1823. This confusion of tenses, this grand solecism of *two presents*, is in a degree common to all postage. But if I sent you word to Bath or Devizes, that I was expecting the aforesaid treat this evening, though at the moment you received the intelligence my full feast of fun would be over, yet there would be for a day or two after, as you would well know, a smack, a relish left upon my mental palate, which would give rational encouragement for you to foster a portion at least of the disagreeable passion, which it was in part my intention to produce. But ten months hence your envy or your sympathy would be as useless as a passion spent upon the dead. Not only does truth, in these long intervals, unessence herself, but (what is harder) one cannot venture a crude fiction for the fear that it may ripen into a truth upon the voyage. What a wild improbable banter I put upon you some three years since – of Will Weatherall having married a servant-maid! I remember gravely consulting you how we were to receive her – for Will's wife was in no case to be rejected; and your no less serious replication in the matter; how tenderly you advised an abstemious introduction of literary topics before the lady, with a caution not to be too forward in bringing on the carpet matters more within the sphere of her intelligence; your deliberate judgment, or rather wise suspension of sentence, how far jacks, and spits, and mops, could with propriety be introduced as subjects; whether the conscious avoiding of all such matters in discourse would not have a worse look than the taking of them casually in our way; in what manner we should carry ourselves to our maid Becky, Mrs William Weatherall being by; whether we show more delicacy, and a truer sense of respect for Will's wife, by treating Becky with our customary chiding before her, or by an unusual deferential civility paid to Becky, as to a person of great worth, but thrown by the caprice of fate into a humble station. There were difficulties, I remember, on both sides, which you did me the favour to state with the precision of a lawyer, united to the tenderness of a friend. I laughed in my sleeve at your solemn pleadings, when lo! while I was valuing myself upon this flam [5] put upon you in New South Wales, the devil in England, jealous possibly of any lie-children not his own, or working after my copy, has actually instigated our friend (not three days since) to the commission of a matrimony, which I had only conjured up for your diversion. William Weatherall has married Mrs Cotterel's maid. But to take it in its truest sense, you will see, my dear F., that news from me must become history to you; which I neither profess to write, nor indeed care much for reading. No person, under a diviner, can with any prospect of veracity conduct a correspondence at such an arm's length. Two prophets, indeed, might thus interchange intelligence with effect; the epoch of the writer (Habakkuk) falling in with the true present time of the receiver (Daniel); but then we are no prophets.

Then as to sentiment. It fares little better with that. This kind of dish, above all, requires to be served up hot; or sent off in water-plates, that your friend may have it almost as warm as yourself. If it have time to cool, it is the most tasteless of all cold meats. I have often smiled at a conceit of the late Lord C.[6] It seems that travelling somewhere about Geneva, he came to some pretty green spot, or nook, where a willow, or something, hung so fantastically and invitingly over a stream – was it? – or a rock? – no matter – but the stillness and the repose, after a weary journey 'tis likely, in a languid moment of his lordship's hot restless life, so took his fancy, that he could imagine no place so proper, in the event of his death, to lay his bones in. This was all very natural and excusable as a sentiment, and shows his character in a very pleasing light. But when from a passing sentiment it came to be an act; and when by a positive testamentary disposal, his remains were actually carried all that way from England; who was there, some desperate sentimentalists excepted, that did not ask the question, Why could not his lordship have found a spot as solitary, a nook as romantic, a tree as green and pendent, with a stream as emblematic to his purpose, in Surrey, in Dorset, or in Devon? Conceive the sentiment boarded up, freighted, entered at the Custom House (startling the tide-waiters with the novelty), hoisted into a ship. Conceive it pawed about and handled between the rude jests of tarpaulin ruffians – a thing of its delicate texture – the salt bilge wetting it till it became as vapid as a damaged lustring. Suppose it in material danger (mariners have some superstition about sentiments) of being tossed over in a fresh gale to some propitiatory shark (spirit of Saint Gothard, save us from a quietus so foreign to the deviser's purpose!) but it has happily evaded a fishy consummation. Trace it then to its lucky landing – at Lyons shall we say? – I have not the map before me – jostled upon four men's shoulders – baiting at this town – stopping to refresh at t'other village – waiting a passport here, a license there; the sanction of the magistracy in this district, the concurrence of the ecclesiastics in that canton; till at length it arrives at its destination, tired out and jaded, from a brisk sentiment, into a feature of silly pride or tawdry senseless affectation. How few sentiments, my dear F., I am afraid we can set down, in the sailor's phrase, as quite seaworthy.

Lastly, as to the agreeable levities, which, though contemptible in bulk, are the twinkling corpuscula which should irradiate a right friendly epistle – your puns and small jests are, I apprehend, extremely circumscribed in their sphere of action. They are so far from a capacity of being packed up and sent beyond sea, they will scarce endure to be transported by hand from this room to the next. Their vigour is as the instant of their birth. Their nutriment for their brief existence is the intellectual atmosphere of the by-standers: or this last, is the fine slime of Nilus – the *melior lutus*,[7] – whose maternal recipiency is as necessary as the *sol pater*[8] to their equivocal generation. A pun hath a hearty kind of present ear-kissing smack with it; you can no more transmit it in its pristine flavour, than you can send a kiss. – Have you not tried in some instances to palm off a yesterday's pun upon a gentleman, and has it answered? Not but it was new to his hearing, but it did not seem to come new from you. It did not hitch in. It was like picking up at a village ale-house a two-days-old newspaper. You have not seen it before, but you resent the stale thing as an affront. This sort of merchandise above all requires a quick return. A pun, and its recognitory laugh, must be co-instantaneous. The one is the brisk lightning, the other the fierce thunder. A moment's interval, and the link is snapped. A pun is reflected from a friend's face as from a mirror. Who would consult his sweet visnomy, if the polished surface were two or three minutes (not to speak of twelve-months, my dear F.) in giving back its copy?

I cannot image to myself whereabout you are. When I try to fix it, Peter Wilkins's island comes across me. Sometimes you seem to be in the *Hades* of *Thieves*. I see Diogenes prying among you with his perpetual fruitless lantern. What must you be willing by this time to give for the sight of an honest man! You must almost have forgotten how *we* look. And tell me, what your Sydneyites do? are they th**v*ng all day long? Merciful heaven! what property can stand against such a depredation! The kangaroos – your Aborigines – do they keep their primitive simplicity un-Europe-tainted, with those little short fore-puds, looking like a lesson framed by nature to the pick-pocket! Marry, for diving into fobs they are rather lamely provided *a priori;* but if the hue and cry were once up, they would show as fair a pair of hind-shifters as the expertest loco-motor in the colony. — We hear the most improbable tales at this distance. Pray, is it true that the young Spartans among you are born with six fingers, which spoils their scanning? — It must look very odd; but use reconciles. For their scansion, it is less to be regretted, for if they take it into their heads to be poets, it is odds but they turn out, the greater part of them, vile plagiarists. Is there much difference to see to between the son of a th**f, and the grandson? or where does the taint stop? Do you bleach[9] in three or in four generations? — I have many questions to put, but ten Delphic voyages can be made in a shorter time than it will take to satisfy my scruples. — Do you grow your own hemp? — What is your staple trade, exclusive of the national profession, I mean? Your lock-smiths, I take it, are some of your great capitalists.

I am insensibly chatting to you as familiarly as when we used to exchange good-morrows out of our old contiguous windows, in pump-famed Hare Court in the Temple. Why did you ever leave that quiet corner? — Why did I? — with its complement of four poor elms, from whose smoke-dyed barks, the theme of jesting ruralists, I picked my first ladybirds! My heart is as dry as that spring sometimes proves in a thirsty August, when I revert to the space that is between us; a length of passage enough to render obsolete the phrases of our English letters before they can reach you. But while I talk, I think you hear me, — thoughts dallying with vain surmise —

> Aye me, while thee the seas and sounding shores
> Hold far away.

Come back, before I am grown into a very old man, so as you shall hardly know me. Come, before Bridget walks on crutches. Girls whom you left children have become sage matrons, while you are tarrying there. The blooming Miss W——r (you remember Sally W——r)[10] called upon us yesterday, an aged crone. Folks, whom you knew, die off every year. Formerly, I thought that death was wearing out, — I stood ramparted about with so many healthy friends. The departure of J. W.,[11] two springs back, corrected my delusion. Since then the old divorcer has been busy. If you do not make haste to return, there will be little left to greet you, of me, or mine.

(*London Magazine*, March 1822)

ON THE ARTIFICIAL COMEDY
OF THE LAST CENTURY

THE artificial Comedy, or Comedy of manners, is quite extinct on our stage. Congreve and Farquhar show their heads once in seven years only, to be exploded and put down instantly. The times cannot bear them. Is it for a few wild speeches, an occasional licence of dialogue? I think not altogether. The business of their dramatic characters will not stand the moral test. We screw every thing up to that. Idle gallantry in a fiction, a dream, the passing pageant of an evening, startles us in the same way as the alarming indications of profligacy in a son or ward in real life should startle a parent or guardian. We have no such middle emotions as dramatic interests left. We see a stage libertine playing his loose pranks of two hours' duration, and of no after consequence, with the severe eyes which inspect real vices with their bearings upon two worlds. We are spectators to a plot or intrigue (not reducible in life to the point of strict morality) and take it all for truth. We substitute a real for a dramatic person, and judge him accordingly. We try him in our courts, from which there is no appeal to the *dramatis personæ*, his peers. We have been spoiled with – not sentimental comedy – but a tyrant far more pernicious to our pleasures which has succeeded to it; the exclusive and all devouring drama of common life; where the moral point is every thing; where, instead of the fictitious half-believed personages of the stage (the phantoms of old comedy) we recognize ourselves, our brothers, aunts, kinsfolk, allies, patrons, enemies, – the same as in life, – with an interest in what is going on so hearty and substantial, that we cannot afford our moral judgment, in its deepest and most vital results, to compromise or slumber for a moment. What is *there* transacting, by no modification is made to affect us in any other manner than the same events or characters would do in our relationships of life. We carry our fire-side concerns to the theatre with us. We do not go thither, like our ancestors, to escape from the pressure of reality, so much as to confirm our experience of it; to make assurance double, and take a bond of fate. We must live our toilsome lives twice over, as it was the mournful privilege of Ulysses to descend twice to the shades. All that neutral ground of character, which stood between vice and virtue; or which in fact was indifferent to neither, where neither properly was called in question; that happy breathing-place from the burthen of a perpetual moral questioning – the sanctuary and quiet Alsatia [1] of hunted casuistry – is broken up and disfranchised, as injurious to the interests of society. The privileges of the place are taken away by law. We dare not dally with images, or names, of wrong. We bark like foolish dogs at shadows. We dread infection from the scenic representation of disorder; and fear a painted pustule. In our anxiety that our morality should not take cold, we wrap it up in a great blanket surtout of precaution against the breeze and sunshine.

I confess for myself that (with no great delinquencies to answer for) I am glad for a season to take an airing beyond the diocese of the strict conscience, – not to live always in the precincts of the law-courts – but now and then, for a dream-while or so, to imagine a world with no meddling restrictions – to get into recesses, whither the hunter cannot follow me –

> – Secret shades
> Of woody Ida's inmost grove,
> While yet there was no fear of Jove –

I come back to my cage and my restraint the fresher and more healthy for it. I wear my shackles more contentedly for having respired the breath of an imaginary freedom. I do not know how it is with others, but I feel the better always for the perusal of one of Congreve's – nay, why should I not add even of Wycherley's – comedies. I am the gayer at least for it; and I could never connect those sports of a witty fancy in any shape with any result to be drawn from them to imitation in real life. They are a world of themselves almost as much as fairy land. Take one of their characters, male or female (with few exceptions they are alike), and place it in a modern play, and my virtuous indignation shall rise against the profligate wretch as warmly as the Catos of the pit [2] could desire; because in a modern play I am to judge of the right and the wrong. The standard of *police* is the measure of *political justice*. The atmosphere will blight it, it cannot live here. It has got into a moral world, where it has no business, from which it must needs fall headlong; as dizzy, and incapable of making a stand, as a Swedenborgian bad spirit that has wandered unawares into the sphere of one of his Good Men or Angels. But in its own world do we feel the creature is so very bad? – The Fainalls and the Mirabels, the Dorimants and the Lady Touchwoods, [3] in their own sphere, do not offend my moral sense; in fact they do not appeal to it at all. They seem engaged in their proper element.

They break through no laws, or conscious restraints. They know of none. They have got out of Christendom into the land – what shall I call it? – of cuckoldry – the Utopia of gallantry, where pleasure is duty, and the manners perfect freedom. It is altogether a speculative scene of things, which has no reference whatever to the world that is. No good person can be justly offended as a spectator, because no good person suffers on the stage. Judged morally, every character in these plays – the few exceptions only are *mistakes* – is alike essentially vain and worthless. The great art of Congreve is especially shown in this, that he has entirely excluded from his scenes, – some little generosities on the part of Angelica[4] perhaps excepted, – not only anything like a faultless character, but any pretensions to goodness or good feelings whatsoever. Whether he did this designedly, or instinctively, the effect is as happy, as the design (if design) was bold. I used to wonder at the strange power which his Way of the World in particular possesses of interesting you all along in the pursuits of characters, for whom you absolutely care nothing – for you neither hate nor love his personages – and I think it is owing to this very indifference for any, that you endure the whole. He has spread a privation of moral light, I will call it, rather than by the ugly name of palpable darkness, over his creations; and his shadows flit before you without distinction or preference. Had he introduced a good character, a single gush of moral feeling, a revulsion of the judgment to actual life and actual duties, the impertinent Goshen[5] would have only lighted to the discovery of deformities, which now are none, because we think them none.

Translated into real life, the characters of his, and his friend Wycherley's dramas, are profligates and strumpets, – the business of their brief existence, the undivided pursuit of lawless gallantry. No other spring of action, or possible motive of conduct, is recognized; principles which, universally acted upon, must reduce this frame of things to a chaos. But we do them wrong in so translating them. No such effects are produced in *their* world. When we are among them, we are amongst a chaotic people. We are not to judge them by our usages. No reverend institutions are insulted by their proceedings, – for they have none among them. No peace of families is violated, – for no family ties exist among them. No purity of the marriage bed is stained, – for none is supposed to have a being. No deep affections are disquieted, – no holy wedlock bands are snapped asunder, – for affection's depth and wedded faith are not of the growth of that soil. There is neither right nor wrong, – gratitude or its opposite, – claim or duty, – paternity or sonship. Of what consequence is it to virtue, or how is she at all concerned about it, whether Sir Simon, or Dapperwit, steal away Miss Martha; or who is the father of Lord Froth's, or Sir Paul Pliant's children.[6]

The whole is a passing pageant, where we should sit as unconcerned at the issues, for life or death, as at a battle of the frogs and mice. But, like Don Quixote, we take part against the puppets, and quite as impertinently. We dare not contemplate an Atlantis, a scheme, out of which our coxcombical moral sense is for a little transitory ease excluded. We have not the courage to imagine a state of things for which there is neither reward nor punishment. We cling to the painful necessities of shame and blame. We would indict our very dreams.

Amidst the mortifying circumstances attendant upon growing old, it is something to have seen the School for Scandal in its glory. This comedy grew out of Congreve and Wycherley, but gathered some allays of the sentimental comedy which followed theirs. It is impossible that it should be now *acted*, though it continues, at long intervals, to be announced in the bills. Its hero, when Palmer played it at least, was Joseph Surface. When I remember the gay boldness, the graceful solemn plausibility, the measured step, the insinuating voice – to express it in a word – the downright *acted* villany of the part, so different from the pressure of conscious actual wickedness, – the hypocritical assumption of hypocrisy, – which made Jack so deservedly a favourite in that character, I must needs conclude the present generation of play-goers more virtuous than myself, or more dense. I freely confess that he divided the palm with me with his better brother; that, in fact, I liked him quite as well. Not but there are passages, – like that, for instance, where Joseph is made to refuse a pittance to a poor relation – incongruities which Sheridan was forced upon by the attempt to join the artificial with the sentimental comedy, either of which must destroy the other – but over these obstructions Jack's manner floated him so lightly, that a refusal from him no more shocked you, than the easy compliance of Charles gave you in reality any pleasure; you got over the paltry question as quickly as you could, to get back into the regions of pure comedy, where no cold moral reigns. The highly artificial manner of Palmer in this character counteracted every disagreeable impression which you might have received from the contrast, supposing them real, between the two brothers. You did not believe in Joseph with the same faith with which you believed in Charles. The latter was a pleasant reality, the former a no less pleasant poetical foil to it. The comedy, I have said, is incongruous; a mixture of Congreve with sentimental incompatibilities; the gaiety upon the whole is buoyant; but it required the consummate art of Palmer to reconcile the discordant elements.

A player with Jack's talents, if we had one now, would not dare to do the part in the same manner. He would instinctively avoid every turn which might tend to unrealize, and so to make the character fascinating. He must take his cue from his spectators, who would expect a bad man and a good man as rigidly opposed to each other as the death-beds of those geniuses are contrasted in the prints, which I am sorry to say have disappeared from the windows of my old friend Carrington Bowles,[7] of St Paul's Churchyard memory – (an exhibition as venerable as the adjacent cathedral, and almost coeval) of the bad and good man at the hour of death; where the ghastly apprehensions of the former, – and truly the grim phantom with his reality of a toasting fork is not to be despised, – so finely contrast with the meek complacent kissing of the rod, – taking it in like honey and butter, – with which the latter submits to the scythe of the gentler bleeder, Time, who wields his lancet with the apprehensive finger of a popular young ladies' surgeon. What flesh, like loving grass, would not covet to meet half-way the stroke of such a delicate mower? – John Palmer was twice an actor in this exquisite part. He was playing to you all the while that he was playing upon Sir Peter and his lady. You had the first intimation of a sentiment before it was on his lips. His altered voice was meant to you, and you were to suppose that his fictitious co-flutterers on the stage perceived nothing at all of it. What was it to you if that half-reality, the husband, was over reached by the puppetry – or the thin thing (Lady Teazle's reputation) was persuaded it was dying of a plethory? The fortunes of Othello and Desdemona were not concerned in it. Poor Jack has passed from the stage in good time, that he did not live to this our age of seriousness. The pleasant old Teazle *King*,[8] too, is gone in good time. His manner would scarce have past current in our day. We must love or hate – acquit or condemn – censure or pity – exert our detestable coxcombry of moral judgment upon everything. Joseph Surface, to go down now, must be a downright revolting villain – no compromise – his first appearance must shock and give horror – his specious plausibilities, which the pleasurable faculties of our fathers welcomed with such hearty greetings, knowing that no harm (dramatic harm even) could come, or was meant to come of them, must inspire a cold and killing aversion. Charles (the real canting person of the scene – for the hypocrisy of Joseph has its ulterior legitimate ends, but his brother's professions of a good heart centre in downright self-satisfaction) must be *loved*, and Joseph *hated*. To balance one disagreeable reality with another, Sir Peter Teazle must be no longer the comic idea of a fretful old bachelor bridegroom, whose teasings (while King acted it) were evidently as much played off at you, as they were meant to concern any body on the stage, – he must be a real person, capable in law of sustaining an injury – a person towards whom duties are to be acknowledged – the genuine crim-con [9] antagonist of the villanous seducer Joseph. To realize him more, his sufferings under his unfortunate match must have the downright pungency of life – must (or should) make you not mirthful but uncomfortable, just as the same predicament would move you in a neighbour or old friend. The delicious scenes which give the play its name and zest, must affect you in the same serious manner as if you heard the reputation of a dear female friend attacked in your real presence. Crabtree, and Sir Benjamin – those poor snakes that live but in the sunshine of your mirth – must be ripened by this hot-bed process of realization into asps or amphisbænas;[10] and Mrs Candour – O! frightful! become a hooded serpent. Oh who that remembers Parsons and Dodd – the wasp and butterfly of the School for Scandal – in those two characters; and charming natural Miss Pope, the perfect gentlewoman as distinguished from the fine lady of comedy, in this latter part – would forego the true scenic delight – the escape from life – the oblivion of consequences – the holiday barring out of the pedant Reflection – those Saturnalia of two or three brief hours, well won from the world – to sit instead at one of our modern plays – to have his coward conscience (that, forsooth must not be left for a moment) stimulated with perpetual appeals – dulled rather, and blunted, as a faculty without repose must be – and his moral vanity pampered with images of notional justice, notional beneficences, lives saved without the spectator's risk, and fortunes given away that cost the author nothing?

No piece was, perhaps, ever so completely cast in all its parts as this *manager's comedy*.[11] Miss Farren had succeeded to Mrs Abingdon in Lady Teazle; and Smith, the original Charles, had retired when I first saw it. The rest of the characters, with very slight exceptions, remained. I remember it was then the fashion to cry down John Kemble, who took the part of Charles after Smith; but I thought, very unjustly. Smith, I fancy, was more airy, and took the eye with a certain gaiety of person. He brought with him no sombre recollections of tragedy. He had not to expiate the fault of having pleased beforehand in lofty declamation. He had no sins of Hamlet or of Richard to atone for. His failure in these parts was a passport to success in one of so opposite a tendency. But, as far as I could judge, the weighty sense of Kemble made up for more personal incapacity than he had to answer for. His harshest tones in this part came steeped and dulcified in good humour. He made his defects a grace. His exact declamatory manner, as he managed wit, only served to convey the points of his dialogue with more precision. It seemed to head the shafts to carry them deeper. Not one of his sparkling sentences was lost. I remember minutely how he delivered each in succession, and cannot by any effort imagine how any of them could be altered for the better. No man could deliver brilliant dialogue – the dialogue of Congreve or Wycherley – because none understood it – half so well as John Kemble. His Valentine, in Love for Love, was, to my recollection, faultless. He flagged sometimes in the intervals of tragic passion. He would slumber over the level parts of an heroic character. His Macbeth has been known to nod. But he always seemed to me to be particularly alive to pointed and witty dialogue. The relaxing levities of tragedy have not been touched by any since him – the playful court-bred spirit in which he condescended to the players in Hamlet – the sportive relief which he threw into the darker shades of Richard – disappeared with him. He had his sluggish moods, his torpors – but they were the halting-stones and resting-places of his tragedy – politic savings, and fetches of the breath – husbandry of the lungs, where nature pointed him to be an economist – rather, I think, than errors of the judgment. They were, at worst, less painful than the eternal tormenting unappeasable vigilance, the 'lidless dragon eyes,' of present fashionable tragedy.

(*London Magazine*, April 1822)

DETACHED THOUGHTS ON BOOKS AND READING

To mind the inside of a book is to entertain one's self with the forced product of another man's brain. Now I think a man of quality and breeding may be much amused with the natural sprouts of his own. – *Lord Foppington in the Relapse.*[1]

AN ingenious acquaintance of my own was so much struck with this bright sally of his Lordship, that he has left off reading altogether, to the great improvement of his originality. At the hazard of losing some credit on this head, I must confess that I dedicate no inconsiderable portion of my time to other people's thoughts. I dream away my life in other's speculations. I love to lose myself in other men's minds. When I am not walking, I am reading; I cannot sit and think. Books think for me.

I have no repugnances. Shaftesbury is not too genteel for me, nor Jonathan Wild[2] too low. I can read anything which I call a *book*. There are things in that shape which I cannot allow for such.

In this catalogue of *books which are no books – biblia abiblia* – I reckon Court Calendars, Directories, Pocket Books, Draught Boards, bound and lettered on the back, Scientific Treatises, Almanacks, Statutes at Large; the works of Hume, Gibbon, Robertson, Beattie, Soame Jenyns, and, generally, all those volumes which 'no gentleman's library should be without': the Histories of Flavius Josephus (that learned Jew), and Paley's Moral Philosophy. With these exceptions, I can read almost anything. I bless my stars for a taste so catholic, so unexcluding.

I confess that it moves my spleen to see these *things in books' clothing* perched upon shelves, like false saints, usurpers of true shrines, intruders into the sanctuary, thrusting out the legitimate occupants. To reach down a well-bound semblance of a volume, and hope it some kind-hearted play-book, then, opening what 'seem its leaves,' to come bolt upon a withering Population Essay. To expect a Steele, or a Farquhar, and find – Adam Smith.[3] To view a well-arranged assortment of blockheaded Encyclopædias (Anglicanas or Metropolitanas)[4] set out in an array of Russia, or Morocco, when a tithe of that good leather would comfortably re-clothe my shivering folios; would renovate Paracelsus himself, and enable old Raymund Lully [5] to look like himself again in the world. I never see these impostors, but I long to strip them, to warm my ragged veterans in their spoils.

To be strong-backed and neat-bound is the desideratum of a volume. Magnificence comes after. This, when it can be afforded, is not to be lavished upon all kinds of books indiscriminately. I would not dress a set of Magazines, for instance, in full suit. The dishabille, or half-binding (with Russia backs [6] ever) is *our* costume. A Shakspeare, or a Milton (unless the first editions), it were mere foppery to trick out in gay apparel. The possession of them confers no distinction. The exterior of them (the things themselves being so common), strange to say, raises no sweet emotions, no tickling sense of property in the owner. Thomson's Seasons, again, looks best (I maintain it) a little torn, and dog's-eared. How beautiful to a genuine lover of reading are the sullied leaves, and worn-out appearance, nay, the very odour (beyond Russia), if we would not forget kind feelings in fastidiousness, of an old 'Circulating Library' Tom Jones, or Vicar of Wakefield! How they speak of the thousand thumbs, that have turned over their pages with delight! – of the lone sempstress, whom they may have cheered (milliner, or hard-working mantua-maker) after her long day's needle-toil, running far into midnight, when she has snatched an hour, ill-spared from sleep, to steep her cares, as in some Lethean cup, in spelling out their enchanting contents! Who would have them a whit less soiled? What better condition could we desire to see them in?

In some respects the better a book is, the less it demands from binding. Fielding, Smollet, Sterne, and all that class of perpetually self-reproductive volumes – Great Nature's Stereotypes – we see them individually perish with less regret, because we know the copies of them to be 'eterne.' But where a book is at once both good and rare – where the individual is almost the species, and when *that* perishes,

> We know not where is that Promethean torch
> That can its light relumine –

such a book, for instance, as the Life of the Duke of Newcastle, by his Duchess [7] – no casket is rich enough, no casing sufficiently durable, to honour and keep safe such a jewel.

Not only rare volumes of this description, which seem hopeless ever to be reprinted; but old editions of writers, such as Sir Philip Sydney, Bishop Taylor, Milton in his prose-works, Fuller – of whom we *have* reprints, yet the books themselves, though they go about, and are talked of here and there, we know, have not endenizened themselves (nor possibly ever will) in the national heart, so as to become stock books – it is good to possess these in durable and costly covers. I do not care for a First Folio of Shakspeare. I rather prefer the common editions of Rowe and Tonson without notes, and with *plates*, which, being so execrably bad, serve as maps, or modest remembrancers, to the text; and without pretending to any supposable emulation with it, are so much better than the Shakspeare gallery *engravings*, which *did*. I have a community of feeling with my countrymen about his Plays, and I like those editions of him best, which have been oftenest tumbled about and handled. – On the contrary, I cannot read Beaumont and Fletcher but in Folio. The Octavo editions are painful to look at. I have no sympathy with them. If they were as much read as the current editions of the other poet, I should prefer them in that shape to the older one. I do not know a more heartless sight than the reprint of the Anatomy of Melancholy. What need was there of unearthing the bones of that fantastic old great man, to expose them in a winding-sheet of the newest fashion to modern censure? what hapless stationer could dream of Burton ever becoming popular? – The wretched Malone [8] could not do worse, when he bribed the sexton of Stratford church to let him white-wash the painted effigy of old Shakspeare, which stood there, in rude but lively fashion depicted, to the very colour of the cheek, the eye, the eyebrow, hair, the very dress he used to wear – the only authentic testimony we had, however imperfect, of these curious parts and parcels of him. They covered him over with a coat of white paint. By — , if I had been a justice of peace for Warwickshire, I would have clapt both commentator and sexton fast in the stocks, for a pair of meddling sacrilegious varlets. I think I see them at their work – these sapient trouble-tombs.

Shall I be thought fantastical, if I confess, that the names of some of our poets sound sweeter, and have a finer relish to the ear – to mine, at least – than that of Milton or of Shakspeare? It may be, that the latter are more staled and rung upon in common discourse. The sweetest names, and which carry a perfume in the mention, are, Kit Marlowe, Drayton, Drummond of Hawthornden, and Cowley.

Much depends upon *when* and *where* you read a book. In the five or six impatient minutes, before the dinner is quite ready, who would think of taking up the Fairy Queen for a stop-gap, or a volume of Bishop Andrewes' sermons?

Milton almost requires a solemn service of music to be played before you enter upon him. But he brings his music, to which, who listens, had need bring docile thoughts, and purged ears.

Winter evenings – the world shut out – with less of ceremony the gentle Shakspeare enters. At such a season, the Tempest, or his own Winter's Tale –

These two poets you cannot avoid reading aloud – to yourself, or (as it chances) to some single person listening. More than one – and it degenerates into an audience.

Books of quick interest, that hurry on for incidents, are for the eye to glide over only. It will not do to read them out. I could never listen to even the better kind of modern novels without extreme irksomeness.

A newspaper, read out, is intolerable. In some of the Bank offices it is the custom (to save so much individual time) for one of the clerks – who is the best scholar – to commence upon the Times, or the Chronicle, and recite its entire contents aloud *pro bono publico*.[9] With every advantage of lungs and elocution, the effect is singularly vapid. In barbers' shops and public-houses a fellow will get up, and spell out a paragraph which he communicates as some discovery. Another follows with *his* selection. So the entire journal transpires at length by piece-meal. Seldom-readers are slow readers, and without this expedient, no one in the company would probably ever travel through the contents of a whole paper.

Newspapers always excite curiosity. No one ever lays one down without a feeling of disappointment.

What an eternal time that gentleman in black, at Nando's,[10] keeps the paper! I am sick of hearing the waiter bawling out incessantly, 'the Chronicle is in hand, Sir.'

Coming in to an inn at night – having ordered your supper – what can be more delightful than to find lying in the window-seat, left there time out of mind by the carelessness of some former guest – two or three numbers of the old Town and Country Magazine, with its amusing *tête-à-tête* pictures – 'The Royal Lover and Lady G—'; 'The Melting Platonic and the Old Beau,' – and such like antiquated scandal? Would you exchange it – at that time, and in that place – for a better book?

Poor Tobin,[11] who latterly fell blind, did not regret it so much for the weightier kinds of reading – the Paradise Lost, or Comus, he could have *read* to him – but he missed the pleasure of skimming over with his own eye a magazine, or a light pamphlet.

I should not care to be caught in the serious avenues of some cathedral alone and reading *Candide*.

I do not remember a more whimsical surprise than having been once detected – by a familiar damsel – reclining at my ease upon the grass, on Primrose Hill (her Cythera),[12] reading – *Pamela*. There was nothing in the book to make a man seriously ashamed at the exposure; but as she seated herself down by me, and seemed determined to read in company, I could have wished it had been – any other book. We read on very sociably for a few pages; and, not finding the author much to her taste, she got up, and – went away. Gentle casuist, I leave it to thee to conjecture, whether the blush (for there was one between us) was the property of the nymph or the swain in this dilemma. From me you shall never get the secret.

I am not much a friend to out-of-doors reading. I cannot settle my spirits to it. I knew a Unitarian minister, who was generally to be seen upon Snow Hill (as yet Skinner's Street *was not*), between the hours of ten and eleven in the morning, studying a volume of Lardner.[13] I own this to have been a strain of abstraction beyond my reach. I used to admire how he sidled along, keeping clear of secular contacts. An illiterate encounter with a porter's knot, or a bread basket, would have quickly put to flight all the theology I am master of, and have left me worse than indifferent to the five points.

There is a class of street-readers, whom I can never contemplate without affection – the poor gentry, who, not having wherewithal to buy or hire a book, filch a little learning at the open stalls – the owner, with his hard eye, casting envious looks at them all the while, and thinking when they will have done. Venturing tenderly, page after page, expecting every moment when he shall interpose his interdict, and yet unable to deny themselves the gratification, they 'snatch a fearful joy.' Martin B—,[14] in this way, by daily fragments, got through two volumes of Clarissa, when the stall-keeper damped his laudable ambition, by asking him (it was in his younger days) whether he meant to purchase the work. M. declares, that under no circumstance in his life did he ever peruse a book with half the satisfaction which he took in those uneasy snatches. A quaint poetess of our day[15] has moralized upon this subject in two very touching but homely stanzas.

> I saw a boy with eager eye
> Open a book upon a stall,
> And read, as he'd devour it all;
> Which when the stall-man did espy,
> Soon to the boy I heard him call,

'You, Sir, you never buy a book,
Therefore in one you shall not look.'
The boy pass'd slowly on, and with a sigh
He wish'd he never had been taught to read,
Then of the old churl's books he should have had no need.

Of sufferings the poor have many,
Which never can the rich annoy:
I soon perceiv'd another boy,
Who look'd as if he had not any
Food, for that day at least – enjoy
The sight of cold meat in a tavern larder.
This boy's case, then thought I, is surely harder,
Thus hungry, longing, thus without a penny,
Beholding choice of dainty-dressed meat:
No wonder if he wish he ne'er had learn'd to eat.

(London Magazine, July 1822)

CONFESSIONS OF A DRUNKARD[1]

DEHORTATIONS[2] from the use of strong liquors have been the favourite topic of sober declaimers in all ages, and have been received with abundance of applause by water-drinking critics. But with the patient himself, the man that is to be cured, unfortunately their sound has seldom prevailed. Yet the evil is acknowledged, the remedy simple. Abstain. No force can oblige a man to raise the glass to his head against his will. 'Tis as easy as not to steal, not to tell lies.

Alas! the hand to pilfer, and the tongue to bear false witness, have no constitutional tendency. These are actions indifferent to them. At the first instance of the reformed will, they can be brought off without a murmur. The itching finger is but a figure in speech, and the tongue of the liar can with the same natural delight give forth useful truths, with which it has been accustomed to scatter their pernicious contraries. But when a man has commenced sot—

O pause, thou sturdy moralist, thou person of stout nerves and a strong head, whose liver is happily untouched, and ere thy gorge riseth at the *name* which I have written, first learn what the *thing* is; how much of compassion, how much of human allowance, thou mayst virtuously mingle with thy disapprobation. Trample not on the ruins of a man. Exact not, under so terrible a penalty as infamy, a resuscitation from a state of death almost as real as that from which Lazarus rose not but by a miracle.

Begin a reformation, and custom will make it easy. But what if the beginning be dreadful, the first steps not like climbing a mountain but going through fire? what if the whole system must undergo a change violent as that which we conceive of the mutation of form in some insects? what if a process comparable to flaying alive be to be gone through? is the weakness that sinks under such struggles to be confounded with the pertinacity which clings to other vices, which have induced no constitutional necessity, no engagement of the whole victim, body and soul?

I have known one in that state, when he has tried to abstain but for one evening, – though the poisonous potion had long ceased to bring back its first enchantments, though he was sure it would rather deepen his gloom than brighten it, – in the violence of the struggle, and the necessity he has felt of getting rid of the present sensation at any rate, I have known him to scream out, to cry aloud, for the anguish and pain of the strife within him.

Why should I hesitate to declare, that the man of whom I speak is myself? I have no puling apology to make to mankind. I see them all in one way or another deviating from the pure reason. It is to my own nature alone I am accountable for the woe that I have brought upon it.

I believe that there are constitutions, robust heads and iron insides, whom scarce any excesses can hurt; whom brandy (I have seen them drink it like wine), at all events whom wine, taken in ever so plentiful measure, can do no worse injury to than just to muddle their faculties, perhaps never very pellucid. On them this discourse is wasted. They would but laugh at a weak brother, who, trying his strength with them, and coming off foiled from the contest, would fain persuade them that such agonistic exercises are dangerous. It is to a very different description of persons I speak. It is to the weak, the nervous; to those who feel the want of some artificial aid to raise their spirits in society to what is no more than the ordinary pitch of all around them without it. This is the secret of our drinking. Such must fly the convivial board in the first instance, if they do not mean to sell themselves for term of life.

Twelve years ago I had completed my six-and-twentieth year. I had lived from the period of leaving school to that time pretty much in solitude. My companions were chiefly books, or at most one or two living ones of my own book-loving and sober stamp. I rose early, went to bed betimes, and the faculties which God had given me, I have reason to think, did not rust in me unused.

About that time I fell in with some companions of a different order. They were men of boisterous spirits, sitters up a-nights, disputants, drunken; yet seemed to have something noble about them. We dealt about the wit, or what passes for it after midnight, jovially. Of the quality called fancy I certainly possessed a larger share than my companions. Encouraged by their applause, I set up for a professed joker! I, who of all men am least fitted for such an occupation, having, in addition to the greatest difficulty which I experience at all times of finding words to express my meaning, a natural nervous impediment in my speech!

Reader, if you are gifted with nerves like mine, aspire to any character but that of a wit. When you find a tickling relish upon your tongue disposing you to that sort of conversation, especially if you find a pre-ternatural flow of ideas setting in upon you at the sight of a bottle and fresh glasses, avoid giving way to it as you would fly your greatest destruction. If you cannot crush the power of fancy, or that within you which you mistake for such, divert it, give it some other play. Write an essay, pen a character or description, – but not as I do now, with tears trickling down your cheeks.

To be an object of compassion to friends, of derision to foes; to be suspected by strangers, stared at by fools; to be esteemed dull when you cannot be witty, to be applauded for witty when you know that you have been dull; to be called upon for the extemporaneous exercise of that faculty which no premeditation can give; to be spurred on to efforts which end in contempt; to be set on to provoke mirth which procures the procurer hatred; to give pleasure and be paid with squinting malice; to swallow draughts of life-destroying wine which are to be distilled into airy breath to tickle vain auditors; to mortgage miserable morrows for nights of madness; to waste whole seas of time upon those who pay it back in little inconsiderable drops of grudging applause, – are the wages of buffoonery and death.

Time, which has a sure stroke at dissolving all connections which have no solider fastening than this liquid cement, more kind to me than my own taste or penetration, at length opened my eyes to the supposed qualities of my first friends. No trace of them is left but in the vices which they introduced, and the habits they infixed. In them my friends survive still, and exercise ample retribution for any supposed infidelity that I may have been guilty of towards them.

My next more immediate companions were and are persons of such intrinsic and felt worth, that though accidentally their acquaintance has proved pernicious to me, I do not know that if the thing were to do over again, I should have the courage to eschew the mischief at the price of forfeiting the benefit. I came to them reeking from the steams of my late over-heated notions of companionship; and the slightest fuel which they unconsciously afforded, was sufficient to feed my old fires into a propensity.

They were no drinkers, but, one from professional habits, and another from a custom derived from his father, smoked tobacco. The devil could not have devised a more subtle trap to re-take a backsliding penitent. The transition, from gulping down draughts of liquid fire to puffing out innocuous blasts of dry smoke, was so like cheating him. But he is too hard for us when we hope to commute. He beats us at barter; and when we think to set off a new failing against an old infirmity, 'tis odds but he puts the trick upon us of two for one. That (comparatively) white devil of tobacco brought with him in the end seven worse than himself.

It were impertinent to carry the reader through all the processes by which, from smoking at first with malt liquor, I took my degrees through thin wines, through stronger wine and water, through small punch, to those juggling compositions, which, under the name of mixed liquors, slur a great deal of brandy or other poison under less and less water continually, until they come next to none, and so to none at all. But it is hateful to disclose the secrets of my Tartarus.[3]

I should repel my readers, from a mere incapacity of believing me, were I to tell them what tobacco has been to me, the drudging service which I have paid, the slavery which I have vowed to it. How, when I have resolved to quit it, a feeling as of ingratitude has started up; how it has put on personal claims and made the demands of a friend upon me. How the reading of it casually in a book, as where Adams takes his whiff in the chimney-corner of some inn in Joseph Andrews, or Piscator in the Complete Angler breaks his fast upon a morning pipe in that delicate room *Piscatoribus Sacrum*,[4] has in a moment broken down the resistance of weeks. How a pipe was ever in my midnight path before me, till the vision forced me to realize it, – how then its ascending vapours curled, its fragrance lulled, and the thousand delicious ministerings conversant about it, employing every faculty, extracted the sense of pain. How from illuminating it came to darken, from a quick solace it turned to a negative relief, thence to a restlessness and dissatisfaction, thence to a positive misery. How, even now, when the whole secret stands confessed in all its dreadful truth before me, I feel myself linked to it beyond the power of revocation. Bone of my bone –

Persons not accustomed to examine the motives of their actions, to reckon up the countless nails that rivet the chains of habit, or perhaps being bound by none so obdurate as those I have confessed to, may recoil from this as from an overcharged picture. But what short of such a bondage is it, which in spite of protesting friends, a weeping wife and a reprobating world, chains down many a poor fellow, of no original indisposition to goodness, to his pipe and his pot?

I have seen a print after Correggio, in which three female figures are ministering to a man who sits fast bound at the root of a tree. Sensuality is soothing him, Evil Habit is nailing him to a branch, and Repugnance at the same instant of time is applying a snake to this side. In his face is feeble delight, the recollection of past rather than perception of present pleasures, languid enjoyment of evil with utter imbecility to good, a Sybaritic effeminacy,[5] a submission to bondage, the springs of the will gone down like a broken clock, the sin and the suffering co-instantaneous, or the latter forerunning the former, remorse preceding action – all this represented in one point of time. – When I saw this, I admired the wonderful skill of the painter. But when I went away, I wept, because I thought of my own condition.

Of *that* there is no hope that it should ever change. The waters have gone over me. But out of the black depths, could I be heard, I would cry out to all those who have but set a foot in the perilous flood. Could the youth, to whom the flavour of his first wine is delicious as the opening scenes of life or the entering upon some newly discovered paradise, look into my desolation, and be made to understand what a dreary thing it is when a man shall feel himself going down a precipice with open eyes and a passive will, – to see his destruction and have no power to stop it, and yet to feel it all the way emanating from himself; to perceive all goodness emptied out of him, and yet not to be able to forget a time when it was otherwise; to bear about the piteous spectacle of his own self-ruins: – could he see my fevered eye, feverish with last night's drinking, and feverishly looking for this night's repetition of the folly; could he feel the body of the death out of which I cry hourly with feebler and feebler outcry to be delivered, – it were enough to make him dash the sparkling beverage to the earth in all the pride of its mantling temptation; to make him clasp his teeth,

> and not undo 'em
> To suffer WET DAMNATION to run thro' 'em.

Yea, but (methinks I hear somebody object) if sobriety be that fine thing you would have us to understand, if the comforts of a cool brain are to be preferred to that state of heated excitement which you describe and deplore, what hinders in your own instance that you do not return to those habits from which you would induce others never to swerve? if the blessing be worth preserving, is it not worth recovering?

Recovering! – O if a wish could transport me back to those days of youth, when a draught from the next clear spring could slake any heats which summer suns and youthful exercise had power to stir up in the blood, how gladly would I return to thee, pure element, the drink of children, and of child-like holy hermit. In my dreams I can sometimes fancy thy cool refreshment purling over my burning tongue. But my waking stomach rejects it. That which refreshes innocence, only makes me sick and faint.

But is there no middle way betwixt total abstinence and the excess which kills you? – For your sake, reader, and that you may never attain to my experience, with pain I must utter the dreadful truth, that there is none, none that I can find. In my stage of habit (I speak not of habits less confirmed – for some of them I believe the advice to be most prudential) in the stage which I have reached, to stop short of that measure which is sufficient to draw on torpor and sleep, the benumbing apoplectic sleep of the drunkard, is to have taken none at all. The pain of the self-denial is all one. And what that is, I had rather the reader should believe on my credit, than know from his own trial. He will come to know it, whenever he shall arrive in that state, in which, paradoxical as it may appear, *reason shall only visit him through intoxication:* for it is a fearful truth, that the intellectual faculties by repeated acts of intemperance may be driven from their orderly sphere of action, their clear day-light ministries, until they shall be brought at last to depend, for the faint manifestation of their departing energies, upon the returning periods of the fatal madness to which they owe their devastation. The drinking man is never less himself than during his sober intervals. Evil is so far his good.*

Behold me then, in the robust period of life, reduced to imbecility and decay. Hear me count my gains, and the profits which I have derived from the midnight cup.

Twelve years ago I was possessed of a healthy frame of mind and body. I was never strong, but I think my constitution (for a weak one) was as happily exempt from the tendency to any malady as it was possible to be. I scarce knew what it was to ail anything. Now, except when I am losing myself in a sea of drink, I am never free from those uneasy sensations in head and stomach, which are so much worse to bear than any definite pains or aches.

At that time I was seldom in bed after six in the morning summer and winter. I awoke refreshed, and seldom without some merry thoughts in my head, or some piece of a song to welcome the new-born day. Now, the first feeling which besets me, after stretching out the hours of re-cumbence to their last possible extent, is a forecast of the wearisome day

* When poor M— painted his last picture, with a pencil in one trembling hand and a glass of brandy and water in the other, his fingers owed the comparative steadiness, with which they were enabled to go through their task in an imperfect manner, to a temporary firmness derived from a repetition of practices, the general effect of which had shaken both them and him so terribly.

that lies before me, with a secret wish that I could have lain on still, or never awaked.

Life itself, my waking life, has much of the confusion, the trouble, and obscure perplexity, of an ill dream. In the day time I stumble upon dark mountains.

Business, which, though never particularly adapted to my nature, yet as something of necessity to be gone through, and therefore best undertaken with cheerfulness, I used to enter upon with some degree of alacrity, now wearies, affrights, perplexes me. I fancy all sorts of discouragements, and am ready to give up an occupation which gives me bread, from a harassing conceit of incapacity. The slightest commission given me by a friend, or any small duty which I have to perform for myself, as giving orders to a tradesman, &c., haunts me as a labour impossible to be got through. So much the springs of action are broken.

The same cowardice attends me in all my intercourse with mankind. I dare not promise that a friend's honour, or his cause, would be safe in my keeping, if I were put to the expense of any manly resolution in defending it. So much the springs of moral action are deadened within me.

My favourite occupations in times past, now cease to entertain. I can do nothing readily. Application for ever so short a time kills me. This poor abstract of my condition was penned at long intervals, with scarcely any attempt at connection of thought, which is now difficult to me.

The noble passages which formerly delighted me in history or poetic fiction, now only draw a few weak tears, allied to dotage. My broken and dispirited nature seems to sink before anything great and admirable.

I perpetually catch myself in tears, for any cause, or none. It is inexpressible how much this infirmity adds to a sense of shame, and a general feeling of deterioration.

These are some of the instances, concerning which I can say with truth, that it was not always so with me.

Shall I lift up the veil of my weakness any further? or is this disclosure sufficient?

I am a poor nameless egotist, who have no vanity to consult by these Confessions. I know not whether I shall be laughed at, or heard seriously. Such as they are, I commend them to the reader's attention, if he find his own case any way touched. I have told him what I am come to. Let him stop in time.

(*London Magazine*, August 1822)

A DISSERTATION
UPON ROAST PIG

MANKIND, says a Chinese manuscript, which my friend M.[1] was obliging enough to read and explain to me, for the first seventy thousand ages ate their meat raw, clawing or biting it from the living animal, just as they do in Abyssinia to this day. This period is not obscurely hinted at by their great Confucius in the second chapter of his Mundane Mutations, where he designates a kind of golden age by the term Cho-fang, literally the Cook's holiday. The manuscript goes on to say, that the art of roasting, or rather broiling (which I take to be the elder brother) was accidentally discovered in the manner following. The swine-herd, Ho-ti, having gone out into the woods one morning, as his manner was, to collect mast for his hogs, left his cottage in the care of his eldest son Bo-bo, a great lubberly boy, who being fond of playing with fire, as younkers of his age commonly are, let some sparks escape into a bundle of straw, which kindling quickly, spread the conflagration over every part of their poor mansion, till it was reduced to ashes. Together with the cottage (a sorry antediluvian make-shift of a building, you may think it), what was of much more importance, a fine litter of new-farrowed pigs, no less than nine in number, perished. China pigs have been esteemed a luxury all over the East from the remotest periods that we read of. Bo-bo was in utmost consternation, as you may think, not so much for the sake of the tenement, which his father and he could easily build up again with a few dry branches, and the labour of an hour or two, at any time, as for the loss of the pigs. While he was thinking what he should say to his father, and wringing his hands over the smoking remnants of one of those untimely sufferers, an odour assailed his nostrils, unlike any scent which he had before experienced. What could it proceed from? – not from the burnt cottage – he had smelt that smell before – indeed this was by no means the first accident of the kind which had occurred through the negligence of this unlucky young fire-brand. Much less did it resemble that of any known herb, weed, or flower. A premonitory moistening at the same time overflowed his nether lip. He knew not what to think. He next stooped down to feel the pig, if there were any signs of life in it. He burnt his fingers, and to cool them he applied them in his booby fashion to his mouth. Some of the crums of the scorched skin had come away with his fingers, and for the first time in his life (in the world's life indeed, for before him no man had known it) he tasted – *crackling!* Again he felt and fumbled at the pig. It did not burn him so much now, still he licked his fingers from a sort of habit. The truth at length broke into his slow understanding, that it was the pig that smelt so, and the pig that tasted so delicious; and, surrendering himself up to the newborn pleasure, he fell to tearing up whole handfuls of the scorched skin with the flesh next it, and was cramming it down his throat in his beastly fashion, when his sire entered amid the smoking rafters, armed with retributory cudgel, and finding how affairs stood, began to rain blows upon the young rogue's shoulders, as thick as hailstones, which Bo-bo heeded not any more than if they had been flies. The tickling pleasure which he experienced in his lower regions, had rendered him quite callous to any inconveniences he might feel in those remote quarters. His father might lay on, but he could not beat him from his pig, till he had fairly made an end of it, when, becoming a little more sensible of his situation, something like the following dialogue ensued.

'You graceless whelp, what have you got there devouring? Is it not enough that you have burnt me down three houses with your dog's tricks, and be hanged to you, but you must be eating fire, and I know not what – what have you got there, I say?'

'O, father, the pig, the pig, do come and taste how nice the burnt pig eats.'

The ears of Ho-ti tingled with horror. He cursed his son, and he cursed himself that ever he should beget a son that should eat burnt pig.

Bo-bo, whose scent was wonderfully sharpened since morning, soon raked out another pig, and fairly rending it asunder, thrust the lesser half by main force into the fists of Ho-ti, still shouting out 'Eat, eat, eat the burnt pig, father, only taste – O Lord,' – with such-like barbarous ejaculations, cramming all the while as if he would choke.

Ho-ti trembled every joint while he grasped the abominable thing, wavering whether he should not put his son to death for an unnatural young monster, when the crackling scorching his fingers, as it had done his son's, and applying the same remedy to them, he in his turn tasted some of its flavour, which, make what sour mouths he would for a pretence, proved not altogether displeasing to him. In conclusion (for the manuscript here is a little tedious), both father and son fairly sat down to the mess, and never left off till they had despatched all that remained of the litter.

Bo-bo was strictly enjoined not to let the secret escape, for the neighbours would certainly have stoned them for a couple of abominable wretches, who could think of improving upon the good meat which God had sent them. Nevertheless, strange stories got about. It was observed that Ho-ti's cottage was burnt down now more frequently than ever. Nothing but fires from this time forward. Some would break out in broad day, others in the night-time. As often as the sow farrowed, so sure was the house of Ho-ti to be in a blaze; and Ho-ti himself, which was the more remarkable, instead of chastising his son, seemed to grow more indulgent to him than ever. At length they were watched, the terrible mystery discovered, and father and son summoned to take their trial at Pekin, then an inconsiderable assize town. Evidence was given, the obnoxious food itself produced in court, and verdict about to be pronounced, when the foreman of the jury begged that some of the burnt pig, of which the culprits stood accused, might be handed into the box. He handled it, and they all handled it, and burning their fingers, as Bo-bo and his father had done before them, and nature prompting to each of them the same remedy, against the face of all the facts, and the clearest charge which judge had ever given, – to the surprise of the whole court, townsfolk, strangers, reporters, and all present – without leaving the box, or any manner of consultation whatever, they brought in a simultaneous verdict of Not Guilty.

The judge, who was a shrewd fellow, winked at the manifest iniquity of the decision: and, when the court was dismissed, went privily, and bought up all the pigs that could be had for love or money. In a few days his Lordship's town house was observed to be on fire. The thing took wing, and now there was nothing to be seen but fires in every direction. Fuel and pigs grew enormously dear all over the district. The insurance offices one and all shut up shop. People built slighter and slighter every day, until it was feared that the very science of architecture would in no long time be lost to the world. Thus this custom of firing houses continued, till in process of time, says my manuscript, a sage arose, like our Locke, who made a discovery, that the flesh of swine, or indeed of any other animal, might be cooked (*burnt*, as they called it) without the necessity of consuming a whole house to dress it. Then first began the rude form of a gridiron. Roasting by the string, or spit, came in a century or two later, I forget in whose dynasty. By such slow degrees, concludes the manuscript, do the most useful, and seemingly the most obvious arts, make their way among mankind –

Without placing too implicit faith in the account above given, it must be agreed, that if a worthy pretext for so dangerous an experiment as setting houses on fire (especially in these days) could be assigned in favour of any culinary object, that pretext and excuse might be found in ROAST PIG.

Of all the delicacies in the whole *mundus edibilis*, I will maintain it to be the most delicate – *princeps obsoniorum*.[2]

I speak not of your grown porkers – things between pig and pork those hobbydehoys – but a young and tender suckling – under a moon old – guiltless as yet of the sty – with no original speck of the *amor immunditiæ*,[3] the hereditary failing of the first parent, yet manifest – his voice as yet not broken, but something between a childish treble, and a grumble – the mild forerunner, or *præludium*,[4] of a grunt.

He must be roasted. I am not ignorant that our ancestors ate them seethed, or boiled – but what a sacrifice of the exterior tegument!

There is no flavour comparable, I will contend, to that of the crisp, tawny, well-watched, not over-roasted, *crackling*, as it is well called – the very teeth are invited to their share of the pleasure at this banquet in overcoming the coy, brittle resistance – with the adhesive oleaginous – O call it not fat – but an indefinable sweetness growing up to it – the tender blossoming of fat – fat cropped in the bud – taken in the shoot – in the first innocence – the cream and quintessence of the child-pig's yet pure food – the lean, no lean, but a kind of animal manna – or, rather, fat and lean, (if it must be so) so blended and running into each other, that both together make but one ambrosial result, or common substance.

Behold him, while he is doing – it seemeth rather a refreshing warmth, than a scorching heat, that he is so passive to. How equably he twirleth round the string! – Now he is just done. To see the extreme sensibility of that tender age, he hath wept out his pretty eyes – radiant jellies – shooting stars –

See him in the dish, his second cradle, how meek he lieth! – wouldst thou have had this innocent grow up to the grossness and indocility which too often accompany maturer swinehood? Ten to one he would have proved a glutton, a sloven, an obstinate, disagreeable animal – wallowing in all manner of filthy conversation – from these sins he is happily snatched away –

> Ere sin could blight, or sorrow fade,
> Death came with timely care —

his memory is odoriferous — no clown curseth, while his stomach half rejecteth, the rank bacon — no coalheaver bolteth him in reeking sausages — he hath a fair sepulchre in the grateful stomach of the judicious epicure — and for such a tomb might be content to die.

He is the best of sapors.[5] Pine-apple is great. She is indeed almost too transcendent — a delight, if not sinful, yet so like to sinning, that really a tender-conscienced person would do well to pause — too ravishing for mortal taste, she woundeth and excoriateth the lips that approach her — like lovers' kisses, she biteth — she is a pleasure bordering on pain from the fierceness and insanity of her relish — but she stoppeth at the palate — she meddleth not with the appetite — and the coarsest hunger might barter her consistently for a mutton chop.

Pig — let me speak his praise — is no less provocative of the appetite, than he is satisfactory to the criticalness of the censorious palate. The strong man may batten on him, and the weakling refuseth not his mild juices.

Unlike to mankind's mixed characters, a bundle of virtues and vices, inexplicably intertwisted, and not to be unravelled without hazard, he is — good throughout. No part of him is better or worse than another. He helpeth, as far as his little means extend, all around. He is the least envious of banquets. He is all neighbours' fare.

I am one of those, who freely and ungrudgingly impart a share of the good things of this life which fall to their lot (few as mine are in this kind) to a friend. I protest I take as great an interest in my friend's pleasures, his relishes, and proper satisfactions, as in mine own. 'Presents,' I often say, 'endear Absents.' Hares, pheasants, partridges, snipes, barn-door chickens (those 'tame villatic fowl'), capons, plovers, brawn, barrels of oysters, I dispense as freely as I receive them. I love to taste them, as it were, upon the tongue of my friend. But a stop must be put somewhere. One would not, like Lear, 'give everything.' I make my stand upon pig. Methinks it is an ingratitude to the Giver of all good flavours, to extra-domiciliate, or send out of the house, slightingly (under pretext of friendship, or I know not what), a blessing so particularly adapted, predestined, I may say, to my individual palate — It argues an in-sensibility.

I remember a touch of conscience in this kind at school. My good old aunt, who never parted from me at the end of a holiday without stuffing a sweetmeat, or some nice thing, into my pocket, had dismissed me one evening with a smoking plum-cake, fresh from the oven. In my way to school (it was over London Bridge) a grey-headed old beggar saluted me (I have no doubt at this time of day that he was a counterfeit). I had no pence to console him with, and in the vanity of self-denial, and the very coxcombry of charity, school-boy-like, I made him a present of – the whole cake! I walked on a little, buoyed up, as one is on such occasions, with a sweet soothing of self-satisfaction; but before I had got to the end of the bridge, my better feelings returned, and I burst into tears, thinking how ungrateful I had been to my good aunt, to go and give her good gift away to a stranger, that I had never seen before, and who might be a bad man for aught I knew; and then I thought of the pleasure my aunt would be taking in thinking that I – I myself, and not another – would eat her nice cake – and what should I say to her the next time I saw her – how naughty I was to part with her pretty present – and the odour of that spicy cake came back upon my recollection, and the pleasure and the curiosity I had taken in seeing her make it, and her joy when she sent it to the oven, and how disappointed she would feel that I had never had a bit of it in my mouth at last – and I blamed my impertinent spirit of alms-giving, and out-of-place hypocrisy of good-ness, and above all I wished never to see the face again of that insidious, good-for-nothing, old grey impostor.

Our ancestors were nice in their method of sacrificing these tender victims. We read of pigs whipt to death with something of a shock, as we hear of any other obsolete custom. The age of discipline is gone by, or it would be curious to inquire (in a philosophical light merely) what effect this process might have towards intenerating[6] and dulcifying a substance, naturally so mild and dulcet as the flesh of young pigs. It looks like refining a violet. Yet we should be cautious, while we con-demn the inhumanity, how we censure the wisdom of the practice. It might impart a gusto –

I remember an hypothesis, argued upon by the young students, when I was at St Omer's,[7] and maintained with much learning and pleasantry on both sides, 'Whether, supposing that the flavour of a pig who obtained his death by whipping (*per flagellationem extremam*) superadded a pleasure upon the palate of a man more intense than any possible suffering we can conceive in the animal, is man justified in using that method of putting the animal to death?' I forget the decision.

His sauce should be considered. Decidedly, a few bread crumbs, done up with his liver and brains, and a dash of mild sage. But, banish, dear Mrs Cook, I beseech you, the whole onion tribe. Barbecue your whole hogs to your palate, steep them in shalots, stuff them out with plantations of the rank and guilty garlic; you cannot poison them, or make them stronger than they are – but consider, he is a weakling – a flower.

(*London Magazine*, September 1822)

A BACHELOR'S COMPLAINT OF THE
BEHAVIOUR OF MARRIED PEOPLE

AS a single man, I have spent a good deal of my time in noting down the infirmities of Married People, to console myself for those superior pleasures, which they tell me I have lost by remaining as I am.

I cannot say that the quarrels of men and their wives ever made any great impression upon me, or had much tendency to strengthen me in those anti-social resolutions, which I took up long ago upon more substantial considerations. What oftenest offends me at the houses of married persons where I visit, is an error of quite a different description; – it is that they are too loving.

Not too loving neither: that does not explain my meaning. Besides, why should that offend me? The very act of separating themselves from the rest of the world, to have the fuller enjoyment of each other's society, implies that they prefer one another to all the world.

But what I complain of is, that they carry this preference so undisguisedly, they perk it up in the faces of us single people so shamelessly, you cannot be in their company a moment without being made to feel, by some indirect hint or open avowal, that *you* are not the object of this preference. Now there are some things which give no offence, while implied or taken for granted merely; but expressed, there is much offence in them. If a man were to accost the first homely-featured or plain-dressed young woman of his acquaintance, and tell her bluntly, that she was not handsome or rich enough for him, and he could not marry her, he would deserve to be kicked for his ill manners; yet no less is implied in the fact, that having access and opportunity of putting the question to her, he has never yet thought fit to do it. The young woman understands this as clearly as if it were put into words; but no reasonable young woman would think of making this a ground of a quarrel. Just as little right have a married couple to tell me by speeches and looks that are scarce less plain than speeches, that I am not the happy man, – the lady's choice. It is enough that I know that I am not: I do not want this perpetual reminding.

The display of superior knowledge or riches may be made sufficiently mortifying: but these admit of a palliative. The knowledge which is brought out to insult me, may accidentally improve me; and in the rich man's houses and pictures, – his parks and gardens, I have a temporary usufruct[1] at least. But the display of married happiness has none of these palliatives; it is throughout pure, unrecompensed, unqualified insult.

Marriage by its best title is a monopoly, and not of the least invidious sort. It is the cunning of most possessors of any exclusive privilege to keep their advantage as much out of sight as possible, that their less favoured neighbours, seeing little of the benefit, may the less be disposed to question the right. But these married monopolists thrust the most obnoxious part of their patent into our faces.

Nothing is to me more distasteful than that entire complacency and satisfaction which beam in the countenances of a new-married couple, – in that of the lady particularly; it tells you, that her lot is disposed of in this world; that *you* can have no hopes of her. It is true, I have none; nor wishes either, perhaps; but this is one of those truths which ought, as I said before, to be taken for granted, not expressed.

The excessive airs which those people give themselves, founded on the ignorance of us unmarried people, would be more offensive if they were less irrational. We will allow them to understand the mysteries belonging to their own craft better than we who have not had the happiness to be made free of the company: but their arrogance is not content within these limits. If a single person presume to offer his opinion in their presence, though upon the most indifferent subject, he is immediately silenced as an incompetent person. Nay, a young married lady of my acquaintance who, the best of the jest was, had not changed her condition above a fortnight before, in a question on which I had the misfortune to differ from her, respecting the properest mode of breeding oysters for the London market, had the assurance to ask with a sneer, how such an old Bachelor as I could pretend to know anything about such matters.

But what I have spoken of hitherto is nothing to the airs which these creatures give themselves when they come, as they generally do, to have children. When I consider how little of a rarity children are, – that every street and blind alley swarms with them, – that the poorest people commonly have them in most abundance, – that there are few marriages that are not blest with at least one of these bargains, – how often they turn out ill, and defeat the fond hopes of their parents, taking to vicious courses, which end in poverty, disgrace, the gallows, &c. – I cannot for my life tell what cause for pride there can possibly be in having them. If they were young phœnixes, indeed, that were born but one in a year, there might be a pretext. But when they are so common –

I do not advert to the insolent merit which they assume with their husbands on these occasions. Let them look to that. But why *we*, who are not their natural-born subjects, should be expected to bring our spices, myrrh, and incense, – our tribute and homage of admiration, – I do not see.

'Like as the arrows in the hand of the giant, even so are the young children:' so says the excellent office in our Prayer-book appointed for the churching of women. 'Happy is the man that hath his quiver full of them:' So say I; but then don't let him discharge his quiver upon us that are weaponless; – let them be arrows, but not to gall and stick us. I have generally observed that these arrows are double-headed; they have two forks, to be sure to hit with one or the other. As for instance, where you come into a house which is full of children, if you happen to take no notice of them (you are thinking of something else, perhaps, and turn a deaf ear to their innocent caresses), you are set down as untractable, morose, a hater of children. On the other hand, if you find them more than usually engaging, – if you are taken with their pretty manners, and set about in earnest to romp and play with them, some pretext or other is sure to be found for sending them out of the room: they are too noisy or boisterous, or Mr — does not like children. With one or other of these forks the arrow is sure to hit you.

I could forgive their jealousy, and dispense with toying with their brats, if it gives them any pain; but I think it unreasonable to be called upon to *love* them, where I see no occasion, – to love a whole family, perhaps, eight, nine, or ten, indiscriminately, – to love all the pretty dears, because children are so engaging.

I know there is a proverb, 'Love me, love my dog:' that is not always so very practicable, particularly if the dog be set upon you to tease you or snap at you in sport. But a dog, or a lesser thing, – any inanimate substance, as a keepsake, a watch or a ring, a tree, or the place where we last parted when my friend went away upon a long absence, I can make shift to love, because I love him, and anything that reminds me of him; provided it be in its nature indifferent, and apt to receive whatever hue fancy can give it. But children have a real character and an essential being of themselves: they are amiable or unamiable *per se;* I must love or hate them as I see cause for either in their qualities. A child's nature is too serious a thing to admit of its being regarded as a mere appendage to another being, and to be loved or hated accordingly: they stand with me upon their own stock, as much as men and woman do. O! but you will say, sure it is an attractive age, – there is something in the tender years of infancy that of itself charms us. That is the very reason why I am more nice about them. I know that a sweet child is the sweetest thing in nature, not even excepting the delicate creatures which bear them; but the prettier the kind of a thing is, the more desirable it is that it should be pretty of its kind. One daisy differs not much from another in glory; but a violet should look and smell the daintiest. – I was always rather squeamish in my women and children.

But this is not the worst: one must be admitted into their familiarity at least, before they can complain of inattention. It implies visits, and some kind of intercourse. But if the husband be a man with whom you have lived on a friendly footing before marriage, – if you did not come in on the wife's side, – if you did not sneak into the house in her train, but were an old friend in fast habits of intimacy before their courtship was so much as thought on, – look about you – your tenure is precarious – before a twelve-month shall roll over your head, you shall find your old friend gradually grow cool and altered towards you, and at last seek opportunities of breaking with you. I have scarce a married friend of my acquaintance, upon whose firm faith I can rely, whose friendship did not commence *after the period of his marriage*. With some limitations they can endure that: but that the good man should have dared to enter into a solemn league of friendship in which they were not consulted, though it happened before they knew him, – before they that are now man and wife ever met, – this is intolerable to them. Every long friendship, every old authentic intimacy, must be brought into their office to be new stamped with their currency, as a sovereign Prince calls in the good old money that was coined in some reign before he was born or thought of, to be new marked and minted with the stamp of his authority, before he will let it pass current in the world. You may guess what luck generally befalls such a rusty piece of metal as I am in these *new mintings*.

Innumerable are the ways which they take to insult and worm you out of their husband's confidence. Laughing at all you say with a kind of wonder, as if you were a queer kind of fellow that said good things, *but an oddity*, is one of the ways; – they have a particular kind of stare for the purpose; – till at last the husband, who used to defer to your judgment, and would pass over some excrescences of understanding and manner for the sake of a general vein of observation (not quite vulgar) which he perceived in you, begins to suspect whether you are not altogether a humorist, – a fellow well enough to have consorted with in his bachelor days, but not quite so proper to be introduced to ladies. This may be called the staring way; and is that which has oftenest been put in practice against me.

Then there is the exaggerating way, or the way of irony: that is, where they find you an object of especial regard with their husband, who is not so easily to be shaken from the lasting attachment founded on esteem which he has conceived towards you; by never-qualified exaggerations to cry up all that you say or do, till the good man, who understands well enough that it is all done in compliment to him, grows weary of the debt of gratitude which is due to so much candour, and by relaxing a little on his part, and taking down a peg or two in his enthusiasm, sinks at length to that kindly level of moderate esteem, – that 'decent affection and complacent kindness' towards you, where she herself can join in sympathy with him without much stretch and violence to her sincerity.

Another way (for the ways they have to accomplish so desirable a purpose are infinite) is, with a kind of innocent simplicity, continually to mistake what it was which first made their husband fond of you. If an esteem for something excellent in your moral character was that which riveted the chain she is to break, upon any imaginary discovery of a want of poignancy in your conversation, she will cry, 'I thought, my dear, you described your friend, Mr — , as a great wit.' If, on the other hand, it was for some supposed charm in your conversation that he first grew to like you, and was content for this to overlook some trifling irregularities in your moral deportment, upon the first notice of any of these she as readily exclaims, 'This, my dear, is your good Mr — .' One good lady whom I took the liberty of expostulating with for not showing me quite so much respect as I thought due to her husband's old friend, had the candour to confess to me that she had often heard Mr — speak of me before marriage, and that she had conceived a great desire to be acquainted with me, but that the sight of me had very much disappointed her expectations; for from her husband's representations of me, she had formed a notion that she was to see a fine, tall, officer-like looking man (I use her very words); the very reverse of which proved to be the truth. This was candid; and I had the civility not to ask her in return, how she came to pitch upon a standard of personal accomplishments for her husband's friends which differed so much from his own; for my friend's dimensions as near as possible approximate to mine; he standing five feet five in his shoes, in which I have the advantage of him by about half an inch; and he no more than myself exhibiting any indications of a martial character in his air or countenance.

These are some of the mortifications which I have encountered in the absurd attempt to visit at their houses. To enumerate them all would be a vain endeavour; I shall therefore just glance at the very common impropriety of which married ladies are guilty, – of treating us as if we were their husbands, and *vice versâ*. I mean, when they use us with familiarity, and their husbands with ceremony. *Testacea*, for instance, kept me the other night two or three hours beyond my usual time of supping, while she was fretting because Mr —— did not come home, till the oysters were all spoiled, rather than she would be guilty of the impoliteness of touching one in his absence. This was reversing the point of good manners: for ceremony is an invention to take off the uneasy feeling which we derive from knowing ourselves to be less the object of love and esteem with a fellow-creature than some other person is. It endeavours to make up, by superior attentions in little points, for that invidious preference which it is forced to deny in the greater. Had *Testacea* kept the oysters back for me, and withstood her husband's importunities to go to supper, she would have acted according to the strict rules of propriety. I know no ceremony that ladies are bound to observe to their husbands, beyond the point of a modest behaviour and decorum: therefore I must protest against the vicarious gluttony of *Cerasia*, who at her own table sent away a dish of Morellas, which I was applying to with great good will, to her husband at the other end of the table, and recommended a plate of less extraordinary gooseberries to my unwedded palate in their stead. Neither can I excuse the wanton affront of –

But I am weary of stringing up all my married acquaintance by Roman denominations. Let them amend and change their manners, or I promise to record the full-length English of their names, to the terror of all such desperate offenders in future.

(*The Reflector*, No. IV, 1811/12 [*London Magazine*, September 1822])

A CHARACTER OF THE LATE ELIA[1]

BY A FRIEND

THIS gentleman, who for some months past had been in a declining way, hath at length paid his final tribute to nature. He just lived long enough (it was what he wished) to see his papers collected into a volume. The pages of the London Magazine will henceforth know him no more.

Exactly at twelve last night his queer spirit departed; and the bells of Saint Bride's rang him out with the old year. The mournful vibrations were caught in the dining room of his friends T. and H.;[2] and the company, assembled there to welcome in another first of January, checked their carousals in mid-mirth, and were silent. Janus wept. The gentle P—r, in a whisper, signified his intention of devoting an elegy; and Allan C—,[3] notably forgetful of his countryman's wrongs, vowed a Memoir to his *manes*[4] full and friendly as a Tale of Lyddalcross.[5]

To say truth, it is time he were gone. The humour of the thing, if there was ever much in it, was pretty well exhausted; and a two years' and half existence has been a tolerable duration for a phantom.

I am now at liberty to confess, that much which I have heard objected to my late friend's writings was well-founded. Crude they are, I grant you – a sort of unlicked, incondite things – villainously pranked in an affected array of antique modes and phrases. They had not been *his*, if they had been other than such; and better it is, that a writer should be natural in a self-pleasing quaintness, than to affect a naturalness (so-called) that should be strange to him. Egotistical they have been pronounced by some who did not know, that what he tells us, as of himself, was often true only (historically) of another; as in his Fourth Essay, (to save many instances) – where under the *first person* (his favourite figure) he shadows forth the forlorn estate of a country-boy placed at a London school, far from his friends and connections – in direct opposition to his own early history. – If it be egotism to imply and twine with his own identity the griefs and affections of another – making himself many, or reducing many unto himself – then is the skilful novelist, who all along brings in his hero, or heroine, speaking of themselves, the greatest egotist of all; who yet has never, therefore, been accused of that narrowness. And how shall the intenser dramatist escape being faulty, who doubtless, under cover of passion uttered by another, oftentimes gives blameless vent to his most inward feelings, and expresses his own story modestly?

My late friend was in many respects a singular character. Those who did not like him, hated him; and some, who once liked him, afterwards became his bitterest haters. The truth is, he gave himself too little concern about what he uttered, and in whose presence. He observed neither time nor place, and would even out with what came uppermost. With the severe religionist, he would pass for a free-thinker; while the other faction set him down for a bigot, or persuaded themselves that he belied his sentiments. Few understood him; and I am not certain that at all times he quite understood himself. He too much affected that dangerous figure – irony. He sowed doubtful speeches, and reaped plain, unequivocal hatred. – He would interrupt the gravest discussion with some light jest; and yet, perhaps, not quite irrelevant in ears that could understand it. Your long and much talkers hated him. The informal habit of his mind, joined to an inveterate impediment of speech, forbade him to be an orator; and he seemed determined that no one else should play that part when he was present. He was *petit* and ordinary in his person and appearance. I have seen him sometimes in what is called good company, but where he has been a stranger, sit silent, and be suspected for an odd fellow; till some unlucky occasion provoking it, he would stutter out some senseless pun (not altogether senseless perhaps, if rightly taken), which has stamped his character for the evening. It was hit or miss with him; but nine times out of ten, he contrived by this device to send away a whole company his enemies. His conceptions rose kindlier than his utterance, and his happiest *impromptus* had the appearance of effort. He has been accused of trying to be witty, when in truth he was but struggling to give his poor thoughts articulation. He chose his companions for some individuality of character which they manifested. – Hence, not many persons of science, and few professed *literati*, were of his councils. They were, for the most part, persons of an uncertain fortune; and, as to such people commonly nothing is more obnoxious than a gentleman of settled (though moderate) income, he passed with most of them for a great miser. To my knowledge this was a mistake. His *intimados*, to confess a truth, were in the world's eye a ragged regiment. He found them floating on the surface of society; and the colour, or something else, in the weed pleased him. The burrs stuck to him – but they were good and loving burrs for all that. He never greatly cared for the society of what are called good people. If any of these were scandalized (and offences were sure to arise), he could not help it. When he had been remonstrated with for not making more concessions to the feelings of good people, he would retort by asking, What one point did these good people ever concede to him? He was temperate in his meals and diversions, but always kept a little on this side of abstemiousness. Only in the use of the Indian weed he might be thought a little excessive. He took it, he would say, as a solvent of speech. Marry – as the friendly vapour ascended, how his prattle would curl up sometimes with it! the ligaments, which tongue-tied him, were loosened, and the stammerer proceeded a statist! [6]

I do not know whether I ought to bemoan or rejoice that my old friend is departed. His jests were beginning to grow obsolete, and his stories to be found out. He felt the approaches of age; and, while he pretended to cling to life, you saw how slender were the ties left to bind him. Discoursing with him latterly on this subject, he expressed himself with a pettishness, which I thought unworthy of him. In our walks about his suburban retreat (as he called it) at Shacklewell, some children belonging to a school of industry had met us, and bowed and courtesied, as he thought, in an especial manner to *him*. 'They take me for a visiting governor,' he muttered earnestly. He had a horror, which he carried to a foible, of looking like any thing important and parochial. He thought that he approached nearer to that stamp daily. He had a general aversion from being treated like a grave or respectable character, and kept a wary eye upon the advances of age that should so entitle him. He herded always, while it was possible, with people younger than himself. He did not conform to the march of time, but was dragged along in the procession. His manners lagged behind his years. He was too much of the boy-man. The *toga virilis* [7] never sat gracefully on his shoulders. The impressions of infancy had burnt into him, and he resented the impertinence of manhood. These were weaknesses; but such as they were, they are a key to explicate some of his writings.

He left little property behind him. Of course, the little that is left (chiefly in India bonds) devolves upon his cousin Bridget. A few critical dissertations were found in his *escritoire*, which have been handed over to the Editor of this Magazine, in which it is to be hoped they will shortly appear, retaining his accustomed signature.

He has himself not obscurely hinted that his employment lay in a public office. The gentlemen in the Export department of the East India

House will forgive me, if I acknowledge the readiness with which they assisted me in the retrieval of his few manuscripts. They pointed out in a most obliging manner the desk, at which he had been planted for forty years; showed me ponderous tomes of figures, in his own remarkably neat hand, which, more properly than his few printed tracts, might be called his 'Works.' They seemed affectionate to his memory, and universally commended his expertness in book-keeping. It seems he was the inventor of some ledger, which should combine the precision and certainty of the Italian double entry (I think they called it) with the brevity and facility of some newer German system – but I am not able to appreciate the worth of the discovery. I have often heard him express a warm regard for his associates in office, and how fortunate he considered himself in having his lot thrown in amongst them. There is more sense, more discourse, more shrewdness, and even talent, among these clerks (he would say) than in twice the number of authors by profession that I have conversed with. He would brighten up sometimes upon the 'old days of the India House,' when he consorted with Woodroffe, and Wissett, and Peter Corbet (a descendant and worthy representative, bating the point of sanctity, of old facetious Bishop Corbet), and Hoole who translated Tasso, and Bartlemy Brown whose father (God assoil him therefore) modernized Walton – and sly warm-hearted old Jack Cole (King Cole they called him in those days), and Campe, and Fombelle – and a world of choice spirits, more than I can remember to name, who associated in those days with Jack Burrell (the *bon vivant* of the South Sea House), and little Eyton (said to be a *facsimile* of Pope – he was a miniature of a gentleman) that was cashier under him, and Dan Voight of the Custom House that left the famous library.

Well, Elia is gone – for aught I know, to be re-united with them – and these poor traces of his pen are all we have to show for it. How little survives of the wordiest authors! Of all they said or did in their lifetime, a few glittering words only! His Essays found some favourers, as they appeared separately; they shuffled their way in the crowd well enough singly; how they will *read*, now they are brought together, is a question for the publishers, who have thus ventured to draw out into one piece his 'weaved-up follies.'

PHIL-ELIA.

THE OLD MARGATE HOY

I AM fond of passing my vacation (I believe I have said so before) at one or other of the Universities. Next to these my choice would fix me at some woody spot, such as the neighbourhood of Henley affords in abundance, on the banks of my beloved Thames. But somehow or other my cousin contrives to wheedle me once in three or four seasons to a watering-place. Old attachments cling to her in spite of experience. We have been dull at Worthing one summer, duller at Brighton another, dullest at Eastbourn, a third, and are at this moment doing dreary penance at – Hastings! – and all because we were happy many years ago for a brief week at Margate. That was our first sea-side experiment, and many circumstances combined to make it the most agreeable holyday of my life. We had neither of us seen the sea, and we had never been from home so long together in company.

Can I forget thee, thou old Margate Hoy,[1] with thy weather-beaten, sun-burnt captain, and his rough accommodations – ill-exchanged for the foppery and fresh-water niceness of the modern steam packet? To the winds and waves thou committedst thy goodly freightage, and didst ask no aid of magic fumes, and spells, and boiling cauldrons. With the gales of heaven thou wentest swimmingly; or, when it was their pleasure, stoodest still with sailor-like patience. Thy course was natural, not forced, as in a hot-bed; nor didst thou go poisoning the breath of ocean with sulphureous smoke – a great sea-chimæra, chimneying and furnacing the deep; or liker to that fire-god parching up Scamander.[2]

Can I forget thy honest, yet slender crew, with their coy reluctant responses (yet to the suppression of anything like contempt) to the raw questions, which we of the great city would be ever and anon putting to them as to the uses of this or that strange naval implement? 'Specially can I forget thee, thou happy medium, thou shade of refuge between us and them, conciliating interpreter of their skill to our simplicity, comfortable ambassador between sea and land! – whose sailor-trowsers did not more convincingly assure thee to be an adopted denizen of the former, than thy white cap and whiter apron over them, with thy neat-fingered practice in thy culinary vocation, bespoke thee to have been of inland nurture heretofore – a master cook of Eastcheap? How busily didst thou ply thy multifarious occupation, cook, mariner, attendant, chamberlain: here, there, like another Ariel, flaming at once about all parts of the deck, yet with kindlier ministration – not to assist the tempest, but, as if touched with a kindred sense of our infirmities, to soothe the qualms which that untried motion might haply raise in our crude land-fancies. And when the o'er-washing billows drove us below deck (for it was far gone in October, and we had stiff and blowing weather) how did thy officious ministerings, still catering for our comfort, with cards, and cordials, and thy more cordial conversation, alleviate the closeness and the confinement of thy else (truth to say) not very savoury, nor very inviting, little cabin!

With these additaments[3] to boot, we had on board a fellow-passenger, whose discourse in verity might have beguiled a longer voyage than we meditated, and have made mirth and wonder abound as far as the Azores. He was a dark, Spanish-complexioned young man, remarkably handsome, with an officer-like assurance, and an insuppressible volubility of assertion. He was, in fact, the greatest liar I had met with then, or since. He was none of your hesitating, half story-tellers (a most painful description of mortals) who go on sounding your belief, and only giving you as much as they see you can swallow at a time – the nibbling pickpockets of your patience – but one who committed downright, day-light depredations upon his neighbour's faith. He did not stand shivering upon the brink, but was a hearty, thorough-paced liar, and plunged at once into the depths of your credulity. I partly believe, he made pretty sure of his company. Not many rich, not many wise, or learned, composed at that time the common stowage of a Margate packet. We were, I am afraid, a set of as unseasoned Londoners (let our enemies give it a worse name) as Aldermanbury, or Watling Street, at that time of day could have supplied. There might be an exception or two among us, but I scorn to make any invidious distinctions among such a jolly, companionable ship's company, as those were whom I sailed with. Something too must be conceded to the *Genius Loci*.[4] Had the confident fellow told us half the legends on land, which he favoured us with on the other element, I flatter myself the good sense of most of us would have revolted. But we were in a new world, with everything unfamiliar about us, and the time and place disposed us to the reception of any prodigious marvel whatsoever. Time has obliterated from my memory much of his wild fablings; and the rest would appear but dull, as written, and to be read on shore. He had been Aide-de-camp (among other rare accidents and fortunes) to a Persian prince, and at one blow had stricken off the head of the King of Carimania on horseback. He, of course, married the Prince's daughter. I forgot what unlucky turn in the politics of that court, combining with the loss of his consort, was the reason of his quitting Persia; but with the rapidity of a magician, he transported himself, along with his hearers, back to England, where we still found him in the confidence of great ladies. There was some story of a Princess – Elizabeth, if I remember – having intrusted to his care an extraordinary casket of jewels, upon some extraordinary occasion – but, as I am not certain of the name or circumstance at this distance of time, I must leave it to the Royal daughters of England to settle the honour among themselves in private. I cannot call to mind half his pleasant wonders; but I perfectly remember, that in the course of his travels he had seen a phœnix; and he obligingly undeceived us of the vulgar error, that there is but one of that species at a time, assuring us that they were not uncommon in some parts of Upper Egypt. Hitherto he had found the most implicit listeners. His dreaming fancies had transported us beyond the 'ignorant present.' But when (still hardying more and more in his triumphs over our simplicity,) he went on to affirm that he had actually sailed through the legs of the Colossus at Rhodes, it really became necessary to make a stand. And here I must do justice to the good sense and intrepidity of one of our party, a youth, that had hitherto been one of his most deferential auditors, who, from his recent reading, made bold to assure the gentleman, that there must be some mistake, as 'the Colossus in question had been destroyed long since'; to whose opinion, delivered with all modesty, our hero was obliging enough to concede thus much, 'the figure was indeed a little damaged.' This was the only opposition he met with, and it did not at all seem to stagger him, for he proceeded with his fables, which the same youth appeared to swallow with still more complacency than ever, – confirmed, as it were, by the extreme candour of that concession. With these prodigies he wheedled us on till we came in sight of the Reculvers,[5] which one of our own company (having been the voyage before) immediately recognising, and pointing out to us, was considered by us as no ordinary seaman.

All this time sat upon the edge of the deck quite a different character. It was a lad, apparently very poor, very infirm, and very patient. His eye was ever on the sea, with a smile; and, if he caught now and then some snatches of these wild legends, it was by accident, and they seemed not to concern him. The waves to him whispered more pleasant stories. He was as one, being with us, but not of us. He heard the bell of dinner ring without stirring; and when some of us pulled out our private stores – our cold meat and our salads – he produced none, and seemed to want none. Only a solitary biscuit he had laid in; provision for the one or two days and nights, to which these vessels then were oftentimes obliged to prolong their voyage. Upon a nearer acquaintance with him, which he seemed neither to court nor decline, we learned that he was going to Margate, with the hope of being admitted into the Infirmary there for sea-bathing. His disease was a scrofula, which appeared to have eaten all over him. He expressed great hopes of a cure; and when we asked him, whether he had any friends where he was going, he replied, 'he *had* no friends.'

These pleasant, and some mournful passages, with the first sight of the sea, co-operating with youth, and a sense of holydays, and out-of-door adventure, to me that had been pent up in populous cities for many months before, – have left upon my mind the fragrance as of summer days gone by, bequeathing nothing but their remembrance for cold and wintry hours to chew upon.

Will it be thought a digression (it may spare some unwelcome comparisons), if I endeavour to account for the *dissatisfaction* which I have heard so many persons confess to have felt (as I did myself feel in part on this occasion), *at the sight of the sea for the first time?* I think the reason usually given – referring to the incapacity of actual objects for satisfying our preconceptions of them – scarcely goes deep enough into the question. Let the same person see a lion, an elephant, a mountain, for the first time in his life, and he shall perhaps feel himself a little mortified. The things do not fill up that space, which the idea of them seemed to take up in his mind. But they have still a correspondency to his first notion, and in time grow up to it, so as to produce a very similar impression: enlarging themselves (if I may say so) upon familiarity. But the sea remains a disappointment. – Is it not, that in *the latter* we had expected to behold (absurdly, I grant, but, I am afraid, by the law of imagination unavoidably) not a definite object, as those wild beasts, or that mountain compassable by the eye, but *all the sea at once*, THE COMMENSURATE ANTAGONIST OF THE EARTH? I do not say we tell ourselves so much, but the craving of the mind is to be satisfied with nothing else. I will suppose the case of a young person of fifteen (as I then was) knowing nothing of the sea, but from description. He comes to it for the first time – all that he has been reading of it all his life, and *that* the most enthusiastic part of life, – all he has gathered from narratives of wandering seamen; what he has gained from true voyages, and what he cherishes as credulously from romance and poetry; crowding their images, and exacting strange tributes from expectation. – He thinks of the great deep, and of those who go down unto it; of its thousand isles, and of the vast continents it washes; of its receiving the mighty Plate, or Orellana,[6] into its bosom, without disturbance, or sense of augmentation; of Biscay swells, and the mariner

> For many a day, and many a dreadful night,
> Incessant labouring round the stormy Cape;

of fatal rocks, and the 'still-vexed Bermoothes'; of great whirlpools, and the water-spout; of sunken ships, and sumless treasures swallowed up in the unrestoring depths: of fishes and quaint monsters, to which all that is terrible on earth –

> Be but as buggs to frighten babes withal,
> Compared with the creatures in the sea's entral;

of naked savages, and Juan Fernandez;[7] of pearls, and shells; of coral beds, and of enchanted isles; of mermaids' grots –

I do not assert that in sober earnest he expects to be shown all these wonders at once, but he is under the tyranny of a mighty faculty, which haunts him with confused hints and shadows of all these; and when the actual object opens first upon him, seen (in tame weather too most likely) from our unromantic coasts – a speck, a slip of sea-water, as it shows to him – what can it prove but a very unsatisfying and even diminutive entertainment? Or if he has come to it from the mouth of a river, was it much more than the river widening? and, even out of sight of land, what had he but a flat watery horizon about him, nothing comparable to the vast o'er-curtaining sky, his familiar object, seen daily without dread or amazement? – Who, in similar circumstances, has not been tempted to exclaim with Charoba, in the poem of Gebir,

> Is this the mighty ocean? is this *all?* [8]

I love town, or country; but this detestable Cinque Port is neither. I hate these scrubbed shoots, thrusting out their starved foliage from between the horrid fissures of dusty innutritious rocks; which the amateur calls 'verdure to the edge of the sea.' I require woods, and they show me stunted coppices. I cry out for the water-brooks, and pant for fresh streams, and inland murmurs. I cannot stand all day on the naked beach, watching the capricious hues of the sea, shifting like the colours of a dying mullet. I am tired of looking out at the windows of this island-prison. I would fain retire into the interior of my cage. While I gaze upon the sea, I want to be on it, over it, across it. It binds me in with chains, as of iron. My thoughts are abroad. I should not so feel in Staffordshire. There is no home for me here. There is no sense of home at Hastings. It is a place of fugitive resort, an heterogeneous assemblage of sea-mews and stock-brokers, Amphitrites[9] of the town, and misses that coquet with the Ocean. If it were what it was in its primitive shape, and what it ought to have remained, a fair honest fishing-town, and no more, it were something – with a few straggling fishermen's huts scattered about, artless as its cliffs, and with their materials filched from them, it were something. I could abide to dwell with Meschek;[10] to assort with fisher-swains, and smugglers. There are, or I dream there are, many of this latter occupation here. Their faces become the place. I like a smuggler. He is the only honest thief. He robs nothing but the revenue, – an abstraction I never greatly cared about. I could go out with them in their mackarel boats, or about their less ostensible business, with some satisfaction. I can even tolerate those poor victims to monotony, who from day to day pace along the beach, in endless progress and recurrence, to watch their illicit countrymen – townsfolk or brethren perchance – whistling to the sheathing and unsheathing of their cutlasses (their only solace), who under the mild name of preventive service, keep up a legitimated civil warfare in the deplorable absence of a foreign one, to show their detestation of run hollands and zeal for old England. But it is the visitants from town, that come here to *say* that they have been here, with no more relish of the sea than a pond perch, or a dace might be supposed to have, that are my aversion. I feel like a foolish dace in these regions, and have as little toleration for myself here, as for them. What can they want here? if they had a true relish of the ocean, why have they brought all this land luggage with them? or why pitch their civilised tents in the desert? What mean these scanty book-rooms – marine libraries as they entitle them – if the sea were, as they would have us believe, a book 'to read strange matter in'? what are their foolish concert-rooms, if they come, as they would fain be thought to do, to listen to the music of the waves? All is false and hollow pretension. They come, because it is the fashion, and to spoil the nature of the place. They are mostly, as I have said, stock-brokers; but I have watched the better sort of them – now and then, an honest citizen (of the old stamp), in the simplicity of his heart, shall bring down his wife and daughters, to taste the sea breezes. I always know the date of their arrival. It is easy to see it in their countenance. A day or two they go wandering on the shingles, picking up cockle-shells, and thinking them great things; but, in a poor week, imagination slackens: they begin to discover that cockles produce no pearls, and then – O then! – if I could interpret for the pretty creatures, (I know they have not the courage to confess it themselves) how gladly would they exchange their sea-side rambles for a Sunday walk on the green-sward of their accustomed Twickenham meadows!

I would ask of one of these sea-charmed emigrants, who think they truly love the sea, with its wild usages, what would their feelings be, if some of the unsophisticated aborigines of this place, encouraged by their courteous questionings here, should venture, on the faith of such assured sympathy between them to return the visit, and come up to see – London. I must imagine them with their fishing-tackle on their back, as we carry our town necessaries. What a sensation would it cause in Lothbury! What vehement laughter would it not excite among

The daughters of Cheapside and wives of Lombard Street.

I am sure that no town-bred, or inland-born subjects, can feel their true and natural nourishment at these sea-places. Nature, where she does not mean us for mariners and vagabonds, bids us stay at home. The salt foam seems to nourish a spleen. I am not half so good-natured as by the milder waters of my natural river. I would exchange these sea-gulls for swans, and scud a swallow for ever about the banks of Thamesis.

(*London Magazine*, July 1823)

THE SUPERANNUATED MAN

Sera tamen respexit
Libertas.   VIRGIL.[1]

A Clerk I was in London gay.
O'KEEFE.[2]

IF peradventure, Reader, it has been thy lot to waste the golden years of
thy life – thy shining youth – in the irksome confinement of an office;
to have thy prison days prolonged through middle age down to de-
crepitude and silver hairs, without hope of release or respite; to have
lived to forget that there are such things as holydays, or to remember
them but as the prerogatives of childhood; then, and then only, will you
be able to appreciate my deliverance.

It is now six and thirty years since I took my seat at the desk in
Mincing Lane. Melancholy was the transition at fourteen from the
abundant playtime, and the frequently intervening vacations of school
days, to the eight, nine, and sometimes ten hours' a-day attendance at a
counting-house. But time partially reconciles us to anything. I gradually
became content – doggedly content, as wild animals in cages.

It is true I had my Sundays to myself; but Sundays, admirable as the
institution of them is for purposes of worship, are for that very reason
the very worst adapted for days of unbending and recreation. In particular, there is a gloom for me attendant upon a city Sunday, a weight
in the air. I miss the cheerful cries of London, the music, and the ballad-
singers – the buzz and stirring murmur of the streets. Those eternal bells
depress me. The closed shops repel me. Prints, pictures, all the glittering
and endless succession of knacks and gewgaws, and ostentatiously displayed wares of tradesmen, which make a week-day saunter through
the less busy parts of the metropolis so delightful – are shut out. No
book-stalls deliciously to idle over – No busy faces to recreate the idle
man who contemplates them ever passing by – the very face of
business a charm by contrast to his temporary relaxation from it.
Nothing to be seen but unhappy countenances – or half-happy at best –
of emancipated 'prentices and little tradesfolks, with here and there a

servant maid that has got leave to go out, who, slaving all the week, with the habit has lost almost the capacity of enjoying a free hour; and livelily expressing the hollowness of a day's pleasuring. The very strollers in the fields on that day looked anything but comfortable.

But besides Sundays I had a day at Easter, and a day at Christmas, with a full week in the summer to go and air myself in my native fields of Hertfordshire. This last was a great indulgence; and the prospect of its recurrence, I believe, alone kept me up through the year, and made my durance tolerable. But when the week came round, did the glittering phantom of the distance keep touch with me? or rather was it not a series of seven uneasy days, spent in restless pursuit of pleasure, and a wearisome anxiety to find out how to make the most of them? Where was the quiet, where the promised rest? Before I had a taste of it, it was vanished. I was at the desk again, counting upon the fifty-one tedious weeks that must intervene before such another snatch would come. Still the prospect of its coming threw something of an illumination upon the darker side of my captivity. Without it, as I have said, I could scarcely have sustained my thraldom.

Independently of the rigours of attendance, I have ever been haunted with a sense (perhaps a mere caprice) of incapacity for business. This, during my latter years, had increased to such a degree, that it was visible in all the lines of my countenance. My health and my good spirits flagged. I had perpetually a dread of some crisis, to which I should be found unequal. Besides my daylight servitude, I served over again all night in my sleep, and would awake with terrors of imaginary false entries, errors in my accounts, and the like. I was fifty years of age, and no prospect of emancipation presented itself. I had grown to my desk, as it were; and the wood had entered into my soul.

My fellows in the office would sometimes rally me upon the trouble legible in my countenance; but I did not know that it had raised the suspicions of any of my employers, when on the 5th of last month, a day ever to be remembered by me, L—, the junior partner in the firm, calling me on one side, directly taxed me with my bad looks, and frankly inquired the cause of them. So taxed, I honestly made confession of my infirmity, and added that I was afraid I should eventually be obliged to resign his service. He spoke some words of course to hearten me, and there the matter rested. A whole week I remained labouring under the impression that I had acted imprudently in my disclosure; that I had foolishly given a handle against myself, and had been anticipating my own dismissal. A week passed in this manner, the most anxious one,

I verily believe, in my whole life, when on the evening of the 12th of April, just as I was about quitting my desk to go home (it might be about eight o'clock) I received an awful summons to attend the presence of the whole assembled firm in the formidable back parlour. I thought now my time is surely come, I have done for myself, I am going to be told that they have no longer occasion for me. L—, I could see, smiled at the terror I was in, which was a little relief to me, – when to my utter astonishment B—, the eldest partner, began a formal harangue to me on the length of my services, my very meritorious conduct during the whole of the time (the deuce, thought I, how did he find out that? I protest I never had the confidence to think as much). He went on to descant on the expediency of retiring at a certain time of life (how my heart panted!), and asking me a few questions as to the amount of my own property, of which I have a little, ended with a proposal, to which his three partners nodded a grave assent, that I should accept from the house, which I had served so well, a pension for life to the amount of two-thirds of my accustomed salary – a magnificent offer! I do not know what I answered between surprise and gratitude, but it was understood that I accepted their proposal, and I was told that I was free from that hour to leave their service. I stammered out a bow, and at just ten minutes after eight I went home – for ever. This noble benefit[3] – gratitude forbids me to conceal their names – I owe to the kindness of the most munificent firm in the world – the house of Boldero, Merryweather, Bosanquet, and Lacy.

Esto perpetua! [4]

For the first day or two I felt stunned, overwhelmed. I could only apprehend my felicity; I was too confused to taste it sincerely. I wandered about, thinking I was happy, and knowing that I was not. I was in the condition of a prisoner in the Old Bastile, suddenly let loose after a forty years' confinement. I could scarce trust myself with myself. It was like passing out of Time into Eternity – for it is a sort of Eternity for a man to have his Time all to himself. It seemed to me that I had more time on my hands than I could ever manage. From a poor man, poor in Time, I was suddenly lifted up into a vast revenue; I could see no end of my possessions; I wanted some steward, or judicious bailiff, to manage my estates in Time for me. And here let me caution persons grown old in active business, not lightly, nor without weighing their own resources, to forego their customary employment all at once, for there may be danger in it. I feel it by myself, but I know that my resources are sufficient; and now that those first giddy raptures have subsided, I have a quiet home-feeling of the blessedness of my condition. I am in no hurry. Having all holidays, I am as though I had none. If Time hung heavy upon me, I could walk it away; but I do *not* walk all day long, as I used to do in those old transient holidays, thirty miles a day, to make the most of them. If Time were troublesome, I could read it away, but I do *not* read in that violent measure, with which, having no Time my own but candlelight Time, I used to weary out my head and eye-sight in by-gone winters. I walk, read, or scribble (as now) just when the fit seizes me. I no longer hunt after pleasure; I let it come to me. I am like the man

> – that's born, and has his years come to him,
>   In some green desert.

'Years,' you will say; 'what is this superannuated simpleton calculating upon? He has already told us he is past fifty.'

I have indeed lived nominally fifty years, but deduct out of them the hours which I have lived to other people, and not to myself, and you will find me still a young fellow. For *that* is the only true Time, which a man can properly call his own, that which he had all to himself; the rest, though in some sense he may be said to live it, is other people's time, not his. The remnant of my poor days, long or short, is at least multiplied for me threefold. My ten next years, if I stretch so far, will be as long as any preceding thirty. 'Tis a fair rule-of-three sum.

Among the strange fantasies which beset me at the commencement of my freedom, and of which all traces are not yet gone, one was, that a vast tract of time had intervened since I quitted the Counting House. I could not conceive of it as an affair of yesterday. The partners, and the clerks with whom I had for so many years, and for so many hours in each day of the year, been so closely associated – being suddenly removed from them – they seemed as dead to me. There is a fine passage, which may serve to illustrate this fancy, in a Tragedy, by Sir Robert Howard;[5] speaking of a friend's death: –

> – 'Twas but just now he went away;
> I have not since had time to shed a tear;
> And yet the distance does the same appear
> As if he had been a thousand years from me.
> Time takes no measure in Eternity.

To dissipate this awkward feeling, I have been fain to go among them once or twice since; to visit my old desk-fellows – my co-brethren of the quill – that I had left below in the state militant. Not all the kindness with which they received me could quite restore to me that pleasant familiarity, which I had heretofore enjoyed among them. We cracked some of our old jokes, but methought they went off but faintly. My old desk; the peg where I hung my hat, were appropriated to another. I knew it must be, but I could not take it kindly. D——l take me if I did not feel some remorse – beast, if I had not, – at quitting my old compeers, the faithful partners of my toils for six and thirty years, that smoothed for me with their jokes and conundrums the ruggedness of my professional road. Had it been so rugged then after all? or was I a coward simply? Well, it is too late to repent; and I also know, that these suggestions are a common fallacy of the mind on such occasions. But my heart smote me. I had violently broken the bands betwixt us. It was at least not courteous. I shall be some time before I get quite reconciled to the separation. Farewell, old cronies, yet not for long, for again and again I will come among ye, if I shall have your leave. Farewell, Ch—, dry, sarcastic, and friendly! Do—, mild, slow to move, and gentlemanly! Pl—, officious to do, and to volunteer, good services! – and thou, thou dreary pile, fit mansion for a Gresham or a Whittington[6] of old, stately House of Merchants; with thy labyrinthine passages, and light-excluding, pent-up offices, where candles for one half the year supplied the place of the sun's light; unhealthy contributor to my weal, stern fosterer of my living, farewell! In thee remain, and not in the obscure collection of some wandering bookseller, my 'works!' There let them rest, as I do from my labours, piled on thy massy shelves, more MSS. in folio than ever Aquinas left, and full as useful! My mantle I bequeath among ye.

A fortnight has passed since the date of my first communication. At that period I was approaching to tranquillity, but had not reached it. I boasted of a calm indeed, but it was comparative only. Something of the first flutter was left; an unsettling sense of novelty; the dazzle to weak eyes of unaccustomed light. I missed my old chains, forsooth, as if they had been some necessary part of my apparel. I was a poor Carthusian, from strict cellular discipline suddenly by some revolution returned upon the world. I am now as if I had never been other than my own master. It is natural to me to go where I please, to do what I please. I find myself at eleven o'clock in the day in Bond Street, and it seems to me that I have been sauntering there at that very hour for years past. I digress into Soho, to explore a book-stall. Methinks I have been thirty years a collector. There is nothing strange nor new in it. I find myself before a fine picture in the morning. Was it ever otherwise? What is become of Fish Street Hill? Where is Fenchurch Street? Stones of old Mincing Lane which I have worn with my daily pilgrimage for six and thirty years, to the footsteps of what toil-worn clerk are your everlasting flints now vocal? I indent the gayer flags of Pall Mall. It is 'Change time, and I am strangely among the Elgin marbles. It was no hyperbole when I ventured to compare the change in my condition to a passing into another world. Time stands still in a manner to me. I have lost all distinction of season. I do not know the day of the week, or of the month. Each day used to be individually felt by me in its reference to the foreign post days; in its distance from, or propinquity to the next Sunday. I had my Wednesday feelings, my Saturday nights' sensations. The genius of each day was upon me distinctly during the whole of it, affecting my appetite, spirits, &c. The phantom of the next day, with the dreary five to follow, sate as a load upon my poor Sabbath recreations. What charm has washed the Ethiop white?[7] —What is gone of Black Monday?[8] All days are the same. Sunday itself — that unfortunate failure of a holiday as it too often proved, what with my sense of its fugitiveness, and over-care to get the greatest quantity of pleasure out of it — is melted down into a week day. I can spare to go to church now, without grudging the huge cantle[9] which it used to seem to cut out of the holiday. I have Time for everything. I can visit a sick friend. I can interrupt the man of much occupation when he is busiest. I can insult over him with an invitation to take a day's pleasure with me to Windsor this fine May-morning. It is Lucretian pleasure[10] to behold the poor drudges, whom I have left behind in the world, carking and caring; like horses in a mill, drudging on in the same eternal round — and what is it all for? A man can never have too much Time to himself, nor too little to do. Had I a little son, I would christen him NOTHING-TO-DO; he should do nothing. Man, I verily believe, is out of his element as long as he is operative. I am altogether for the life contemplative. Will no kindly earthquake come and swallow up those accursed cotton mills? Take me that lumber of a desk there, and bowl it down

> As low as to the fiends.

I am no longer ******, clerk to the firm of, &c. I am Retired Leisure. I am to be met with in trim gardens. I am already come to be known by my vacant face and careless gesture, perambulating at no fixed pace nor with any settled purpose. I walk about; not to and from.

They tell me, a certain *cum dignitate* [11] air, that has been buried so long with my other good parts, has begun to shoot forth in my person. I grow into gentility perceptibly. When I take up a newspaper it is to read the state of the opera. *Opus operatum est.* [12] I have done all that I came into this world to do. I have worked task-work, and have the rest of the day to myself.

(*London Magazine*, May 1825)

THE CONVALESCENT[1]

A PRETTY severe fit of indisposition which, under the name of a nervous fever, has made a prisoner of me for some weeks past, and is but slowly leaving me, has reduced me to an incapacity of reflecting upon any topic foreign to itself. Expect no healthy conclusions from me this month, reader; I can offer you only sick men's dreams.

And truly the whole state of sickness is such; for what else is it but a magnificent dream for a man to lie a-bed, and draw daylight curtains about him; and, shutting out the sun, to induce a total oblivion of all the works which are going on under it? To become insensible to all the operations of life, except the beatings of one feeble pulse?

If there be a regal solitude, it is a sick bed. How the patient lords it there; what caprices he acts without control! how king-like he sways his pillow – tumbling, and tossing, and shifting, and lowering, and thumping, and flatting, and moulding it, to the ever varying requisitions of his throbbing temples.

He changes *sides* oftener than a politician. Now he lies full length, then half-length, obliquely, transversely, head and feet quite across the bed; and none accuses him of tergiversation.[2] Within the four curtains he is absolute. They are his Mare Clausum.[3]

How sickness enlarges the dimensions of a man's self to himself! he is his own exclusive object. Supreme selfishness is inculcated upon him as his only duty. 'Tis the Two Tables of the Law to him. He has nothing to think of but how to get well. What passes out of doors, or within them, so he hear not the jarring of them, affects him not.

A little while ago he was greatly concerned in the event of a law-suit, which was to be the making or the marring of his dearest friend. He was to be seen trudging about upon this man's errand to fifty quarters of the town at once, jogging this witness, refreshing that solicitor. The cause was to come on yesterday. He is absolutely as indifferent to the decision, as if it were a question to be tried at Pekin. Peradventure from some whispering, going on about the house, not intended for his hearing, he picks up enough to make him understand, that things went cross-grained in the Court yesterday, and his friend is ruined. But the word 'friend,' and the word 'ruin,' disturb him no more than so much jargon. He is not to think of any thing but how to get better.

What a world of foreign cares are merged in that absorbing consideration!

He has put on his strong armour of sickness, he is wrapped in the callous hide of suffering, he keeps his sympathy, like some curious vintage, under trusty lock and key, for his own use only.

He lies pitying himself, honing and moaning to himself; he yearneth over himself; his bowels are even melted within him, to think what he suffers; he is not ashamed to weep over himself.

He is for ever plotting how to do some good to himself; studying little stratagems and artificial alleviations.

He makes the most of himself; dividing himself, by an allowable fiction, into as many distinct individuals, as he hath sore and sorrowing members. Sometimes he meditates – as of a thing apart from him – upon his poor aching head, and that dull pain which, dozing or waking, lay in it all the past night like a log, or palpable substance of pain, not to be removed without opening the very skull, as it seemed, to take it thence. Or he pities his long, clammy, attenuated fingers. He compassionates himself all over; and his bed is a very discipline of humanity, and tender heart.

He is his own sympathiser; and instinctively feels that none can so well perform that office for him. He cares for few spectators to his tragedy. Only that punctual face of the old nurse pleases him, that announces his broths, and his cordials. He likes it because it is so unmoved, and because he can pour forth his feverish ejaculations before it as unreservedly as to his bed-post.

To the world's business he is dead. He understands not what the callings and occupations of mortals are; only he has a glimmering conceit of some such thing, when the doctor makes his daily call: and even in the lines on that busy face he reads no multiplicity of patients, but solely conceives of himself as *the sick man*. To what other uneasy couch the good man is hastening, when he slips out of his chamber, folding up his thin douceur [4] so carefully for fear of rustling – is no speculation which he can at present entertain. He thinks only of the regular return of the same phenomenon at the same hour to-morrow.

Household rumours touch him not. Some faint murmur, indicative of life going on within the house, soothes him, while he knows not distinctly what it is. He is not to know any thing, not to think of any thing. Servants gliding up or down the distant staircase, treading as upon velvet, gently keep his ear awake, so long as he troubles not himself further than with some feeble guess at their errands. Exacter knowledge would be a burthen to him: he can just endure the pressure of conjecture. He opens his eye faintly at the dull stroke of the muffled knocker, and closes it again without asking 'Who was it?' He is flattered by a general notion that inquiries are making after him, but he cares not to know the name of the inquirer. In the general stillness, and awful hush of the house, he lies in state, and feels his sovereignty.

To be sick is to enjoy monarchal prerogatives. Compare the silent tread, and quiet ministry, almost by the eye only, with which he is served – with the careless demeanour, the unceremonious goings in and out (slapping of doors, or leaving them open) of the very same attendants, when he is getting a little better – and you will confess, that from the bed of sickness (throne let me rather call it) to the elbow chair of convalescence, is a fall from dignity, amounting to a deposition.

How convalescence shrinks a man back to his pristine stature! where is now the space, which he occupied so lately, in his own, in the family's eye?

The scene of his regalities, his sick room, which was his presence chamber, where he lay and acted his despotic fancies – how is it reduced to a common bed-room! The trimness of the very bed has something petty and unmeaning about it. It is *made* every day. How unlike to that wavy, many-furrowed, oceanic surface, which it presented so short a time since, when to *make* it was a service not to be thought of at oftener than three or four day revolutions, when the patient was with pain and grief to be lifted for a little while out of it, to submit to the encroachments of unwelcome neatness, and decencies which his shaken frame deprecated; then to be lifted into it again, for another three or four days' respite, to flounder it out of shape again, while every fresh furrow was a historical record of some shifting posture, some uneasy turning, some seeking for a little ease; and the shrunken skin scarce told a truer story than the crumpled coverlid.

Hushed are those mysterious sighs – those groans – so much more awful, while we knew not from what caverns of vast hidden suffering they proceeded. The Lernean pangs are quenched. The riddle of sickness is solved; and Philoctetes is become an ordinary personage.

Perhaps some relic of the sick man's dream of greatness survives in the still lingering visitations of the medical attendant. But how is he too changed with every thing else! Can this be he – this man of news – of chat – of anecdote – of every thing but physic – can this be he, who so lately came between the patient and his cruel enemy, as on some solemn embassy from Nature, erecting herself into a high mediating party? – Pshaw! 'tis some old woman.

Farewell with him all that made sickness pompous – the spell that hushed the household – the desert-like stillness, felt throughout its inmost chambers – the mute attendance – the inquiry by looks – the still softer delicacies of self-attention – the sole and single eye of distemper alonely fixed upon itself – world-thoughts excluded – the man a world unto himself – his own theatre –

What a speck is he dwindled into!

In this flat swamp of convalescence, left by the ebb of sickness, yet far enough from the terra firma[5] of established health, your note, dear Editor, reached me, requesting – an article. In Articulo Mortis,[6] thought I; but it is something hard – and the quibble, wretched as it was, relieved me. The summons, unseasonable as it appeared, seemed to link me on again to the petty businesses of life, which I had lost sight of; a gentle call to activity, however trivial; a wholesome weaning from that preposterous dream of self-absorption – the puffy state of sickness – in which I confess to have lain so long, insensible to the magazines and monarchies of the world alike; to its laws and to its literature. The hypochondriac flatus is subsiding; the acres, which in imagination I had spread over – for the sick man swells in the sole contemplation of his single sufferings, till he becomes a Tityus[7] to himself – are wasting to a span; and for the giant of self-importance, which I was so lately, you have me once again in my natural pretensions – the lean and meagre figure of your insignificant Essayist.

(*London Magazine*, July 1825)

STAGE ILLUSION

A PLAY is said to be well or ill acted in proportion to the scenical illusion produced. Whether such illusion can in any case be perfect, is not the question. The nearest approach to it, we are told, is, when the actor appears wholly unconscious of the presence of spectators. In tragedy – in all which is to affect the feelings – this undivided attention to his stage business seems indispensable. Yet it is, in fact, dispensed with every day by our cleverest tragedians; and while these references to an audience, in the shape of rant or sentiment, are not too frequent or palpable, a sufficient quantity of illusion for the purposes of dramatic interest may be said to be produced in spite of them. But, tragedy apart, it may be inquired whether, in certain characters in comedy, especially those which are a little extravagant, or which involve some notion repugnant to the moral sense, it is not a proof of the highest skill in the comedian when, without absolutely appealing to an audience, he keeps up a tacit understanding with them; and makes them, unconsciously to themselves, a party in the scene. The utmost nicety is required in the mode of doing this; but we speak only of the great artists in the profession.

The most mortifying infirmity in human nature, to feel in ourselves, or to contemplate in another, is, perhaps, cowardice. To see a coward *done to the life* upon a stage would produce anything but mirth. Yet we most of us remember Jack Bannister's cowards.[1] Could anything be more agreeable, more pleasant? We loved the rogues. How was this effected by but the exquisite art of the actor in a perpetual sub-insinuation to us, the spectators, even in the extremity of the shaking fit, that he was not half such a coward as we took him for? We saw all the common symptoms of the malady upon him; the quivering lip, the cowering knees, the teeth chattering; and could have sworn 'that man was frightened.' But we forgot all the while – or kept it almost a secret to ourselves – that he never once lost his self-possession; that he let out by a thousand droll looks and gestures – meant to *us*, and not at all supposed to be visible to his fellows in the scene, that his confidence in his own resources had never once deserted him. Was this a genuine picture of a coward? or not rather a likeness, which the clever artist contrived to palm upon us instead of an original; while we secretly connived at the delusion for the purpose of greater pleasure, than a more genuine counterfeiting of the imbecility, helplessness, and utter self-desertion, which we know to be concomitants of cowardice in real life, could have given us?

Why are misers so hateful in the world, and so endurable on the stage, but because the skilful actor, by a sort of sub-reference, rather than direct appeal to us, disarms the character of a great deal of its odiousness, by seeming to engage *our* compassion for the insecure tenure by which he holds his money bags and parchments? By this subtle vent half of the hatefulness of the character – the self-closeness with which in real life it coils up from the sympathies of men – evaporates. The miser becomes sympathetic; *i.e.* is no genuine miser. Here again a diverting likeness is substituted for a very disagreeable reality.

Spleen, irritability – the pitiable infirmities of old men, which produce only pain to behold in the realities, counterfeited upon a stage, divert not altogether for the comic appendages to them, but in part from an inner conviction that they are *being acted* before us; that a likeness only is going on, and not the thing itself. They please by being done under the life, or beside it; not *to the life*. When Gatty[2] acts an old man, is he angry indeed? or only a pleasant counterfeit, just enough of a likeness to recognise, without pressing upon us the uneasy sense of a reality.

Comedians, paradoxical as it may seem, may be too natural. It was the case with a late actor. Nothing could be more earnest or true than the manner of Mr Emery;[3] this told excellently in his Tyke, and characters of a tragic cast. But when he carried the same rigid exclusiveness of attention to the stage business, and wilful blindness and oblivion of everything before the curtain into his comedy, it produced a harsh and dissonant effect. He was out of keeping with the rest of the *Personæ Dramatis*. There was as little link between him and them as betwixt himself and the audience. He was a third estate, dry, repulsive, and unsocial to all. Individually considered, his execution was masterly. But comedy is not this unbending thing; for this reason, that the same degree of credibility is not required of it as to serious scenes. The degrees of credibility demanded to the two things may be illustrated by the different sort of truth which we expect when a man tells us a mournful or a merry story. If we suspect the former of falsehood in any one tittle, we reject it altogether. Our tears refuse to flow at a suspected imposition. But the teller of a mirthful tale has latitude allowed him. We are content with less than absolute truth. 'Tis the same with dramatic illusion. We confess we love in comedy to see an audience naturalised behind the scenes, taken into the interest of the drama, welcomed as by-standers however. There is something ungracious in a comic actor holding himself aloof from all participation or concern with those who are come to be diverted by him. Macbeth must see the dagger, and no ear but his own be told of it; but an old fool in farce may think he *sees something*, and by conscious words and looks express it, as plainly as he can speak, to pit, box, and gallery. When an impertinent in tragedy, an Osric, for instance, breaks in upon the serious passions of the scene, we approve of the contempt with which he is treated. But when the pleasant impertinent of comedy, in a piece purely meant to give delight, and raise mirth out of whimsical perplexities, worries the studious man with taking up his leisure, or making his house his home, the same sort of contempt expressed (however *natural*) would destroy the balance of delight in the spectators. To make the intrusion comic, the actor who plays the annoyed man must a little desert nature; he must, in short, be thinking of the audience, and express only so much dissatisfaction and peevishness as is consistent with the pleasure of comedy. In other words, his perplexity must seem half put on. If he repel the intruder with the sober set face of a man in earnest, and more especially if he deliver his expostulations in a tone which in the world must necessarily provoke a duel; his real-life manner will destroy the whimsical and purely dramatic existence of the other character (which to render it comic demands an antagonist comicality on the part of the character opposed to it), and convert what was meant for mirth, rather than belief, into a downright piece of impertinence indeed, which would raise no diversion in us, but rather stir pain, to see inflicted in earnest upon any worthy person. A very judicious actor (in most of his parts) seems to have fallen into an error of this sort in his playing with Mr Wrench[4] in the farce of Free and Easy.

Many instances would be tedious; these may suffice to show that comic acting at least does not always demand from the performer that strict abstraction from all reference to an audience which is exacted of it; but that in some cases a sort of compromise may take place, and all the purposes of dramatic delight be attained by a judicious understanding, not too openly announced, between the ladies and gentlemen – on both sides of the curtain.

(*London Magazine*, August 1825)

SANITY OF TRUE GENIUS

so far from the position holding true, that great wit (or genius, in our modern way of speaking) has a necessary alliance with insanity, the greatest wits, on the contrary, will ever be found to be the sanest writers. It is impossible for the mind to conceive a mad Shakspeare. The greatness of wit, by which the poetic talent is here chiefly to be understood, manifests itself in the admirable balance of all the faculties. Madness is the disproportionate straining or excess of any one of them. 'So strong a wit,' says Cowley, speaking of a poetical friend,

> '– did Nature to him frame,
> As all things but his judgment overcame;
> His judgment like the heavenly moon did show,
> Tempering that mighty sea below.' [1]

The ground of the mistake is, that men, finding in the raptures of the higher poetry a condition of exaltation, to which they have no parallel in their own experience, besides the spurious resemblance of it in dreams and fevers, impute a state of dreaminess and fever to the poet. But the true poet dreams being awake. He is not possessed by his subject, but has dominion over it. In the groves of Eden he walks familiar as in his native paths. He ascends the empyrean heaven, and is not intoxicated. He treads the burning marl without dismay; he wins his flight without self-loss through realms of chaos 'and old night.' Or if, abandoning himself to that severer chaos of a 'human mind untuned,' he is content awhile to be mad with Lear, or to hate mankind (a sort of madness) with Timon, neither is that madness, nor this misanthropy, so unchecked, but that, – never letting the reins of reason wholly go, while most he seems to do so, – he has his better genius still whispering at his ear, with the good servant Kent suggesting saner counsels, or with the honest steward Flavius recommending kindlier resolutions. Where he seems most to recede from humanity, he will be found the truest to it. From beyond the scope of Nature if he summon possible existences, he subjugates them to the law of her consistency. He is beautifully loyal to that sovereign directress, even when he appears most to betray and desert her. His ideal tribes submit to policy; his very monsters are tamed to his hand, even as that wild sea-brood, shepherded by Proteus. He tames and he clothes them with attributes of flesh and blood, till they wonder at themselves, like Indian Islanders forced to submit to European vesture. Caliban, the Witches, are as true to the laws of their own nature (ours with a difference), as Othello, Hamlet, and Macbeth. Herein the great and the little wits are differenced; that if the latter wander ever so little from nature or actual existence, they lose themselves, and their readers. Their phantoms are lawless; their visions nightmares. They do not create, which implies shaping and consistency. Their imaginations are not active — for to be active is to call something into act and form — but passive, as men in sick dreams. For the super-natural, or something super-added to what we know of nature, they give you the plainly non-natural. And if this were all, and that these mental hallucinations were discoverable only in the treatment of subjects out of nature, or transcending it, the judgment might with some plea be pardoned if it ran riot, and a little wantonised: but even in the describing of real and everyday life, that which is before their eyes, one of these lesser wits shall more deviate from nature — show more of that inconsequence, which has a natural alliance with frenzy, — than a great genius in his 'maddest fits,' as Wither [2] somewhere calls them. We appeal to any one that is acquainted with the common run of Lane's novels, [3] — as they existed some twenty or thirty years back, — those scanty intellectual viands of the whole female reading public, till a happier genius arose, and expelled for ever the innutritious phantoms, — whether he has not found his brain more 'betossed,' his memory more puzzled, his sense of when and where more confounded, among the improbable events, the incoherent incidents, the inconsistent characters, or no-characters, of some third-rate love intrigue — where the persons shall be a Lord Glendamour and a Miss Rivers, and the scene only alternate between Bath and Bond Street — a more bewildering dreaminess induced upon him, than he has felt wandering over all the fairy grounds of Spenser. In the productions we refer to, nothing but names and places is familiar; the persons are neither of this world nor of any other conceivable one; an endless string of activities without purpose, or purposes destitute of motive: — we meet phantoms in our known walks; *fantasques* [4] only christened. In the poet we have names which announce fiction; and we have absolutely no place at all, for the things and persons of the Fairy Queen prate not of their 'whereabout.' But in their inner nature, and the law of their speech and actions, we are at home and upon acquainted ground. The one turns life into a dream; the other to the wildest dreams gives the sobrieties of every-day occurrences. By what subtle art of tracing the mental processes it is effected, we are not philosophers enough to explain, but in that wonderful episode of the cave of Mammon,[5] in which the Money God appears first in the lowest form of a miser, is then a worker of metals, and becomes the god of all the treasures of the world: and has a daughter, Ambition, before whom all the world kneels for favours – with the Hesperian fruit, the waters of Tantalus, with Pilate washing his hands vainly, but not impertinently, in the same stream – that we should be at one moment in the cave of an old hoarder of treasures, at the next at the forge of the Cyclops, in a palace and yet in hell, all at once, with the shifting mutations of the most rambling dream, and our judgment yet all the time awake, and neither able nor willing to detect the fallacy, – is a proof of that hidden sanity which still guides the poet in the widest seeming-aberrations.

It is not enough to say that the whole episode is a copy of the mind's conceptions in sleep; it is, in some sort – but what a copy! Let the most romantic of us, that has been entertained all night with the spectacle of some wild and magnificent vision, recombine it in the morning, and try it by his waking judgment. That which appeared so shifting, and yet so coherent, while that faculty was passive, when it comes under cool examination, shall appear so reasonless and so unlinked, that we are ashamed to have been so deluded; and to have taken, though but in sleep, a monster for a god. But the transitions in this episode are every whit as violent as in the most extravagant dream, and yet the waking judgment ratifies them.

(*New Monthly Magazine*, May 1826)

BARRENNESS OF THE IMAGINATIVE FACULTY IN THE PRODUCTIONS OF MODERN ART

HOGARTH excepted, can we produce any one painter within the last fifty years, or since the humour of exhibiting began, that has treated a story *imaginatively?* By this we mean, upon whom his subject has so acted, that it has seemed to direct *him* – not to be arranged by him? Any upon whom its leading or collateral points have impressed themselves so tyrannically, that he dared not treat it otherwise, lest he should falsify a revelation? Any that has imparted to his compositions, not merely so much truth as is enough to convey a story with clearness, but that individualising property, which should keep the subject so treated distinct in feature from every other subject, however similar, and to common apprehensions almost identical; so as that we might say, this and this part could have found an appropriate place in no other picture in the world but this? Is there any thing in modern art – we will not demand that it should be equal – but in any way analogous to what Titian has effected, in that wonderful bringing together of two times in the 'Ariadne,' in the National Gallery? Precipitous, with his reeling Satyr rout about him, re-peopling and re-illuming suddenly the waste places, drunk with a new fury beyond the grape, Bacchus, born in fire, fire-like flings himself at the Cretan. This is the time present. With this telling of the story – an artist, and no ordinary one, might remain richly proud. Guido, in his harmonious version of it, saw no further. But from the depth of the imaginative spirit Titian has recalled past time, and laid it contributory with the present to one simultaneous effect. With the desert all ringing with the mad cymbals of his followers, made lucid with the presence and new offers of a god, – as if unconscious of Bacchus, or but idly casting her eyes as upon some unconcerning pageant – her soul undistracted from Theseus – Ariadne is still pacing the solitary shore in as much heart-silence, and in almost the same local solitude, with which she awoke at day-break to catch the forlorn last glances of the sail that bore away the Athenian.

Here are two points miraculously co-uniting; fierce society, with the feeling of solitude still absolute, noon-day revelations, with the accidents of the dull grey dawn unquenched and lingering; the *present* Bacchus, with the *past* Ariadne; two stories, with double Time; separate, and harmonising. Had the artist made the woman one shade less indifferent to the God; still more, had she expressed a rapture at his advent, where would have been the story of the mighty desolation of the heart previous? merged in the insipid accident of a flattering offer met with a welcome acceptance. The broken heart for Theseus was not lightly to be pieced up by a God.

We have before us a fine rough print, from a picture by Raphael in the Vatican. It is the Presentation of the new-born Eve to Adam by the Almighty. A fairer mother of mankind we might imagine, and a goodlier sire perhaps of men since born. But these are matters subordinate to the conception of the *situation*, displayed in this extraordinary production. A tolerable modern artist would have been satisfied with tempering certain raptures of connubial anticipation, with a suitable acknowledgement to the Giver of the blessing, in the countenance of the first bridegroom; something like the divided attention of the child (Adam was here a child man) between the given toy, and the mother who had just blest it with the bauble. This is the obvious, the first-sight view, the superficial. An artist of a higher grade, considering the awful presence they were in, would have taken care to subtract something from the expression of the more human passion, and to heighten the more spiritual one. This would be as much as an exhibition goer, from the opening of Somerset House[1] to last year's show, has been encouraged to look for. It is obvious to hint at a lower expression yet, in a picture, that for respects of drawing and colouring, might be deemed not wholly inadmissible within these art-fostering walls, in which the raptures should be as ninety-nine, the gratitude as one, or perhaps Zero! By neither the one passion nor the other has Raphael expounded the situation of Adam. Singly upon his brow sits the absorbing sense of wonder at the created miracle. The *moment* is seized by the intuitive artist, perhaps not self-conscious of his art, in which neither of the conflicting emotions — a moment how abstracted — have had time to spring up, or to battle for indecorous mastery. — We have seen a landscape of a justly admired neoteric,[2] in which he aimed at delineating a fiction, one of the most severely beautiful in antiquity — the gardens of the Hesperides. To do Mr — justice he had painted a laudable orchard, with fitting seclusion, and a veritable dragon (of which a Polypheme, by Poussin, is somehow a fac-simile for the situation) looking over into the world shut out backwards, so that none but a 'still-climbing Hercules' could hope to catch a peep at the admired Ternary of Recluses.

No conventual porter could keep his eyes better than this custos[3] with the 'lidless eyes.' He not only sees that none *do* intrude into that privacy, but, as clear as daylight, that none but *Hercules aut Diabolus*[4] by any manner of means *can*. So far all is well. We have absolute solitude here or nowhere. *Ab extra*[5] the damsels are snug enough. But here the artist's courage seems to have failed him. He began to pity his pretty charge, and, to comfort the irksomeness, has peopled their solitude with a bevy of fair attendants, maids of honour, or ladies of the bed-chamber, according to the approved etiquette at a court of the nineteenth century; giving to the whole scene the air of a *fête champêtre*, if we will but excuse the absence of the gentlemen. This is well, and Watteauish. But what is become of the solitary mystery – the

> Daughters three,
> That sing around the golden tree?[6]

This is not the way in which Poussin would have treated this subject.

The paintings, or rather the stupendous architectural designs, of a modern artist,[7] have been urged as objections to the theory of our motto. They are of a character, we confess, to stagger it. His towered structures are of the highest order of the material sublime. Whether they were dreams, or transcripts of some elder workmanship – Assyrian ruins old – restored by this mighty artist, they satisfy our most stretched and craving conceptions of the glories of the antique world. It is a pity that they were ever peopled. On that side, the imagination of the artist halts, and appears defective. Let us examine the point of the story in the 'Belshazzar's Feast.' We will introduce it by an apposite anecdote.

The court historians of the day record, that at the first dinner given by the late King[8] (then Prince Regent) at the Pavilion, the following characteristic frolic was played off. The guests were select and admiring; the banquet profuse and admirable; the lights lustrous and oriental; the eye was perfectly dazzled with the display of plate, among which the great gold salt-cellar, brought from the regalia in the Tower for this especial purpose, itself a tower! stood conspicuous for its magnitude. And now the Revd ***, the then admired court Chaplain, was proceeding with the grace, when, at a signal given, the lights were suddenly overcast, and a huge transparency was discovered, in which glittered in gold letters –

'BRIGHTON – EARTHQUAKE – SWALLOW-UP-ALIVE!'

Imagine the confusion of the guests; the Georges and garters, jewels, bracelets, moulted upon the occasion! The fans dropped, and picked up the next morning by the sly court pages! Mrs Fitz-what's-her-name fainting, and the Countess of * * * holding the smelling-bottle, till the good-humoured Prince caused harmony to be restored by calling in fresh candles, and declaring that the whole was nothing but a pantomime *hoax*, got up by the ingenious Mr Farley,[9] of Covent Garden, from hints which his Royal Highness himself had furnished! Then imagine the infinite applause that followed, the mutual rallyings, the declarations that 'they were not much frightened,' of the assembled galaxy.

The point of time in the picture exactly answers to the appearance of the transparency in the anecdote. The huddle, the flutter, the bustle, the escape, the alarm, and the mock alarm; the prettinesses heightened by consternation; the courtier's fear which was flattery, and the lady's which was affectation; all that we may conceive to have taken place in a mob of Brighton courtiers, sympathising with the well-acted surprise of their sovereign; all this, and no more, is exhibited by the well-dressed lords and ladies in the Hall of Belus. Just this sort of consternation we have seen among a flock of disquieted wild geese at the report only of a gun having gone off!

But is this vulgar fright, this mere animal anxiety for the preservation of their persons, – such as we have witnessed at a theatre, when a slight alarm of fire has been given – an adequate exponent of a supernatural terror? the way in which the finger of God, writing judgments, would have been met by the withered conscience? There is a human fear, and a divine fear. The one is disturbed, restless, and bent upon escape. The other is bowed down, effortless, passive. When the spirit appeared before Eliphaz in the visions of the night, and the hair of his flesh stood up, was it in the thoughts of the Temanite to ring the bell of his chamber, or to call up the servants?[10] But let us see in the text what there is to justify all this huddle of vulgar consternation.

From the words of Daniel[11] it appears that Belshazzar had made a great feast to a thousand of his lords, and drank wine before the thousand. The golden and silver vessels are gorgeously enumerated, with the princes, the king's concubines, and his wives. Then follows –

'In the same hour came forth fingers of a man's hand, and wrote over against the candlestick upon the plaster of the wall of the king's palace; and the *king* saw the part of the hand that wrote. Then the *king's* countenance was changed, and his thoughts troubled him, so that the joints of his loins were loosened, and his knees smote one against another.'

This is the plain text. By no hint can it be otherwise inferred, but that the appearance was solely confined to the fancy of Belshazzar, that his single brain was troubled. Not a word is spoken of its being seen by any else there present, not even by the queen herself, who merely undertakes for the interpretation of the phenomenon, as related to her, doubtless, by her husband. The lords are simply said to be astonished; *i.e.*, at the trouble and the change of countenance in their sovereign. Even the prophet does not appear to have seen the scroll, which the king saw. He recalls it only, as Joseph did the Dream to the King of Egypt. 'Then was the part of the hand sent from him [the Lord], and this writing was written.' He speaks of the phantasm as past.

Then what becomes of this needless multiplication of the miracle? this message to a royal conscience, singly expressed – for it was said, 'thy kingdom is divided,' – simultaneously impressed upon the fancies of a thousand courtiers, who were implied in it neither directly not grammatically?

But admitting the artist's own version of the story, and that the sight was seen also by the thousand courtiers – let it have been visible to all Babylon – as the knees of Belshazzar were shaken, and his countenance troubled, even so would the knees of every man in Babylon, and their countenances, as of an individual man, have been troubled; bowed, bent down, so would they have remained, stupor-fixed, with no thought of struggling with that inevitable judgment.

Not all that is optically possible to be seen, is to be shown in every picture. The eye delightedly dwells upon the brilliant individualities in a 'Marriage at Cana,' by Veronese, or Titian, to the very texture and colour of the wedding garments, the ring glittering upon the bride's fingers, the metal and fashion of the wine-pots; for at such seasons there is leisure and luxury to be curious. But in a 'day of judgment,' or in a 'day of lesser horrors, yet divine,' as at the impious feast of Belshazzar, the eye should see, as the actual eye of an agent or patient in the immediate scene would see, only in masses and indistinction. Not only the female attire and jewelry exposed to the critical eye of fashion, as minutely as the dresses in a lady's magazine, in the criticised picture, – but perhaps the curiosities of anatomical science, and studied diversities of posture in the falling angels and sinners of Michael Angelo, – have no business in their great subjects. There was no leisure for them.

By a wise falsification, the great masters of painting got at their true conclusions; by not showing the actual appearances, that is, all that was to be seen at any given moment by an indifferent eye, but only what the eye might be supposed to see in the doing or suffering of some portentous action. Suppose the moment of the swallowing up of Pompeii.[12] There they were to be seen – houses, columns, architectural proportions, differences of public and private buildings, men and women at their standing occupations, the diversified thousand postures, attitudes, dresses, in some confusion truly, but physically they were visible. But what eye saw them at that eclipsing moment, which reduces confusion to a kind of unity, and when the senses are upturned from their proprieties, when sight and hearing are a feeling only? A thousand years have passed, and we are at leisure to contemplate the weaver fixed standing at his shuttle, the baker at his oven, and to turn over with antiquarian coolness the pots and pans of Pompeii.

'Sun, stand thou still upon Gibeon, and thou, Moon, in the valley of Ajalon.'[13] Who, in reading this magnificent Hebraism, in his conception, sees aught but the heroic son of Nun, with the outstretched arm, and the greater and lesser light obsequious? Doubtless there were to be seen hill and dale, and chariots and horsemen, on open plain, or winding by secret defiles, and all the circumstances and stratagems of war. But whose eyes would have been conscious of this array at the interposition of the synchronic miracle? Yet in the picture of this subject by the artist of the 'Belshazzar's Feast' – no ignoble work either – the marshalling and landscape of the war is everything, the miracle sinks into an anecdote of the day; and the eye may 'dart though rank and file traverse' for some minutes, before it shall discover, among his armed followers, *which is Joshua!* Not modern art alone, but ancient, where only it is to be found if anywhere, can be detected erring, from defect of this imaginative faculty. The world has nothing to show of the preternatural in painting, transcending the figure of Lazarus bursting his grave-clothes, in the great picture at Angerstein's.[14] It seems a thing between two beings. A ghastly horror at itself struggles with newly-apprehending gratitude at second life bestowed. It cannot forget that it was a ghost. It has hardly felt that it is a body. It has to tell of the world of spirits. – Was it from a feeling, that the crowd of half-impassioned by-standers, and the still more irrelevant herd of passers-by at a distance, who have not heard or but faintly have been told of the passing miracle, admirable as they are in design and hue – for it is a glorified work – do not respond adequately to the action – that the single figure of the Lazarus has been attributed to Michael Angelo, and the mighty Sebastian unfairly robbed of the fame of the greater half of the interest? Now that there were not indifferent passers-by, within actual scope of the eyes of those present at the miracle, to whom the sound of it had but faintly, or not at all, reached, it would be hardihood to deny; but would they see them? or can the mind in the conception of it admit of such un-concerning objects? can it think of them at all? or what associating league to the imagination can there be between the seers, and the seers not, of a presential miracle?

Were an artist to paint upon demand a picture of a Dryad, we will ask whether, in the present low state of expectation, the patron would not, or ought not be fully satisfied with a beautiful naked figure re-cumbent under wide-stretched oaks? Disseat those woods, and place the same figure among fountains, and a fall of pellucid water, and you have a – Naiad! Not so in a rough print we have seen after Julio Romano, we think – for it is long since – *there*, by no process, with mere change of scene, could the figure have reciprocated characters. Long, grotesque, fantastic, yet with a grace of her own, beautiful in convolution and distortion, linked to her connatural tree, co-twisting with its limbs her own, till both seemed either – these, animated branches; those, dis-animated members – yet the animal and vegetable lives sufficiently kept distinct – *his* Dryad lay – an approximation of two natures, which to conceive, it must be seen; analogous to, not the same with, the delicacies of Ovidian transformations.

To the lowest subjects, and, to a superficial comprehension, the most barren, the Great Masters gave loftiness and fruitfulness. The large eye of genius saw in the meanness of present objects their capabilities of treatment from their relations to some grand Past or Future. How has Raphael – we must still linger about the Vatican – treated the humble craft of the ship-builder, in *his* 'Building of the Ark'? It is in that scriptural series, to which we have referred, and which, judging from some fine rough old graphic sketches of them which we possess, seem to be of a higher and more poetic grade than even the Cartoons. The dim of sight are the timid and the shrinking. There is a cowardice in modern art. As the Frenchmen, of whom Coleridge's friend made the prophetic guess at Rome, from the beard and horns of the Moses of Michael Angelo collected no inferences beyond that of a He Goat and a Cornuto; [15] so from this subject, of mere mechanic promise, it would instinctively turn away, as from one incapable of investiture with any grandeur. The dock-yards at Woolwich would object derogatory associations. The depôt at Chatham would be the mote and the beam in its intellectual eye. But not to the nautical preparations in the shipyards of Civita Vecchia did Raphael look for instructions, when he imagined the Building of the Vessel that was to be conservatory of the wrecks of the species of drowned mankind. In the intensity of the action, he keeps ever out of sight the meanness of the operation. There is the Patriarch, in calm forethought, and with holy prescience, giving directions. And there are his agents – the solitary but sufficient Three [16] – hewing, sawing, every one with the might and earnestness of a Demiurgus; [17] under some instinctive rather than technical guidance! giant-muscled; every one a Hercules, or liker to those Vulcanian Three, that in sounding caverns under Mongibello wrought in fire – Brontes, and black Steropes, and Pyracmon. [18] So work the workmen that should repair a world!

Artists again err in the confounding of *poetic* with *pictorial subjects*. In the latter, the exterior accidents are nearly everything, the unseen qualities as nothing. Othello's colour – the infirmities and corpulence of a Sir John Falstaff – do they haunt us perpetually in the reading? or are they obtruded upon our conceptions one time for ninety-nine that we are lost in admiration at the respective moral or intellectual attributes of the character? But in a picture Othello is *always* a Blackamoor; and the other only Plump Jack. Deeply corporealised, and enchained hopelessly in the grovelling fetters of externality, must be the mind, to which, in its better moments, the image of the high-souled, high-intelligenced Quixote – the errant Star of Knighthood, made more tender by eclipse – has never presented itself, divested from the unhallowed accompaniments of a Sancho, or a rabblement at the heels of Rosinante. That man has read his book by halves; he has laughed, mistaking his author's purport, which was – tears. The artist that pictures Quixote – (and it is in this degrading point that he is every season held up at our Exhibitions) in the shallow hope of exciting mirth, would have joined the rabble at the heels of his starved steed. We wish not to see *that* counterfeited, which we would not have wished to see in the reality. Conscious of the heroic inside of the noble Quixote, who, on hearing that his withered person was passing, would have stepped over his threshold to gaze upon his forlorn habiliments, and the 'strange bed-fellows which misery brings a man acquainted with'? Shade of Cervantes! who in thy Second Part could put into the mouth of thy Quixote those high aspirations of a super-chivalrous gallantry, where he replies to one of the shepherdesses, apprehensive that he would spoil their pretty net-works, and inviting him to be a guest with them, in accents like these: 'Truly, fairest Lady, Actæon was not more astonished when he saw Diana bathing herself at the fountain, than I have been in beholding your beauty: I commend the manner of your pastime, and thank you for your kind offers; and, if

I may serve you, so I may be sure you will be obeyed, you may command me: for my profession is this, To show myself thankful, and a doer of good to all sorts of people, especially of the rank that your person shows you to be; and if those nets, as they take up but a little piece of ground, should take up the whole world, I would seek out new worlds to pass through, rather than break them: and (he adds) that you may give credit to this my exaggeration, behold at least he that promiseth you this, is Don Quixote de la Mancha, if haply this name hath come to your hearing.' Illustrious Romancer! were the 'fine frenzies,' which possessed the brain of thy own Quixote, a fit subject, as in this Second Part, to be exposed to the jeers of Duennas and Serving Men? to be monstered, and shown up at the heartless banquets of great men? Was that pitiable infirmity, which in thy First Part misleads him, *always from within*, into half-ludicrous, but more than half-compassionable and admirable errors, not infliction enough from heaven, that men by studied artifices must devise and practise upon the humour, to inflame where they should soothe it? Why, Goneril would have blushed to practise upon the abdicated king at this rate, and the she-wolf Regan not have endured to play the pranks upon his fled wits, which thou hast made thy Quixote suffer in Duchesses' halls, and at the hands of that unworthy nobleman.*

In the First Adventures, even, it needed all the art of the most consummate artist in the Book way that the world hath yet seen, to keep up in the mind of the reader the heroic attributes of the character without relaxing; so as absolutely that they shall suffer no alloy from the debasing fellowship of the clown. If it ever obtrudes itself as a disharmony, are we inclined to laugh; or not, rather, to indulge a contrary emotion? – Cervantes, stung, perhance, by the relish with which *his* Reading Public had received the fooleries of the man, more to their palates than the generosities of the master, in the sequel let his pen run riot, lost the harmony and the balance, and sacrificed a great idea to the taste of his contemporaries. We know that in the present day the Knight has fewer admirers than the Squire. Anticipating, what did actually happen to him – as afterwards it did to his scarce inferior follower, the Author of 'Guzman de Alfarache'[19] – that some less knowing hand would prevent him by a spurious Second Part; and judging, that it would be easier for his competitor to out-bid him in the comicalities, than in the *romance*, of his work, he abandoned his Knight, and has fairly set up the Squire for

* Yet from this Second Part, our cried-up pictures are mostly selected, the waiting women with beards, &c.

his Hero. For what else has he unsealed the eyes of Sancho; and instead of that twilight state of semi-insanity – the madness at second-hand – the contagion, caught from a stronger mind infected – that war between native cunning, and hereditary deference, with which he has hitherto accompanied his master – two for a pair almost – does he substitute a downright Knave, with open eyes, for his own ends only following a confessed Madman; and offering at one time to lay, if not actually laying, hands upon him! From the moment that Sancho loses his reverence, Don Quixote is become – a treatable lunatic. Our artists handle him accordingly.

(*Athenaeum*, 12, 19, 26 January and 2 February 1833)

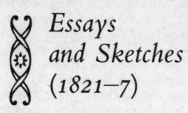

*Essays
and Sketches
(1821–7)*

REVIEW OF THE FIRST VOLUME
OF HAZLITT'S *TABLE-TALK*, 1821
(unpublished)

A SERIES of Miscellaneous Essays, however well executed in the parts, if
it have not some pervading character to give a unity to it, is ordinarily
as tormenting to get through as a set of aphorisms, or a jest-book. – The
fathers of Essay writing in ancient and modern times – Plutarch in a
measure, and Montaigne without mercy or measure – imparted their
own personal peculiarities to their themes. By this balm are they preserved. The Author of the Rambler in a less direct way has attained the
same effect. Without professing egotism, his work is as essentially egotistical as theirs. He deals out opinion, which he would have you take
for argument; and is perpetually obtruding his own particular views of
life for universal truths. This is the charm which binds us to his writings,
and not any steady conviction we have of the solidity of his thinking.
Possibly some of those Papers, which are generally understood to be
failures in the Rambler – its ponderous levities for instance, and un-
wieldy efforts at being sprightly – may detract less from the general
effect, than if something better in kind, but less in keeping, had been
substituted in place of them. If the author had taken his friend Goldsmith
into partnership, and they had furnished their quotas for alternate days,
the world had been gainer by the arrangement, but what a heterogeneous mass the work itself would have presented!

Another class of Essayists, equally impressed with the advantages of
this sort of appeal to the reader, but more dextrous at shifting off the
invidiousness of a perpetual self-reference, substituted for themselves an
ideal character; which left them a still fuller licence in the delivery of their
peculiar humours and opinions, under the masqued battery of a fictitious
appellation. Truths, which the world would have startled at from the
lips of the gay Captain Steele, it readily accepted from the pen of old
Isaac Bickerstaff. But the breed of the Bickerstaffs, as it began, so alas! it
expired with him. It shewed indeed a few feeble sparks of revival in
Nestor Ironside,[1] but soon went out. Addison had stepped in with his
wit, his criticism, his morality – the cold generalities which extinguish
humour – and the *Spectator*, and its Successor, were little more than
bundles of Essays (valuable indeed, and elegant reading above our praise)

but hanging together with very slender principles of bond or union. In fact we use the word *Spectator*, and mean a Book. At mention of the *Tatler* we sigh, and think of Isaac Bickerstaff. Sir Roger de Coverly, Will Wimble, Will Honeycomb, live for ever in memory – but who is their *silent Friend?* – Except that he never opens his mouth, we know nothing about him. He writes finely upon all subjects – but himself. He sets every thing in a proper light – but we do not see through his spectacles. He colours nothing with his own hues. The Lucubrations[2] come as from an old man, an old bachelor to boot, and a humourist. The *Spectator* too, we are told, *is* all this. But a young man, a young married man moreover, or any description of man, or woman, with no sort of character beyond general shrewdness, and a power of observation, might have strung together all that discordant assemblage of Papers, which call the *Spectator* father. They describe indeed with the utmost felicity all ages & conditions of men, but they themselves smack of no peculiar age or condition. He writes, we are told, because he cannot bring himself to speak, but why he cannot bring himself to speak is the riddle. He is used to good company. Why he should conceal his name, while he lavishly proclaims that of his companions, is equally a secret. Was it to remove him still further from any possibility of our sympathies? – or wherein, we would be informed, lurks the mystery of his short chin? – As a visitor at the Club (a sort of *umbra*) he might have shewn to advantage among those short but masterly sketches – but the mass of matter, spread through eight volumes, is really somewhat too miscellaneous and diffuse, to hang together for identity upon such a shade, such a tenuity!

Since the days of the *Spectator* and *Guardian*, Essayists, who have appeared under a fictitious appellation, have for the most part contented themselves with a brief description of their character and story in the opening Paper; after which they dismiss the Phantom of an Editor, and let the work shift for itself, as wisely and wittily as it is able, unsupported by any characteristic pretences, or individual colouring. – In one particular indeed the followers of Addison were long and grievously misled. For many years after the publication of his celebrated 'Vision of Mirza',[3] no book of Essays was thought complete without a Vision. It set the world dreaming. Take up any one of the volumes of this description, published in the last century; – you will possibly alight upon two or three successive papers, depicting, with more or less gravity, sober views of life *as it is* – when – pop – you come upon a Vision, which you trembled at beforehand from a glimpse you caught at certain abstractions in Capitals, Fame, Riches, Long Life, Loss of Friends, Punishment by Exile – a set of denominations part simple, part compounded – existing in single, double, and triple hypostases. – You cannot think on their fantastic essences without giddiness, or describe them short of a solecism. – These authors seem not to have been content to entertain you with their day-light fancies, but you *must* share their vacant slumbers & common-place reveries. The humour, thank Heaven, is pretty well past. These Visions, any thing but visionary – (for who ever dreamt of Fame, but by metaphor, some mad Orientalist perhaps excepted?) – so tamely extravagant, so gothically classical – these inspirations by downright malice aforethought – these heartless, bloodless literalities – these 'thin consistencies',[4] dependent for their personality upon Great Letters – for write them small, and the tender essences fade into abstractions – have at length happily melted away before the progress of good sense; or the absurdity has worn itself out. We might else have still to lament, that the purer taste of their inventor should have so often wandered aside into these caprices; or to wish, if he had chosen to indulge in an imitation of Eastern extravagance, that he had confined himself to that least obnoxious specimen of his skill, the Allegory of Mirza. –

The Author before us is, in this respect at least, no visionary. He talks to you in broad day-light. He comes in no imaginary character. He is of the class of Essayists first mentioned. He attracts, or repels, by strong realities of individual observation, humour, and feeling.

The title, which Mr Hazlitt has chosen, is characteristic enough of his Essays. The tone of them is uniformly conversational; and they are not the less entertaining, that they resemble occasionally the *talk* of a very clever person, when he begins to be animated in a convivial party. You fancy that a disputant is always present, and feel a disposition to take up the cudgels yourself [o]n behalf of the other side of the question. *Table-Talk* is not calculated for cold or squeamish readers. The average thinker will find his common notions a little too roughly disturbed. He must brace up his ears to the reception of some novelties. Strong traits of character stand out in the work; and it is not so much a series of well argued treatises, as a bold confession, or exposition, of Mr Hazlitt's own ways of feeling upon the subjects treated of. It is in fact a piece of Autobiography; and, in our minds, a vigorous & well-executed one. The Writer almost every where adopts the style of a discontented man. This assumption of a character, if it be not truly (as we are inclined to believe) his own, is that which gives force & life to his writing. He murmurs most musically through fourteen ample Essays. He quarrels with People that have but one idea, and with the Learned that are oppressed with many; with the man of Paradox, and the man of Common-Place; with the Fashionable, and with the Vulgar; with Dying Men that make a Will, and those who die & leave none behind them; with Sir Joshua Reynolds for setting up study above genius, and with the same person for disparaging study in respect of genius; lastly, he quarrels with himself, with book-making, with his friends, with the present time, and future – (the last he has an especial grudge to, and strives hard to prove that it has no existence) – in short, with every thing in the world, *except what he likes* – his past recollections which he describes in a way to make every one else like them too; the Indian Jugglers; Cavanagh, the Fives-Player; the noble art and practice of Painting, which he contends will make men both healthy and wise; and the Old Masters. –

He thus describes (*con amore*) his first visit to the Louvre, at its golden period before Taste had cause to lament the interposition of ruthless Destiny.

I had made some progress in painting when I went to the Louvre to study, and I never did anything afterwards. I never shall forget conning over the Catalogue which a friend lent me just before I set out. The pictures, the names of the painters, seemed to relish in the mouth. There was one of Titian's Mistress at her toilette. Even the colours with which the painter had adorned her hair were not more golden, more amiable to sight, than those which played round and tantalised my fancy ere I saw the picture. There were two portraits by the same hand – 'A young Nobleman with a glove' – Another, 'a companion to it' – I read the description over and over with fond expectancy, and filled up the imaginary outline with whatever I could conceive of grace, and dignity, and an antique *gusto* – all but equal to the original. There was the Transfiguration too. With what awe I saw it in my mind's eye, and was overshadowed with the spirit of the artist! Not to have been disappointed with these works afterwards, was the highest compliment I can pay to their transcendent merits. Indeed, it was from seeing other works of the same great masters that I had formed a vague, but no disparaging idea of these. The first day I got there, I was kept for some time in the French Exhibition-room, and thought I should not be able to get a sight of the old masters. I just caught a peep at them through the door (vile hindrance!) like looking out of purgatory into paradise – from Poussin's noble mellow-looking landscapes to where Rubens hung out his gaudy banner, and down the glimmering vista to the rich jewels of Titian and the Italian school. At last, by much importunity, I was admitted, and lost not an instant in making use of my new privilege. – It was *un beau jour* to me. I marched delighted through a quarter of a mile of the proudest efforts of the mind of man, a whole creation of genius, a universe of art! I ran the gauntlet of all the schools from the bottom to the top; and in the end got admitted into the inner room, where they had been repairing some of their greatest works. Here the Transfiguration, the St Peter Martyr, and the St Jerome of Domenichino stood on the floor, as if they had bent their knees, like camels stooping, to unlade their riches to the spectator. On one side, on an easel, stood Hippolito de Medici (a portrait by Titian), with a boar-spear in his hand, looking through those he saw, till you turned away from the keen glance; and thrown together in heaps were landscapes of the same hand, green pastoral hills and vales, and shepherds piping to their mild mistresses underneath the flowering shade. Reader, 'if thou hast not seen the Louvre, thou are damned!' – for thou hast not seen the choicest remains of the works of art; or thou hast not seen all these together, with their mutually reflected glories. I say nothing of the statues; for I know but little of sculpture, and never liked any till I saw the Elgin Marbles ... Here, for four months together, I strolled and studied, and daily heard the warning sound – *'Quatres heures passées, il faut fermer, Citoyens'* – (Ah! why did they ever change their style?) muttered in coarse provincial French; and brought away with me some loose draughts and fragments, which I have been forced to part with, like drops of life-blood, for 'hard money.' How often, thou tenantless mansion of godlike magnificence – how often has my heart since gone a pilgrimage to thee!

(From *The Pleasures of Painting*)

With all this enthusiasm for the Art, and the intense application which at one time he seems to have been disposed to give to it, the wonder is, that Mr Hazlitt did not turn out a fine painter, rather than writer. Did he lack encouragement? or did his powers of application fail him from some doubt of ultimate success?

One of my first attempts was a picture of my father, who was then in a green old age, with strong-marked features, and scarred with the small-pox. I drew it out with a broad light crossing the face, looking down, with spectacles on, reading. The book was Shaftesbury's Characteristics, in a fine old binding, with Gribelin's etchings. My father would as lieve it had been any other book; but for him to read was to be content, was 'riches fineless.' The sketch promised well; and I set to work to finish it, determined to spare no time nor pains. My father was willing to sit as long as I pleased; for there is a natural desire in the mind of man to sit for one's picture, to be the object of continued attention, to have one's likeness multiplied; and besides his satisfaction in the picture, he had some pride in the artist, though he would rather I should have written a sermon than painted like Rembrandt or like Raphael. Those winter days, with the gleams of sunshine coming through the chapel-windows, and cheered by the notes of the robin-redbreast in our garden (that 'ever in the haunch of winter sings'), – as my afternoon's work drew to a close, – were among the happiest of my life. When I gave the effect I intended to any part of the picture for which I had prepared my colours; when I imitated the roughness of the skin by a lucky stroke of the pencil; when I hit the clear pearly tone of a vein; when I gave the ruddy complexion of health, the blood circulating under the broad shadows of one side of the face, I thought my fortune made; or rather it was already more than made, in my fancying that I might one day be able to say with Correggio, '*I also am a painter!*' It was an idle thought, a boy's conceit; but it did not make me less happy at the time. I used regularly to set my work in the chair to look at it through the long evenings; and many a time did I return to take leave of it before I could go to bed at night. I remember sending it with a throbbing heart to the Exhibition, and seeing it hung up there by the side of one of the Honourable Mr Skeffington (now Sir George). There was nothing in common between them, but that they were the portraits of two very good-natured men. I think, but am not sure, that I finished this portrait (or another afterwards) on the same day that the news of the battle of Austerlitz came; I walked out in the afternoon, and, as I returned, saw the evening star set over a poor man's cottage with other thoughts and feelings than I shall ever have again. Oh for the revolution of the great Platonic year, that those times might come over again! I could sleep out the three hundred and sixty-five thousand intervening years very contentedly! – The picture is left: the table, the chair, the window where I learned to construe Livy, the chapel where my father preached, remain where they were; but he himself is gone to rest, full of years, of faith, of hope, and charity!

(From *The Pleasures of Painting*)

There is a *naivete* commingled with pathos in this little scene, which cannot be enough admired. The old dissenting clergyman's pride at his son's getting on in his profession as an artist, still with a wish rather that he had taken to his own calling; and then an under-vanity of his own in 'having his picture drawn' coming in to comfort him; the preference he would have given to some more orthodox book, with some sort of satisfaction still that he was drawn with a book – above all, the tenderness in the close – make us almost think we are perusing some strain of Mackenzie; or some of the better (because the more pathetic) parts of the Tatler. Indeed such passages are not unfrequent in this writer; and break in upon us, amidst the spleen and severity of his commoner tone, like springs bursting out in the desert. The author's wayward humour, turning inwards from the contemplation of real or imagined grievances – or exhausting itself in gall and bitterness at the things *that be* – reverts for its solace, with a mournfully contrasting spirit of satisfaction, to the past. The corruption of Hope quickens into life again the perishing flowers of the Memory. – In this spirit, in the third, and the most valuable of his Essays, that 'On the past and future', – in which he maintains the reality of the former as a possession in hand, against those who pretend that the future is every thing and the past nothing – after some reasoning, rather too subtle and metaphysical for the general reader – he exclaims with an eloquence that approximates to the finest poetry –

Is it nothing to have been, and to have been happy or miserable? Or is it a matter of no moment to think whether I have been one or the other? Do I delude myself, do I build upon a shadow or a dream, do I dress up in the gaudy garb of idleness and folly a pure fiction, with nothing answering to it in the universe of things and the records of truth, when I look back with fond delight or with tender regret to that which was at one time to me *my all*, when I revive the glowing image of some bright reality,

> 'The thoughts of which can never from my heart?'

Do I then muse on nothing, do I bend my eyes on nothing, when I turn back in fancy to 'those suns and skies so pure' that lighted up my early path? Is it to think of nothing, to set an idle value upon nothing, to think of all that has happened to me, and of all that can ever interest me? Or, to use the language of a fine poet (who is himself among my earliest and not least painful recollections) –

> 'What though the radiance which was once so bright
> Be now for ever vanish'd from my sight,
> Though nothing can bring back the hour
> Of glory in the grass, of splendour in the flow'r' –

yet am I mocked with a lie, when I venture to think of it? Or do I not drink in and breathe again the air of heavenly truth, when I but 'retrace its footsteps, and its skirts far off adore?' I cannot say with the same poet –

> 'And see how dark the backward stream,
> A little moment past so smiling' –

for it is the past that gives me most delight and most assurance of reality. What to me constitutes the great charm of the Confessions of Rousseau is their turning so much upon this feeling. He seems to gather up the past moments of his being like drops of honey-dew to distil a precious liquor from them; his alternate pleasures and pains are the bead-roll that he tells over, and piously worships; he makes a rosary of the flowers of hope and fancy that strewed his earliest years. When he begins the last of the Reveries of a Solitary Walker, '*Il y a aujourd'hui, jour des Pâques Fleuris, cinquante ans depuis que j'ai premier vu Madame Warens,*' what a yearning of the soul is implied in that short sentence! Was all that had happened to him, all that he had thought and felt in that sad interval of time, to be accounted nothing? Was that long, dim, faded retrospect of years happy or miserable – a blank that was not to make his eyes fail and his heart faint within him in trying to grasp all that had once filled it and that had since vanished, because it was not a prospect into futurity? Was he wrong in finding more to interest him in it than in the next fifty years – which he did not live to see; or if he had, what then? Would they have been worth thinking of, compared with the times of his youth, of his first meeting with Madame Warens, with those times which he has traced with such truth and pure delight 'in our heart's tables?' When 'all the life of life was flown,' was he not to live the first and best part of it over again, and once more be all that he then was? – Ye woods that crown the clear lone brow of Norman Court, why do I revisit ye so oft, and feel a soothing consciousness of your presence, but that your high tops waving in the wind recal to me the hours and years that are for ever fled; that ye renew in ceaseless murmurs the story of long-cherished hopes and bitter disappointment; that in your solitudes and tangled wilds I can wander and lose myself as I wander on and am lost in the solitude of my own heart; and that as your rustling branches give the loud blast to the waste below – borne on the thoughts of other years, I can look down with patient anguish at the cheerless desolation which I feel within! Without that face pale as the primrose with hyacinthine locks, for ever shunning and for ever haunting me, mocking my waking thoughts as in a dream; without that smile which my heart could never turn to scorn; without those eyes dark with their own lustre, still bent on mine, and drawing the soul into their liquid mazes like a sea of love; without that name trembling in fancy's ear; without that form gliding before me like Oread or Dryad in fabled groves, what should I do? how pass away the listless leaden-footed hours? Then wave, wave on, ye woods of Tuderley, and loft your high tops in the air; my sighs and vows uttered by your mystic voice breathe into me my former being, and enable me to bear the thing I am!

The Tenth Essay, 'On Living to One's-self', has this singular passage.

Even in the common affairs of life, in love, friendship, and marriage, how little security have we when we trust our happiness in the hands of others! Most of the friends I have seen have turned out the bitterest enemies or cold, uncomfortable acquaintance. Old companions are like meats served up too often, that lose their relish and their wholesomeness.

We hope that this is more dramatically than truly written. We recognise nothing like it in our own circle. We had always thought that Old Friends, and Old Wine were the best. – We should conjecture that Mr Hazlitt has been singularly unfortunate, or injudicious, in the choice of his acquaintance, did not one phenomenon stagger us. We every now & then encounter in his Essays with a *character*, apparently from the life, too mildly drawn for an enemy, too sharply for a friend. We suspect that Mr Hazlitt does not always play quite fairly with his associates. There is a class of critics – and he may be of them – who pry into men with 'too respective eyes.'[5] They will 'anatomize Regan',[6] when Cordelia would hardly bear such dissection. We are not acquainted with Mr Hazlitt's 'familiar faces',[7] but when we see certain Characters exposed & hung up, not in Satire – for the exaggerations of *that* cure themselves by their excess, as we make allowance for the over-charged features in a caricature – but certain poor whole-length figures dangling with all the *best & worst* of humanity about them displayed with cool and unsparing impartiality – Mr Hazlitt must excuse us if we cannot help suspecting some of them to be the shadows of defunct Friendships. – This would be a recipe indeed, a pretty sure one, for converting friends 'into bitterest enemies or cold, uncomfortable acquaintance'. – The most expert at drawing Characters, are the very persons most likely to be deceived in individual & home instances. They will seize an infirmity, which irritates them deservedly in a companion, and go on piling up every kindred weakness they have found by experience apt to coalesce with that failing (gathered from a thousand instances) till they have built up in their fancies an *Abstract*, widely differing indeed from their poor *concrete friend*! What blunders Steele, or Sterne, may not in this way have made *at home*! – But we forget. Our business is with books. We profess not, with Mr Hazlitt, to be Reviewers of Men. – We are willing to give our readers a specimen of what this writer can do, when the moody fit is off him. One of the pleasantest and lightest of his Essays is 'On People with one Idea'. We quote his first instance.

There is Major Cartwright: he has but one idea or subject of discourse, Parliamentary Reform. Now Parliamentary Reform is (as far as I know) a very good thing, a very good idea, and a very good subject to talk about; but why should it be the only one? To hear the worthy and gallant Major resume his favourite topic, is like law-business, or a person who has a suit in Chancery going on. Nothing can be attended to, nothing can be talked of but that. Now it is getting on, now again it is standing still; at one time the Master has promised to pass judgment by a certain day, at another he has put it off again and called for more papers, and both are equally reasons for speaking of it. Like the piece of packthread in the barrister's hands, he turns and twists it all ways, and cannot proceed a step without it. Some school-boys cannot read but in their own book: and the man of one idea cannot converse out of his own subject. Conversation it is not; but a sort of recital of the preamble of a bill, or a collection of grave arguments for a man's being of opinion with himself. It

would be well if there was anything of character, of eccentricity in all this; but
that is not the case. It is a political homily personified, a walking common-
place we have to encounter and listen to. It is just as if a man was to insist
on your hearing him go through the fifth chapter of the Book of Judges
every time you meet, or like the story of the Cosmogony in the Vicar of
Wakefield. It is a tune played on a barrel-organ. It is a common vehicle of
discourse into which they get and are set down when they please, without
any pains or trouble to themselves. Neither is it professional pedantry or
trading quackery: it has no excuse. The man has no more to do with the question which he saddles on all his hearers than you have. This is what makes
the matter hopeless. If a farmer talks to you about his pigs or his poultry, or
a physician about his patients, or a lawyer about his briefs, or a merchant
about stock, or an author about himself, you know how to account for this,
it is a common infirmity, you have a laugh at his expense, and there is no
more to be said. But here is a man who goes out of his way to be absurd,
and is troublesome by a romantic effort of generosity. You cannot say to
him, 'All this may be interesting to you, but I have no concern in it:' you
cannot put him off in that way. He retorts the Latin adage upon you – Nihil
humani a me alienum puto. He has got possession of a subject which is of universal and paramount interest (not 'a fee-grief, due to some single breast') –
and on that plea may hold you by the button as long as he chooses. His
delight is to harangue on what nowise regards himself: how then can you
refuse to listen to what as little amuses you? Time and tide wait for no man.
The business of the state admits of no delay. The question of Universal Suffrage and Annual Parliaments stands first on the order of the day – takes
precedence in its own right of every other question. Any other topic, grave
or gay, is looked upon in the light of impertinence, and sent to Coventry.
Business is an interruption; pleasure a digression from it. It is the question
before every company where the Major comes, which immediately resolves
itself into a committee of the whole world upon it, is carried on by means of
a perpetual virtual adjournment, and it is presumed that no other is entertained while this is pending – a determination which gives its persevering
advocate a fair prospect of expatiating on it to his dying day. As Cicero says
of study, it follows him into the country, it stays with him at home: it sits
with him at breakfast, and goes out with him to dinner. It is like a part of
his dress, of the costume of his person, without which he would be at a loss
what to do. If he meets you in the street, he accosts you with it as a form of
salutation: if you see him at his own house, it is supposed you come upon
that. If you happen to remark, 'It is a fine day, or the town is full,' it is
considered as a temporary compromise of the question; you are suspected of
not going the whole length of the principle. As Sancho, when reprimanded
for mentioning his homely favourite in the Duke's kitchen, defended himself
by saying – 'There I thought of Dapple, and there I spoke of him' – so the
true stickler for Reform neglects no opportunity of introducing the subject

wherever he is. Place its veteran champion under the frozen north, and he will celebrate sweet smiling Reform: place him under the mid-day Afric suns, and he will talk of nothing but Reform – Reform so sweetly smiling and so sweetly promising for the last forty years –

> *'Dulce ridentem Lalagen,*
> *Dulce loquentem!'*

This is all extremely clever, and about as true as it is necessary for such half-imaginary sketches to be. The veteran subject of it has had his name bandied to & fro, for praise & blame, the better part of a century, and has learned to stand harder knocks than these. He will laugh, we dare say, very heartily at this Chimaera of himself from the pen of a *brother-reformer*. We would venture a wager that the writer of it, with all his appearance of drawing from the life, never spent a day in company with the Major. We have passed many, & can assure the Essayist, that Major C— has many things in his head, and in his mouth too, besides Parliamentary Reform. We know that he is more solicitous to evade the question, than to obtrude it, in private company; and will chuse to turn the conversation purposely to topics of philology & polite literature, of which he is no common master. He will not shun a metaphysical point even if it come in his way, though he professes not to enter into that sort of science so deeply as Mr Hazlitt; and will discuss any point 'at sight' from history & chronology, his favourite subjects, down to the merits of his scarcely less darling Norfolk dumpling. We suspect that Mr Hazlitt knows nothing of the veteran beyond his political speeches, which to be sure are pretty monotonous upon one subject, and has carved the rest out of his own brain. But to deduce a man's general conversation from what falls from him in public meetings, expressly convened to discuss a particular topic, is about as good logic, as it would be in the case of another sort of *Reformer*, who, like Major C—, but in an humbler sphere, goes about professing to *remove nuisances* if we should infer, that the good man's whole discourse, at bed & board, in the ale-house & by the roadside, was confined to two cuckoo syllables, because in the exercise of his public function we had never heard him utter anything beyond Dust O!

The 'Character of Cobbett' (Sixth Essay) comes nearer the mark. It has the freedom of a sketch, and the truth of an elaborated portrait. Nothing is extenuated, nothing overdone. It is 'without o'erflowing full'.[8] It may be read with advantage by the partisans & opponents of the most extraordinary political personage that has appeared in modern times. It is too long to quote, too good for abridgment. We prefer closing our extracts with a portion of the Twelfth Essay, both for variety-sake, and because it seems no inappropriate conclusion to leave off with that which is ordinarily the latest of human actions – 'the last infirmity of common minds' [9] – the making of a Will. [Lamb quotes with omissions the passage beginning 'Few things shew the human character . . . that we came into it!']

We cannot take leave of this agreeable and spirited volume without bearing our decided testimony to Mr Hazlitt's general merits as a writer. He is (we have no hesitation in saying) one of the ablest prose-writers of the age. To an extraordinary power of original observation he adds an equal power of familiar and striking expression. There is a ground-work of patient and curious thinking in almost every one of these Essays, while the execution is in a high degree brilliant and animated. The train of reasoning or line of distinction on which he insists is often so fine as to escape common observation; at the same time that the quantity of picturesque and novel illustration is such as to dazzle and overpower common attention. He is however a writer perfectly free from affectation, and never rises into that tone of rapid and glowing eloquence of which he is a master, but when the occasion warrants it. Hence there is nothing more directly opposite to his usual style than what is understood by *poetical prose*. – If we were to hazard an analytical conjecture on this point, we should incline to think that Mr H. as a critic and an Essayist has blended two very different and opposite lines of study and pursuit, a life of internal reflection, and a life of external observation, together; or has, in other words, engrafted the Painter on the Metaphysician; and in our minds, the union, if not complete or in all respects harmonious, presents a result not less singular than delightful. If Mr H. criticises an author, he paints him. If he draws a character, he dissects it; and some of his characters 'look a little the worse' (as Swift says) 'for having the skin taken off'.[10] If he describes a feeling, he is not satisfied till he embodies it as a real sensation in all its individuality and with all the circumstances that give it interest. If he enters upon some distinction too subtle and recondite to be immediately understood, he relieves it by some palpable and popular illustration. In fact, he all along acts as his own interpreter, and is continually translating his thoughts out of their original metaphysical obscurity into the language of the senses and of common observation. This appears to us to constitute the excellence and to account for the defects of his writings. There is a display (to profusion) of various and striking powers; but they do not tend to the same object. The thought and the illustration do not always hang well together: the one puzzles, and the other startles. From this circumstance it is that to many people Mr Hazlitt appears an obscure and unconnected and to others a forced and extravagant writer. He may be said to paint caricatures on gauze or cobwebs; to explain the mysteries of the Cabbala by Egyptian hieroglyphics. Another fault is that he draws too entirely on his own resources. He never refers to the opinions of other authors (ancient or modern) or to the common opinions afloat on any subject, or if he does, it is to treat them with summary or elaborate contempt. Neither does he consider a subject in all its possible or most prominent bearings, but merely in those points (sometimes minute and extraneous, at other times more broad and general) in which it happens to have pressed close on his own mind or to have suggested some ingenious solution. He follows out his own view of a question, however, fearlessly and patiently; and puts the reader in possession without reserve of all he has thought upon it. There is no writer who seems to pay less attention to the common prejudices of the vulgar; or the common-places of the learned; and who has consequently given greater offence to the bigoted, the self-sufficient, and the dull. We have nothing to do with Mr Hazlitt as a controversial writer; and even as a critic, he is perhaps too much of a partisan, he is too eager and exclusive in his panegyrics or invectives; but as an Essayist, his writings can hardly fail to be read with general satisfaction and with the greatest by those who are most able to appreciate characteristic thought and felicitous expression.

LETTER OF ELIA
TO ROBERT SOUTHEY, ESQUIRE

SIR, – You have done me an unfriendly office,[1] without perhaps much considering what you were doing. You have given an ill name to my poor Lucubrations. In a recent Paper on Infidelity, you usher in a conditional commendation of them with an exception; which, preceding the encomium,[2] and taking up nearly the same space with it, must impress your readers with the notion, that the objectional parts in them are at least equal in quantity to the pardonable. The censure is in fact the criticism; the praise – a concession merely. Exceptions usually follow, to qualify praise or blame. But there stands your reproof, in the very front of your notice, in ugly characters, like some bugbear, to frighten all good Christians from purchasing. Through you I become an object of suspicion to preceptors of youth, and fathers of families. '*A book which wants only a sounder religious feeling to be as delightful as it is original.*' With no further explanation, what must your readers conjecture, but that my little volume is some vehicle for heresy or infidelity? The quotation which you honour me by subjoining, oddly enough, is of a character which bespeaks a temperament in the writer the very reverse of *that* your reproof goes to insinuate. Had you been taxing me with superstition, the passage would have been pertinent to the censure. Was it worth your while to go so far out of your way to affront the feelings of an old friend, and commit yourself by an irrelevant quotation, for the pleasure of reflecting upon a poor child, an exile at Genoa?[3]

I am at a loss what particular Essay you had in view (if my poor ramblings amount to that appellation) when you were in such a hurry to thrust in your objection, like bad news, foremost. – Perhaps the paper on 'Saying Graces' was the obnoxious feature. I have endeavoured there to rescue a voluntary duty – good in place, but never, as I remember, literally commanded – from the charge of an undecent formality. Rightly taken, Sir, that Paper was not against Graces, but Want of Grace; not against the ceremony, but the carelessness and slovenliness so often observed in the performance of it.

Or was it *that* on the 'New Year' – in which I have described the feelings of the merely natural man, on a consideration of the amazing change, which is supposable to take place on our removal from this fleshly scene? – If men would honestly confess their misgivings (which few men will) there are times when the strongest Christian of us, I believe, has reeled under questions of such staggering obscurity. I do not accuse you of this weakness. There are some who tremblingly reach out shaking hands to the guidance of Faith – others who stoutly venture into the dark (their Human Confidence their leader, whom they mistake for Faith); and, investing themselves beforehand with Cherubic wings, as they fancy, find their new robes as familiar, and fitting to the supposed growth and stature in godliness, as the coat they left off yesterday – Some whose hope totters upon crutches – Others who stalk into futurity upon stilts.

The contemplation of a Spiritual World, – which, without the addition of a misgiving conscience, is enough to shake some natures to their foundation – is smoothly got over by others, who shall float over the black billows, in their little boat of No-Distrust, as unconcernedly as over a summer sea. The difference is chiefly constitutional.

One man shall love his friends and his friends' faces; and, under the uncertainty of conversing with them again, in the same manner and familiar circumstances of sight, speech, &c. as upon earth – in a moment of no irreverent weakness – for a dream-while – no more – would be almost content, for a reward of a life of virtue (if he could ascribe such acceptance to his lame performances), to take up his portion with those he loved, and was made to love, in this good world, which he knows – which was created so lovely, beyond his deservings. Another, embracing a more exalted vision – so that he might receive indefinite additaments of power, knowledge, beauty, glory, &c. – is ready to forgo the re-cognition of humbler individualities of earth, and the old familiar faces. The shapings of our heavens are the modifications of our constitutions; and Mr Feeble Mind, or Mr Great Heart, is born in every one of us.

Some (and such have been accounted the safest divines) have shrunk from pronouncing upon the final state of any man; nor dare they pronounce the case of Judas to be desperate. Others (with stronger optics), as plainly as with the eye of flesh, shall behold a *given king* in bliss,[4] and a *given chamberlain* in torment; even to the eternising of a cast of the eye in the latter, his own self-mocked and good-humouredly-borne deformity on earth, but supposed to aggravate the uncouth and hideous expression of his pangs in the other place. That one man can presume so far, and that another would with shuddering disclaim confidences, is, I believe, an effect of the nerves purely.

If in either of these Papers, or elsewhere, I have been betrayed into some levities – not affronting the sanctuary, but glancing perhaps at some of the outskirts and extreme edges, the debateable land between the holy and profane regions – (for the admixture of man's inventions, twisting themselves with the name of religion itself, has artfully made it difficult to touch even the alloy, without, in some men's estimation, soiling the fine gold) – if I have sported within the purlieus of serious matter – it was, I dare say, a humour – be not startled, sir, – which I have unwittingly derived from yourself. You have all your life been making a jest of the Devil. Not of the scriptural meaning of that dark essence – personal or allegorical; for the nature is no where plainly delivered. I acquit you of intentional irreverence. But indeed you have made wonderfully free with, and been mighty pleasant upon, the popular idea and attributes of him. A noble Lord,[5] your brother Visionary, has scarcely taken greater liberties with the material keys, and merely Catholic notion of St Peter. You have flattered him in prose: you have chanted him in goodly odes. You have been his Jester; Volunteer Laureat, and self-elected Court Poet to Beëlzebub.

You have never ridiculed, I believe, what you thought to be religion, but you are always girding at what some pious, but perhaps mistaken folks, think to be so. For this reason I am sorry to hear that you are engaged upon a life of George Fox. I know you will fall into the error of intermixing some comic stuff with your seriousness. The Quakers tremble at the subject in your hands. The Methodists are as shy of you, upon account of *their* founder.[6] But, above all, our Popish brethren are most in your debt. The errors of that church have proved a fruitful source to your scoffing vein. Their Legend has been a Golden one to you. And here, your friends, Sir, have noticed a notable inconsistency. To the imposing rites, the solemn penances, devout austerities of that communion; the affecting though erring piety of their hermits; the silence and solitude of the Chartreux – their crossings, their holy waters – their Virgin, and their saints – to these, they say, you have been indebted for the best feelings, and the richest imagery, of your Epic poetry. You have drawn copious drafts upon Loretto. We thought at one time you were going post to Rome – but that in the facetious commentaries, which it is your custom to append so plentifully, and (some say) injudiciously, to your loftiest performances in this kind, you spurn the uplifted toe, which you but just now seemed to court; leave his holiness in the lurch; and show him a fair pair of Protestant heels under your Romish vestment. When we think you already at the wicket, suddenly a violent cross wind blows you transverse –

> Ten thousand leagues awry
> Then might we see
> Cowls, hoods, and habits, with their wearers, tost
> And flutter'd into rags; then reliques, beads,
> Indulgences, dispenses, pardons, bulls,
> The sport of winds.

You pick up pence by showing the hallowed bones, shrine, and crucifix; and you take money a second time by exposing the trick of them afterwards. You carry your verse to Castle Angelo[7] for sale in a morning; and, swifter than a pedlar can transmute his pack, you are at Canterbury with your prose ware before night.

Sir, is it that I dislike you in this merry vein? The very reverse. No countenance becomes an intelligent jest better than your own. It is your grave aspect, when you look awful upon your poor friends, which I would deprecate.

In more than one place, if I mistake not, you have been pleased to compliment me at the expense of my companions. I cannot accept your compliment at such a price. The upbraiding a man's poverty naturally makes him look about him, to see whether he be so poor indeed as he is presumed to be. You have put me upon counting my riches. Really, Sir, I did not know I was so wealthy in the article of friendships.[8] There is — , and — , whom you never heard of, but exemplary characters both, and excellent churchgoers; and N., mine and my father's friend for nearly half a century; and the enthusiast for Wordsworth's poetry, T. N. T., a little tainted with Socinianism, it is to be feared, but constant in his attachments, and a capital critic; and — , a sturdy old Athanasian, so that sets all to rights again; and W., the light, and warm-as-light-hearted, Janus of the London; and the translator of Dante, still a curate, modest and amiable C.; and Allan C., the large-hearted Scot; and P—r, candid and affectionate as his own poetry; and A—p, Coleridge's friend; and G—n, his more than friend; and Coleridge himself, the same to me still, as in those old evenings, when we used to sit and speculate (do you remember them, Sir?) at our old Salutation tavern, upon Pantisocracy[9] and golden days to come on earth; and W—th (why, Sir, I might drop my rent-roll here, such goodly farms and manors have I reckoned up already. In what possession has not this last name alone estated me? – but I will go on) – and M., the noble-minded kinsman, by wedlock, of W—th; and H. C. R., unwearied in the offices of a friend; and Clarkson, almost above the narrowness of that relation, yet condescending not seldom heretofore from the labours of his world-embracing charity to bless my humble roof; and the gall-less and single-minded Dyer; and the high-minded associate of Cook, the veteran Colonel, with his lusty heart still sending cartels of defiance to old Time; and, not least, W. A., the last and steadiest left to me of that little knot of whist-players, that used to assemble weekly, for so many years, at the Queen's Gate (you remember then, Sir?) and called Admiral Burney friend.

I will come to the point at once. I believe you will not make many exceptions to my associates so far. But I have purposely omitted some intimacies, which I do not yet repent of having contracted, with two gentlemen, diametrically opposed to yourself in principles. You will understand me to allude to the authors of Rimini and of the Table-Talk.[10] And first, of the former.

It is an error more particularly incident to persons of the correctest principles and habits, to seclude themselves from the rest of mankind, as from another species; and form into knots and clubs. The best people herding thus exclusively, are in danger of contracting a narrowness. Heat and cold, dryness and moisture, in the natural world do not fly asunder, to split the globe into sectarian parts and separations; but mingling, as they best may, correct the malignity of any single predominance. The analogy holds, I suppose, in the moral world. If all the good people were to ship themselves off to Terra Incognitas, what, in humanity's name, is to become of the refuse? If the persons, whom I have chiefly in view, have not pushed matters to this extremity yet, they carry them as far as they can go. Instead of mixing with the infidel and the freethinker – in the room of opening a negociation, to try at least to find out at which gate the error entered – they huddle close together, in a weak fear of infection, like that pusillanimous underling in Spenser –

> This is the wandering wood, this Error's den;
> A monster vile, whom God and man does hate:
> Therefore, I reed, beware. Fly, fly, quoth then
> The fearful Dwarf.

and, if they be writers in orthodox journals, addressing themselves only to the irritable passions of the unbeliever, – they proceed in a safe system of strengthening the strong hands, and confirming the valiant knees; of converting the already converted, and proselyting their own party. I am the more convinced of this from a passage in the very Treatise which occasioned this letter. It is where, having recommended to the doubter the writings of Michaelis and Lardner, you ride triumphant over the necks of all infidels, sceptics, and dissenters, from this time to the world's end, upon the wheels of two unanswerable deductions. I do not hold it meet to set down, in a Miscellaneous Compilation like this, such religious words as you have thought fit to introduce into the pages of a petulant Literary Journal. I therefore beg leave to substitute *numerals*, and refer to the Quarterly Review (for July) for filling of them up. 'Here,' say you, 'as in the history of 7, if these books are authentic, the events which they relate must be true; if they were written by 8, 9 is 10 and 11.' Your first deduction, if it means honestly, rests upon two identical propositions; though I suspect an unfairness in one of the terms, which this would not be quite the proper place for explicating. At all events, *you* have no cause to triumph; you have not been proving the premises, but refer for satisfaction therein to very long and laborious works, which may well employ the sceptic a twelvemonth or two to digest, before he can possibly be ripe for your conclusion. When he has satisfied himself about the premises, he will concede to you the inference, I dare say, most readily. – But your latter deduction, *viz*., that because 8 has written a book concerning 9, therefore 10 and 11 was certainly his meaning, is one of the most extraordinary conclusions *per saltum* [11] that I have had the good fortune to meet with. As far as 10 is verbally asserted in the writings, all sects must agree with you; but you cannot be ignorant of the many various ways in which the doctrine of the * * * * * * * * * has been understood, from a low figurative expression (with the Unitarians) up to the most mysterious actuality; in which highest sense alone you and your church take it. And for 11, that there is *no other possible conclusion* – to hazard this in the face of so many thousands of Arians and Socinians, &c., who have drawn so opposite a one, is such a piece of theological hardihood, as, I think, warrants me in concluding that, when you sit down to pen theology, you do not at all consider your opponents, but have in your eye, merely and exclusively, readers of the same way of thinking with yourself, and therefore have no occasion to trouble yourself with the quality of the logic, to which you treat them.

Neither can I think, if you had had the welfare of the poor child – over whose hopeless condition you whine so lamentably and (I must think) unseasonably – seriously at heart, that you could have taken the step of sticking him up *by name* – T. H. is as good as *naming* him – to perpetuate an outrage upon the parental feelings, as long as the Quarterly Review shall last. – Was it necessary to specify an individual case, and give to Christian compassion the appearance of a personal attack? Is this the way to conciliate unbelievers, or not rather to widen the breach irreparably?

I own I could never think so considerably of myself as to decline the society of an agreeable or worthy man upon difference of opinion only. The impediments and the facilitations to a sound belief are various and inscrutable as the heart of man. Some believe upon weak principles; others cannot feel the efficacy of the strongest. One of the most candid, most upright, and single-meaning men, I ever knew, was the late Thomas Holcroft. I believe he never said one thing and meant another, in his life; and, as near as I can guess, he never acted otherwise than with the most scrupulous attention to conscience. Ought we to wish the character false, for the sake of a hollow compliment to Christianity?

Accident introduced me to the acquaintance of Mr L. H. – and the experience of his many friendly qualities confirmed a friendship between us. You, who have been misrepresented yourself, I should hope, have not lent an idle ear to the calumnies which have been spread abroad respecting this gentleman. I was admitted to his household for some years, and do most solemnly aver that I believe him to be in his domestic relations as correct as any man. He chose an ill-judged subject[12] for a poem; the peccant humours of which have been visited on him tenfold by the artful use, which his adversaries have made, of an *equivocal term*. The subject itself was started by Dante, but better because brieflier treated of. But the crime of the Lovers, in the Italian and the English poet, with its aggravated enormity of circumstance, is not of a kind (as the critics of the latter well knew) with those conjunctions, for which Nature herself has provided no excuse, because no temptation. – It has nothing in common with the black horrors, sung by Ford and Massinger. The familiarising of it in the tale and fable may be for that reason incidentally more contagious. In spite of Rimini, I must look upon its author as a man of taste, and a poet. He is better than so, he is one of the most cordial-minded men I ever knew, and matchless as a fire-side companion. I mean not to affront or wound your feelings when I say that in his more genial moods, he has often reminded me of you. There is the same air of mild dogmatism – the same condescending to a boyish sportiveness – in both your conversations. His hand-writing is so much the same with your own, that I have opened more than one letter of his, hoping, nay, not doubting, but it was from you, and have been disappointed (he will bear with my saying so) at the discovery of my error. L. H. is unfortunate in holding some loose and not very definite speculations (for at times I think he hardly knows whither his premises would carry him) on marriage – the tenets, I conceive, of the Political Justice [13] carried a little further. For any thing I could discover in his practice, they have reference, like those, to some future possible condition of society, and not to the present times. But neither for these obliquities of thinking (upon which my own conclusions are as distant as the poles asunder) – nor for his political asperities and petulancies, which are wearing out with the heats and vanities of youth – did I select him for a friend; but for qualities which fitted him for that relation. I do not know whether I flatter myself with being the occasion, but certain it is, that, touched with some misgivings for sundry harsh things which he had written aforetime against our friend C.,[14] – before he left this country he sought a reconciliation with that gentleman (himself being his own introducer), and found it.

L. H. is now in Italy; on his departure to which land, with much regret I took my leave of him and his little family – seven of them, Sir, with their mother – and as kind a set of little people (T. H. and all), as affectionate children, as ever blessed a parent. Had you seen them, Sir, I think you could not have looked upon them as so many little Jonases – but rather as pledges of the vessel's safety, that was to bear such a freight of love.

I wish you would read Mr H.'s lines to that same T. H. 'six years old, during a sickness:' –

> Sleep breaks at last from out thee,
> My little patient boy –

(they are to be found on the 47th page of 'Foliage') – and ask yourself how far they are out of the spirit of Christianity. I have a letter from Italy, received but the other day, into which L. H. has put as much heart, and as many friendly yearnings after old associates, and native country, as, I think, paper can well hold. It would do you no hurt to give that the perusal also.

From the *other gentleman* I neither expect nor desire (as he is well assured) any such concessions as L. H. made to C. What hath soured him, and made him to suspect his friends of infidelity towards him, when there was no such matter, I know not. I stood well with him for fifteen years (the proudest of my life), and have ever spoke my full mind of him to some, to whom his panegyric must naturally be least tasteful. I never in thought swerved from him, I never betrayed him, I never slackened in my admiration of him, I was the same to him (neither better nor worse) though he could not see it, as in the days when he thought fit to trust me. At this instant, he may be preparing for me some compliment, above my deserts, as he has sprinkled many such among his admirable books, for which I rest his debtor; or, for any thing I know, or can guess to the contrary, he may be about to read a lecture on my weaknesses. He is welcome to them (as he was to my humble hearth), if they can divert a spleen, or ventilate a fit of sullenness. I wish he would not quarrel with the world at the rate he does; but the reconciliation must be effected by himself, and I despair of living to see that day. But, protesting against much that he has written, and some things which he chooses to do; judging him by his conversation which I enjoyed so long, and relished so deeply; or by his books, in those places where no clouding passion intervenes – I should belie my own conscience, if I said less, than that I think W. H. to be, in his natural and healthy state, one of the wisest and finest spirits breathing. So far from being ashamed of that intimacy, which was betwixt us, it is my boast that I was able for so many years to have preserved it entire; and I think I shall go to my grave without finding, or expecting to find, such another companion. But I forget my manners – you will pardon me, Sir – I return to the correspondence. –

Sir, you were pleased (you know where) to invite me to a compliance with the wholesome forms and doctrines of the Church of England. I take your advice with as much kindness, as it was meant. But I must think the invitation rather more kind than seasonable. I am a Dissenter. The last sect, with which you can remember me to have made common profession, were the Unitarians. You would think it not very pertinent, if (fearing that all was not well with you), I were gravely to invite you (for a remedy) to attend with me a course of Mr Belsham's Lectures [15] at Hackney. Perhaps I have scruples to some of your forms and doctrines. But if I come, am I secure of civil treatment? – The last time I was in any of your places of worship was on Easter Sunday last. I had the satisfaction of listening to a very sensible sermon of an argumentative turn, delivered with great propriety, by one of your bishops. The place was Westminster Abbey. As such religion, as I have, has always acted on me more by way of sentiment than argumentative process, I was not unwilling, after sermon ended, by no unbecoming transition, to pass over to some serious feelings, impossible to be disconnected from the sight of those old tombs, &c. But, by whose order I know not, I was debarred that privilege even for so short a space as a few minutes; and turned, like a dog or some profane person, out into the common street;

with feelings, which I could not help, but not very congenial to the day or the discourse. I do not know that I shall ever venture myself again into one of your Churches.

You had your education at Westminster; and doubtless among those dim aisles and cloisters, you must have gathered much of that devotional feeling in those young years, on which your purest mind feeds still – and may it feed! The antiquarian spirit, strong in you, and gracefully blending ever with the religious, may have been sown in you among those wrecks of splendid mortality. You owe it to the place of your education; you owe it to your learned fondness for the architecture of your ancestors; you owe it to the venerableness of your ecclesiastical establishment, which is daily lessened and called in question through these practices – to speak aloud your sense of them; never to desist raising your voice against them, till they be totally done away with and abolished; till the doors of Westminster Abbey be no longer closed against the decent, though low-in-purse, enthusiast, or blameless devotee, who must commit an injury against his family economy, if he would be indulged with a bare admission within its walls. You owe it to the decencies, which you wish to see maintained in its impressive services, that our Cathedral be no longer an object of inspection to the poor at those times only, in which they must rob from their attendance on the worship every minute which they can bestow upon the fabrick. In vain the public prints have taken up this subject, in vain such poor nameless writers as myself express their indignation. A word from you, Sir – a hint in your Journal – would be sufficient to fling open the doors of the Beautiful Temple again, as we can remember them when we were boys. At that time of life, what would the imaginative faculty (such as it is) in both of us, have suffered, if the entrance to so much reflection had been obstructed by the demand of so much silver! – If we had scraped it up to gain an occasional admission (as we certainly should have done) would the sight of those old tombs have been as impressive to us (while we had been weighing anxiously prudence against sentiment) as when the gates stood open, as those of the adjacent Park; when we could walk in at any time, as the mood brought us, for a shorter or longer time, as *that* lasted? Is the being shown over a place the same as silently for ourselves detecting the genius of it? In no part of our beloved Abbey now can a person find entrance (out of service time) under the sum of *two shillings*. The rich and the great will smile at the anticlimax, presumed to lie in those two short words. But you can tell them, Sir, how much quiet worth, how much capacity for enlarged feeling, how much taste and genius, may coexist, especially in youth, with a purse incompetent to this demand. – A respected friend of ours, during his late visit to the metropolis, presented himself for admission to Saint Paul's. At the same time a decently clothed man, with as decent a wife, and child, were bargaining for the same indulgence. The price was only two-pence each person. The poor but decent man hesitated, desirous to go in; but there were three of them, and he turned away reluctantly. Perhaps he wished to have seen the tomb of Nelson. Perhaps the Interior of the Cathedral was his object. But in the state of his finances, even sixpence might reasonably seem too much. Tell the Aristocracy of the country (no man can do it more impressively); instruct them of what value these insignificant pieces of money, these minims to their sight, may be to their humbler brethren. Shame these Sellers out of the Temple. Show the poor, that you can sometimes think of them in some other light than as mutineers and mal-contents. Conciliate them by such kind methods to their superiors, civil and ecclesiastical. Stop the mouths of the railers; and suffer your old friends, upon the old terms, again to honour and admire you. Stifle not the suggestions of your better nature with the stale evasion, that an indiscriminate admission would expose the Tombs to violation. Remember your boy-days. Did you ever see, or hear, of a mob in the Abbey, while it was free to all? Do the rabble come there, or trouble their heads about such speculations? It is all that you can do to drive them into your churches; they do not voluntarily offer themselves. They have, alas! no passion for antiquities; for tomb of king or prelate, sage or poet. If they had, they would be no longer the rabble.

For forty years that I have known the Fabrick, the only well-attested charge of violation adduced, has been – a ridiculous dismemberment committed upon the effigy of that amiable spy, Major Andre. And is it for this – the wanton mischief of some schoolboy, fired perhaps with raw notions of Transatlantic Freedom – or the remote possibility of such a mischief occurring again, so easily to be prevented by stationing a constable within the walls, if the vergers are incompetent to the duty – is it upon such wretched pretences, that the people of England are made to pay a new Peter's Pence, so long abrogated; or must content themselves with contemplating the ragged Exterior of their Cathedral? The mischief was done about the time that you were a scholar there. Do you know any thing about the unfortunate relic? – can you help us in this emergency to find the nose? – or can you give Chantry a notion (from memory) of its pristine life and vigour? I am willing for peace's sake to subscribe my guinea towards the restoration of the lamented feature.

I am, Sir, Your humble servant,
ELIA.

(*London Magazine*, October 1823)

READERS AGAINST THE GRAIN

NO one can pass through the streets, alleys, and blindest thoroughfares of this Metropolis, without surprise at the number of shops opened everywhere for the sale of cheap publications – not blasphemy and sedition – nor altogether flimsy periodicals, though the latter abound to a surfeit – but I mean fair reprints of good old books. Fielding, Smollett, the Poets, Historians, are daily becoming accessible to the purses of poor people. I cannot behold this result from the enlargement of the reading public without congratulations to my country. But as every blessing has its wrong side, it is with aversion I behold springing up with this phenomenon a race of *Readers against the grain*. Young men who thirty years ago would have been play-goers, punch-drinkers, cricketers, etc. with one accord are now – Readers! – a change in some respects, perhaps, salutary; but I liked the old way best. Then people read because they liked reading. He must have been indigent indeed, and, as times went then, probably unable to enjoy a book, who from one little circulating library or another (those slandered benefactions to the public) could not pick out an odd volume to satisfy the intervals of the workshop and the desk. Then, if a man told you that he 'loved reading mightily, but had no books,' you might be sure that in the first assertion at least he was mistaken. Neither had he, perhaps, the materials that should enliven a punch-bowl in his own cellar; but if the rogue loved his liquor, he would quickly find out where the arrack,[1] the lemons, and the sugar dwelt – he would speedily find out the circulating shop for them. I will illustrate this from my own observation.

It may detract a little from the gentility of your columns when I tell your Readers that I am – what I hinted at in my last – a Bank Clerk. Three-and-thirty years ago, when I took my first station at the desk, out of as many fellows in office one or two there were that had read a little. One could give a pretty good account of the *Spectator*. A second knew *Tom Jones*. A third recommended *Telemachus*. One went so far as to quote *Hudibras*, and was looked on as a phenomenon. But the far greater number neither cared for books, nor affected to care. They were, as I said, in their leisure hours, cricketers, punch-drinkers, play-goers, and the rest. Times are altered now. We are all readers; our young men are split up into so many book-clubs, knots of literati; we criticize; we read the *Quarterly* and *Edinburgh*, I assure you; and instead of the old, honest, unpretending literature so becoming to our profession – we read and *judge* of everything. I have something to do in these book-clubs, and know the trick and mystery of it. Every new publication that is likely to make a noise, must be had at any rate. By some they are devoured with avidity. These would have been readers in the old time I speak of. The only loss is, that for the good old reading of Addison or Fielding's days is substituted that never-ending flow of thin novelties which are kept up like a ball, leaving no possible time for better things, and threatening in the issue to bury or sweep away from the earth the memory of their nobler predecessors. We read to say that we have read. No reading can keep pace with the writing of this age, but we pant and toil after it as fast as we can. I smile to see an honest lad, who ought to be at trap-ball,[2] labouring up hill against this giant load, taking his toil for a pleasure, and with that utter incapacity for reading which *betrays itself by a certain silent movement of the lips when the reader reads to himself,* undertaking the infinite contents of fugitive poetry, or travels, what not – to see them with their snail-pace undertaking so vast a journey as might make faint a giant's speed; keeping a volume, which a real reader would get through in an hour, three, four, five, six days, and returning it with the last leaf but one folded down. These are your readers against the grain, who yet *must* read or be thought nothing of – who, crawling through a book with tortoise-pace, go creeping to the next Review to learn what they shall say of it. Upon my soul, I pity the honest fellows mightily. The self-denials of virtue are nothing to the patience of these self-tormentors. If I hate one day before another, it is the accursed first day of the month, when a load of periodicals is ushered in and distributed to feed the reluctant monster. How it gapes and takes in its prescribed diet, as little savoury as that which Daniel ministered to that Apocryphal dragon,[3] and not more wholesome! Is there no stopping the eternal wheels of the Press for a half century or two, till the nation recover its senses? Must we *magazine* it and *review* at this sickening rate for ever? Shall we never again read to be *amused?* but to judge, to criticize, to talk about it and about it? Farewell, old honest delight taken in books not quite contemporary, before this plague-token of modern endless novelties broke out upon us – farewell to reading for its own sake!

Rather than follow in the train of this insatiable monster of modern reading, I would forswear my spectacles, play at put, mend pens, kill fleas, stand on one leg, shell peas, or do whatsoever ignoble diversion you shall put me to. Alas! I am hurried on in the vortex. I die of new books, or the everlasting talk about them. I faint of Longmans. I sicken of the Constables. Blackwood and Cadell[4] have me by the throat.

I will go and relieve myself with a page of honest John Bunyan, or Tom Brown. Tom anybody will do, so long as they are not of this whiffling century.

Your Old-fashioned Correspondent
Lepus.

(*New Times*, 13 January 1825)

A VISION OF HORNS

MY thoughts had been engaged last evening in solving the problem, why in all times and places the *horn* has been agreed upon as the symbol, or honourable badge, of married men. Moses's horn, the horn of Ammon, of Amalthea, and a cornucopia of legends besides, came to my recollection, but afforded no satisfactory solution, or rather involved the question in deeper obscurity. Tired with the fruitless chase of inexplicant analogies, I fell asleep, and dreamed in this fashion.

Methought certain scales or films fell from my eyes, which had hitherto hindered these little tokens from being visible. I was somewhere in the Cornhill (as it might be termed) of some Utopia. Busy citizens jostled each other, as they may do in our streets, with care (the care of making a penny) written upon their foreheads; and *something else*, which is rather imagined, than distinctly imaged, upon the brows of my own friends and fellow-townsmen.

In my first surprise I supposed myself gotten into some forest – Arden, to be sure, or Sherwood; but the dresses and deportment, all civic, forbade me to continue in that delusion. Then a scriptural thought crossed me (especially as there were nearly as many Jews as Christians among them), whether it might not be the Children of Israel going up to besiege Jericho. I was undeceived of both errors by the sight of many faces which were familiar to me. I found myself strangely (as it will happen in dreams) at one and the same time in an unknown country, with known companions. I met old friends, not with new faces, but with their old faces oddly adorned in front, with each man a certain corneous excrescence. Dick Mitis, the little cheesemonger in St *'s Passage, was the first that saluted me, with his hat off – you know Dick's way to a customer – and, I not being aware of him, he thrust a strange beam into my left eye, which pained and grieved me exceedingly; but, instead of apology, he only grinned and fleered in my face, as much as to say, 'It is the custom of the country,' and passed on.

I had scarce time to send a civil message to his lady, whom I have always admired as a pattern of a wife, – and do indeed take Dick and her to be a model of conjugal agreement and harmony, – when I felt an ugly smart in my neck, as if something had gored it behind, and turning round, it was my old friend and neighbour, Dulcet, the confectioner, who, meaning to be pleasant, had thrust his protuberance right into my nape, and seemed proud of his power of offending.

Now I was assailed right and left, till in my own defence I was obliged to walk sideling and wary, and look about me, as you guard your eyes in London streets; for the horns thickened, and came at me like the ends of umbrellas poking in one's face.

I soon found that these towns-folk were the civillest best-mannered people in the world, and that if they had offended at all, it was entirely owing to their blindness. They do not know what dangerous weapons they protrude in front, and will stick their best friends in the eye with provoking complacency. Yet the best of it is, they can see the beams on their neighbours' foreheads, if they are as small as motes, but their own beams they can in no wise discern.

There was little Mitis, that I told you I just encountered – he has simply (I speak of him at home in his own shop) the smoothest forehead in his own conceit – he will stand you a quarter of an hour together contemplating the serenity of it in the glass, before he begins to shave himself in a morning – yet you saw what a desperate gash he gave me.

Desiring to be better informed of the ways of this extraordinary people, I applied myself to a fellow of some assurance, who (it appeared) acted as a sort of interpreter to strangers – he was dressed in a military uniform, and strongly resembled Colonel — , of the guards; – and 'pray, Sir,' said I, 'have all the inhabitants of your city these troublesome excrescences? I beg pardon; I see you have none. You perhaps are single.' 'Truly, sir,' he replied with a smile, 'for the most part we have, but not all alike. There are some, like Dick, that sport but one tumescence. Their ladies have been tolerably faithful – have confined themselves to a single aberration or so – these we calls Unicorns. Dick, you must know, is my Unicorn. [He spoke this with an air of invincible assurance.] Then we have Bicorns, Tricorns, and so on up to Millecorns. [Here methought I crossed and blessed myself in my dream.] Some again we have – there goes one – you see how happy the rogue looks – how he walks smiling and perking up his face, as if he thought himself the only man. He is not married yet, but on Monday next he leads to the altar the accomplished widow Dacres, relict of our late sheriff.'

'I see, Sir,' said I, 'and observe that he is happily free from the national *goitre* (let me call it), which distinguishes most of your countrymen.'

'Look a little more narrowly,' said my conductor.

I put on my spectacles; and observing the man a little more diligently, above his forehead I could mark a thousand little twinkling shadows dancing the hornpipe, little hornlets, and rudiments of horn, of a soft and pappy consistence (for I handled some of them), but which, like coral out of water, my guide informed me would infallibly stiffen and grow rigid within a week or two from the expiration of his bachelorhood.

Then I saw some horns strangely growing out behind, and my interpreter explained these to be married men whose wives had conducted themselves with infinite propriety since the period of their marriage, but were thought to have antedated their good men's titles, by certain liberties they had indulged themselves in, prior to the ceremony. This kind of gentry wore their horns backwards, as has been said, in the fashion of the old pig-tails; and as there was nothing obtrusive or ostentatious in them, nobody took any notice of it.

Some had pretty little budding antlers, like the first essays of a young faun. These, he told me, had wives, whose affairs were in a hopeful way, but not quite brought to a conclusion.

Others had nothing to show, only by certain red angry marks and swellings in their foreheads, which itched the more they kept rubbing and chafing them; it was to be hoped that something was brewing.

I took notice that every one jeered at the rest, only none took notice of the sea-captains; yet these were as well provided with their tokens as the best among them. This kind of people, it seems, taking their wives upon so contingent tenures, their lot was considered as nothing but natural, – so they wore their marks without impeachment, as they might carry their cockades,[1] and nobody respected them a whit the less for it.

I observed, that the more sprouts grew out of a man's head, the less weight they seemed to carry with them; whereas, a single token would now and then appear to give the wearer some uneasiness. This shows that use is a great thing.

Some had their adornings gilt, which needs no explanation; while others, like musicians, went sounding theirs before them – a sort of music which I thought might very well have been spared.

It was pleasant to see some of the citizens encounter between themselves; how they smiled in their sleeves at the shock they received from their neighbour, and none seemed conscious of the shock which their neighbour experienced in return.

Some had great corneous stumps, seemingly torn off and bleeding.

These, the interpreter warned me, were husbands who had retaliated upon their wives, and the badge was in equity divided between them.

While I stood discerning of these things, a slight tweak on my cheek unawares, which brought tears into my eyes, introduced to me my friend Placid, between whose lady and a certain male cousin, some idle flirtations I remember to have heard talked of; but that was all. He saw he had somehow hurt me, and asked my pardon with that round unconscious face of his, and looked so tristful and contrite for his no-offence, that I was ashamed for the man's penitence. Yet I protest it was but a scratch. It was the least little hornet of a horn that could be framed. 'Shame on the man,' I secretly exclaimed, 'who could thrust so much as the value of a hair into a brow so unsuspecting and inoffensive. What then must they have to answer for, who plant great, monstrous, timber-like, projecting antlers upon the heads of those whom they call their friends, when a puncture of this atomical tenuity made my eyes to water at this rate. All the pincers at Surgeons' Hall cannot pull out for Placid that little hair.'

I was curious to know what became of these frontal excrescences when the husbands died; and my guide informed me that the chemists in their country made a considerable profit by them, extracting from them certain subtile essences: – and then I remembered, that nothing was so efficacious in my own for restoring swooning matrons, and wives troubled with the vapours, as a strong sniff or two at the composition, appropriately called hartshorn – far beyond *sal volatile*.

Then also I began to understand, why a man, who is the jest of the company, is said to be the butt – as much as to say, such a one butteth with the horn.

I inquired if by no operation these wens were ever extracted; and was told that there was indeed an order of dentists, whom they call canonists in their language, who undertook to restore the forehead to its pristine smoothness; but that ordinarily it was not done without much cost and trouble; and when they succeeded in plucking out the offending part it left a painful void, which could not be filled up; and that many patients who had submitted to the excision, were eager to marry again, to supply with a good second antler the baldness and deformed gap left by the extraction of the former, as men losing their natural hair substitute for it a less becoming periwig.

Some horns I observed beautifully taper, smooth, and (as it were) flowering. These I understand were the portions brought by handsome women to their spouses; and I pitied the rough, homely, unsightly deformities on the brows of others, who had been deceived by plain and ordinary partners. Yet the latter I observed to be by far the most common – the solution of which I leave to the natural philosopher.

One tribute of married men I particularly admired at, who, instead of horns, wore, engrafted on their forehead, a sort of horn-book. 'This,' quoth my guide, 'is the greatest mystery in our country, and well worth an explanation. You must know that all infidelity is not of the senses. We have as well intellectual, as material, wittols.[2] These, whom you see decorated with the Order of the Book – are triflers, who encourage about their wives' presence the society of your men of genius (their good friends, as they call them) – literary disputants, who ten to one out-talk the poor husband, and commit upon the understanding of the woman a violence and estrangement in the end, little less painful than the coarser sort of alienation. Whip me these knaves – [my conductor here expressed himself with a becoming warmth] – whip me them, I say, who with no excuse from the passions, in cold blood seduce the minds, rather than the persons, of their friends' wives; who, for the tickling pleasure of hearing themselves prate, dehonestate[3] the intellects of married women, dishonouring the husband in what should be his most sensible part. If I must be — [here he used a plain word] let it be by some honest sinner like myself, and not by one of these gad-flies, these debauchers of the understanding, these flattery-buzzers.' He was going on in this manner, and I was getting insensibly pleased with my friend's manner (I had been a little shy of him at first), when the dream suddenly left me, vanishing – as Virgil speaks – through the gate of Horn.

ELIA.

(*London Magazine*, January 1825)

THE ILLUSTRIOUS DEFUNCT 3272/

> Nought but a blank remains, a dead void space,
> A step of life that promised such a race. – DRYDEN

NAPOLEON has now sent us back from the grave sufficient echoes of his living renown: the twilight of posthumous fame has lingered long enough over the spot where the sun of his glory set; and his name must at length repose in the silence, if not in the darkness of night. In this busy and evanescent scene, other spirits of the age are rapidly snatched away, claiming our undivided sympathies and regrets, until in turn they yield to some newer and more absorbing grief. Another name is now added to the list of the mighty departed, a name whose influence upon the hopes and fears, the fates and fortunes of our countrymen, has rivalled, and perhaps eclipsed that of the defunct 'child and champion of Jacobinism,' while it is associated with all the sanctions of legitimate government, all the sacred authorities of social order and our most holy religion. We speak of one, indeed, under whose warrant heavy and incessant contributions were imposed upon our fellow-citizens, but who exacted nothing without the signet and sign-manual of most devout Chancellors of the Exchequer. Not to dally longer with the sympathies of our readers, we think it right to premonish them that we are composing an epicedium[2] upon no less distinguished a personage than the Lottery, whose last breath, after many penultimate puffs, has been sobbed forth by sorrowing contractors, as if the world itself were about to be converted into a blank. There is a fashion of eulogy, as well as of vituperation; and though the Lottery stood for some time in the latter predicament, we hesitate not to assert that '*multis ille bonis flebilis occidit.*'[3] Never have we joined in the senseless clamour which condemned

---

* Since writing this article, we have been informed that the object of our funeral-oration is not definitively dead, but only moribund.[1] So much the better; we shall have an opportunity of granting the request made to Walter by one of the children in the wood, and 'kill him two times.' The Abbé de Vertot having a siege to write, and not receiving the materials in time, composed the whole from his invention. Shortly after its completion, the expected documents arrived, when he threw them aside, exclaiming – 'You are of no use to me now; I have carried the town.'

the only tax whereto we became voluntary contributors, the only re-source which gave the stimulus without the danger or infatuation of gambling, the only alembic which in these plodding days sublimised our imaginations, and filled them with more delicious dreams than ever flitted athwart the sensorium of Alnaschar.[4]

Never can the writer forget when, as a child, he was hoisted upon a servant's shoulder in Guildhall, and looked down upon the installed and solemn pomp of the then drawing Lottery. The two awful cabinets of iron, upon whose massive and mysterious portals, the royal initials were gorgeously emblazoned, as if after having deposited the unfulfilled prophecies within, the King himself had turned the lock and still retained the key in his pocket; – the blue-coat boy,[5] with his naked arm, first converting the invisible wheel, and then diving into the dark recess for a ticket; – the grave and reverend faces of the commissioners eyeing the announced number; – the scribes below calmly committing it to their huge books; – the anxious countenances of the surrounding populace, while the giant figures of Gog and Magog, like presiding deities, looked down with a grim silence upon the whole proceeding, – constituted altogether a scene, which combined with the sudden wealth supposed to be lavished from those inscrutable wheels, was well calculated to impress the imagination of a boy with reverence and amazement. Jupiter, seated between the two fatal urns of good and evil, the blind Goddess with her cornucopia, the Parcæ wielding the distaff, the thread of life, and the abhorred shears, seemed but dim and shadowy abstractions of myth-ology, when I had gazed upon an assemblage exercising, as I dreamt, a not less eventful power, and all presented to me in palpable and living operation. Reason and experience, ever at their old spiteful work of catching and destroying the bubbles which youth delighted to follow, have indeed dissipated much of this illusion, but my mind so far retained the influence of that early impression, that I have ever since continued to deposit my humble offerings at its shrine whenever the ministers of the Lottery went forth with type and trumpet to announce its periodical dispensations; and though nothing has been doled out to me from its undiscerning coffers but blanks, or those more vexatious tantalizers of the spirit, denominated small prizes, yet do I hold myself largely indebted to this most generous diffuser of universal happiness. Ingrates that we are! are we to be thankful for no benefits that are not palpable to sense, to recognise no favours that are not of marketable value, to acknowledge no wealth unless it can be counted with the five fingers? If we admit the mind to be the sole depositary of genuine joy, where is the bosom that has not been elevated into a temporary elysium by the magic of the Lottery? Which of us has not converted his ticket, or even his sixteenth share of one, into a nest-egg of Hope, upon which he has sate brooding in the secret roosting-places of his heart, and hatched it into a thousand fantastical apparitions?

What a startling revelation of the passions if all the aspirations engendered by the Lottery could be made manifest! Many an impecuniary epicure has gloated over his locked-up warrant for future wealth, as a means of realizing the dream of his namesake in the 'Alchemist,'[6] –

> My meat shall all come in in Indian shells, –
> Dishes of agate set in gold, and studded
> With emeralds, sapphires, hyacinths, and rubies;
> The tongues of carps, dormice, and camel's heels
> Boiled i' the spirit of Sol, and dissolved in pearl,
> (Apicius' diet 'gainst the epilepsy;)
> And I will eat these broths with spoons of amber,
> Headed with diamant and carbuncle. –
> My footboy shall eat pheasants, calvered salmons,
> Knots, godwits, lampreys; I myself will have
> The beards of barbels served: – instead of salads
> Oil'd mushrooms, and the swelling unctuous paps
> Of a fat pregnant sow, newly cut off.
> Dress'd with an exquisite and poignant sauce,
> For which I'll say unto my cook – 'There's gold,
> Go forth, and be a knight.'

Many a doating lover has kissed the scrap of paper whose promissory shower of gold was to give up to him his otherwise unattainable Danaë: Nimrods have transformed the same narrow symbol into a saddle, by which they have been enabled to bestride the backs of peerless hunters; while nymphs have metamorphosed its Protean form into –

> Rings, gaudes, conceits,
> Knacks, trifles, nosegays, sweetmeats,

and all the braveries of dress, to say nothing of the obsequious husband, the two-footman'd carriage, and the opera-box. By the simple charm of this numbered and printed rag, gamesters have, for a time at least, recovered their losses, spendthrifts have cleared off mortgages from their estates, the imprisoned debtor has leapt over his lofty boundary of circumscription and restraint, and revelled in all the joys of liberty and fortune; the cottage walls have swelled out into more goodly proportion than those of Baucis and Philemon; poverty has tasted the luxuries of competence, labour has lolled at ease in a perpetual arm-chair of idleness, sickness has been bribed into banishment, life has been invested with new charms, and death deprived of its former terrors. Nor have the affections been less gratified than the wants, appetites, and ambitions of mankind. By the conjurations of the same potent spell, kindred have lavished anticipated benefits upon one another, and charity upon all. Let it be termed a delusion; a fool's paradise is better than the wise man's Tartarus: be it branded as an Ignis fatuus,[7] it was at least a benevolent one, which instead of beguiling its followers into swamps, caverns, and pitfalls, allured them on with all the blandishments of enchantment to a garden of Eden, an ever-blooming elysium of delight. True, the pleasures it bestowed were evanescent, but which of our joys are permanent? and who so inexperienced as not to know that anticipation is always of higher relish than reality, which strikes a balance both in our sufferings and enjoyments. 'The fear of ill exceeds the ill we fear,' and fruition, in the same proportion, invariably falls short of hope. 'Men are but children of a larger growth,' who may amuse themselves for a long time in gazing at the reflection of the moon in the water, but, if they jump in to grasp it, they may grope for ever, and only get the farther from their object. He is the wisest who keeps feeding upon the future, and refrains as long as possible from undeceiving himself, by converting his pleasant speculations into disagreeable certainties.

The true mental epicure always purchased his ticket early, and postponed enquiry into its fate to the last possible moment, during the whole of which intervening period he had an imaginary twenty thousand locked up in his desk, – and was not this well worth all the money? Who would scruple to give twenty pounds interest for even the ideal enjoyment of as many thousands during two or three months? '*Crede quod habes, et habes,*'[8] and the usufruct of such a capital is surely not dear at such a price. Some years ago, a gentleman in passing along Cheapside saw the figures 1069, of which number he was the sole proprietor, flaming on the window of a lottery office as a capital prize. Somewhat flurried by this discovery, not less welcome than unexpected, he resolved to walk round St Paul's that he might consider in what way to communicate the happy tidings to his wife and family; but, upon repassing the shop, he observed that the number was altered to 10,069, and upon inquiry, had the mortification to learn that his ticket was a blank, and had only been stuck up in the window by a mistake of the clerk. This effectually calmed his agitation, but he always speaks of himself as having once possessed twenty thousand pounds, and maintains that his ten-minutes' walk round St Paul's was worth ten times the purchase-money of the ticket. A prize thus obtained, has, moreover, this special advantage; – it is beyond the reach of fate, it cannot be squandered, bankruptcy cannot lay siege to it, your friends cannot pull it down, nor enemies blow it up; it bears a charmed life, and none of woman born can break its integrity, even by the dissipation of a single fraction. Show me the property in these perilous times that is equally compact and impregnable. We can no longer become enriched for a quarter of an hour; we can no longer succeed in such splendid failures; all our chances of making such a miss have vanished with the last of the Lotteries.

Life will now become a flat, prosaic routine of matter-of-fact, and sleep itself, erst so prolific of numerical configurations and mysterious stimulants to lottery adventure, will be disfurnished of its figures and figments. People will cease to harp upon the one lucky number suggested in a dream, and which forms the exception, while they are scrupulously silent upon the ten thousand falsified dreams which constitute the rule. Morpheus will stifle Cocker with a handful of poppies, and our pillows will be no longer haunted by the book of numbers.

And who, too, shall maintain the art and mystery of puffing, in all its pristine glory, when the lottery professors shall have abandoned its cultivation? They were the first, as they will assuredly be the last, who fully developed the resources of that ingenious art; who cajoled and decoyed the most suspicious and wary reader into a perusal of their advertisements by devices of endless variety and cunning: who baited their lurking schemes with midnight murders, ghost stories, crim-cons,[9] bon-mots, balloons, dreadful catastrophes, and every diversity of joy and sorrow, to catch newspaper-gudgeons. Ought not such talents to be encouraged? Verily the abolitionists have much to answer for!

And now, having established the felicity of all those who gained imaginary prizes, let us proceed to show that the equally numerous class who were presented with real blanks, have not less reason to consider themselves happy. Most of us have cause to be thankful for that which is bestowed, but we have all, probably, reason to be still more grateful for that which is withheld, and more especially for our being denied the sudden possession of riches. In the Litany, indeed, we call upon the Lord to deliver us 'in all time of our wealth;' but how few of us are sincere in deprecating such a calamity! Massinger's Luke, and Ben Jonson's Sir Epicure Mammon, and Pope's Sir Balaam, and our own daily observation, might convince us that the devil 'now tempts by making rich, not making poor.' We may read in the Guardian a circumstantial account of a man who was utterly ruined by gaining a capital prize: – we may recollect what Dr Johnson said to Garrick, when the latter was making a display of his wealth at Hampton Court, – 'Ah, David! David! these are the things that make a death-bed terrible;' – we may recall the Scripture declaration, as to the difficulty a rich man finds in entering into the kingdom of Heaven, and combining all these denunciations against opulence, let us heartily congratulate one another upon our lucky escape from the calamity of a twenty or thirty thousand pound prize! The fox in the fable, who accused the unattainable grapes of sourness, was more of a philosopher than we are generally willing to allow. He was an adept in that species of moral alchemy, which turns every thing to gold, and converts disappointment itself into a ground of resignation and content. Such we have shown to be the great lesson inculcated by the Lottery when rightly contemplated; and if we might parody M. de Chateaubriand's jingling expression, – '*le Roi est mort: vive le Roi*,' we should be tempted to exclaim, 'The Lottery is no more – long live the Lottery!'

(*New Monthly Magazine*, January 1825)

MANY FRIENDS

UNFORTUNATE is the lot of that man, who can look round about the wide world, and exclaim with truth, *I have no friend!* Do you know any such lonely sufferer? For mercy sake send him to me. I can afford him plenty. He shall have them good, cheap. I have enough and to spare. Truly society is the balm of human life. But you may take a surfeit from sweetest odours administered to satiety. Hear my case, dear *Variorum*,[1] and pity me. I am an elderly gentleman – not old – a sort of middle-aged-gentleman-and-a-half – with a tolerable larder, cellar, &c.; and a most unfortunately easy temper for the callous front of impertinence to try conclusions on. My day times are entirely engrossed by the business of a public office, where I am anything but alone from nine till five. I have forty fellow-clerks about me during those hours; and, though the human face be divine, I protest that so many human faces seen every day do very much diminish the homage I am willing to pay to that divinity. It fares with these divine resemblances as with a Polytheism. Multiply the object and you infallibly enfeeble the adoration. 'What a piece of work is Man! how excellent in faculty,' &c. But a great many men together – a hot huddle of rational creatures – Hamlet himself would have lowered his contemplation a peg or two in my situation. *Tædet me harum quotidianarum formarum.*[2] I go home every day to my late dinner, absolutely famished and face-sick. I am sometimes fortunate enough to go off unaccompanied. The relief is restorative like sleep; but far oftener, alas! some one of my fellows, who lives *my way* (as they call it) does me the sociality of walking with me. He sees me to the door; and now I figure to myself a snug fire-side – comfortable meal – a respiration from the burthen of society – and the blessedness of a single knife and fork. I sit down to my solitary mutton, happy as Adam when a bachelor. I have not swallowed a mouthful, before a startling ring announces the visit of a *friend*. O! for an everlasting muffle upon that appalling instrument of torture! A knock makes me nervous; but a ring is a positive fillip to all the sour passions of my nature: – and yet such is my effeminacy of temperament, I neither tie up the one nor dumbfound the other. But these accursed friends, or fiends, that torment me thus! They come in with a full consciousness of their being unwelcome –

with a sort of grin of triumph over your weakness. My soul sickens
within when they enter. I can scarcely articulate a 'how d'ye.' My
digestive powers fail. I have enough to do to maintain them in any
healthiness when alone. Eating is a solitary function; you may drink in
company. Accordingly the bottle soon succeeds; and such is my infirmity, that the reluctance soon subsides before it. The visitor becomes
agreeable. I find a great deal that is good in him; wonder I should have
felt such aversion on his first entrance; we get chatty, conversible; insensibly comes midnight; and I am dismissed to the cold bed of celibacy
(the only place, alas! where I am suffered to be alone) with the reflection
that another day has gone over my head without the possibility of
enjoying my own free thoughts in solitude even for a solitary moment.
O for a Lodge in some vast wilderness! the den of those Seven Sleepers[3]
(conditionally the other six were away) – a *Crusoe* solitude!

What most disturbs me is, that my chief annoyers are mostly young
men. Young men, let them think as they please, are no company *singly*
for a gentleman of my years. They do mighty well in a mixed society,
and where there are females to take them off, as it were. But to have the
load of one of them to one's own self for successive hours conversation
is unendurable.

There was my old friend Captain Beacham – he died some six years
since, bequeathing to my friendship three stout young men, his sons,
and seven girls, the tallest in the land. Pleasant, excellent young women
they were, and for their sakes I did, and could endure much. But they
were too tall. I am superstitious in that respect, and think that to a just
friendship, something like proportion in stature as well as mind is desirable. Now I am five feet and a trifle more. Each of these young
women rose to six, and one exceeded by two inches. The brothers are
proportionably taller. I have sometimes taken the altitude of this
friendship; and on a modest computation I may be said to have known
at one time a whole furlong of Beachams. But the young women are
married off, and dispersed among the provinces. The brothers are left.
Nothing is more distasteful than these relics and parings of past
friendships – unmeaning records of agreeable hours flown. There are
three of them. If they hunted in triples, or even couples, it were something; but by a refinement of persecution, they contrive to come singly;
and so spread themselves out into three evenings molestation in a week.
Nothing is so distasteful as the sight of their long legs, couched for
continuance upon my fender. They have been mates of Indiamen; and
one of them in particular has a story of a shark swallowing a boy in the

bay of Calcutta. I wish the shark had swallowed *him*. Nothing can be more useless than their conversation to me, unless it is mine to them. We have no ideas (save of eating and drinking) in common. The shark story has been told till it cannot elicit a spark of attention; but it goes on just as usual. When I try to introduce a point of literature, or common life, the mates gape at me. When I fill a glass, they fill one too. Here is sympathy. And for this poor correspondency of having a gift of swallowing and retaining liquor in common with my fellow-creatures, I am to be tied up to an ungenial intimacy abhorrent from every sentiment, and every sympathy besides. But I cannot break the bond. They are sons of my old friend.

LEPUS.[4]

(*New Times*, 8 January 1825)

DOG DAYS

'Now Sirius rages'

TO THE EDITOR OF THE EVERY-DAY BOOK[1]

SIR, — I am one of those unfortunate creatures, who at this season of the year are exposed to the effects of an illiberal prejudice. Warrants are issued out in form, and whole scores of us are taken up and executed annually, under an obsolete statute, on what is called suspicion of lunacy. It is very hard that a sober, sensible dog, cannot go quietly through a village about his business, without having his motions watched, or some impertinent fellow observing that there is an 'odd look about his eyes.' My pulse, for instance, at this present writing, is as temperate as yours, Mr Editor, and my head as little rambling, but I hardly dare to show my face out of doors for fear of these scrutinizers. If I look up in a stranger's face, he thinks I am going to bite him. If I go with my eyes fixed upon the ground, they say I have got the mopes, which is but a short stage from the disorder. If I wag my tail, I am too lively; if I do not wag it, I am sulky — either of which appearances passes alike for a prognostic. If I pass a dirty puddle without drinking, sentence is infallibly pronounced upon me. I am perfectly swilled with the quantity of ditch-water I am forced to swallow in a day, to clear me from imputations — a worse cruelty than the water ordeal of your old Saxon ancestors. If I snap at a bone, I am furious; if I refuse it, I have got the sullens, and that is a bad symptom. I dare not bark outright, for fear of being adjudged to rave. It was but yesterday, that I indulged in a little innocent *yelp* only, on occasion of a cart-wheel going over my leg, and the populace was up in arms, as if I had betrayed some marks of flightiness in my conversation.

Really our case is one which calls for the interference of the chancellor. He should see, as in cases of other lunatics, that commissions are only issued out against proper objects; and not a whole race be proscribed, because some dreaming Chaldean, two thousand years ago, fancied a canine resemblance in some star or other, that was supposed to predominate over addle brains, with as little justice as Mercury was held to be influential over rogues and swindlers; no compliment I am sure to either star or planet. Pray attend to my complaint, Mr Editor, and speak a good word for us this hot weather.

> Your faithful, though sad dog,
> POMPEY.

(*Every-day Book*, July 1825)

A CHARACTER

A DESK at the Bank of England is *primâ facie* not the point in the world that seems best adapted for an insight into the characters of men; yet something may be gleaned from the barrenest soil. There is EGOMET,[1] for instance. By the way, how pleasant it is to string up one's acquaintance thus, in the grumbler's corner of some newspaper, and for them to know nothing at all about it; nay, for them to read their own characters and suspect nothing of the matter. Blessings on the writer who first made use of Roman names. It is only calling Tomkins – Caius; and Jenkins – Titus; or whipping Hopkins upon the back of Scævola, and you have the pleasure of executing sentence with no pain to the offender. This hanging in effigy is delightful; it evaporates the spleen without souring the blood, and is altogether the most gentlemanly piece of Jack-Ketchery[2] imaginable.

EGOMET, then, has been my desk-fellow for thirty years. He is a remarkable species of selfishness. I do not mean that he is attentive to his own gain; I acquit him of that common-place manifestation of the foible. I shoot no such small deer. But his sin is a total absorption of mind in things relating to himself – *his* house – *his* horse – *his* stable – *his* gardener, &c. Nothing that concerns himself can he imagine to be indifferent to you. – He does my sympathy too much honour. The worst is, he takes no sort of interest whatever in *your* horse, house, stable, gardener, &c. If you begin a discourse about your own household economy and small matters, he treats it with the most mortifying indifference. He has discarded all pronouns for the first-personal. His inattention, or rather aversion, to hear, is no more than what is a proper return to a self-important babbler of his own little concerns; but then, if he will not give, why should he expect to receive, a hearing? 'There is no reciprocity in this.'

There is an egotism of vanity; but his is not that species either. He is not vain of any talent, or indeed properly of any thing he possesses; but his doings and sayings, his little pieces of good or ill luck, the sickness of his maid, the health of his pony, the question whether he shall ride or walk home to-day to Clapham, the shape of his hat or make of his boot; his poultry, and how many eggs they lay daily – are the never ending topics of his talk. *Your* goose might lay golden eggs without exciting in him a single curiosity to hear about it.

He is alike throughout; his large desk, which abuts on mine – *nimium vicini*,[3] alas! is a vast lumber chest composed of every scrap of most insignificant paper, even to dinner invitation cards, every fragment that has been addressed to him, or in any way has concerned himself. My elbow aches with being perpetually in the way of his sudden jerking of it up, which he does incessantly to hunt for some worthless scrap of the least possible self-reference; this he does without notice, and without ceremony. I should like to make a bonfire of the ungainful mass – but I should not like it either; with it would fall down at once all the structure of his pride – his fane of Diana,[4] his treasure, his calling, the business he came into the world to do.

I said before, he is not avaricious – not egotistical in the vain sense of the word either; therefore the term selfishness, or egotism, is improperly applied to his distemper; it is the sin of self-fullness. Neither is himself, properly speaking, an object of his contemplation at all; it is the things which belong or refer to himself. His conversation is one entire soliloquy; or it may be said to resemble Robinson Crusoe's self-colloquies in his island: you are the parrot sitting by. Begin a story, however modest, of your own concerns (something of real interest perhaps), and the little fellow contracts and curls up into his little self immediately, and, with shut ears, sits unmoved, self-centred, as remote from your joys or sorrows as a Pagod[5] or a Lucretian Jupiter.

LEPUS.

(*New Times*, 25 August 1825)

CHARLES LAMB'S AUTOBIOGRAPHY[1]

CHARLES LAMB, born in the Inner Temple, 10th February, 1775; educated in Christ's Hospital; afterwards a clerk in the Accountants' Office, East India House; pensioned off from that service, 1825, after thirty-three years' service; is now a gentleman at large, can remember few specialities in his life worth noting, except that he once caught a swallow flying (*teste suâ manu*).[2] Below the middle stature; cast of face slightly Jewish, with no Judaic tinge in his complexional religion; stammers abominably, and is therefore more apt to discharge his occasional conversation in a quaint aphorism, or a poor quibble, than in set and edifying speeches; has consequently been libelled as a person always aiming at wit, which, as he told a dull fellow that charged him with it, is at least as good as aiming at dulness: a small eater, but not drinker; confesses a partiality for the production of the Juniper-Berry; was a fierce smoker of tobacco, but may be resembled to a volcano burnt out, emitting only now and then a casual puff. Has been guilty of obtruding upon the Public a Tale, in prose, called Rosamund Gray; a Dramatic sketch, named John Woodvil; a Farewell Ode to Tobacco, with sundry other Poems, and light prose matter, collected in Two slight crown octavos, and pompously christened his Works, tho' in fact they were his Recreations; and his true works may be found on the Shelves of Leadenhall Street,[3] filling some hundred folios. He is also the true Elia, whose Essays are extant in a little volume, published a year or two since; and rather better known from that name without a meaning, than from any thing he has done, or can hope to do, in his own. He also was the first to draw the Public attention to the old English Dramatists, in a work called 'Specimens of English Dramatic Writers who lived about the Time of Shakspeare,' published about fifteen years since. In short, all his merits and demerits to set forth would take to the end of Mr Upcott's book, and then not be told truly.

He died   18 , much lamented.*

Witness his hand,
CHARLES LAMB.
10th Apr. 1827.

* To anybody. – Please to fill up these dates.

 *Letters*

[27 May 1796]

Dear C—

Make yourself perfectly easy about May.[1] I paid his bill, when I sent your clothes. I was flush of money, & am so still to all the purposes of a single life, so give yourself no further concern about it. The money would be superfluous to me, if I had it.

With regard to Allen,[2] – the woman he has married has some money, I have heard about £200 a year, enough for the maintenance of herself & children; one of whom is a girl **nine years old!** so Allen has dipt betimes into the cares of a family. I very seldom see him, & do not know whether he has given up the Westminster hospital.

When Southey becomes as modest as his predecessor Milton, & publishes his Epics in duodecimo I will read 'em, – a Guinea a book is somewhat exorbitant, nor have I the opportunity of borrowing the work. The extracts from it in the Monthly Review & the short passages in your Watchman[3] seem to me much superior to any thing in his partnership account with Lovell –

Your poems I shall procure forthwith. There were noble lines in what you inserted in one of your Numbers from Religious musings, but I thought them elaborate. I am somewhat glad you have given up that Paper – it must have been dry, unprofitable, & of 'dissonant mood' to your disposition. I wish you success in all your undertakings & am glad to hear you are employed about the Evidences of Religion. There is need of multiplying such books an hundred fold in this philosophical age to *prevent* converts to Atheism, for they seem too tough disputants to meddle with afterwards –. I am sincerely sorry for Allen, as a family man particularly –

Le Grice[4] is gone to make puns in Cornwall. He has got a tutorship to a young boy, living with his Mother a widow Lady. He will of course initiate him quickly in 'whatsoever things are lovely, honorable, & of good report.' He has cut Miss Hunt compleately, – the poor Girl is very ill on the Occasion, but he laughs at it, & justifies himself by saying 'she does not see him laugh!' Coleridge, I know not what suffering scenes you have gone through at Bristol, – my life has been somewhat diversified of late. The 6 weeks that finished last year & began this your very humble servant spent very agreeably in a **mad house at Hoxton** –. I am got somewhat rational now, & **dont bite any one**.

But **mad** I was – & many a vagary my imagination played with me, enough to make a **volume** if all **told** –

My Sonnets I have extended to the **Number of nine** since I saw you, & will some day communicate to you –

I am beginning a poem in blank **verse**, which if I finish I publish –

White[5] is on the eve of publishing (he took the hint from **Vortigern**) Original letters of Falstaff Shallow &c – a copy you shall have when it comes out. They are without exception the best imitations I ever saw –

Coleridge it may convince you of my regards for you when I tell you my head ran on you in my madness as much almost as on another Person, who I am inclined to think was the more immediate cause of my temporary frenzy –. The sonnet I send you has small merit as poetry but you will be curious to read it when I tell you it was written in my prison house in one of my lucid Intervals

to my sister

If from my lips some angry accents fell,
 Peevish complaint, or harsh reproof unkind,
 Twas but the Error of a sickly mind,
And troubled thoughts, clouding the purer well,
 & waters clear, of Reason: & for me
Let this my verse the poor atonement be,
My verse, which thou to praise: wast ever inclined
 Too highly, & with a partial eye to see
No Blemish: thou to me didst ever shew
 Fondest affection, & woudst oftimes lend
An ear to the desponding, love sick Lay,
 Weeping my sorrows with me, who repay
But ill the mighty debt, of love I owe,
 Mary, to thee, my sister & my friend –

With these lines, & with that sisters kindest remembrances to C— I conclude –

Yours Sincerely
LAMB

Your conciones ad populum[6] are the most eloquent politics that ever came in my way.

Write, when convenient – not as a task, for here is nothing in this letter to **answer** –

You may inclose under cover to me at the India house what letters you please, for they come post free. – –

We cannot send our remembrances to Mrs C— not having seen her, but believe me our best good wishes attend you both –

My civic & poetic compt's to Southey if at Bristol –. Why, he is a very Leviathan of Bards – the small minow I –

2. TO SAMUEL TAYLOR COLERIDGE

[27 September 1796]

My dearest friend –

White or some of my friends or the public papers by this time may have informed you of the terrible calamities that have fallen on our family. I will only give you the outlines. My poor dear dearest sister in a fit of insanity has been the death of her own mother. I was at hand only time enough to snatch the knife out of her grasp. She is at present in a mad house, from whence I fear she must be moved to an hospital. God has preserved to me my senses, – I eat and drink and sleep, and have my judgment I believe very sound. My poor father was slightly wounded, and I am left to take care of him and my aunt. Mr Norris of the Bluecoat school has been very kind to us, and we have no other friend, but thank God I am very calm and composed, and able to do the best that remains to do. Write, – as religious a letter as possible – but no mention of what is gone and done with – with me the former things are passed away, and I have something more to do than to feel –

God almighty

have us all in
his keeping. –

C. Lamb

mention nothing of poetry. I have destroyed every vestige of past vanities of that kind. Do as you please, but if you publish, publish mine (I give free leave) without name or initial, and never send me a book, I charge you, you[r] own judgment will convince you not to take any notice of this yet to your dear wife. – You look after your family, – I have reason and strength left to take care of mine. I charge you don't think of coming to see me. Write. I will not see you if you come. God almighty love you and all of us –

3. TO SAMUEL TAYLOR COLERIDGE

[3 October 1796]

My dearest friend,

   your letter was an inestimable treasure to me. It will be a comfort to
you, I know, to know that our prospects are somewhat brighter. My
poor dear dearest sister, the unhappy & unconscious instrument of the
Almighty's judgments to our house, is restored to her senses; to a dreadful
sense & recollection of what has past, awful to her mind & impressive
(as it must be to the end of life) but temper'd with religious resignation,
& the reasonings of a sound judgment, which in this early stage knows
how to distinguish between a deed committed in a transient fit of
frenzy, & the terrible guilt of a **Mother's** murther. **I have seen her.** I
found her this morning calm & serene, far very very far from an
indecent forgetful serenity; she has a most affectionate & tender concern
for what has happened. Indeed from the beginning, frightful & hopeless
as her disorder seemed, I had confidence enough in her strength of
mind, & religious principle, to look forward to a time when *even she*
might recover tranquillity. God be praised, Coleridge, wonderful as it is
to tell, I have never once been otherwise than collected, & calm; even
on the dreadful day & in the midst of the terrible scene I preserved a
tranquillity, which bystanders may have construed into indifference, a
tranquillity not of despair; is it folly or sin in me to say that it was a
religious principle that *most* supported me? I allow much to other
favorable circumstances. I felt that I had something else to do than to
regret; on that first evening my Aunt was laying insensible, to all appearance like one dying, – my father, with his poor forehead plaisterd over
from a wound he had received from a daughter dearly loved by him, &
who loved him no less dearly, – my mother a dead & murder'd corpse
in the next room – yet was I wonderfully supported. I closed not my
eyes in sleep that night, but lay without terrors & without despair. I
have lost no sleep since. I had been long used not to rest in things of
sense, had endeavord after a comprehension of mind, unsatisfied with
the 'ignorant present time,' & this kept me up. I had the whole weight
of the family thrown on me, for my brother, little disposed (I speak not
without tenderness for him) at any time to take care of old age &
infirmities had now, with his bad leg, an exemption from such duties, &
I was now **left alone**. One little incident may serve to make you
understand my way of managing my mind. Within a day or 2 after the
fatal **one**, we drest for dinner a tongue, which we had had salted for some
weeks in the house. As I sat down a feeling like **remorse** struck me, –

this tongue poo[r] Mary got for **me**, & can I partake of it **now**, when she is far **away** – a thought occurred & relieve[d] me, – if I give into this way of feeling, there is not a chair, a room, an object in our rooms, that will not awaken the keenest griefs, I must rise above such weaknesses –. I hope this was not want of true feeling. I did not let this carry me tho' too far. On the very 2d day (I date from the day of **horrors**) as is usual in such cases there were a matter of 20 people I do think supping in our **room** –. They prevailed on me to eat *with them* (for to eat I never refused) they were all making merry! in the room, – some had come from friendship, some from busy curiosity, & some from **Interest**; I was going to partake with **them**, when my recollection came that my poor dead mother was lying in the next room, the very next room, a mother who thro' life wished nothing but her children's welfare – indignation, the rage of grief, something like remorse, rushed upon my mind in an agony of emotion, – I found my way mechanically to the adjoin[in]g room, & fell on my knees by the **side** of her coffin, asking forgiveness of heaven, & sometimes of her, for forgetting her **so soon**. Tranquillity returned, & it was the only violent emotion that master'd me, & I think it did me good. –

I mention these things because I hate concealment, & love to give a faithful journal of what passes within **me**. Our friends have been very good. Sam LeGrice [1] who was then in town was with me the 3 or 4 first days, & was as a brother to me, gave up every hour of his time, to the very hurting of his health & spirits, in constant attendance & humoring my poor father. Talk'd with him, read to him, play'd at cr[ib]bage with Him (for so **short** is the old man's recollection, that he was playing at cards, as tho' nothing had happened, while the Coroner's Inquest was sitting over the way!) Samuel wept tenderly when he went away, for his Mother wrote him a very severe letter on his loitering so long in town, & he was forced to go. Mr Norris of Christ Hospital has been as a father to me, Mrs Norris as a Mother, tho' we had few claims on them. A Gentleman brother to my Godmother, from whom we never had right or reason to expect any such assistance, sent my father twenty pounds, – & to crown all these God's blessings to our family at such a time, an old Lady, a cousin of my father & Aunts, a Gentlewoman of fortune, is to take my Aunt & make her comfortable for the short remainder of her days. –

My Aunt is recover'd & as well as ever, & highly pleased at thoughts of going, – & has generously given up the interest of her little money (which was formerly paid my Father for her board) wholely & solely to my **Sister's** use. Reckoning this we have, **Daddy & I** for our two selves & an old maid servant to look after him, when I am out, which will be necessary, £170 or £180 (rather) a year out of which we can spare 50 or 60 at least for Mary, while she stays at Islington, where she must & shall stay during her father's life for his & her comfort. I know John will make speeches about it, but she shall not go into an **hospital**. The good Lady of the Mad house, & her daughter, an elegant sweet behaved young Lady, love her & are taken with her amazingly, & I know from her **own** mouth she loves them, & longs to be with them as much –. Poor thing, they say she was but the other morning saying, she knew she must go to **Bethlem** for life; that one of her brother's would have it so, but the other would wish it Not, but he obliged to go with the stream; that she had often as she passed **Bedlam** thought it likely 'here it may be my fate to end my days' – conscious of a certain flightiness in her poor head oftentimes, & mindful of more than one severe illness of that Nature before. A Legacy of £100 which my father will have at **Xmas**, & this 20 I mentioned before with what is in the house, will much more than set us **Clear**, – if my father, an old servant maid, & I can't **live** & live **comfortably** on £130 or £120 a year[2] we ought to burn by slow fires, & I almost would, that Mary might not go into an hospital. Let me not leave one unfavorable impression on your **mind** respecting my Brother. Since this has happened he has been very kind & brotherly; but I fear for his mind, – he has taken his ease in the world, & is not fit himself to struggle with difficulties, nor has much accustomed himself to throw himself into their way, – & I know his language is already, 'Charles, you must take care of yourself, you must not abridge yourself of a single pleasure you have been used to' &c &c. & in that style of talking. But you, a necessarian,[3] can respect a difference of mind, & love what *is amiable* in a character not perfect. He has been very good, but I fear for his mind. Thank God, I can unconnect myself with him, & shall manage all my father's monies in future **myself**, if I take charge of Daddy, which **poor** John has not even hinted a wish, at any future time even, to share with **me** –

The Lady at this Mad house assures me that I may dismiss immediately both Doctor & Apothecary, retaining occasionally an opening draught or so for a while, & there is a less expensive establishment in her house, where she will only not have a **room & nurse** to herself for £50 or guineas a year – the outside would be 60 –. You know by œconomy how much more, even, I shall be able to spare for her comforts –

She will, I fancy, if she stays, make one of the family, rather than of the patients, & the old & young ladies I like **exceedingly**, & she loves dearly, & they, as the saying is take to her **very** extraordinaryily, if it is extraordinary that people who see my sister should love her. Of all the people I ever saw in the world my poor sister was most & throughly devoi[d] of the least tincture of **selfishness** –. I will enlarge upon her qualities, poor dear dearest soul, in a future letter for my own comfort, for I understood her throughly; & if I mistake not in the most trying situation that a human being can be found in, she will be found (I speak not with sufficient humility, I fear, but humanly & foolishly speaking) she will be found, I trust, uniformly great & amiable; God keep her in her present Mind, to whom be thanks & praise for all his dispensations to mankind –

LAMB

Coleridge, continue to **write**, but do not for ever offend me by talking of sending me cash; sincerely & on my soul we do not want it. God love you both –

Send me word, how it fares with Sara.[4] I repeat it, your letter was & will be an inestimable treasure to **me**; you have a view of what my situation demands of me like my own view; & I trust a just one –

These mentioned good fortunes & change of prospects had almost brought my mind **over** to the extreme the very opposite to **Despair**; I was in danger of making myself too happy; your letter brought me back to a view of things which I had entertained from the beginning; I hope (for Mary I can answer) but I hope that *I* shall thro' life never have less recollection nor a fainter impression of what has happened than I have now; tis not a light thing, nor meant by the Almighty to be received lightly; I must be serious, circumspect, & deeply religious thro' lif[e;] & by such means may *both* of us escape madness in future if it so pleases the Almighty –

I will write again very Soon; do you directly –

4. TO SAMUEL TAYLOR COLERIDGE

[17 October 1796]

My dearest friend,

I grieve from my very soul to observe you in your plans of life, veering about from this hope to the other, & settling no where. Is it an untoward fatality (speaking humanly) that does this for you?, a stubborn irresistible concurrence of events? or lies the fault, as I fear it does, in your **own** mind? You seem to be taking up splendid schemes of fortune only to lay them down again, & your fortunes are an ignis fatuus that has been conducting you, in thought, from Lancaster Court, Strand, to somewhere near Matlock, then jumping across to Dr Somebody's whose sons' tutor you were likely to be, & would to God, the dancing demon *may* conduct you at last in peace & comfort to the 'life & labors of a cottager.' You see from the above awkward playfulness of fancy that my spirits are not quite depress'd; I should ill deserve God's blessings, which since the late terrible event have come down in Mercy upon us, if I indulged regret or querulousnes, – Mary continues serene & chearful, – I have not by me a little letter she wrote to me, for tho' I see her almost every day yet we delight to write to one another (for we can scarce see each other but in company with some of the people of the house), I have not the letter by me but will quote from memory what she wrote in it. 'I have no bad terrifying dreams. At midnight when I happen to awake, the nurse sleeping by the side of **me**, with the noise of the poor mad people around me, I have no fear. The spirit of my mother seems to descend, & smile upon me, & bid me **live** to enjoy the life & reason which the Almighty has given me –. I shall see her again in heaven; she will then understand me better, my Grandmother too will understand me better, & will then say no more as she used to Do, 'Polly, what are those poor crazy moyther'd brains of yours thinkg. of always?' – Poor Mary, my mother indeed *never understood* her right. She loved her, as she loved us all with a **Mother's love**, but in opinion, in feeling, & sentiment, & disposition, bore so distant a resemblance to her daughter, that she never understood her right. Never could believe how much *she* loved her – but met her caresses, her protestations of filial affection, too frequently with coldness & **repulse**, – Still she was a good mother, God forbid I should think of her but *most* respectfully, *most* affectionately. Yet she would always love my brother above Mary, who was not worthy of one tenth of that affection, which Mary had a right to claim. But it is my Sister's gratifying recollection, that every act of duty & of love she could pay, every kindness (& I speak true, when I say to the hurting of her health, & most probably in great part to the derangement of her senses) thro' a long course of infirmities & sickness, she could shew her, **she ever did**. I will some day, as I promised enlarge to you upon my Sister's excellencies; twill seem like exaggeration, but I will do it. At present **short letters** suit my **state of mind best. So take** my kindest wishes for your comfort and establishment in life [an]d for Sara's welfare and comforts with you. God love you; God love us all —

C. LAMB

5. TO SAMUEL TAYLOR COLERIDGE

Sunday Evening, October 24 [23], 1796

Coleridge,

I feel myself much your debtor for that spirit of confidence and friendship which dictated your last letter. May your soul find peace at last in your cottage life! I only wish you were *but* settled. Do continue to write to me. I read your letters with my sister, and they give us both abundance of delight. Especially they please us two, when you talk in a religious strain, — not but we are offended occasionally with a certain freedom of expression, a certain air of mysticism, more consonant to the conceits of pagan philosophy, than consistent with the humility of genuine piety. To instance now in your last letter — you say, 'it is by the press, that God hath given finite spirits both evil and good (I suppose you mean *simply* bad men and good men) a portion as it were of His Omnipresence!' Now, high as the human intellect comparatively will soar, and wide as its influence, malign or salutary, can extend, is there not, Coleridge, a distance between the Divine Mind and it, which makes such language blasphemy? Again, in your first fine consolatory epistle you say, 'you are a temporary sharer in human misery, that you may be an eternal partaker of the Divine Nature.' What more than this do those men say, who are for exalting the man Christ Jesus into the second person of an unknown Trinity, — men, whom you or I scruple not to call idolaters? Man, full of imperfections, at best, and subject to wants which momentarily remind him of dependence; man, a weak and ignorant being, 'servile' from his birth 'to all the skiey influences,' with eyes sometimes open to discern the right path, but a head generally too dizzy to pursue it; man, in the pride of speculation, forgetting his nature, and hailing in himself the future God, must make the angels laugh. Be not angry with me, Coleridge; I wish not to cavil; I know I cannot *instruct* you; I only wish to *remind* you of that humility which best becometh the Christian character. God, in the New Testament (*our best guide*), is represented to us in the kind, condescending, amiable, familiar light of a *parent:* and in my poor mind 'tis best for us so to consider of Him, as our *heavenly* Father, and our *best Friend*, without indulging too bold conceptions of His nature. Let us learn to think humbly of ourselves, and rejoice in the appellation of 'dear children,' 'brethren,' and 'co-heirs with Christ of the promises,' seeking to know no further.

I am not insensible, indeed I am not, of the value of that first letter of yours, and I shall find reason to thank you for it again and again long after that blemish in it is forgotten. It will be a fine lesson of comfort to us, whenever we read it; and read it we often shall, Mary and I.

Accept our loves and best kind wishes for the welfare of yourself and wife, and little one.[1] Nor let me forget to wish you joy on your birthday so lately past; I thought you had been older. My kind thanks and remembrances to Lloyd.

God love us all, and may He continue to be the father and the friend of the whole human race!

C. LAMB

6. TO SAMUEL TAYLOR COLERIDGE

December 10, 1796

I had put my letter into the post rather hastily, not expecting to have to acknowledge another from you so soon. This morning's present has made me alive again: my last night's epistle was childishly querulous; but you have put a little life into me, and I will thank you for your remembrance of me, while my sense of it is yet warm; for if I linger a day or two I may use the same phrase of acknowledgment, or similar; but the feeling that dictates it now will be gone. I shall send you a *caput mortuum*, not a *cor vivens*.[1] Thy Watchman's, thy bellman's, verses,[2] I do retort upon thee, thou libellous varlet, – why, you cried the hours yourself, and who made you so proud? But I submit, to show my humility, most implicitly to your dogmas. I reject entirely the copy of verses you reject. With regard to my leaving off versifying, you have said so many pretty things, so many fine compliments, ingeniously decked out in the garb of sincerity, and undoubtedly springing from a present feeling somewhat like sincerity, that you might melt the most un-muse-ical soul, – did you not (now for a Rowland compliment for your profusion of Olivers)[3] – did you not in your very epistle, by the many pretty fancies and profusion of heart displayed in it, dissuade and discourage me from attempting anything after you. At present I have not leisure to make verses, nor anything approaching to a fondness for the exercise. In the ignorant present time, who can answer for the future man? 'At lovers' perjuries Jove laughs' – and poets have sometimes a disingenuous way of forswearing their occupation. This though is not my case. The tender cast of soul, sombred with melancholy and subsiding recollections, is favourable to the Sonnet or the Elegy; but from

> The sainted growing woof,
> The teasing troubles keep aloof.

The music of poesy may charm for a while the importunate teasing cares of life; but the teased and troubled man is not in a disposition to make that music.

You sent me some very sweet lines relative to Burns, but it was at a time when, in my highly agitated and perhaps distorted state of mind, I thought it a duty to read 'em hastily and burn 'em. I burned all my own verses, all my book of extracts from Beaumont and Fletcher and a thousand sources: I burned a little journal of my foolish passion which I had a long time kept:

> Noting ere they past away
> The little lines of yesterday.

I almost burned all your letters, – I did as bad, I lent 'em to a friend to keep out of my brother's sight, should he come and make inquisition into our papers, for, much as he dwelt upon your conversation while you were among us, and delighted to be with you, it has been his fashion ever since to depreciate and cry you down, – you were the cause of my madness – you and your damned foolish sensibility and melancholy – and he lamented with a true brotherly feeling that we ever met, even as the sober citizen, when his son went astray upon the mountains of Parnassus, is said to have 'cursed wit and Poetry and Pope.' I quote wrong, but no matter. These letters I lent to a friend to be out of the way for a season; but I have claimed them in vain, and shall not cease to regret their loss. Your packets, posterior to the date of my misfortunes, commencing with that valuable consolatory epistle, are every day accumulating – they are sacred things with me.

Publish your *Burns* when and how you like, it will be new to me, – my memory of it is very confused, and tainted with unpleasant associations. Burns was the god of my idolatry, as Bowles of yours. I am jealous of your fraternising with Bowles, when I think you relish him more than Burns or my old favourite, Cowper. But you conciliate matters when you talk of the 'divine chit-chat' of the latter: by the expression I see you thoroughly relish him. I love Mrs Coleridge for her excuses an hundredfold more dearly than if she heaped 'line upon line,' out-Hannah-ing Hannah More,[4] and had rather hear you sing 'Did a very little baby' by your family fire-side, than listen to you when you were repeating one of Bowles's sweetest sonnets in your sweet manner, while we two were indulging sympathy, a solitary luxury, by the fireside at the Salutation. Yet have I no higher ideas of heaven. Your company was one 'cordial in this melancholy vale' – the remembrance of it is a blessing partly, and partly a curse. When I can abstract myself from things present, I can enjoy it with a freshness of relish; but it more constantly operates to an unfavourable comparison with the un-interesting; converse I always and *only* can partake in. Not a soul loves Bowles here; scarce one has heard of Burns; few but laugh at me for reading my Testament – they talk a language I understand not: I conceal sentiments that would be a puzzle to them. I can only converse with you by letter and with the dead in their books. My sister indeed, is all I can wish in a companion; but our spirits are alike poorly, our reading and knowledge from the self-same sources, our communication with the scenes of the world alike narrow: never having kept separate company, or any 'company' *'together'* – never having read separate books, and few books *together* – what knowledge have we to convey to each other? In our little range of duties and connexions, how few sentiments can take place, without friends, with few books, with a taste for religion rather than a strong religious habit! We need some support, some leading-strings to cheer and direct us. You talk very wisely, and be not sparing of *your advice.* Continue to remember us, and to show us you do remember us: we will take as lively an interest in what concerns you and yours. All I can add to your happiness, will be sympathy. You can add to mine *more;* you can teach me wisdom. I am indeed an unreasonable correspondent; but I was unwilling to let my last night's letter go off without this qualifier: you will perceive by this my mind is easier, and you will rejoice. I do not expect or wish you to write, till you are moved; and of course shall not, till you announce to me that event, think of writing myself. Love to Mrs Coleridge and David Hartley, and my kind remembrance to Lloyd, if he is with you.

C. LAMB

I will get 'Nature and Art,'[5] – have not seen it yet – nor any of Jeremy Taylor's works.

7. TO SAMUEL TAYLOR COLERIDGE

London
Saturday [7 January–
Tuesday, 10 January 1797]

I am completely reconciled to that second strophe,[1] & wave all objection. In spite of the Grecian Lyrists, I persist in thinking your brief personification of Madness useless; reverence forbids me to say, impertinent. Golden locks & snow white glories are as incongruous as your former, & if the great Italian painters, of whom my friend knows about as much as the man in the moon, if these great gentlemen be on your side, I see no harm in retaining the purple – the glories, that *I* have observed to encircle the heads of saints & madonnas, in those old paintings, have been mostly of a dirty drab-color'd yellow – a dull gambogium.[2] Keep your old line: it will excite a confused kind of pleasurable idea in the reader's mind, not clear enough to be call'd a conception, nor just enough, I think, to reduce to painting. It is a rich line, you say; & riches hide a many faults. I maintain, that in the 2d antist: you *do* disjoin Nature & the world, & contrary to your conduct in the 2d strophe. 'Nature joins her groans' joins with *whom*, a god's name, but the world or earth in line preceding? but this is being over curious, I acknowledge. Nor *did* I call the *last* line useless, I only objected to 'unhur[l'd']. I cannot be made to like the former part of that 2d Epode; I cannot be made to feel it, as I do the parallel places in Isaiah, Jeremy, & Daniel. Whether it is that in the pr[e]sent case the rhyme impairs the efficacy – or that the circumstances are feigned, & we are conscious of a made up lye in the case, & the narrative is too long winded to preserve the semblance of truth; or that lines 8. 9. 10. 14 in partic: 17 & 18 are mean & unenthusiastic – or that lines 5 to 8 in their change of rhyme shew like art – I dont know, but it strikes me as something meant to affect, & failing in its purpose. Remember, my waywardness of feeling is single, & singly stands opposed to all your friends, & what is one among many! This I know, that your quotations from the prophets have never escaped me, & never fail'd to affect me strongly –. I hate that simile, –. – I am glad you have amended that parenthesis in the account of Destruction. I like it well now. only alter that history of child bearing, & all will do well. let the obnoxious Epode remain, to terrify such of your friends, as are willing to be terrified. I think, I would omit the Notes, not as not good per se, but as uncongenial with the dignity of the **Ode**. I need not repeat my wishes to have my little sonnets printed verbatim my last way; In particular, I fear lest you should prefer printing my first sonnet, as you have done more than once, 'did the wand of Merlin wave?'[3] it looks so like *Mr* **Merlin**[4] the ingenius successor of the immortal Merlin, now living in good health & spirits, & flourishing in Magical Reputation, in Oxford Street & on my life, one half who read *it*, would understand it so. – Do put 'em forth finally as I have, in various letters, settled it, – for first a man's self is to be pleased, & then his friends, – & of course, the greater number of his friends, if they differ inter se.[5] Thus taste may safely be put to the vote – I do long to see our names together – not for vanity's-sake, & naughty pride of heart altogether, for not a living soul, **I know** or am intimate with, will scarce read the book – so I shall gain nothing quoad famam,[6] – & yet there is a little vanity mixes in it, I cannot help denying. –. I am aware of the **unpoetical cast** of the 6 last lines of my last sonnet, & think myself unwarranted in smuggling so tame a thing into the book; only the sentiments of those 6 lines are throughly conginial to me in my state of mind, & I wish to accumulate perpetuating tokens of my affection to poor **Mary** – that it has no originality in its cast, nor anything in the feelings, but what is common & natural to thousands, nor aught properly called poetry, **I see**; stil[l] it will tend to keep present to my mind a view of things which I ought to indulge –. These 6 lines, too have not, to a reader, a connectedness with the foregoing. **omit it if you like** –. What a treasure it is to my poor indolent & unemployed mind, thus to lay hold on a subject to talk about, tho' tis but a sonnet & that of the lowest order. How mournfully inactive I am! – Tis night: good night –

[Sunday evening]

My sister, I thank God, is nigh recover'd. She was seriously ill. **Do**, in your next letter, & that right soon, give me some satisfaction respecting your present situation at Stowey. Is it a farm you have got? & what does your worship know about farming? Coleridge, I want you to write an Epic poem. Nothing short of it can satisfy the vast capacity of true poetic genius. Having one great End to direct all your poetical faculties to, & on which to lay out your hopes, your ambition, will shew you to what you are equal. By the sacred energies of Milton, by the dainty sweet & soothing phantasies of honey tongued Spencer, I adjure you to attempt the Epic –. **Or** do something, more ample, than the writing an occasional brief ode or sonnet; something 'to make yourself for ever known, – to make the age to come your own' – but I prate; doubtless, you meditate something. When you are exalted among the **Lords** of Epic fame, I shall recall with pleasure & exultingly, the days of your humility, when you disdaind not to put forth in the same volume with mine, your religious musings, & that other poem from the Joan of Arc, those promising first fruits of high renown to come –. You have learning, you have fancy, you have enthusiasm – you have strength & amplitude of wing enow for flights like those I recommend –

In the vast & unexplored regions of fairyland, there is ground enough unfound & uncultivated; search there, & realize your favorite Susquehanah scheme –.[7] In all our comparisons of taste, I do not know whether I have ever heard your opinion of a poet, very dear to me, the now out of fashion **Cowley** – favor **me** with your judgment of him – & tell me if his prose essays, in particular, as well as no inconsiderable part of his verse, be not delicious. I prefer the graceful rambling of his essays, even to the courtly elegance & ease of Addison – abstracting from this latter's exquisite humour. **Why is not your poem on Burns** in the Monthly magazine? I was much disappointed. I have a pleasurable but confused remembrance of it. When the little volume is printed, send me 3 or 4, at all events not more than 6 copies. & tell me if I put you to any additional expense, by printing with you. I have no thought of the kind, & in that case, must reimburse you –. My epistle is a model of unconnectedness, but I have no partic: subject to write on, & must proportion my scribble in some degree to the increase of postage. It is not quite fair, considering how burdensome your correspondence from different quarters must be, to add to it, with so little shew of reason. I will make an end for this evening. Sunday even: – Farewell –

[Monday evening]

Priestly, whom I sin in almost adoring, speaks of 'such a choice of company, as tends to keep up that right bent, & firmness of mind, which a nec[e]ssary intercourse with the world would otherwise warp & relax. Such fellowship is the true ba[l]sam of life, it[s] cement is infinitely more durable than that of the friendships of the world, & it looks for its proper fruit, & complete gratification, to the life beyond the Grave.' Is there a possible chance for such an one as me to realize in this world, such friendships? Where am I to look for 'em? what testimonials shall I bring of my being worthy of such friendship? Alas! the great & good go together in separate **Herds**, & leave such as me to lag far far behind in all intellectual, & far more grievous to say, in all moral accomplishments –. Coleridge, I have not one truly elevated character among my acquaintance: not one Christian: not one, but undervalues Christianity – singly what am I to do. Wesley (have you read his life?, was *he* not an elevated Character?) Wesley has said, '**Religion** is not a solitary thing.' Alas! it necessarily is so with me, or next to solitary. Tis true, you write to me. But correspondence by letter, & personal intimacy, are very widely different. Do, do write to me, & do some good to my mind, already how much **'warped & relaxed'** by the world! – 'Tis the conclusion of another evening –. Goodnight. God have us all in his Keeping –

If you are sufficiently at leisure, oblige me with an account of your plan of life at Stowey – your literary occupations & prospects – in short make me acquainted with every circumstance, which, as relating to you, can be interesting to me. Are you yet a Berkleyan? [8] Make me one. I rejoyce in being, speculatively, a necessarian. – Would to God, I were habitually a practical one. Confirm me in the faith of that great & glorious doctrine, & keep me steady in the contemplation of it. You sometime since exprest an intention you had of finishing some extensive work on the Evidences of Natural & Revealed Religion. Have you let that intention go? Or are you doing any thing towards it? Make to yourself other ten talents: My letter is full of nothingness. I talk of nothing. But I must talk. I love to write to you. I take a pride in it –. It makes me think less meanly of myself. It makes me think myself not totally disconnected from the better part of Mankind. I know, I am too dissatisfied with the beings around me, – but I cannot help occasionally exclaiming '**Woe** is me, that I am constrained to dwell with Mesheck, & to have my habitation among the tents of Kedar' [9] – I know, I am no ways better in practice than my neighbors – but I have a taste for religion, an occasional earnest aspiration after perfection, which they have not. I gain nothing by being with such as myself – we encourage one another in mediocrity – I am always longing to be with men more excellent than myself. All this must sound odd to you, but these are my predominant feelings, when I sit down to write to you, & I should put force upon my mind, were I to reject them. Yet I rejoyce, & feel my privilege with gratitude, when I have been reading some wise book, such as I have just been reading, **Priestly** on Philosophical necessity, in the thought that I enjoy a kind of Communion, a kind of friendship even, with the great & good. Books are to me instead of friends, – I wish they did not resemble the latter in their scarceness. – And how does **little David Hartley**? 'Ecquid in antiquam virtutem?' [10] – does his mighty name work wonders yet upon his little frame, & opening mind? I did not distinctly understand you, – you dont mean to make an actual plownman of him?! **Mrs C**— is no doubt well, – give my kindest respects to her –. Is Lloyd with you yet? – are you intimate with Southey? what poems is he about to publish – he hath a most prolific brain, & is indeed a most sweet poet. But how can you answer all the various mass of interrogation I have put to you in the course of the sheet –. Write back just what you like, only write something, however brief –. I have now nigh finished my page, & got to the **end** of another evening (Monday evening) – & my eyes are heavy & sleepy, & my brain unsuggestive –. I have just heart enough awake to say **Good night once more**, & God love you my dear friend, God love us all –. Mary bears an affectionate remembrance of you –

the 10th January 1797   CHARLES LAMB

8. TO SAMUEL TAYLOR COLERIDGE

[28 January 1798]

You have writ me Many kind letters, and I have answered none of them –. I do'nt deserve your attentions – an unnatural indifference has been creeping on me, since my last misfortunes, or I should have seized the first opening of a correspondence with *you* – to you I owe much, under God – in my brief acquaintance with you in London your conversations won me to the better cause, and rescued me from the polluting spirit of the world –. I might have been a worthless character without you – as it is, I do possess a certain improveable portion of devotional feelings – tho' when I view myself in the light of divine truth, and not according to the common measures of human judgment, I am altogether corrupt & sinful – this is no cant – I am very sincere –

These last afflictions, Coleridge, have failed to soften and bend my will – they found me unprepared – my former calamities produced in me a spirit of humility, and a spirit of prayer –. I thought, they had sufficiently disciplined me – but the event ought to humble me – if God's judgments now fail to take away from me the heart of stone, what more grievous trials ought I not to expect! – –. I have been very querulous – impatient under the rod – full of little jealousies & heart-burnings – –. I had well nigh quarrelled with Charles Lloyd – & for no other reason, I believe, than that the good creature did all he could to make me happy – –. the truth is, I thought he tried to force my mind from its natural & proper bent, he continually wished me to be from home, he was drawing me *from* the consideration of my poor dear Mary's situation, rather than assisting me to gain a proper view of it, with religious consolations –. I wanted to be left to the tendency of my own mind in a solitary state, which in times past, I knew, had led to quietness & a patient bearing of the yoke – he was hurt, that I was not more constantly with him – but he was living with **White**, a man to whom I had never been accustomed to impart my *dearest feelings* – tho' from long habits of friendliness, & many a social & good quality, I loved him very much –. I met company there sometimes – – indiscriminate company, any society almost, when I am in affliction, is sorely painful to me –. I seem to breathe more freely, to thin[k] more collectedly, to feel more properly & calmly, when alone – all these things the good creature did with the kindest intentions in the world – but they produced in me nothing but soreness and discontent –. I became, as he complained, 'jaundiced' towards him –. . but he has forgiven me – and his smile, I hope, will draw all such humours from me –. I am recovering, God be praised for it, a healthiness of mind – something like calmness – but I want more religion –. I am jealous of human helps & leaning-places.

I rejoyce in your good fortunes – – may God at the last **settle** you – you have had many & painful trials – – – humanly speaking, they are going to end –. – – but we should rather pray, that discipline may attend us thro' the whole of our lives . . . a careless and a dissolute spirit has advanced upon *me* with large strides – pray God, that my present afflictions may be sanctified to me –. Mary is recovering . . . but I see no opening yet of a situation for her – your invitation went to my very heart – but you have a power of exciting interest, [o]f leading all hearts captive, too forcible [to] admit of Mary's being with you –. I consider her as perpetually on the brink of madness –. I think, you would almost make her dance within an inch of the precipice – she must be with duller fancies, & cooler intellects . . . I know a young man of this description, who has suited her these twenty years, & may live to do so still – if we are one day restor'd to each other –. In answer to your suggestions of occupation for me, I must say that I do not think my capacity altogether suited for disqui[si]tions of that kind . . . I have read little, I have a very weak memory & retain little of what I read, am unused to compositions in which any methodizing is required – – but I thank you sincerely for the hint, and shall receive it as far as I am able – that is, endeavor to engage my mind in some constant & innocent pursuit – – – –. I know my capacities better than you do –

Accept my kindest love – & believe me

Yours as ever

C L

9. TO SAMUEL TAYLOR COLERIDGE

[The Lloyds', Birmingham

ca. 23 May–6 June] 1798

Theses Quædam Theologicæ.[1]

1. Whether God loves a lying Angel better than a true Man?

2. Whether the Archangel Uriel *could* affirm an untruth? & if he *could* whether he *would*?

3. Whether Honesty be an angelic virtue? or not rather to be reckoned among those qualities which the Schoolmen term *Virtutes minus splendidæ, et terræ et hominis participes?*[2]

4. Whether the higher order of Seraphim Illuminati ever sneer?

5. Whether pure Intelligences can love?

6. Whether the Seraphim Ardentes do not manifest their virtues by the way of vision & theory? & whether practice be not a sub-celestial & merely human virtue?

7. Whether the Vision Beatific be anything more or less than a perpetual represention to each individual Angel of his own present attainments & future capabilities, somehow in the manner of mortal looking-glasses, reflecting a perpetual complacency & self-satisfaction?

8 & last. Whether an immortal & amenable soul may not come to be damned at last, & the man never suspect it beforehand?

Learned Sir, my Friend,

Presuming on our long habits of friendship, & emboldened further by your late liberal permission to avail myself of your correspondence, in case I want any knowledge, (which I intend to do when I have no Encyclopædia, or Lady's Magazine at hand to refer to in any matter of science,) I now submit to your enquiries the above Theological Propositions, to be by you defended, or oppugned, or both, in the Schools of Germany, whither I am told you are departing, to the utter dissatisfaction of your native Devonshire, & regret of universal England; but to my own individual consolation, if thro the channel of your wished return, Learned Sir, my Friend, may be transmitted to this our Island, from those famous Theological Wits of Leipsic & Gottingen, any rays of illumination, in vain to be derived from the home growth of our English Halls and Colleges. Finally, wishing Learned Sir, that you may see Schiller, & swing in a wood (*vide* Poems)[3], & sit upon a Tun, & eat fat hams of Westphalia,

> I remain
> Your friend and docile Pupil to instruct
> CHARLES LAMB

To S. T. Coleridge

10. TO THOMAS MANNING

[1 March 1800]

I hope by this time you are prepared to say, the Falstaff's Letters[1] are a bundle of the sharpest, queerest, profoundest humours, of any these juice-drained latter times have spawned. – I should have advertiz'd you, that the meaning is frequently hard to be got at; and so are the future Guineas, that now lie ripening & aurifying in the womb of some undiscoverd Potosi;[2] but dig, dig, dig, dig, Manning. . . .

I set to, with an unconquerable propulsion to write, with a lamentable want of what to write. My private goings on are orderly as the movements of the spheres, and stale as their music to angel's ears. Public affairs – except as they touch upon me, & so turn into private – I cannot whip my mind up to feel any interest in. – – I grieve indeed that War and Nature & Mr Pitt that hangs up in Lloyd's best parlour, should have conspired to call up three necessaries, simple commoners as our fathers knew them, into the upper house of Luxuries – –. Bread, and Beer, and Coals,[3] Manning. – But as to France and Frenchman, And the Abbe Sieyes[4] & his constitutions, I cannot make these present times present to me. I read histories of the past, and I live in them; altho' to abstract senses they are far less momentous, than the noises which keep Europe awake. I am reading Burnet's Own Times.[5] – Did you ever read that garrulous, pleasant history? He tells his story like an old man, past political service, bragging to his sons, on winter evenings, of the part he took in public transactions, when 'his old cap was new.' Full of scandal, which all true history is. No palliatives, but all the stark wickedness, that actually gives the momentum to national actors. Quite the prattle of age & out lived importance. Truth & sincerity staring out upon you perpetually in alto relievo. – Himself a party man, he makes you a party man. None of the Damned Philosophical Humeian indifference, so cold

& unnatural & unhuman. None of the damned Gibbonian fine writing so fine & composite. None of Mr Robertson's periods with three members. None of Mr Roscoe's sage remarks, all so apposite & coming in so clever, lest the reader should have had the trouble of drawing an inference. Burnet's good old prattle I can bring present to my mind; I can make the revolution present to me –. the French Revolution, by a converse perversity in my nature, I fling as far *from* me. –

To quit this damned subject, and to relieve you from two or three dismal yawns, which I hear in spirit, I here conclude my more than commonly obtuse letter; dull, up to the dullness of a Dutch commentator on Shakspere –

My love to Lloyd and to Sophia

C L

11. TO SAMUEL TAYLOR COLERIDGE

Land of Shadows
Shadow-month [April]
the 16th or 17th, 1800

I send you, in this parcel, my play, which I beg you to present in my name, with my respect and love, to Wordsworth and his sister. You blame us for giving your direction to Miss Wesley;[1] the woman has been ten times after us about it, and we gave it her at last, under the idea that no further harm would ensue, but she would *once* write to you, and you would bite your lips and forget to answer it, and so it would end. You read us a dismal homily upon 'Realities.' We know, quite as well as you do, what are shadows and what are realities. You, for instance, when you are over your fourth or fifth jorum,[2] chirping about old school occurrences, are the best of realities. Shadows are cold, thin things, that have no warmth or grasp in them. Miss Wesley and her friend, and a tribe of authoresses that come after you here daily, and, in defect of you, hive and cluster upon us, are the shadows. You encouraged that mopsey, Miss Wesley, to dance after you, in the hope of having her nonsense put into a nonsensical Anthology. We have pretty well shaken her off, by that simple expedient of referring her to you; but there are more burrs in the wind. I came home t'other day from business, hungry as a hunter, to dinner, with nothing, I am sure, of *the author but hunger* about me, and whom found I closeted with Mary but a friend of this Miss Wesley, one Miss Benje, or Benjey – I don't know how she spells her name. I just came in time enough, I believe, luckily to prevent them from exchanging vows of eternal friendship. It seems she is one of your authoresses, that you first foster, and then upbraid us with. But I forgive you. 'The rogue has given me potions to make me love him.' Well; go she would not, nor step a step over our threshold, till we had promised to come and drink tea with her next night. I had never seen her before, and could not tell who the devil it was that was so familiar. We went, however, not to be impolite. Her lodgings are up two pairs of stairs in East Street. Tea and coffee, and macaroons – a kind of cake I much love. We sat down. Presently Miss Benje broke the silence, by declaring herself quite of a different opinion from D'Israeli,[3] who supposes the differences of human intellect to be the mere effect of organization. She begged to know my opinion. I attempted to carry it off with a pun upon organ; but that went off very flat. She immediately conceived a very low opinion of my metaphysics; and, turning round to Mary, put some question to her in French, – possibly having heard that neither Mary nor I understood French. The explanation that took place occasioned some embarrassment and much wondering. She then fell into an insulting conversation about the comparative genius and merits of all modern languages, and concluded with asserting that the Saxon was esteemed the purest dialect in Germany. From thence she passed into the subject of poetry; where I, who had hitherto sat mute and a hearer only, humbly hoped I might now put in a word to some advantage, seeing that it was my own trade in a manner. But I was stopped by a round assertion, that no good poetry had appeared since Dr Johnson's time. It seems the Doctor has suppressed many hopeful geniuses that way by the severity of his critical strictures in his 'Lives of the Poets.' I here ventured to question the fact, and was beginning to appeal to *names*, but I was assured 'it was certainly the case.' Then we discussed Miss More's book on education, which I had never read. It seems Dr Gregory, another of Miss Benjey's friends, has found fault with one of Miss More's metaphors. Miss More has been at some pains to vindicate herself – in the opinion of Miss Benjey, not without success. It seems the Doctor is invariably against the use of broken or mixed metaphor, which he reprobates against the authority of Shakspeare himself. We next discussed the question, whether Pope was a poet? I find Dr Gregory is of opinion he was not, though Miss Seward does not at all concur with him in this. We then sat upon the comparative merits of the ten translations of 'Pizarro,' and Miss Benjey or Benje advised

Mary to take two of them home; she thought it might afford her some pleasure to compare them *verbatim;* which we declined. It being now nine o'clock, wine and macaroons were again served round, and we parted, with a promise to go again next week, and meet the Miss Porters, who, it seems, have heard much of Mr Coleridge, and wish to meet *us*, because we are *his* friends. I have been preparing for the occasion. I crowd cotton in my ears. I read all the reviews and magazines of the past month against the dreadful meeting, and I hope by these means to cut a tolerable second-rate figure.

Pray let us have no more complaints about shadows. We are in a fair way, *through you*, to surfeit sick upon them.

Our loves and respects to your host and hostess. Our dearest love to Coleridge.

Take no thought about your proof-sheets; they shall be done as if Woodfall[4] himself did them. Pray send us word of Mrs Coleridge and little David Hartley, your little reality.

Farewell, dear Substance. Take no umbrage at any thing I have written.

C. LAMB, *Umbra*

Coleridge, I find loose among your papers a copy of 'Christabel.' It wants about thirty lines; you will very much oblige me by sending me the beginning as far as that line, –

And the spring comes slowly up this way;

and the intermediate lines between –

The lady leaps up suddenly,
The lovely Lady Christabel;

and the lines, –

She folded her arms beneath her cloak,
And stole to the other side of the oak.

The trouble to you *will be small*, and the benefit to us *very great!* A pretty antithesis! A figure in speech I much applaud.

Godwin has called upon us. He spent one evening here. Was very friendly. Kept us up till midnight. Drank punch, and talked about you. He seems, above all men, mortified at your going away. Suppose you were to write to that good-natured heathen – 'or is he a *shadow?*' If I do not *write*, impute it to the long postage, of which you have so much cause to complain. I have scribbled over a *queer letter*, as I find by perusal; but it means no mischief.

I am, and will be, yours ever, in sober sadness,

C. L.

Write your *German* as plain as sunshine, for that must correct itself. You know I am homo unius linguæ: in English, illiterate, a dunce, a ninny.

12. TO THOMAS MANNING

[P.M. 20 May 1800]

Dear Manning,

I feel myself unable to thank you sufficiently for your kind letter. It was doubly acceptable to me, both for the choice poetry and the kind honest prose which it contained. It was just such a letter as I should have expected from Manning.

I am in much better spirits than when I wrote last. I have had a very eligible offer to lodge with a friend in town. He will have rooms to let at midsummer, by which time I hope my sister will be well enough to join me. It is a great object to me to live in town, where we shall be much more *private*, and to quit a house and neighbourhood where poor Mary's disorder, so frequently recurring, has made us a sort of marked people. We can be nowhere private except in the midst of London. We shall be in a family where we visit very frequently . . . only my landlord and I have not yet come to a conclusion. He has a partner to consult. I am still on the tremble, for I do not know where we could go into lodgings that would not be, in many respects, highly exceptionable. Only God send Mary well again, and I hope all will be well! The prospect, such as it is, has made me quite happy. I have just time to tell you of it, as I know it will give you pleasure. – Farewell.

C. LAMB.

13. TO ROBERT LLOYD

[No date: July 1800]

Dear Robert,

My mind has been so barren and idle of late, that I have done nothing. I have received many a summons from you, and have repeatedly sat down to write, and broke off from despair of sending you anything worthy your acceptance. I have had such a deadness about me. Man delights not me nor woman neither. I impute it in part, or altogether, to the stupefying effect which continued fine weather has upon me. I want some rains, or even snow and intense cold winter nights, to bind me to my habitation, and make me value it as a home — a sacred character which it has not attained with me hitherto. I cannot read or write when the sun shines: I can only walk.

I must tell you that, since I wrote last I have been two days at Oxford, on a visit (long put off) to Gutch's family (my landlord). I was much gratified with the Colleges and Libraries and what else of Oxford I could see in so short a time. In the All Souls' Library is a fine head of Bishop Taylor,[1] which was one great inducement to my Oxford visit. In the Bodleian are many Portraits of illustrious Dead, the only species of painting I value at a farthing. But an indubitable good Portrait of a great man is worth a pilgrimage to go and see. Gutch's family is a very fine one, consisting of well-grown sons and daughters, and all likely and well-favour'd. What is called a Happy family — that is, according to my interpretation, a numerous assemblage of young men and women, all fond of each other to a certain degree, and all happy together, but where the very number forbids any two of them to get close enough to each other to share secrets and *be friends*. That close intercourse can only exist (commonly, I think,) in a family of two or three. I do not envy large families. The fraternal affection by diffusion and multi–partici–pation is ordinarily thin and weak. They don't get near enough to each other.

I expected to have had an account of Sophia's being brought to bed[2] before this time; but I remain in confidence that you will send me the earliest news. I hope it will be happy.

Coleridge is settled at Keswick, so that the probability is that he will be once again united with your Brother. Such men as he and Words-worth would exclude solitude in the Hebrides or Thule.

Pray have you seen the New Edition of Burns, including his post-humous works? I want very much to get a sight of it, but cannot afford to buy it, my Oxford Journey, though very moderate, having pared away all superfluities.

Will you accept of this short letter, accompanied with professions of deepest regard for you?

Yours unalterably,

C. Lamb.

14. TO SAMUEL TAYLOR COLERIDGE

Aug. 6th, 1800.

Dear Coleridge,

I have taken to-day, and delivered to Longman and Co., *Imprimis*: your books, viz., three ponderous German dictionaries, one volume (I can find no more) of German and French ditto, sundry other German books unbound, as you left them, Percy's Ancient Poetry, and one volume of Anderson's Poets. I specify them, that you may not lose any. *Secundo*: a dressing-gown (value, fivepence), in which you used to sit and look like a conjuror, when you were translating 'Wallenstein.' A case of two razors and a shaving-box and strap. This it has cost me a severe struggle to part with. They are in a brown-paper parcel, which also contains sundry papers and poems, sermons, *some few Epic* Poems, – one about Cain and Abel, which came from Poole, &c., &c., and also your tragedy; with one or two small German books, and that drama in which Got-fader performs. *Tertio*: a small oblong box containing *all your letters*, collected from all your waste papers, and which fill the said little box. All other waste papers, which I judged worth sending, are in the paper parcel aforesaid. But you will find *all* your letters in the box by themselves. Thus have I discharged my conscience and my lumber-room of all your property, save and except a folio entitled Tyrrell's Bibliotheca Politica, which you used to learn your politics out of when you wrote for the Post,[1] *mutatis mutandis*, *i.e.*, applying past inferences to modern *data*. I retain that, because I am sensible I am very deficient in the politics myself; and I have torn up – don't be angry, waste paper has risen forty per cent., and I can't afford to buy it – all Buonaparte's Letters, Arthur Young's Treatise on Corn, and one or two more light-armed infantry, which I thought better suited the flippancy of London discussion than the dignity of Keswick thinking. Mary says you will be in a damned passion about them when you come to miss them; but you must study philosophy. Read Albertus Magnus de Chartis Amissis five times over after phlebotomising, – 'tis Burton's recipe[2] – and then be angry with an absent friend if you can. I have just heard that Mrs Lloyd is delivered of a fine boy, and mother and boy are doing well. Fie on sluggards, what is thy Sara doing? Sara is obscure. Am I to understand by her letter, that she sends a *kiss* to Eliza Buckingham? Pray tell your wife that a note of interrogation on the superscription of a letter is highly ungrammatical – she proposes writing my name *Lamb?* Lambe[3] is quite enough. I have had the Anthology,[4] and like only one thing in it, *Lewti*; but of that the last stanza is detestable, the rest most exquisite!

– the epithet *enviable* would dash the finest poem. For God's sake (I never was more serious), don't make me ridiculous any more by terming me gentle-hearted in print, or do it in better verses.[5] It did well enough five years ago when I came to see you, and was moral coxcomb enough at the time you wrote the lines, to feed upon such epithets; but, besides that, the meaning of gentle is equivocal at best, and almost always means poor-spirited, the very quality of gentleness is abhorrent to such vile trumpetings. My *sentiment* is long since vanished. I hope my *virtues* have done *sucking*. I can scarce think but you meant it in joke. I hope you did, for I should be ashamed to think that you could think to gratify me by such praise, fit only to be a cordial to some green-sick sonneteer.

I have hit off the following in imitation of old English poetry, which, I imagine, I am a dab at. The measure is unmeasureable; but it most resembles that beautiful ballad of the 'Old and Young Courtier;' and in its feature of taking the extremes of two situations for just parallel, it resembles the old poetry certainly. If I could but stretch out the circumstances to twelve more verses, *i.e.*, if I had as much genius as the writer of that old song, I think it would be excellent. It was to follow an imitation of Burton in prose, which you have not seen. But fate 'and wisest Stewart' say No.[6]

I can send you 200 pens and six quires of paper *immediately*, if they will answer the carriage by coach. It would be foolish to pack 'em up *cum multis libris et cæteris*,[7] – they would all spoil. I only wait your commands to coach them. I would pay five-and-forty thousand carriages to read W.'s tragedy, of which I have heard so much and seen so little – only what I saw at Stowey. Pray give me an order in writing on Longman for 'Lyrical Ballads.' I have the first volume, and, truth to tell, six shillings is a broad shot. I cram all I can in, to save a multiplying of letters – those pretty comets with swingeing tails.

I'll just crowd in God bless you! C. LAMB.
Wednesday night.

15. TO THOMAS MANNING

[P.M. 9 August 1800]

Dear Manning,

I suppose you have heard of Sophia Lloyd's good fortune, and paid the customary compliments to the parents. Heaven keep the new-born infant from star-blasting and moon-blasting, from epilepsy, marasmus, and the devil! May he live to see many days, and they good ones; some friends, and they pretty regular correspondents, with as much wit as [? and] wisdom as will eat their bread and cheese together under a poor roof without quarrelling; as much goodness as will earn heaven if there be such a place and deserve it if there be not, but, rather than go to bed solitary, would truckle with the meanest succubus on her bed of brimstone. Here I must leave off, my benedictory powers failing me. I could *curse* the sheet full; so much stronger is corruption than grace in the Natural Man.

And now, when shall I catch a glimpse of your honest face-to-face countenance again – your fine *dogmatical sceptical* face, by punch-light? O! one glimpse of the human face, and shake of the human hand, is better than whole reams of this cold, thin correspondence – yea, of more worth than all the letters that have sweated the fingers of sensibility from Madame Sevigné and Balzac (observe my Larning!) to Sterne and Shenstone.

Coleridge is settled with his wife (with a child in her guts) and the young philosopher at Keswick with the Wordsworths. They have contrived to spawn a new volume of lyrical ballads, which is to see the light in about a month, and causes no little excitement in the *literary world*. George Dyer too, that good-natured heathen, is more than nine months gone with his twin volumes of ode, pastoral, sonnet, elegy, Spenserian, Horatian, Akensidish, and Masonic verse – Clio prosper the birth! it will be twelve shillings out of somebody's pocket. I find he means to exclude 'personal satire,' so it appears by his truly original advertisement. Well, God put it into the hearts of the English gentry to come in shoals and subscribe to his poems, for He never put a kinder heart into flesh of man than George Dyer's!

Now farewell: for dinner is at hand, and yearning guts do chide.

C. L.

16. TO SAMUEL TAYLOR COLERIDGE

Thursday, Aug. 14, 1800.

Read on and you'll come to the *Pens*.

My head is playing all the tunes in the world, ringing such peals. It has just finished the 'Merry Christ Church Bells,' and absolutely is beginning 'Turn again, Whittington.' Buz, buz, buz: bum, bum, bum: wheeze, wheeze, wheeze: feu, feu, feu: tinky, tinky, tinky: *craunch*. I shall certainly come to be damned at last. I have been getting drunk for two days running. I find my moral sense in the last stage of a consumption, and my religion burning as blue and faint as the tops of burning bricks. Hell gapes and the Devil's great guts cry cupboard for me. In the midst of this infernal torture, Conscience (and be damn'd to her) is barking and yelping as loud as any of them.

I have sat down to read over again your satire upon me [1] in the Anthology and I think I do begin to spy out something with beauty and design in it. I perfectly accede to all your alterations, and only desire that you had cut deeper, when your hand was in.

In the next edition of the 'Anthology' (which Phœbus avert and those nine other wandering maids also!) please to blot out *gentle-hearted*, and substitute: drunken dog, ragged-head, seld-shaven, odd-eyed, stuttering, or any other epithet which truly and properly belongs to the gentleman in question. And for Charles read Tom, or Bob, or Richard *for more delicacy*. Damn you, I was beginning to forgive you and believe in earnest that the lugging in of my proper name was purely unintentional on your part, when looking back for further conviction, stares me in the face *Charles Lamb of the India House. Now* I am convinced it was all done in malice, heaped sack-upon-sack, congregated, studied malice. You Dog! your 141st page shall not save you. I own I was just ready to acknowledge that there is a something not unlike good poetry in that page, if you had not run into the unintelligible abstraction-fit about the manner of the Deity's making spirits perceive his presence. God, nor created thing alive, can receive any honour from such thin show-box attributes.

By-the-by, where did you pick up that scandalous piece of private history about the angel and the Duchess of Devonshire? [2] If it is a fiction of your own, why truly it is a very modest one *for you*. Now I do affirm that 'Lewti' is a very beautiful poem. I *was* in earnest when I praised it. It describes a silly species of one not the wisest of passions. *Therefore* it cannot deeply affect a disenthralled mind. But such imagery, such novelty, such delicacy, and such versification never got into an 'Anthology' before. I am only sorry that the cause of all the passionate complaint is not greater than the trifling circumstance of Lewti being out of temper one day. In sober truth, I cannot see any great merit in the little Dialogue called 'Blenheim.' It is rather novel and pretty; but the thought is very obvious and children's poor prattle, a thing of easy imitation. *Pauper vult videri et* EST.[3]

'Gaulberto' certainly has considerable originality, but sadly wants finishing. It is, as it is, one of the very best in the book. Next to 'Lewti' I like the 'Raven,' which has a good deal of humour. I was pleased to see it again, for you once sent it me, and I have lost the letter which contained it. Now I am on the subject of Anthologies, I must say I am sorry the old Pastoral way has fallen into disrepute. The Gentry which now indite Sonnets are certainly the legitimate descendants of the ancient shepherds. The same simpering face of description, the old family face, is visibly continued in the line. Some of their ancestors' labours are yet to be found in Allan Ramsay's and Jacob Tonson's *Miscellanies*. But, miscellanies decaying and the old Pastoral way dying of mere want, their successors (driven from their paternal acres) now-a-days settle and hive upon Magazines and Anthologies. This Race of men are uncommonly addicted to superstition. Some of them are Idolators and worship the Moon. Others deify qualities, as love, friendship, sensibility, or bare accidents, as Solitude. Grief and Melancholy have their respective altars and temples among them, as the heathens builded theirs to Mors, Febris, Pallor.[4] They all agree in ascribing a peculiar sanctity to the number fourteen. One of their own legislators affirmeth, that whatever exceeds that number 'encroacheth upon the province of the Elegy' – *vice versa*, whatever 'cometh short of that number abutteth upon the premises of the Epigram.' I have been able to discover but few *Images* in their temples, which, like the Caves of Delphos of old, are famous for giving *Echoes*. They impute a religious importance to the letter O, whether because by its roundness it is thought to typify the moon, their principal goddess, or for its analogies to their own labours, all ending where they began; or whatever other high and mystical reference, I have never been able to discover, but I observe they never begin their invocations to their gods without it, except indeed one insignificant sect among them, who use the Doric A, pronounced like Ah! broad, instead. These boast to have restored the old Dorian mood.

Now I am on the subject of poetry, I must announce to you, who, doubtless, in your remote part of the Island, have not heard tidings of so great a blessing, that GEORGE DYER hath prepared two ponderous volumes full of Poetry and Criticism. They impend over the town, and are threatened to fall in the winter. The first volume contains every sort of poetry except personal satire, which George, in his truly original prospectus, renounceth for ever, whimsically foisting the intention in between the price of his book and the proposed number of subscribers. (If I can, I will get you a copy of his *handbill*.) He has tried his *vein* in every species besides – the Spenserian, Thomsonian, Masonic and Akensidish more especially. The second volume is all criticism; wherein he demonstrates to the entire satisfaction of the literary world, in a way that must silence all reply for ever, that the pastoral was introduced by Theocritus and polished by Virgil and Pope – that Gray and Mason (who always hunt in couples in George's brain) have a good deal of poetical fire and true lyric genius – that Cowley was ruined by excess of wit (a warning to all moderns) – that Charles Lloyd, Charles Lamb, and William Wordsworth, in later days, have struck the true chords of poesy. O, George, George, with a head uniformly wrong and a heart uniformly right, that I had power and might equal to my wishes! – then I would call the Gentry of thy native Island, and they should come in troops, flocking at the sound of thy Prospectus Trumpet, and crowding who shall be first to stand in thy List of Subscribers. I can only put twelve shillings into thy pocket (which, I will answer for them, will not stick there long), out of a pocket almost as bare as thine. [*Lamb here erases six lines.*]

Is it not a pity so much fine writing should be erased? But, to tell the truth, I began to scent that I was getting into that sort of style which Longinus and Dionysius Halicarnassus aptly call 'the affected.' But I am suffering from the combined effect of two days' drunkenness, and at such times it is not very easy to think or express in a natural series. The ONLY useful OBJECT of this Letter is to apprize you that on Saturday I shall transmit the PENS by the same coach I sent the Parcel. So enquire them out. You had better write to Godwin *here*, directing your letter to be forwarded to him. I don't know his address. You know your letter must at any rate come to London first.

C. L.

17. TO THOMAS MANNING

[P.M. 16 October 1800]

Dear Manning,

Had you written one week before you did, I certainly should have obeyed your injunction; you should have seen me before my letter. I will explain to you my situation. There are six of us in one department. Two of us (within these four days) are confined with severe fevers; and two more, who belong to the Tower Militia,[1] expect to have marching orders on Friday. Now six are absolutely necessary. I have already asked and obtained two young hands to supply the loss of the *Feverites*; and, with the other prospect before me, you may believe I cannot decently ask leave of absence for myself. All I can promise (and I do promise with the sincerity of *Saint* Peter, and the contrition of *Sinner* Peter if I fail) that I will come *the very first spare week*, and go nowhere till I have been at Camb. No matter if you are in a state of pupilage when I come; for I can employ myself in Cambridge very pleasantly in the mornings. Are there not Libraries, Halls, Colleges, Books, Pictures, Statues?

I wish to God you had made London in your way. There is an exhibition quite uncommon in Europe, which could not have escaped *your genius*, – a LIVE RATTLESNAKE, 10 feet in length, and the thickness of a big leg. I went to see it last night by candlelight. We were ushered into a room very little bigger than ours at Pentonville. A man and woman and four boys live in this room, joint tenants with nine snakes, most of them such as no remedy has been discovered for their bite. We walked into the middle, which is formed by a half-moon of wired boxes, all mansions of *snakes*, – whip-snakes, thunder-snakes, pig-nose-snakes, American vipers, and *this monster*. He lies curled up in folds; and immediately a stranger enters (for he is used to the family, and sees them play at cards,) he set up a rattle like a watchman's in London, or near as loud, and reared up a head, from the midst of these folds, like a toad, and shook his head, and showed every sign a snake can show of irritation. I had the foolish curiosity to strike the wires with my finger, and the devil flew at me with his toad-mouth wide open: the inside of his mouth is quite white. I had got my finger away, nor could he well have bit me with his damn'd big mouth, which would have been certain death in five minutes. But it frightened me so much, that I did not recover my voice for a minute's space. I forgot, in my fear, that he was secured. You would have forgot too, for 'tis incredible how such a monster can be confined in small gauzy-looking wires. I dreamed of snakes in the night. I wish to heaven you could see it. He absolutely swelled with passion to the bigness of a large thigh. I could not retreat without infringing on another box, and just behind, a little devil not an inch from my back, had got his nose out, with some difficulty and pain, quite through the bars! He was soon taught better manners. All the snakes were curious, and objects of terror: but this monster, like Aaron's serpent, swallowed up the impression of the rest. He opened his damn'd mouth, when he made at me, as wide as his head was broad. I hallooed out quite loud, and felt pains all over my body with the fright.

I have had the felicity of hearing George Dyer read out one book of 'The Farmer's Boy.'[2] I thought it rather childish. No doubt, there is originality in it, (which, in your self-taught geniuses, is a most rare quality, they generally getting hold of some bad models in a scarcity of books, and forming their taste on them,) but no *selection*. *All* is described.

Mind, I have only heard read one book.

Yours sincerely,
Philo-Snake,   C. L.

18. TO THOMAS MANNING

[P.M. 3 November 1800]

Ecquid meditatur Archimedes?[1] What is Euclid doing? What has happened to learned Trismegist? – Doth he take it in ill part, that his humble friend did not comply with his courteous invitation? Let it suffice, I could not come – are impossibilities nothing – be they abstractions of the intellects or not (rather) most sharp and mortifying realities? nuts in the Will's mouth too hard for her to crack? brick and stone walls in her way, which she can by no means eat through? sore lets, *impedimenta viarum*,[2] no thoroughfares? *racemi nimium alte pendentes?*[3] Is the phrase classic? I allude to the grapes in Æsop, which cost the fox a strain, and gained the world an aphorism. Observe the superscription of this letter. In adapting the size of the letters, which constitute *your* name and Mr *Crisp's*[4] name respectively, I had an eye to your different stations in life. 'Tis really curious, and must be soothing to an *aristocrat*. I wonder it has never been hit on before my time.

I have made an acquisition latterly of a *pleasant hand*, one Rickman, to whom I was introduced by George Dyer, not the most flattering auspices under which one man can be introduced to another. George brings all sorts of people together, setting up a sort of agrarian law, or common property, in matter of society; but for once he has done me a great pleasure, while he was only pursuing a principle, as *ignes fatui may* light you home. This Rickman lives in our Buildings, immediately opposite our house; the finest fellow to drop in a' nights, about nine or ten o'clock – cold bread-and-cheese time – just in the *wishing* time of the night, when you *wish* for somebody to come in, without a distinct idea of a probable anybody. Just in the nick, neither too early to be tedious, nor too late to sit a reasonable time. He is a most pleasant hand: a fine rattling fellow, has gone through life laughing at solemn apes; himself hugely literate, oppressively full of information in all stuff of conversation, from matter of fact to Xenophon and Plato – can talk Greek with Porson, politics with Thelwall,[5] conjecture with George Dyer, nonsense with me, and anything with anybody: a great farmer, somewhat concerned in an agricultural magazine – reads no poetry but Shakspeare, very intimate with Southey, but never reads his poetry: relishes George Dyer, thoroughly penetrates into the ridiculous where-ever found, understands the *first time* (a great desideratum in common minds) – you need never twice speak to him; does not want explanations, translations, limitations, as Professor Godwin does when you make an assertion: *up* to anything, *down* to everything – whatever *sapit hominem*.[6] A perfect *man*. All this farrago, which must perplex you to read, and has put me to a little trouble to *select*, only proves how impossible it is to describe a *pleasant hand*. You must see Rickman to know him, for he is a species in one. A new class. An exotic, any slip of which I am proud to put in my garden-pot. The clearest-headed fellow. Fullest of matter with least verbosity. If there be any alloy in my fortune to have met with such a man, it is that he commonly divides his time between town and country, having some foolish family ties at Christchurch, by which means he can only gladden our London hemisphere with returns of light. He is now going for six weeks.

At last I have written to Kemble,[7] to know the event of my play, which was presented last Christmas. As I suspected, came an answer back that the copy was lost, and could not be found – no hint that anybody had to this day ever looked into it – with a courteous (reason-able!) request of another copy (if I had one by me,) and a promise of a definite answer in a week. I could not resist so facile and moderate a demand, so scribbled out another, omitting sundry things, such as the witch story, about half of the forest scene (which is too leisurely for story), and transposing that damn'd soliloquy about England getting drunk, which, like its reciter, stupidly stood alone, nothing prevenient or antevenient, and cleared away a good deal besides; and sent this copy, written *all out* (with alterations, &c., *requiring judgment*) in one day and a half! I sent it last night, and am in weekly expectation of the tolling-bell and death-warrant.

This is all my Lunnon news. Send me some from the *banks of Cam*, as the poets delight to speak, especially George Dyer, who has no other name, nor idea, nor definition of Cambridge: namely, its being a market-town, sending members to Parliament, never entered into his definition: it was and is, simply, the banks of the Cam or the fair Cam, as Oxford is the banks of the Isis or the fair Isis. Yours in all humility, most illustrious Trismegist,

C. LAMB.

(Read on; there's more at the bottom.)

You ask me about the 'Farmer's Boy' – don't you think the fellow who wrote it (who is a shoemaker) has a poor mind? Don't you find he is always silly about *poor Giles*, and those abject kind of phrases, which mark a man that looks up to wealth? None of Burns's poet–dignity. What do you think? I have just opened him; but he makes me sick. Dyer knows the shoemaker (a damn'd stupid hound in company); but George promises to introduce him indiscriminately to all friends and all combinations.

19. TO THOMAS MANNING

[P.M. 28 November 1800]

Dear Manning,

I have received a very kind invitation from Lloyd and Sophia to go and spend a month with them at the Lakes. Now it fortunately happens (which is so seldom the case!) that I have spare cash by me, enough to answer the expenses of so long a journey; and I am determined to get away from the office by some means. The purpose of this letter is to request of you (my dear friend) that you will not take it unkind if I decline my proposed visit to Cambridge *for the present*. Perhaps I shall be able to take Cambridge *in my way*, going or coming. I need not describe to you the expectations which such an one as myself pent up all my life in a dirty city, have formed of a tour to the Lakes. Consider Grasmere! Ambleside! Wordsworth! Coleridge! I hope you will.* Hills, woods, lakes, and mountains, to the eternal devil. I will eat snipes with thee, Thomas Manning. Only confess, confess, a *bite*.

P.S. I think you named the 16th; but was it not modest of Lloyd to send such an invitation! It shows his knowledge of *money* and *time*. I would be loth to think he meant

Ironic satire sidelong sklented
On my poor pursie. – BURNS.

For my part, with reference to my friends northward, I must confess that I am not romance-bit about *Nature*. The earth, and sea, and sky (when all is said) is but as a house to dwell in. If the inmates be courteous, and good liquors flow like the conduits at an old coronation; if they can talk sensibly and feel properly; I have no need to stand staring upon the gilded looking-glass (that strained my friend's purse-strings in the purchase), nor his five-shilling print over the mantelpiece of old Nabbs the carrier (which only betrays his false taste). Just as important to me (in a sense) is all the furniture of my world — eye-pampering, but satisfies no heart. Streets, streets, streets, markets, theatres, churches, Covent Gardens, shops sparkling with pretty faces of industrious milliners, neat sempstresses, ladies cheapening, gentlemen behind counters lying, authors in the street with spectacles, George Dyers (you may know them by their gait), lamps lit at night, pastry-cooks' and silversmiths' shops, beautiful Quakers of Pentonville,[1] noise of coaches, drowsy cry of mechanic watchmen at night, with bucks reeling home drunk; if you happen to wake at midnight, cries of Fire and Stop thief; inns of court, with their learned air, and halls, and butteries, just like Cambridge colleges; old book-stalls, Jeremy Taylors, Burtons on Melancholy, and Religio Medicis on every stall. These are thy pleasures, O London with-the-many-sins. O City abounding in whores, for these may Keswick and her giant brood go hang!

C. L.

20. TO THOMAS MANNING

December 27th, 1800.

At length George Dyer's phrenesis has come to a crisis; he is raging and furiously mad. I waited upon the heathen, Thursday was a se'nnight; the first symptom which struck my eye and gave me incontrovertible proof of the fatal truth was a pair of nankeen pantaloons four times too big for him, which the said Heathen did pertinaciously affirm to be new.

They were absolutely ingrained with the accumulated dirt of ages; but he affirmed them to be clean. He was going to visit a lady that was nice about those things, and that's the reason he wore nankeen that day. And then he danced, and capered, and fidgeted, and pulled up his pantaloons, and hugged his intolerable flannel vestment closer about his poetic loins; anon he gave it loose to the zephyrs which plentifully insinuate their tiny bodies through every crevice, door, window or wainscot, expressly formed for the exclusion of such impertinents. Then he caught at a proof sheet, and catched up a laundress's bill instead — made a dart at Blomfield's Poems, and threw them in agony aside. I could not bring him to one direct reply; he could not maintain his jumping mind in a right line for the tithe of a moment by Clifford's Inn clock. He must go to the printer's immediately — the most unlucky accident — he had struck off five hundred impressions of his Poems, which were ready for delivery to subscribers, and the Preface must all be expunged. There were eighty pages of Preface, and not till that morning had he discovered that in the very first page of said Preface he had set out with a principle of Criticism fundamentally wrong, which vitiated all his following reasoning. The Preface must be expunged, although it cost him £30 — the lowest calculation, taking in paper and printing! In vain have his real friends remonstrated against this Midsummer madness. George is as obstinate as a Primitive Christian — and wards and parries off all our thrusts with one unanswerable fence; — 'Sir, it's of great consequence that the *world* is not *misled!*'

As for the other Professor,[1] he has actually begun to dive into Tavernier and Chardin's *Persian* Travels for a story, to form a new drama for the sweet tooth of this fastidious age. Hath not Bethlehem College a fair action for non-residence against such professors? Are poets so *few* in *this age*, that He must write poetry? *Is morals* a subject so exhausted, that he must quit that line? Is the metaphysic well (without a bottom) drained dry?

If I can guess at the wicked pride of the Professor's heart, I would take a shrewd wager that he disdains ever again to dip his pen in *Prose*. Adieu, ye splendid theories! Farewell, dreams of political justice! Law-suits, where I was counsel for Archbishop Fenelon *versus* my own mother, in the famous fire cause![2]

Vanish from my mind, professors, one and all! I have metal more attractive on foot.

Man of many snipes, — I will sup with thee, Deo volente et diabolo nolente,[3] on Monday night the 5th of January, in the new year, and crush a cup to the infant century.

A word or two of my progress. Embark at six o'clock in the morning, with a fresh gale, on a Cambridge one-decker; very cold till eight at night; land at St Mary's light-house, muffins and coffee upon table (or any other curious production of Turkey or both Indies), snipes exactly at nine, punch to commence at ten, with *argument;* difference of opinion is expected to take place about eleven; perfect unanimity, with some haziness and dimness, before twelve. – N.B. My single affection is not so singly wedded to snipes; but the curious and epicurean eye would also take a pleasure in beholding a delicate and well-chosen assortment of teals, ortolans,[4] the unctuous and palate-soothing flesh of geese wild and tame, nightingales' brains, the sensorium of a young sucking-pig, or any other Christmas dish, which I leave to the judgment of you and the cook of Gonville.

C. LAMB.

21. TO WILLIAM WORDSWORTH

[P.M. 30 January 1801]

Thanks for your Letter and Present.[1] I had already borrowed your second volume. What most please me are, the Song of Lucy. . . . *Simon's sickly daughter* in the Sexton made me *cry*. Next to these are the description of the continuous Echoes in the story of Joanna's laugh, where the mountains and all the scenery absolutely seem alive – and that fine Shakesperian character of the Happy Man, in the Brothers,

> – that creeps about the fields,
> Following his fancies by the hour, to bring
> Tears down his cheek, or solitary smiles
> Into his face, *until the Setting Sun*
> *Write Fool upon his forehead.*

I will mention one more: the delicate and curious feeling in the wish for the Cumberland Beggar, that he may have about him the melody of Birds, altho' he hear them not. Here the mind knowingly passes a fiction upon herself, first substituting her own feelings for the Beggar's, and, in the same breath detecting the fallacy, will not part with the wish. – The Poet's Epitaph is disfigured, to my taste by the vulgar satire upon parsons and lawyers in the beginning, and the coarse epithet of pin point in the 6th stanza. All the rest is eminently good, and your own. I will just add that it appears to me a fault in the Beggar, that the instructions conveyed in it are too direct and like a lecture: they don't slide into the mind of the reader, while he is imagining no such matter. An intelligent reader finds a sort of insult in being told, I will teach you how to think upon this subject. This fault, if I am right, is in a ten-thousandth worse degree to be found in Sterne and many many novelists

& modern poets, who continually put a sign post up to shew where you are to feel. They set out with assuming their readers to be stupid. Very different from Robinson Crusoe, the Vicar of Wakefield, Roderick Random, and other beautiful bare narratives. There is implied an unwritten compact between Author and reader; I will tell you a story, and I suppose you will understand it. Modern novels 'St Leons' [2] and the like are full of such flowers as these 'Let not my reader suppose,' 'Imagine, *if you can*' — modest! — &c. — I will here have done with praise and blame. I have written so much, only that you may not think I have passed over your book without observation. — I am sorry that Coleridge has christened his Ancient Marinere 'a poet's Reverie' — it is as bad as Bottom the Weaver's declaration that he is not a Lion but only the scenical representation of a Lion. What new idea is gained by this Title, but one subversive of all credit, which the tale should force upon us, of its truth? For me, I was never so affected with any human Tale. After first reading it, I was totally possessed with it for many days — I dislike all the miraculous part of it, but the feelings of the man under the operation of such scenery dragged me along like Tom Piper's magic whistle. I totally differ from your idea that the Marinere should have had a character and profession. This is a Beauty in Gulliver's Travels, where the mind is kept in a placid state of little wonderments; but the Ancient Marinere undergoes such Trials, as overwhelm and bury all individuality or memory of what he was, like the state of a man in a Bad dream, one terrible peculiarity of which is: that all consciousness of personality is gone. Your other observation is I think as well a little unfounded: the Marinere from being conversant in supernatural events *has* acquired a supernatural and strange cast of *phrase*, eye, appearance, &c. which frighten the wedding guest. You will excuse my remarks, because I am hurt and vexed that you should think it necessary, with a prose apology, to open the eyes of dead men that cannot see. To sum up a general opinion of the second vol. — I do not feel any one poem in it so forcibly as the Ancient Marinere, the Mad Mother, and the Lines at Tintern Abbey in the first. — I could, too, have wished the Critical preface had appeared in a separate treatise. All its dogmas are true and just, and most of them new, *as* criticism. But they associate a *diminishing* idea with the Poems which follow, as having been written for *Experiment* on the public taste, more than having sprung (as they must have done) from living and daily circumstances. — I am prolix, because I am gratifyed in the opportunity of writing to you, and I don't well know when to leave off. I ought before this to have reply'd to your very kind invitation into Cumberland. With you and your Sister I could gang any where. But I am afraid whether I shall ever be able to afford so desperate a Journey. Separate from the pleasure of your company, I don't much care if I never see a mountain in my life. I have passed all my days in London, until I have formed as many and intense local attachments, as any of you mountaineers can have done with dead nature. The Lighted shops of the Strand and Fleet Street, the innumerable trades, tradesmen and customers, coaches, waggons, playhouses, all the bustle and wickedness round about Covent Garden, the very women of the Town, the Watchmen, drunken scenes, rattles, – life awake, if you awake, at all hours of the night, the impossibility of being dull in Fleet Street, the crowds, the very dirt & mud, the Sun shining upon houses and pavements, the print shops, the old book stalls, parsons cheap'ning books, coffee houses, steams of soups from kitchens, the pantomimes, London itself a pantomime and a masquerade, – all these things work themselves into my mind and feed me, without a power of satiating me. The wonder of these sights impells me into night-walks about her crowded streets, and I often shed tears in the motley Strand from fulness of joy at so much Life. – All these emotions must be strange to you. So are your rural emotions to me. But consider, what must I have been doing all my life, not to have lent great portions of my heart with usury to such scenes? –

My attachments are all local, purely local. I have no passion (or have had none since I was in love, and then it was the spurious engendering of poetry & books) to groves and vallies. The rooms where I was born, the furniture which has been before my eyes all my life, a book case which has followed me about (like a faithful dog, only exceeding him in knowledge) wherever I have moved – old chairs, old tables, streets, squares, where I have sunned myself, my old school, – these are my mistresses. Have I not enough, without your mountains? I do not envy you. I should pity you, did I not know, that the Mind will make friends of any thing. Your sun & moon and skys and hills & lakes affect me no more, or scarcely come to me in more venerable characters, than as a gilded room with tapestry and tapers, where I might live with handsome visible objects. I consider the clouds above me but as a roof, beautifully painted but unable to satisfy the mind, and at last, like the pictures of the apartment of a connoisseur, unable to afford him any longer a pleasure. So fading upon me, from disuse, have been the Beauties of Nature, as they have been confinedly called; so ever fresh & green and warm are all the inventions of men and assemblies of men in this great city. I should certainly have laughed with dear Joanna.

Give my kindest love, *and my sister's*, to D. & your*self* and a kiss from me to little Barbara Lewthwaite.[3]

C. LAMB

Thank you for Liking my Play!![4]

22. TO ROBERT LLOYD

February 7, 1801.

Dear Robert,

I shall expect you to bring me a brimful account of the pleasure which Walton[1] has given you, when you come to town. It must square with your mind. The delightful innocence and healthfulness of the Angler's mind will have blown upon yours like a Zephyr. Don't you already feel your spirit *filled* with the scenes? – the banks of rivers – the cowslip beds – the pastoral scenes – the neat alehouses – and hostesses and milkmaids, as far exceeding Virgil and Pope, as the 'Holy Living' is beyond Thomas à Kempis.[2] Are not the eating and drinking joys painted to the Life? Do they not inspire you with an immortal hunger? Are not you ambitious of being made an Angler? What edition have you got? is it Hawkins's, with plates of Piscator, &c.? That sells very dear. I have only been able to purchase the last edition without the old Plates which pleased my childhood; the plates being worn out, and the old Edition difficult and expensive to procure. The 'Complete Angler' is the only Treatise written in Dialogues that is worth a halfpenny. Many elegant dialogues have been written (such as Bishop Berkeley's 'Minute Philosopher'), but in all of them the Interlocutors are merely abstract arguments personify'd; not living dramatic characters, as in Walton, where *every thing* is *alive*; the fishes are absolutely *charactered*; and birds and animals are as interesting as men and women.

I need not be at much pains to get the 'Holy Livings.' We can procure them in ten minutes' search at any stall or shop in London. By your engaging one for Priscilla,[3] it should seem *she* will be in Town – is that the case? I thought she was fix'd at the Lakes.

I perfectly understand the nature of your solitariness at Birm., and wish I could divide myself, 'like a bribed haunch'[4] between London and it. But courage! you will soon be emancipated, and (it may be) have a frequent power of visiting this great place. Let them talk of lakes and mountains and romantic dales – all that fantastic stuff; give me a ramble by night, in the winter nights in London – the Lamps lit – the pavements of the motley Strand crowded with to and fro passengers – the shops all brilliant, and stuffed with obliging customers and obliged tradesmen – give me the old bookstalls of London – a walk in the bright Piazzas of Covent Garden. I defy a man to be dull in such places – perfect Mahometan paradises upon earth! I have lent out my heart with usury to such scenes from my childhood up, and have cried with fulness of joy at the multitudinous scenes of Life in the crowded streets of ever dear London. I wish you could fix here. I don't know if you quite comprehend my low Urban Taste; but depend upon it that a man of any feeling will have given his heart and his love in childhood and in boyhood to any scenes where he has been bred, as well to dirty streets (and smoky walls as they are called) as to green lanes, 'where live nibbling sheep,' and to the everlasting hills and the Lakes and ocean. A mob of men is better than a flock of sheep, and a crowd of happy faces justling into the playhouse at the hour of six is a more beautiful spectacle to man than the shepherd driving his 'silly' sheep to fold. Come to London and learn to sympathise with my unrural notions.

Wordsworth has published a second vol. – 'Lyrical Ballads.' Most of them very good, but not so good as first vol. What more can I tell you? I believe I told you I have been to see *Manning*. He is a dainty chiel. – A man of great Power – an enchanter almost. – Far beyond Coleridge or any man in power of impressing – when he gets you alone, he can act the wonders of Egypt. Only he is lazy, and does not always put forth all his strength; if he did, I know no man of genius at all comparable to him.

Yours as ever,
C. L.

23. TO THOMAS MANNING

Feb. 15, 1801.

I had need be cautious henceforward what opinion I give of the 'Lyrical Ballads.' All the North of England are in a turmoil. Cumberland and Westmoreland have already declared a state of war. I lately received from Wordsworth a copy of the second volume, accompanied by an acknowledgement of having received from me many months since a copy of a certain Tragedy, with excuses for not having made any acknowledgement sooner, it being owing to an 'almost insurmountable aversion from Letter-writing.' This letter I answered in due form and time, and enumerated several of the passages which had most affected me, adding, unfortunately, that no single piece had moved me so forcibly as the *Ancient Mariner*, *The Mad Mother*, or the *Lines at Tintern Abbey*. The Post did not sleep a moment. I received almost instantaneously a long letter of four sweating pages from my Reluctant Letter-Writer, the purport of which was, that he was sorry his 2d vol. had not given me more pleasure (Devil a hint did I give that it had *not pleased me*), and 'was compelled to wish that my range of sensibility was more extended, being obliged to believe that I should receive large influxes of happiness and happy Thoughts' (I suppose from the L. B.) – With a deal of stuff about a certain Union of Tenderness and Imagination, which in the sense he used Imagination was not the characteristic of Shakspeare, but which Milton possessed in a degree far exceeding other Poets: which Union, as the highest species of Poetry, and chiefly deserving that name, 'He was most proud to aspire to'; then illustrating the said Union by two quotations [1] from his own 2d vol. (which I had been so unfortunate as to miss). 1st Specimen – a father addresses his son:

> When thou
> First camest into the World, as it befalls
> To new-born Infants, thou didst sleep away
> Two days: and *Blessings from Thy father's Tongue*
> *Then fell upon thee*.

The lines were thus undermarked, and then followed 'This Passage, as combining in an extraordinary degree that Union of Imagination and Tenderness which I am speaking of, I consider as one of the Best I ever wrote!'

2d Specimen. – A youth, after years of absence, revisits his native place, and thinks (as most people do) that there has been strange alteration in his absence: –

> And that the rocks
> And everlasting Hills themselves were changed.

You see both these are good Poetry: but after one has been reading Shakspeare twenty of the best years of one's life, to have a fellow start up, and prate about some unknown quality, which Shakspeare possessed in a degree inferior to Milton and *somebody else!!* This was not to be *all* my castigation. Coleridge, who had not written to me some months before, starts up from his bed of sickness to reprove me for my hardy presumption: four long pages, equally sweaty and more tedious, came from him; assuring me that, when the works of a man of true genius such as W. undoubtedly was, do not please me at first sight, I should suspect the fault to lie 'in me and not in them,' etc. etc. etc. etc. etc. What am I to do with such people? I certainly shall write them a very merry Letter. Writing to *you*, I may say that the 2d vol. has no such pieces as the three I enumerated. It is full of original thinking and an observing mind, but it does not often make you laugh or cry. — It too artfully aims at simplicity of expression. And you sometimes doubt if Simplicity be not a cover for Poverty. The best Piece in it I will send you, being *short*. I have grievously offended my friends in the North by declaring my undue preference; but I need not fear you: —

> She dwelt among the untrodden ways
>   Beside the Springs of Dove,
> A maid whom there were few [none] to praise
>   And very few to love.
>
> A violet, by a mossy stone,
>   Half hidden from the eye.
> Fair as a star when only one
>   Is shining in the sky.
>
> She lived unknown; and few could know,
>   When Lucy ceased to be.
> But she is in the [her] grave, and oh!
>   The difference to me.

This is choice and genuine, and so are many, many more. But one does not like to have 'em rammed down one's throat. 'Pray, take it — it's very good — let me help you — eat faster.'

At length George Dyer's first volume is come to a birth. One volume of three — subscribers being allowed by the prospectus to pay for all at once (tho' it's very doubtful if the rest ever come to anything, this having been already some years getting out). I paid two guineas for you and myself, which entitle us to the whole. I will send you your copy, if you are in *a great hurry*. Meantime you owe me a guinea.

George skipped about like a scorched pea at the receipt of so much cash. To give you a specimen of the beautiful absurdity of the notes, which defy imitation, take one: 'Discrimination is not the *aim* of the present volume. It will be more strictly attended to in the next.' One of the sonnets purports to have been written in Bedlam! This for a man to own!

The rest are addressed to Science, Genius, Melancholy – &c. &c. – two, to the River Cam – an Ode to the Nightingale. Another to Howard, beginning: 'Spirit of meek Philanthropy!' One is entitled *The Madman* –'being collected by the author from several Madhouses.' It begins: 'Yes, yes, – 'tis He!' A long poetical satire is addressed to 'John Disney, D.D. – his wife and daughter!!!'

Now to my own affairs. I have not taken that thing to Colman,[2] but I have proceeded one step in the business. I have enquired his address, and am promised it in a few days: Meantime three acts and a half are finished galloping, of a Play on a Persian story[3] which I must father in April. But far, very far, from *Antonio* in composition. O Jephtha, Judge of Israel, what a fool I was!

C. LAMB

24. TO THOMAS MANNING

[Late February 1801]

You masters of logic ought to know (logic is nothing more than a knowledge of *words*, as the Greek etymon implies), that all words are no more to be taken in a literal sense at all times than a promise given to a tailor. When I expressed an apprehension that you were mortally offended, I meant no more than by the application of a certain formula of efficacious sounds, which had *done* in similar cases before, to rouse a sense of decency in you, and a remembrance of what was due to me! You masters of logic should advert to this phenomenon in human speech, before you arraign the usage of us dramatic geniuses. Imagination is a good blood mare, and goes well; but the misfortune is, she has too many paths before her. 'Tis true I might have imaged to myself, that you had trundled your frail carcass to Norfolk. I might also, and did imagine, that you had not, but that you were lazy, or inventing new properties in a triangle, and for that purpose moulding and squeezing Landlord Crisp's three-cornered beaver into fantastic experimental forms; or that Archimedes was meditating to repulse the French, in case of a Cambridge invasion, by a geometric hurling of folios on their red caps; or, peradventure, that you were in extremities, in great wants, and just set out for Trinity-bogs when my letters came. In short, my genius (which is a short word now-a-days for what-a-great-man-am-I) was absolutely stifled and overlaid with its own riches. Truth is one and poor, like the cruse of Elijah's widow.[1] Imagination is the bold face that multiplies its oil: and thou, the old cracked pipkin,[2] that could not believe it could be put to such purposes. Dull pipkin, to have Elijah for thy cook! Imbecile recipient of so fat a miracle! I send you George Dyer's Poems, the richest production of the lyric muse *this century* can justly boast: for Wordsworth's L. B. were published, or at least written, before Christmas.

Please to advert to pages 291 to 296 for the most astonishing account of where Shakspeare's muse has been all this while. I thought she had been dead, and buried in Stratford Church, with the young man *that kept her company*, —

> But it seems, like the Devil,
> Buried in Cole Harbour.
> Some say she's risen again,
> 'Gone prentice to a Barber.

N.B. — I don't charge anything for the additional manuscript notes, which are the joint productions of myself and a learned translator of Schiller, John Stoddart, Esq.

N.B. the 2nd — I should not have blotted your book, but I had sent my own out to be bound, as I was in duty bound. A liberal criticism upon the several pieces, lyrical, heroical, amatory, and satirical, would be acceptable.

So, you don't think there's a Word's—worth of good poetry in the great L. B.! I daren't put the dreaded syllables at their just length, for my back tingles from the northern castigation. I send you the three letters, which I beg you to return along with those former letters, which I hope you are not going to print by your detention. But don't be in a hurry to send them. When you come to town will do. Apropos of coming to town, last Sunday was a fortnight, as I was coming to town from the Professor's, inspired with new rum, I tumbled down, and broke my nose. I drink nothing stronger than malt liquors.

I am going to change my lodgings, having received a hint that it would be agreeable, at our Lady's next feast. I have partly fixed upon most delectable rooms, which look out (when you stand a tiptoe) over the Thames and Surrey Hills, at the upper end of King's Bench walks in the Temple. There I shall have all the privacy of a house without the encumbrance, and shall be able to lock my friends out as often as I desire to hold free converse with my immortal mind; for my present lodgings resemble a minister's levee, I have so increased my acquaintance (as they call 'em), since I have resided in town. Like the country mouse, that had tasted a little of urban manners, I long to be nibbling my own cheese by my dear self without mouse-traps and time-traps. By my new plan, I shall be as airy, up four pair of stairs, as in the country; and in a garden, in the midsts of [that] enchanting, more than Mahometan paradise, London, whose dirtiest drab-frequented alley, and her lowest bowing tradesman, I would not exchange for Skiddaw, Helvellyn, James, Walter, and the parson into the bargain. O! her lamps of a night! her rich goldsmiths, print-shops, toyshops, mercers, hardwaremen, pastrycooks! St Paul's Churchyard! the Strand! Exeter Change! Charing Cross, with the man *upon* a black horse! These are thy gods, O London! Ain't you mightily moped on the banks of the Cam! Had not you better come and set up here? You can't think what a difference. All the streets and pavements are pure gold, I warrant you. At least I know an alchemy that turns her mud into that metal, – a mind that loves to be at home in crowds.

'Tis half-past twelve o'clock, and all sober people ought to be a-bed. Between you and me, the *Lyrical Ballads* are but drowsy performances.

C. LAMB (as you may guess)

25. TO ROBERT LLOYD

June 26, 1801.

Cooke[1] in 'Richard the Third' is a perfect caricature. He gives you the *monster* Richard, but not the *man* Richard. Shakspeare's bloody character impresses you with awe and deep admiration of his witty parts, his consummate hypocrisy, and indefatigable prosecution of purpose. You despise, detest, and loathe the cunning, vulgar, low and fierce Richard, which Cooke substitutes in his place. He gives you no other idea than of a vulgar villain, rejoicing in his being able to over-reach, and not possessing that joy in *silent* consciousness, but betraying it, like a *poor* villain, in sneers and distortions of the face, like a droll at a country fair; not to add that cunning so self-betraying and manner so vulgar could never have deceived the politic Buckingham nor the soft Lady Anne: *both* bred in courts, would have turned with disgust from such a fellow. Not but Cooke has *powers;* but not of discrimination. His manner is strong, coarse, and vigorous, and well adapted to some characters. But the lofty imagery and high sentiments and high passions of *Poetry* come black and prose-smoked from his prose Lips. I have not seen him in Overreach,[2] but from what I remember of the character, I think he could not have chosen one more fit. I thought the play a highly finished one when I read it some time back. I *remember* a most noble image. Sir Giles, drawing his sword in the last scene, says:

> Some undone widow sits upon mine arm,
> And takes away the use on't.

This is horribly fine, and I am not sure that it did not suggest to me my conclusion of *Pride's Cure;* but my imitation is miserably inferior:

> This arm was busy in the day of Naseby:
> 'Tis paralytic now, and knows no use of weapons.

Pierre and Jaffier are the best things in Otway. Belvidera is a poor Creature, and has had more than her due fame. Monimia is a little better, but she *whines*. I like Calista in the *Fair Penitent* better than either of Otway's women. Lee's *Massacre of Paris* is a noble play, very chastely and finely written. His Alexander is full of that madness 'which rightly should possess a poet's brain.' Œdipus is also a fine play, but less so than these two. It is a joint production of Lee and Dryden. *All For Love* begins with uncommon Spirit, but soon flags, and is of no worth upon the whole. The last scene of Young's *Revenge*[3] is sublime: the rest of it not worth 1d.

I want to have your opinion and Plumstead's[4] on Cooke's *Richard the Third*. I am possessed with an admiration of the genuine Richard, his genius, and his mounting spirit, which no consideration of his cruelties can depress. Shakspeare has not made Richard so black a Monster as is supposed. Wherever he is monstrous, it was to conform to vulgar opinion. But he is generally a Man. Read his most exquisite address to the Widowed Queen to court her daughter for him – the topics of maternal feeling, of a deep knowledge of the heart, are such as no monster could have supplied. Richard must have *felt* before he could feign so well; tho' ambition choked the good seed. I think it the most finished piece of Eloquence in the world; of *persuasive* oratory far above Demosthenes, Burke, or any man, far exceeding the courtship of Lady Anne. *Her* relenting is barely natural, after all; the more perhaps S.'s merit to make *impossible* appear *probable*, but the *Queen's consent* (taking in all the circumstances and topics, *private* and *public*, with his angelic address, able to draw the host of [piece cut out of letter] Lucifer) is *probable;* and [piece cut out of letter] resisted it. This observation applies to many other parts. All the inconsistency is, that Shakspeare's better genius was forced to struggle against the prejudices which made a monster of Richard. He set out to paint a *monster*, but his human sympathies produced a *man*.

Are you not tired with all this *ingenious* criticism? I am.

Richard itself is totally metamorphosed in the wretched *acting play* of that name, which you will see, altered by *Cibber*.

God bless you. C. LAMB.

26. TO WALTER WILSON

August 14th, 1801.
Dear Wilson,

I am extremely sorry that any serious difference should subsist between us on account of some foolish behaviour of mine at Richmond; you knew me well enough before – that a very little liquor will cause a considerable alteration in me.

I beg you to impute my conduct solely to that, and not to any deliberate intention of offending you, from whom I have received so many friendly attentions. I know that you think a very important difference in opinion with respect to some more serious subjects between us makes me a dangerous companion; but do not rashly infer, from some slight and light expressions which I may have made use of in a moment of levity in your presence, without sufficient regard to your feelings – do not conclude that I am an inveterate enemy to all religion. I have had a time of seriousness, and I have known the importance and reality of a religious belief. Latterly, I acknowledge, much of my seriousness has gone off, whether from new company or some other new associations; but I still retain at bottom a conviction of the truth, and a certainty of the usefulness of religion. I will not pretend to more gravity or feeling than I at present possess; my intention is not to persuade you that any great alteration is probable in me; sudden converts are superficial and transitory; I only want you to believe that I have *stamina* of seriousness within me, and that I desire nothing more than a return of that friendly intercourse which used to subsist between us, but which my folly has suspended.

Believe me, very affectionately yours, C. LAMB.

27. TO ROBERT LLOYD

[18 November 1801]

I am not dead nor asleep. But Manning is in town, & Coleridge is in town, and I am making a thorough alteration in the structure of my play for Publication. My brain is overwrought with variety of worldly-intercourse. I have neither time nor mind for scribbling. Who shall deliver me from the body of this Death? –

Only continue to write & to believe that when the **Hour** comes, I shall strike like Jack of the Clock, id est, I shall once more become a regular correspondent of Robt. & Plumstead. How is the benevolent, loud-talking, Shakspere-loving, Brewer? – [1]

To your enquiry respecting a selection from B'p Taylor I answer – it cannot be done, & if it could it would not *take* with John Bull. – It cannot be done, for who can disentangle and unthread the rich texture of Nature & Poetry sewn so thick into a stout coat of theology, without spoiling both *lace* & *coat*? how beggarly and how bald do even Shakespeares Princely Pieces look, when thus violently divorced from *connexion* & *circumstance*! when we meet with To be or not to be – or Jacques's moralizings upon the Deer – or Brutus and Cassius' quarrel & reconciliation – in an Enfield speaker or in Elegant Extracts – how we stare & will scarcely acknowledge to ourselves (what we are conscious we feel) that they are flat & have no power. Something exactly like this have I experienced when I have picked out similes & stars from Holy Dying and shewn them per se, as you'd show specimens of minerals or pieces of rock –. Compare the grand effect of the Star-paved firmament – & imagine a boy capable of picking out those pretty twinklers **one by one** & playing at chuck farthing with them. – Every thing in heaven & earth, in man and in story, in books & in fancy, acts by **Confederacy**, by juxaposition, by circumstance & **place** –. Consider a fine family – (if I were not writing to you I might instance your own) of sons & daughters with a respectable father & a handsome mother at their head, all met in one house, & happy round one table –. Earth cannot shew a more lovely & venerable sight, such as the Angels in heaven might lament that in their country there is no marrying or giving in marriage –. Take & split this Body into individuals – shew the separate caprices, vagaries, &c. of Charles, Rob. or Plum. one a quaker, another a churchman. – The eldest daughter seeking a husband out of the pale of parental faith – another warping perhaps – the father a prudent, circumspective, do-me-good sort of a man *blest* with children whom no ordinary rules can circumscribe –. I have not room for all particulars – but just as this happy & venerable Body of a family loses by splitting & considering individuals too nicely, so it is when we pick out **Best Bits** out of a great writer. Tis the *Sum* total of his mind which *affects* us

C [L]

28. TO THOMAS MANNING

Monday 15th February 1802

Not a sentence, not a syllable, of **Trismegistus** shall be lost through my neglect. I am his word-banker,[1] his store-keeper of puns & syllogisms. You cannot conceive (and if Trismegistus cannot, no man can) the strange joy, which I felt at the Receipt of a Letter from Paris. It seemed to give me a learned importance, which placed me above all, who had not Parisian Correspondents. Believe, that I shall carefully husband every Scrap, which will save you the trouble of memory, when you come back. You cannot write things so trifling, let them only be about Paris, which I shall not treasure. In particular, I must have parallels of Actors & Actresses. I must be told if any Building in Paris is at all comparable to St Paul's, which contrary to the usual mode of that part of our Nature, called Admiration, I have looked up to with unfading Wonder, every morning at ten oClock, ever since it has lain in my way to business. At noon I casually glance upon it, being hungry; and Hunger has not much taste for the fine arts. Is any night-walk comparable to a Walk from St Pauls to Charing Cross, for Lighting, & Paving, Crowds going & coming without respite, the rattle of coaches, & the chearfulness of shops? Have you seen a man Guillotined yet? is it as good as Hanging? are the Women *all* painted, & the men *all* monkeys? or are there not a few that look like *rational* of *both sexes?* Are you & the first Consul *thick?* All this expence of ink I may fairly put you to, as your Letters will not be solely for my proper pleasure, but are to serve as memoranda & notices, helps for short memory, a kind of Rumfordizing[2] recollection, for yourself on your return. Your Letter was just what a letter should be, crammed, and very funny. Every part of it pleased me, till you came to Paris, & your damned philosophical indolence or indifference stung me. You cannot stir from your rooms till you know the Language! what the Devil! are men nothing but word-trumpets?, are men all tongue & ear? have these creatures, that you & I profess to know *something about*, no faces, gestures, gabble, no folly, no

absurdity, no induction of French education upon the Abstract Idea of
Men & Women, no similitude nor dissimilitude to English! Why, thou
damned **Smelfungus!** [3] Your account of your Landing and reception &
Bullen (I forget how you spelt it) it was spelt *my* way in Harry the 8ths
ti[me,] was exactly in that *minute* styl[e] which strong impressions
inspire (writing to a Frenchman I write as a Frenchman would) –. It
appears to me, as if I should die with joy at the first Landing in a foreign
Country. It is the nearest Pleasure, which a grown man can substitute
for that unknown one, which he can never know, the pleasure of the
first entrance into Life from the Womb. – I dare say, in a short time my
Habits would come back lik[e] a 'stronger man' armed, and drive out
that new pleasure; & I should soon sicken for known objects. Nothing
has transpired h[ere] that seems to me of sufficient importance to send
dry-shod over the Water: but I suppose you will want to be told some
news. The Best & the Worst to me is, that I have given up Two Guineas
a week at the Post, & regained my health & spirits, whic[h] were upon
the wane. I grew **sick**, & Stuart [4] unsatisfied. Ludisti satis, tempus abire
est.[5] I must cut closer that's all. In all this time I have done but one
thing, which I reckon tolerable: & that I will transcribe, because it may
give you pleasure, being a Picture of *my* hungers. You will find it in my
last Page. It absurdly is a first Number of a Series, thu[s] strangled in
Embryo. **More News**. The Professor's Rib [6] has come out to be a
damn'd disagreeable woman, so much as to drive me & some more old
Cronies from his House. If a man will keep **Snakes** in his House, he
must not wonder if People are shy of coming to see him **because of the
Snakes. Mister Fell** or as you with your usual **faceteness** and drollery
call him Mr F + ll has stopt short in the middle of his Play, like what is
called **being taken short**. Some *friend* has told him that it has not the
least merit in it. O! that I had the rectifying of the Litany! I would put in
a Libera *Nos* (*Scriptores* videlicet) ab *amicis!* [7] That's all the **News**. *A pro
pos* (is it *Pedantry*, writing to a Frenchman, to express myself sometimes
by a French Word, when an English one would not do as well? methinks,
my thoughts fall naturally into it)

A pro pos, I think you wrong about *my* Play. *All* the **omissions**
are *right*. And the supplementary Scene in which Sandford *narrates* the
manner in which his master is affected, is the **Best** in the Book. It
stands, where a Hodge podge of German puerilities used to stand. I
insist upon it, that you like that Scene. Love me, love that scene. I will
now transcribe the Londoner (No. 1) & wind up all with Affection &
Humble Servant at the end. **The Londoner** [8] (I write *small*, in regard to

your good eyesight): 'In compliance with my own particular humour, no less than with thy laudable curiosity, Reader, I proceed to give thee some accot. of my history & habits. I was born under the Nose of St. Dunstan's Steeple, just where the conflux of the eastern & western inhabitants of this two-fold City meet & justle in friendly opposition at Temple Bar. The same day, which gave me to the world, saw London happy in the celebration of her great Annual Feast. This I cannot help looking upon as a lively type or omen of the great good will, which I was destined to bear toward the City, resembling in kind that Solicitude, which every Chief Magistrate is supposed to feel for whatever concerns her interest & well being. Indeed I consider myself in some sort a *speculative Lord Mayor of London:* for tho' circumstances *un*happily preclude me from ever arriving at the dignity of a gold chain & spital sermon, yet thus much will I say of myself in truth, that Whittington himself with his *Cat* (just emblem of *vigilance* & a *furred gown*) never went beyond me in affection, which I bear to the Citizens. Shut out from serving them in the most honorable mode, I aspire to do them benefit in another scarcely less honorable: & if I cannot by virtue of office commit vice & irregularity to the *material Counter*, I will at least erect a *spiritual one*, where they shall be laid fast by the heels. In plain words, I will do my best endeavors to write them down. To return to Myself (from whence my zeal for the public good is perpetually causing me to digress) I will let thee, Reader, into certain more of my peculiarities. I was born (as you have heard) bred, & have past most part of my time in a *crowd*. This has begot in me an entire affection for that way of life, amounting to an almost insurmountable aversion from solitude & rural scenes. This aversion was never in[terrup]ted or suspended, except for a few years in the younger part of my Life, during a period, in whi[ch I ha]d fixed my affections upon a charming young woman. Every man, while the **Passion** is upon him, [is for a] ti[m]e at least addited to groves & meadows & purling streams. During this short period of my existence, I contracted just enough familiarity with rural objects, to understand tolerably well ever after the **Poets**, when they declaim in such passionate terms in favor of a country Life. For my own part, now the fit is long past, I have no hesitation in declaring, that a mob of happy faces, crowding up at the **Pit Door** of Drury Lane Theatre just at the hour of 5, give me ten thou'san[d] finer pleasures, than I ever received from all the flocks of silly sheep, that have whitened the plains of Arcadia or **Epsom Downs**. This passion for Crowds is no where feasted so full as in London. The man must have a rare recipe

for melancholy, who can be dull in Fleet Street. I am naturally inclined to Hypochrondria; but in London it vanishes, like all other
ills –. Often, when I have felt a weariness or distaste at home, have I
rushed out into her crowded *Strand*, and fed my humour till tears
have wetted my cheek for inutterable sympathies with the multitudinous moving picture, which she never fails to present at all
hours, like the shifting scenes of a skilful Pantomime. The very deformities of London, which give distaste to others, from habit do not
displease me. The endless succession of Shops, where Fancy (miscalled
Folly) is supplied with perpetual new gauds & toys, excite in me no
puritanical aversion. I gladly behold every appetite supplied with its
proper food. The obliging Customer, & the obliged Tradesman –
things which live by bowing, & things which exist but for homage,
do not affect me with disgust; from habit, I perceive nothing but
urbanity, where other men, more refined, discover meanness. I love
the very Smoke of London, because it has been the medium most
familiar to my vision. I see grand principles of honor at work in the
dirty ring, which encompasses two Combatants with fists, & principles of no less eternal justice in the tumultuous detectors of a pick-
pocket. The salutary astonishment, with which an Execution is
surveyed, convinces me more forcibly than an 100 vols. of abstract
Polity, that the universal instinct of man in all ages has leaned
to Order & good government. Thus, an **Art** of extracting morality
from the commonest incidents of a Town **Life** is attained by the
same well-natured Alchemy, with which the *Forresters* of *Arden*,
in a beautiful country, 'Found tongues in trees, books in the
running brooks, Sermons in stones, & Good in ev'ry thing.' Where
has **Spleen** her food but in London? – humour, interest, curiosity, suck
at her measureless breasts without a possibility of being satiated.
Nursed amid her noise, her crowds, her beloved smoke, what have I
been doing all my life, if I have not lent out my heart with *usury* to
such scenes? Reader, in the course of my perigrinations about this
Great City; it is hard, if I have not picked up Matters which may
serve to amuse thee, as it has done me, a summer evening long.
Farewell.' –

What is all this about?, said Mrs Shandy –. A story of a Cock & a Bull,
said Yorick;[9] & so it is – but Manning will take good-naturedly what
God will send him across the water: only I hope he wont *shut* his *eyes* &
open his *mouth*, as the Children say, for that is a way to *gape* & not to
read. Manning, continue your Laudable Purpose of making me your

Register. I will render back all your **Remarks**, & *I, not you*, shall have received **Usury** by having read them. –

In the mean time, may the **Great Spirit**, have you in his keeping; & preserve our English-man from the inoculation of frivolity & sin upon French Earth. –

Allons (or what is it you say instead of *good-bye?*) –

Mary sends her kind Remembrance, & covets the Remarks equally with me.

C. LAMB

29. TO THOMAS MANNING

London
24th Sep. 1802

My dear Manning

Since the date of my last letter I have been a traveller. A strong desire seized me of visiting remote regions. My first impulse was to go and see Paris. It was a trivial objection to my aspiring mind, that I did not understand a word of the language: since, I certainly intend some time in my life to see **Paris** and equally certainly intend never to learn the language: therefore that could be no objection. However I am very glad I did not go, because you had left Paris (I see) before I could have set out. – I believe, Stoddart[1] promising to go with me another year prevented that plan. My next scheme (for to my restless ambitious mind London was become a bed of thorns) was to visit the far famed Peak in Derbyshire, where the Devil sits, they say, without breeches. *This* my purer mind rejected, as indelicate. And my final resolve was a Tour to the Lakes. I set out with Mary to Keswick, without giving Coleridge any notice, for my time being precious did not admit of it; he received us with all the hospitality in the world, and gave up his time to shew us all the wonders of the country. He dwells upon a small hill by the side of Keswick, in a comfortable house, quite enveloped on all sides by a net of mountains: great floundering bears & monsters they seem'd, all couchant & asleep. We got in in the evening, travelling in a Post Chaise from Pe[n]rith, in the midst of a gorgeous sun shine, which transmuted all the mountains into colours, purple &c. &c. We thought we had got into Fairy Land. But that went off (as it never came again, while we stayed, we had no more fine sun sets) and we entered Coleridge's comfortable study just in the dusk, when the mountains were all dark with clouds upon their heads. Such an impression I never received from objects of sight before, nor do I suppose that I can ever again. Glorious creatures, fine old fellows, Skiddaw &c. I never shall forget ye, how ye lay about that night, like an intrenchment, gone to bed as it seemed for the night, but promising that ye were to be seen in the morning. Coleridge had got a blazing fire in his study, which is a large antique ill-shaped room, with an old fashioned organ, never play'd upon, big enough for a church, Shelves of scattered folios, an Eolian Harp, & an old sofa, half bed &c. And all looking out upon the last fading view of Skiddaw & his broad-breasted brethren: What a night! – Here we staid three full weeks, in which time I visited Wordsworth's cottage, where we stayed a day or two with the Clarksons [2] (good people & most hospitable, at whose house we tarried one day & night) & saw Lloyd. Wordsworths were gone to Calais. They have since been in London, & past much time with us: he is now gone into Yorkshire to be married, to a girl of small fortune, but he is in expectation of augmenting his own, in consequence of the death of Lord Lonsdale, who kept him out of his own, in conformity with a plan my Lord had taken up in early life of making every body unhappy. So we have seen Keswick, Grasmere, Ambleside, Ulswater (where the Clarksons live) and a place at the other end of Ulswater, I forget the name, to which we travelled on a very sultry day over the middle of Helvellyn. – We h[a]ve clambered up to the top of Skiddaw, & I have waded up the bed of Lodore. In fine I have satisfied myself, that there is such a thing as that, which tourists call *romantic*, which I very much suspected before: they make such a spluttering about it, and toss their splendid epithets around them, till they give as dim a light, as four oClock next morning the Lamps do after an illumination. Mary was excessively tired, when she got about half way up Skiddaw, but we came to a cold rill (than which nothing can be imagined more cold, running over cold stones) & with the reinforcemt. of a draught of cold water, she surmounted it most manfully. – O its fine black head & the bleak air a top of it, with a prospect of mountains all about & about, making you giddy, & then Scotland afar off & the border countries so famous in song & ballad –. It was a day that will stand out, like a mountain, I am sure, in my life. – But I am returned (I have now been come home near 3 weeks (I was a month out)) & you cannot conceive the degradation I felt at first, from being accustommed to wander free as air among mountains, & bathe in rivers without being controuled by any one, to come home & *work:* I felt very *little*. I had been dreaming I was a very great man. But that is going off, & I find I shall conform in time to that state of Life, to which it has pleased God to call me. Besides, after all, Fleet Street & the Strand are better places to live in for good & all than among Skiddaw: Still, I turn back to those great places, where I wandered about, participating in their greatness. After all I could not *live* in Skiddaw: I could spend a year, two, three years, among them, but I must have a prospect of seeing Fleet Street at the End of that time: or I should mope & pine away, I know. Still Skiddaw is a fine Creature. My habits are changing, I think; i.e. from drunk to sober: whether I shall be happier or no, remains to be proved. I shall certainly be more happy in a morning, but whether I shall not sacrifice the fat & the marrow & the kidneys, i.e. the Night, the glor[iou]s, care-drowning, night, that heals all our wrongs, pours wine into our mortifications, changes the scene from indifferent & flat to bright & brilliant –. O Manning, if I should have formed a diabolical resolution, by the time you come to England, of not admitting any spirituous liquors into my house, will you be my guest on such shame worthy terms? Is life, with such limitations, worth trying. – The truth is that my liquors bring a nest of friendly harpies about my house, who consume me. –

This is a pitiful tale to be read at St Gothard: [3] but it is just now nearest my heart. – Fenwick [4] is a ruined man. He is hiding himself from his Creditors, and has sent his wife & children into the Country. Fell, my other drunken companion (that has been: nam hic cæstus artemque repono) [5] is turned Editor of a Naval Chronicle. Godwin (with a pitiful artificial Wife) continues a steady friend: tho' the same facility does not remain of visiting him often. That Bitch has detached Marshall [6] from his house: Marshall, the man who went to sleep when the Ancient Mariner was reading, the old steady, unalterable, friend of the Professor – –. Holcroft [7] is not yet come to town. I expect to see him & will deliver your messag[e.] Ho[w I hat]e *this part* of a letter. [T]hings come crowding in to say, & no room for 'em. Some things are too little to be told, i.e. to have a preference: some are too big & circumstantial. – Thanks for yours, which was most delicious. Would I had been with you, benighted &c – I fear, my head is turned with wandering. I shall never be the same acquiesct. being. – farewell. –

Write again **quickly**, for I shall not like to hazard a letter, not knowing where the fates have carried you. farewell, my dear fellow.

C LAMB

30. TO THOMAS MANNING

London
19th February 1803

My dear Manning,

The general scope of your letter afforded no indications of insanity, but some particular points raised a scruple. For God's sake don't think any more of 'Independent Tartary.' What have you to do among such Ethiopians? Is there no *lineal descendant* of Prester John?[1]

Is the chair empty? Is the sword unswayed? – depend upon't they'll never make you their king, as long as any branch of that great stock is remaining. I tremble for your Christianity. They'll certainly circumcise you. Read Sir John Mandevil's travels to cure you, or come over to England. There is a Tartarman now exhibiting at Exeter Change. Come and talk with him, and hear what he says first. Indeed, he is no very favorable specimen of his Countrymen! But perhaps the best thing you can do, is to *try* to get the idea out of your head. For this purpose repeat to yourself every night, after you have said your prayers, the words Independent Tartary, Independent Tartary, two or three times, and associate with them the *idea of oblivion* ('tis Hartley's method[2] with obstinate memories), or say, Independent, Independent, have I not already got an *Independence?* That was a clever way of the old puritans – pun-divinity. My dear friend, think what a sad pity it would be to bury such *parts* in heathen countries, among nasty, unconversable, horse-belching, Tartar people! Some say, they are Cannibals; and then conceive a Tartar-fellow *eating* my friend, and adding the *cool malignity* of mustard and vinegar! I am afraid 'tis the reading of Chaucer has misled you; his foolish stories about Cambuscan and the ring, and the horse of brass.[3] Believe me, there's no such things, 'tis all the poet's *invention;* but if there were such *darling* things as old Chaucer sings, I would *up* behind you on the Horse of Brass, and frisk off for Prester John's Country. But these are all tales; a Horse of Brass never flew, and a King's daughter never talked with Birds! The Tartars, really, are a cold, insipid, smouchey set. You'll be sadly moped (if you are not eaten) among them. Pray *try* and cure yourself. Take Hellebore[4] (the counsel is Horace's, 'twas none of my thought *originally*). Shave yourself oftener. Eat no saffron, for saffron-eaters contract a terrible Tartar-like yellow. Pray, to avoid the fiend. Eat nothing that gives the heart-burn. *Shave the upper lip.* Go about like an European. Read no books of voyages (they're nothing but lies): only now and then a Romance, to keep the fancy *under*. Above all, don't go to any sights of *wild beasts. That has been your* ruin. Accustom yourself to write familiar letters on common subjects to your friends in England, such as are of a moderate understanding. And think about common things more. There's your friend Holcroft now, has written a play. You used to be fond of the drama. Nobody went to see it. Notwithstanding this, with an audacity perfectly original, he faces the town down in a preface, that they *did like* it very much. I have heard a waspish punster say, 'Sir, why did you not laugh at my jest?' But for a man boldly to face me out with, 'Sir, I maintain it, you did laugh at my jest,' is a little too much. I have seen H. but once. He spoke of you to me in honorable terms. H. seems to me to be drearily dull. Godwin is dull, but then he has a dash of affectation, which smacks of the coxcomb, and your coxcombs are always agreeable. I supped last night with Rickman, and met a merry *natural* captain, who pleases himself vastly with once having made a Pun at Otaheite in the O. language. 'Tis the same man who said Shakspeare he liked, because he was so *much of the Gentleman*. Rickman is a man 'absolute in all numbers.' I think I may one day bring you acquainted, if you do not go to Tartary first; for you'll never come back. Have a care, my dear friend, of Anthropophagi! their stomachs are always craving. But if you do go among [them] pray contrive to *stink* as soon as you can that you may [not (?)] hang a [on (?)] hand at the Butcher's. 'Tis terrible to be weighed out for 5d. a-pound. To sit at table (the reverse of fishes in Holland), not as a guest, but as a meat.[5]

God bless you: do come to England. Air and exercise may do great things. Talk with some Minister. Why not your father?

God dispose all for the best. I have discharged my duty.

Your sincere frd,

C. LAMB

31. TO THOMAS MANNING

16 Mitre Court Buildings Inner Temple
Saturday 24 [23] feb. 1805

Dear Manning,

We have executed your commissions. There was nothing for you at the White Horse. I have been very unwell since I saw you. A sad depression of spirits, a most unaccountable nervousness: from which I have been partially relieved by an odd accident. You knew **Dick Hopkins** the searing Scullion of Caius'? This fellow by industry and agility has thrust himself into the important situations (no sinecures believe me) of Cook to Trinity Hall & Cauis College: and the generous creature has

contrived with the greatest delicacy imaginable to send me a present of
Cambridge Brawn. What makes it the more extraordinary is that the
man never saw me in his life that I know of. I suppose he has *heard* of
me. I did not immediately recognize the donor: but one of Richard's
cards, which had accidentally fallen into the straw, detected him in a
moment. **Dick** you know was always remarkable for flourishing. His
card imports that 'Orders (to-wit for Brawn) from any part of England,
Scotland, or Ireland will be duly executed' &c.. At first I thought of
declining the present: but Richard knew my blind side when he pitched
upon **Brawn**. Tis of all my hobbies the supreme in the eating way. He
might have sent, sops from the pan, skimmings, crumplets, chips, hog's
lard, the tender brown judiciously scalped from a fillet of veal (dextr-
ously replaced by a salamander) the tops of asparagus, fugitive livers,
runaway gizzards of fowls, the eyes of martyr'd Pigs, tender effusions of
laxative woodcocks, the red spawn of lobsters, leveret's ears, and such
pretty filchings common to cooks: but these had been ordinary presents,
the every-day courtesies of Dish-washers to their sweethearts. Brawn
was a noble thought. It is not every common Gullet-fancier than can
properly esteem of it. It is like a picture of one of the choice old Italian
masters. It's gusto is of that hidden sort. As Wordsworth sings of a
modest poet: you must love him ere to you he will seem worthy of
your love:[1] so Brawn, you must taste it ere to you it will seem to have
any taste at all. But tis nuts to the adept: those that will send out their
tongue and feelers to find it out. It will be wooed & not unsought be
won. Now **Ham-essence,** lobsters, turtle, such popular minions absolute *court you,* lay themselves out to strike you at first smack, like one of
David's Pictures (they call him *Darveed*) compared with the plain
russet-coated wealth of a Titian or a Corregio, as I illustrated above.
Such are the obvious glaring **heathen** virtues of a Corporation dinner
compared with the reserved collegiate worth of Brawn.

Do me the favor to leave off the business which you may be at
present upon, and go immediately to the Kitchens of Trinity & Caius',
and make my most respectful compli[ments] to Mr Richard Hopkins,
and assure him that his Brawn is most excellent, and that I am moreover
obliged to him for his **inuendo** about Salt water & Bran: which I shall
not fail to improve. I leave it to you whether you shall chuse to pay
him the civility of asking him to dinner while you stay in Cambridge,
or in whatever other way you may best like to shew your gratitude to
my friend. Richard Hopkins considered in many points of view is a
very extraordinary character.. – **Adieu**. I hope to see you to supper in

London soon, where we will taste Richard's brawn, and drink his health in a chearful but moderate cup. We have not many such men in any rank of life as Mr R. Hopkins. **Crisp** the Barber of St Mary's was just such another. I wonder *he* never sent me any little token, some chestnuts, or a puff, or two pound of hair: just to remember him by. **Gifts** are like nails. **Præsens** ut **absens**: that is, your *Present* makes amends for your absence. –

Yours.
C LAMB

32. TO THOMAS MANNING

Jan. 2nd, 1810

Dear Manning,

When I last wrote to you, I was in lodgings. I am now in chambers, No. 4, Inner Temple Lane, where I should be happy to see you any evening. Bring any of your friends, the Mandarins, with you. I have two sitting-rooms: I call them so *par excellence*, for you may stand, or loll, or lean, or try any posture in them; but they are best for sitting; not squatting down Japanese fashion, but the more decorous use of the posteriors which European usage has consecrated. I have two of these rooms on the third floor, and five sleeping, cooking, &c., rooms, on the fourth floor. In my best room is a choice collection of the works of Hogarth, an English painter of some humour. In my next best are shelves containing a small but well-chosen library. My best room commands a court, in which there are trees and a pump, the water of which is excellent – cold with brandy, and not very insipid without. Here I hope to set up my rest, and not quit till Mr Powell, the under-taker, gives me notice that I may have possession of my last lodging. He lets lodgings for single gentlemen. I sent you a parcel of books by my last, to give you some idea of the state of European literature. There comes with this two volumes, done up as letters, of minor poetry, a sequel to 'Mrs Leicester';[1] the best you may suppose mine; the next best are my coadjutor's; you may amuse yourself in guessing them out; but I must tell you mine are both one-third in quantity of the whole. So much for a very delicate subject. It is hard to speak of one's self, &c. Holcroft had finished his life when I wrote to you, and Hazlitt has since finished his life – I do not mean his own life, but he has finished a life of Holcroft,[2] which is going to press. Tuthill is Dr Tuthill. I continue Mr Lamb. I have published a little book for children on titles of honour: and to give them some idea of the difference of rank and gradual rising,

I have made a little scale, supposing myself to receive the following various accessions of dignity from the king, who is the fountain of honour – As at first, 1, Mr C. Lamb; 2, C. Lamb, Esq.; 3, Sir C. Lamb, Bart; 4, Baron Lamb of Stamford; * 5, Viscount Lamb; 6, Earl Lamb; 7, Marquis Lamb; 8, Duke Lamb. It would look like quibbling to carry it on further, and especially as it is not necessary for children to go beyond the ordinary titles of sub-regal dignity in our own country, otherwise I have sometimes in my dreams imagined myself still advancing, as 9th, King Lamb; 10th, Emperor Lamb; 11th, Pope Innocent, higher than which is nothing but the Lamb of God. Puns I have not made many (nor punch much), since the date of my last; one I cannot help relating. A constable in Salisbury Cathedral was telling me that eight people dined at the top of the spire of the cathedral; upon which I remarked, that they must be very sharp-set. But in general I cultivate the reasoning part of my mind more than the imaginative. Do you know Kate *********? I am stuffed out so with eating turkey for dinner, and another turkey for supper yesterday (turkey in Europe and turkey in Asia), that I can't jog on. It is New-Year here. That is, it was New-Year half a-year back, when I was writing this. Nothing puzzles me more than time and space, and yet nothing puzzles me less, for I never think about them. Miss Knap is turned midwife. Never having had a child herself, she can't draw any wrong analogies from her own case. Dr Stoddart has had Twins. There was five shillings to pay the Nurse. Mrs Godwin was impannelled on a jury of Matrons last Session. She saved a criminal's life by giving it as her opinion that –. The judge listened to her with the greatest deference. The Persian ambassador is the principal thing talked of now. I sent some people to see him worship the sun on Primrose Hill at half past six in the morning, 28th November; but he did not come, which makes me think the old fire-worshippers are a sect almost extinct in Persia. Have you trampled on the Cross yet? The Persian ambassador's name is Shaw Ali Mirza. The common people call him Shaw Nonsense. While I think of it, I have put three letters besides my own three into the India post for you, from your brother, sister, and some gentleman whose name I forget. Will they, have they, did they, come safe? The distance you are at, cuts up tenses by the root. I think you said you did not know Kate *********. I express her by nine stars, though she is but one, but if ever one star differed from another in glory –. You must have seen her at her father's. Try and remember her.

* Where my family come from. I have chosen that if ever I should have my choice.

Coleridge is bringing out a paper in weekly numbers, called the 'Friend,' which I would send, if I could; but the difficulty I had in getting the packets of books out to you before deters me; and you'll want something new to read when you come home. It is chiefly intended to puff off Wordsworth's poetry; but there are some noble things in it by the by. Except Kate, I have had no vision of excellence this year, and she passed me like the queen on her coronation day; you don't know whether you saw her or not. Kate is fifteen: I go about moping, and sing the old pathetic ballad I used to like in my youth –

> She's sweet Fifteen,
> I'm *one year more.*

Mrs Bland sung it in boy's clothes the first time I heard it. I sometimes think the lower notes in my voice are like Mrs. Bland's. That glorious singer Braham, one of my lights, is fled. He was for a season. He was a rare composition of the Jew, the gentleman, and the angel, yet all these elements mixed up so kindly in him, that you could not tell which predominated; but he is gone, and one Phillips is engaged instead. Kate is vanished, but Miss B****** is always to be met with!

> Queens drop away, while blue-legg'd Maukin thrives;
> And courtly Mildred dies while country Madge survives.

That is not my poetry, but Quarles's; but haven't you observed that the rarest things are the least obvious? Don't show anybody the names in this letter. I write confidentially, and wish this letter to be considered as *private.* Hazlitt has written a *grammar* for Godwin; Godwin sells it bound up with a treatise of his own on language, but the *grey mare is the better horse.* I don't allude to Mrs Godwin, but to the word *grammar,* which comes near to *grey mare,* if you observe, in sound. That figure is called paranomasia in Greek. I am sometimes happy in it. An old woman begged of me for charity. 'Ah! sir,' said she, 'I have seen better days'; 'So have I, good woman,' I replied; but I meant literally, days not so rainy and overcast as that on which she begged: she meant more prosperous days. Mr Dawe is made associate of the Royal Academy. By what law of association I can't guess. Mrs Holcroft, Miss Holcroft, Mr and Mrs Godwin, Mr and Mrs Hazlitt, Mrs Martin and Louisa, Mrs Lum, Capt. Burney, Mrs Burney, Martin Burney, Mr Rickman, Mrs Rickman, Dr Stoddart, William Dollin, Mr Thompson, Mr and Mrs Norris, Mr Fenwick, Mrs Fenwick, Miss Fenwick, a man that saw you at our house one day, and a lady that heard me speak of you; Mrs Buffam that heard

Hazlitt mention you, Dr Tuthill, Mrs Tuthill, Colonel Harwood, Mrs Harwood, Mr Collier, Mrs Collier, Mr Sutton, Nurse, Mr Fell, Mrs Fell, Mr Marshall, are very well, and occasionally inquire after you.

[I remain yours ever,
Ch. LAMB

Mary sends her love.

33. TO WILLIAM WORDSWORTH

9th Aug 1815

Dear Wordsworth,

We acknowledge with pride the receit of both your handwritings, and desire to be ever had in kindly remembrance by you both & by Dorothy. Miss Hutchinson had just transmitted us a letter containing, among other chearful matter, the annunication of a child born. Nothing of consequence has turned up in our parts since your departure. Mary and I felt quite queer after your taking leave (you W. W.) of us in St Giles's. We wished we had seen more of you, but felt we had scarce been sufficiently acknowleging for the share we had enjoyed of your company. We felt as if we had been not enough *expressive* of our pleasure. But our manners *both* are a little too much on this side of too-much-cordiality. We want presence of mind and presence of heart. What we feel comes too late like an after thought impromptu. But perhaps you observed nothing of that which we have been painfully conscious of and are every day in our intercourse with those we stand affected to through all the degrees of love. Robinson is on the Circuit. Our Pangyrist I thought had forgotten one of the objects of his youthful admiration, but I was agreeably removed from that scruple by the laundress knocking at my door this morning almost before I was up with a present of fruit from my young friend &c –. There is something inexpressibly pleasant to me in these *presents*. Be it fruit, or fowl, or brawn, or *what not. Books* are a legitimate cause of acceptance. If presents be not the soul of friendship, undoubtedly they are the most spiritual part of the body of that intercourse. There is too much narrowness of thinking in this point. The punctilio of acceptance methinks is too confined and straitlaced. I could be content to receive money, or clothes, or a joint of meat from a friend; why should he not send me a dinner as well as a dessert? I would taste him in the beasts of the field and thro' all creation. Therefore did the basket of fruit of the juvenile Talfourd not displease me. Not that I have any thoughts of bartering or reciprocating these things. To send him any thing in return would be to reflect suspicion of mercenariness upon what I know he meant a free will offering. Let him overcome me in bounty. In this strife a generous nature loves to be overcome. Alsager [1] (whom you term **Alsinger** – and indeed he is rather *singer* than *sager*, no reflection upon his naturals neither) is well and in harmony with himself & the world. I dont know how he and those of his constitution keep their nerves so nicely balanced as they do. Or have they any? or are they made of packthread? He is proof against weather, ingratitude, meat under done, every weapon of fate. I have just now a jagged end of a tooth pricking against my tongue, which meets it half way in a wantonness of provocation, and there they go at it, the tongue pricking itself like the viper against the file, and the tooth galling all the gum inside & out to torture, tongue & tooth, tooth & tongue, hard at [it], and I to pay the reckoning, till all my mouth is as hot as brimstone, & I'd venture the roof of my mouth that at this moment, at which I conjecture my full-happinessed friend is picking his crackers, that not one of the double rows of ivory in his privileged mouth has as much as a flaw in it, but all perform their functions, & having performed it, expect to be picked (luxurious steeds!) & rubbed down. I dont think he could be robbed, or could have his house set on fire, or ever want money. I have heard him express a similar opinion of his own impassibility. I keep acting here Heautontimorumenos. [2] M. Burney has been to Calais & has come home a travelld monsieur. He speaks nothing but the Gallic Idiom. Field is on circuit. So now I believe I have given account of most that you saw at our cabin. Have you seen a curious letter in Morn Chron by C. Ll. the Genius of Absurdity respecting Bonapartes suing out his Habeas Corpus. [3] That man is his own **Moon**. He has no need of ascending into that gentle planet for mild influences. You wish me some of your leisure. I have a glimmering aspect, a chink-light of liberty before me which I pray God prove not fallacious. My remonstrances have stirred up others to remonstrate, and altogether there is a plan for separating certain parts of business from our department, which if it take place will produce me more time, i.e. my evenings free. It may be a means of placing me in a more conspicuous situation which will knock at my nerves another way, but I wait the issue in submission. If I can but begin my own day at 4 oClock in the afternoon, I shall think myself to have Eden days of peace & liberty to what I have had. As you say, how a man can fill 3 volumes up with an Essay on the Drama [4] is wonderful. I am sure a very few sheets would hold all I had to say on the subject, and yet I dare say ********** as **Von Slagel** ***. Did you ever read Charron on Wisdom? or Patrick's Pilgrim? [5] if neither, you have two great pleasures to come. I mean some day to attack Caryl on Job, six Folios. What any man can write, surely I may read. [8] If I do but get rid of auditing Warehousekeepers Accts. & get no worse-harassing task in the place of it, what a lord of Liberty I shall be. I shall dance & skip and make mouths at the invisible event, and pick the thorns out of my pillow & throw them at rich mens night caps, & talk blank verse hoity toity, and sing a **Clerk I** was in **London** Gay, ban, ban Ca-caliban, like the emancipated monster & go where I like up this street or down that ally –

Adieu & pray that it may be my luck. Good be to you all

C LAMB

34. TO WILLIAM WORDSWORTH

SIR,

PLEASE TO STATE THE WEIGHTS AND AMOUNTS OF THE FOLLOWING LOTS OF SOLD   SALE, 181   FOR

YOUR OBEDIENT SERVANT,

Chas Lamb

ACCOUNTANT'S OFFICE,
26 Apr 1816

Dear W..

I have just finished the pleasing task of correcting the Revise of the Poems and letter. [1] I hope they will come out faultless. One blunder I saw and shuddered at. The hallucinating rascal had printed **battered** for **battened**, this last not conveying any distinct sense to his gaping soul. The Reader (as they call 'em) had discovered it & given it the marginal brand, but the substitutory **n** had not yet appeared. I accompanied his notice with a most pathetic address to the printer not to neglect the Correction. I know how such a blunder would '**batte\b at your Peace.**' With regard to the works, the Letter I read with unabated satisfaction. Such a thing was wanted, called for. The parallel of Cotton with Burns I heartily approve; Iz. Walton hallows any page in which his reverend name appears. 'Duty archly bending to purposes of general benevolence' is exquisite. The Poems I endeavored not to understand, but to read them with my eye alone, and I think I succeeded. (Some people will do that when they come out, you'll say.) As if I were to luxuriate tomorrow at some Picture Gallery I was never at before, and going by to day by chance, found the door open, had but 5 minutes to look about me, peeped in, just such a *chastised* peep I took with my mind at the lines my luxuriating eye was coursing over unrestrained, – not to anticipate another days fuller satisfaction. Coleridge is printing Xtabel by Ld. Byron's recommendation to Murray, with what he calls a vision Kubla Khan – which said vision he repeats so enchantingly that it irradiates & brings heaven & Elysian bowers into my parlour while he sings or says it, but there is an observation Never tell thy dreams, and I am almost afraid that Kubla Khan is an owl that wont bear day light, I fear lest it should be discovered by the lantern of typography & clear reducting to letters, no better than nonsense or no sense. When I was young I used to chant with extacy **mild Arcadians ever blooming,** [2] till somebody told me it was meant to be nonsense. Even yet I have a lingering attachment to it, and think it better than **Windsor forest, Dying Xtians address &c –**. C has sent his Tragedy to D. L. T. it cannot be acted this season, & by their manner of receiving it, I hope he will be able to alter it to make them accept it for next. He is at present under the medical care of a Mr **Gilman** [3] (**Killman?**) a Highgate Apothecary, where he **plays at leaving off Laud—m.** – I think his essentials not touched, he is very bad, but then he wonderfully picks up another day, and his face when he repeats his verses hath its ancient glory, an Arch angel a little damaged. –

Will Miss H. pardon our not replying at length to her kind Letter? We are not quiet enough. Morgan is with us every day, going betwixt Highgate & the Temple. Coleridge is absent but 4 miles, & the neighborhood of such a man is as exciting as the presence of 50 ordinary Persons. Tis enough to be within the whiff & wind of **his** genius, for us not to possess our souls in quiet. If I lived with him or the *Author of the Excursion*, I should in a very little time lose my own identity, & be dragged along in the current of other peoples thoughts, hampered in a net. How cool I sit in this office, with no possible interruption further than what I may term *material*; there is not as much metaphysics in 36 of the people here as there is in the first page of Lockes treatise on the Human understanding, or as much poetry as in any ten lines of the Pleasure of Hope or more natural Beggars Petition.[4] I never entangle myself in any of their speculations. Interruption's, if I try to write a letter even, I have dreadful. Just now within 4 lines I was call'd off for ten minutes to consult dusty old books for the settlement of obsolete Errors. I hold you a guinea you dont find the Chasm where I left off, so excellently the wounded sense closed again & was healed. – N. B. Nothing said above to the contrary but that I hold the personal presence of the two mentioned potent spirits at a rate as high as any, but I pay dearer, what amuses others **robs me of my self**, my mind is positively discharged into their greater currents, but flows with a welling violence. As to your question about work, it is far less oppressive to me than it was, from circumstances; it takes all the golden part of the day away, a solid lump from ten to four, but it does not kill my peace as before. Someday or other I shall be in a taking[5] again. My head akes & you have had enough. God bless you.

London   C LAMB

Twenty Sixth April 1816

35. TO WILLIAM WORDSWORTH

from Leadin Hall
Septemr something [23 September] 1816

My dear Wordsworth,

It seems an age since we have corresponded, but indeed the interim has been stuffd out with more variety than usually checquers my same-seeming existence –. Mercy on me, what a traveller have I been since I wrote you last! what foreign wonders have been explored! I have seen Bath, King Bladuds ancient well, fair Bristol seed-plot of suicidal Chatterton, Marlbro, Chippenham, Calne, famous for nothing in particular that I know of – but such a vertigo of locomotion has not seized us for years –. We spent a month with the Morgans at the last named Borough, – August – and such a change has the change wrought in us that we could not stomach wholesome Temple air, but are absolutely rusticating (o the gentility of it) at Dalston, about one mischievous boy's stone's throw off Kingsland Turnpike, one mile from Shoreditch church, thence we emanate in various directions to Hackney, Clapton, Totnam, and such like romantic country. That my lungs should ever prove so dainty as to fancy they perceive differences of **air!** but so it is, tho' I am almost ashamed of it, like Milton's devil (turn'd truant to his old Brimstone) I am purging off the foul air of my once darling tobacco in this **Eden**, absolutely snuffing up pure gales, **like** old worn out Sin playing at being innocent which never comes again, for in spite of good books & good thoughts there is something in a **Pipe** that virtue cannot give tho' she give her unendowed person for a dowry. Have you read the review of Coleridges character, person, physiognomy &c. in the Examiner,[1] – his features even to his *nose* – O horrible license beyond the old Comedy –. **He** is himself gone to the sea side with his favorite Apothecary, having left for publication as I hear a prodigious mass of composition for a Sermon to the middling ranks of people to persuade them they are not so distressed as is commonly supposed. Methinks he should recite **it** to a congregation of Bilston Colliers, – the fate of **Cinna** the **Poet**[2] would instantaneously be his. God bless him, but certain that rogue-Examiner has beset him in most unmannerly strains. Yet there is a kind of respect shines thro' the disrespect that to those who know the rare compound (that is the subject of it) almost balances the reproof, but then those who know him but partially or at a distance are so extremely apt to drop the qualifying part thro' their fingers. The 'after all, Mr Wordsworth is a man of great talents, if he did not abuse them'[3] comes so dim upon the eyes of an Edinbro' review reader, that have been gloating-open chuckle-wide upon the preceding detail of abuses, it scarce strikes the pupil with any consciousness of the letters being there, like letters writ in lemon –. There was a cut at me a few months back by the same hand, but my agnomen or agni-nomen[4] not being calculated to strike the popular **ear**, it dropt anonymous, but it was a pretty compendium of observation which the author has collected in my disparagement, from some hundreds of social evenings which we had spent together, – however in spite of all, there is something tough in my attachment to H—[5] which these violent strainings cannot quite dislocate or sever asunder. I get no conversation in London that is absolutely worth attending to but his. There is monstrous little sense in the world, or I am monstrous clever, or squeamish or something, but there is nobody to talk to – to talk *with* I should say – and to go talking to ones self all day long is too much of a good thing, besides subjecting one to the imputation of being out of ones senses, which does no good to ones temporal interest at all. By the way, I have seen Colerge. but once this 3 or 4 months, he is an odd person, when he first comes to town he is quite hot upon visiting, and then he turns off & absolutely never comes at all, but seems to forget there are anysuch people in the world. I made one attempt to visit him (a morning call) at Highgate, but there was something in him or his Apothecary which I found so unattractively-repulsing-from any temptation to call again, that I stay away as naturally as a Lover visits. The rogue gives you Love Powders, and then a strong horse drench to bring 'em off your stomach that they may'nt hurt you. I was very sorry the printing of your Letter was not quite to your mind, but I surely did not think but you had arranged the manner of breaking the paragraphs from some principle known to your own mind, and for some of the Errors, I am confident that **Note** of Admiration, in the middle of two words did not stand so when I had it, it must have dropt out & been replaced wrong, so odious a blotch could not have escaped me. Gifford (whom God curse) has persuaded squinting Murray (whom may God not bless) not to accede to an offer Field made for me to print 2 vols. of Essays, to include the one on Hogrth. & 1 or 2 more, but most of the matter to be new, but I dare say I should never have found time to make them; **M** would have had 'em, but shewed specimens from the Reflector to **G**— as he acknowledged to Field, & Crispin did for me.[6] 'Not on his soal but on his soul damn'd Jew' may the malediction of my eternal antipathy light –. We desire much to hear from you, and of you all, including Miss Hutchinson for not writing to whom Mary feels a weekly (and did for a long time, feel a daily) Pang. How is Southey? – I hope his pen will continue to move many years smoothly & continuously for all the rubs of the rogue Examiner. A pertinacious **foul** mouthed villain **it is!** –

This is written for a rarity at the seat of business, it is but little time I can generally command from secular calligraphy, the pen seems to know as much and makes letters like figures – an obstinate clerkish thing. It shall make a couplet in spite of its nib before I have done with it,

> **'and so I end**
> Commending me to your love my dearest **friend.'**

C LAMB

36. TO CHARLES CHAMBERS

[1 September 1817]

with regard to a **John Dory**, which you desire to be particularly informed about – I honour the fish, but it is rather on account of **Quin**[1] who patronized it, and whose taste (of a *dead* man) I had as lieve go by as any body's, (**Apicius** and **Heliogabulus** excepted[2] – this latter started nightingales brains and peacock's tongues as a garnish –)

Else, in *itself*, and trusting to my own poor single judgment, it hath not that moist mellow oleaginous gliding smooth descent from the tongue to the palate, thence to the stomach &c. as your Brighton Turbot hath, which I take to be the most friendly and familiar flavor of any that swims – most genial & at home to the palate –

nor has it on the other hand that fine falling off flakiness, that obsequious peeling off (as it were like a **sea onion**) which endears your cods head & shoulders to some appitites, that manly firmness combined with a sort of womanish coming-in-pieces which the same cods head & shoulders hath – where the *whole* is easily separable, pliant to a knife or a spoon, but each *individual flake* presents a pleasing resistance to the opposed tooth – you understand me – these delicate subjects are necessarily obscure –

but it has a third flavor of its own, totally distinct from Cod or Turbot, which it must be owned may to some not injudicious palates render it acceptable – but to my unpractised tooth it presented rather a crude river-fish-flavour, like your Pike or Carp, and perhaps like them should have been tamed & corrected by some laborious & well chosen **sauce**. Still, I always suspect a fish which requires so much of artificial settings off. Your choicest relishes (like native loveliness) need not the foreign aid of ornament, but are when unadorned (that is, with nothing but a little plain anchovy & a squeeze of lemon) are then adorned the most. However, I shall go to Brighton again, next Summer, and shall have an opportunity of correcting my judgment, if it is not sufficiently informed. I can only say that when **Nature** was pleased to make the **John Dory so** notoriously deficient in outward graces (as to be sure **he** is the very **Rhinoceros** of fishes, the ugliest dog that swims, except perhaps the **Sea Satyr** which I never saw, but which they say is terrible) when she formed him with so few external advantages, she might have bestowed a more elaborate finish on his parts internal, & have given him a **relish**, a **sapor**, to recommend him; as she made **Pope** a **Poet** to make up for making him crooked.

I am sorry to find that you have got a knack of saying things which are not true, to shew your wit. If I had no wit, but what I must shew at the expence of my virtue or my modesty, I had as lieve be as stupid **as ***** at the **Tea Warehouse**. Depend upon it, [m]y dea[r] Chambers, that an ounce of integrity at our death bed will stand us in more avail than all the Wit of Congreve or ********. For instance you tell me a fine story about Truss,[3] and his playing at Leamington, which I know to be false, because I have advice from Derby that he was whipt through the Town on that very day you say he appeared in some character or other, for robbing an old woman at church of a seal ring. And Dr Parr has been two months dead.[4] So it wont do to scatter these random stories about **among people** that **know** any thing. Besides, your forte is not invention. It is *judgment*, particularly shewn in your choice of dishes. We seem in that instance born under one star. I like you for liking hare. I esteem you for disrelishing minced veal. Liking is too cold a word, I **love** you for your noble attachment to the fat unctuous juices of **deers** flesh & the **green unspeakable** of turtle. I honor you for your endeavors to esteem and approve of my favorite which I ventured to recommend to you, as substitute for hare, bullock's heart; and I am not offended that you cannot taste it with *my* palate. A true son of Epicurus should reserve one taste peculiar to himself. For a long time I kept the secret about the exceeding deliciousness of the **marrow** of boiled knuckle of veal, till my tongue weakly run out in its praises, and now it is prostitute & common. – But I have made one discovery, which I will not impart till my dying scene is over, perhaps it will be my last mouthful in this world, delicious thought, enough to sweeten (or rather make savoury) the hour of death. It is  a little square bit about this size in or near the huckle bone of a fried joint of *********** fat I cant call it, nor lean neither altogether, it is that beautiful com pound which Nature must have made in Paradise Park venison, before she separ ated the two substances, the dry & the oleaginous, to punish sinful mankind; Adam ate them entire & inseparate, and this little taste of Eden in the huckle bone of a fried ***** seems the only relique of a Paradisaical state. When I die, an exact description of its topography shall be left in a cupboard with a key, ins[c]ribed on which these words, 'C. Lamb – dying imparts this to C. Chambers as the only worthy depositary of such a secret.' You'll drop a tear – – – – –

37. TO MRS WILLIAM WORDSWORTH

18 feb. 1818. East India House.

(Mary shall send you all the *news*, which I find I have left out.)

My dear Mrs Wordsworth,

I have repeatedly taken pen in hand to answer your kind letter. My sister should more properly have done it, but she having failed, I consider myself answerable for her debts. I am now trying to do it in the midst of Commercial noises, and with a quill which seems more ready to glide into arithmetical figures and names of Goods, Cassia, Cardemoms, Aloes, Ginger, Tea, than into kindly responses and friendly recollections.

The reason why I cannot write letters at home is, that I am never alone. Plato's (I write to *W. W.* now) Plato's double animal parted never longed [? more] to be reciprocally reunited in the system of its first creation, than I sometimes do to be but for a moment single and separate. Except my morning's walk to the office, which is like treading on sands of gold for that reason, I am never so. I cannot walk home from office but some officious friend offers his damn'd unwelcome courtesies to accompany me. All the morning I am pestered. I could sit and gravely cast up sums in great Books, or compare sum with sum, and write PAID against this and UNP'D against t'other, and yet reserve in some 'corner of my mind' some darling thoughts all my own – faint memory of some passage in a Book – or the tone of an absent friend's Voice – a snatch of Miss Burrell's [1] singing – a gleam of Fanny Kelly's [2] divine plain face – The two operations might be going on at the same time without thwarting, as the sun's two motions (earth's I mean), or as I sometimes turn round till I am giddy, in my back parlour, while my sister is walking longitudinally in the front – or as the shoulder of veal twists round with the spit, while the smoke wreathes up the chimney – but there are a set of amateurs of the Belle Lettres – the gay science – who come to me as a sort of rendezvous, putting questions of criticism, of British Institutions, Lalla Rooks [3] &c., what Coleridge said at the Lecture last night – who have the form of reading men, but, for any possible use Reading can be to them but to talk of, might as well have been Ante-Cadmeans born, or have lain sucking out the sense of an Egypt[n]. hieroglyph as long as the Pyramids will last before they should find it. These pests worrit me at business and in all its intervals, perplexing my accounts, poisoning my little salutary warming-time at the fire, puzzling my paragraphs if I take a newspaper, cramming in between my own free thoughts and a column of figures which had come to an amicable compromise but for them. Their noise ended, one of them, as I said, accompanys me home lest I should be solitary for a moment; he at length takes his welcome leave at the door, up I go, mutton on table, hungry as hunter, hope to forget my cares and bury them in the agreeable abstraction of mastication, knock at the door, in comes Mrs Hazlitt, or M. Burney, or Morgan, or Demogorgon, or my brother, or somebody, to prevent my eating alone, a Process absolutely necessary to my poor wretched digestion. O the pleasure of eating alone! – eating my dinner alone! let me think of it. But in they come, and make it absolutely necessary that I should open a bottle of orange – for my meat turns into stone when any one dines with me, if I have not wine – wine can mollify stones. Then *that* wine turns into acidity, acerbity, misanthropy, a hatred of my interrupters (God bless 'em! I love some of 'em dearly), and with the hatred a still greater aversion to their going away. Bad is the dead sea they bring upon me, choaking and death-doing, but worse is the deader dry sand they leave me on if they go before bed time. Come never, I would say to these spoilers of my dinner, but if you come, never go. The fact is, this interruption does not happen very often, but every time it comes by surprise that present bane of my life, orange wine, with all its dreary stifling consequences, follows. Evening Company I should always like had I any mornings, but I am saturated with human faces (*divine* forsooth) and voices all the golden morning, and five evenings in a week would be as much as I should covet to be in company, but I assure you that is a wonderful week in which I can get two, or one, to myself. I am never C. L. but always C. L. and Co.

He, who thought it not good for man to be alone, preserve me from the more prodigious monstrosity of being never by myself. I forget bed time, but even there these sociable frogs clamber up to annoy me. Once a week, generally some singular evening that, being alone, I go to bed at the hour I ought always to be abed, just close to my bedroom window, is the club room of a public house, where a set of singers, I take them to be chorus-singers of the two theatres (it must be *both of them*), begin their orgies. They are a set of fellows (as I conceive) who being limited by their talents to the burthen of the song at the play houses, in revenge have got the common popular airs by Bishop or some cheap composer arranged for choruses, that is, to be sung all in chorus. At least I never can catch any of the text of the plain song, nothing but the Babylonish choral howl at the tail on't. 'That fury being quenchd' – the howl I mean – a curseder burden succeeds, of shouts and clapping and knocking of the table. At length over tasked nature drops under it and escapes for a few hours into the society of the sweet silent creatures of Dreams, which go away with mocks and mows at cockcrow. And then I think of the words Christobel's father used (bless me, I have dipt in the wrong ink) to say every morning by way of variety when he awoke – 'Every knell, the Baron saith, Wakes us up to a world of death,' or something like it. All I mean by this senseless interrupted tale is that by my central situation I am a little over companied. Not that I have any animosity against the good creatures that are so anxious to drive away the Harpy solitude from me. I like 'em, and cards, and a chearful glass, but I mean merely to give you an idea between office confinement and after office society, how little time I can call my own. I mean only to draw a picture, not to make an inference. I would not that I know of have it otherwise. I only wish sometimes I could exchange some of my faces and voices for the faces and voices which a late visitation brought most welcome and carried away leaving regret, but more pleasure, even a kind of gratitude at being so often favored with that kind northern visitation. My London faces and noises don't hear me – I mean no disrespect – or I should explain myself that instead of their return 220 times a year and the return of W. W. &c. 7 times in 104 weeks, some more equal distribution might be found. I have scarce room to put in Mary's kind love and my poor name.

CH. LAMB.

This to be read last.

W. H. goes on lecturing against W. W. and making copious use of quotations from said W. W. to give a zest to said lectures. S. T. C. is lecturing with success. I have not heard either him or H. but I dined with S. T. C. at Gilman's a Sunday or two since and he was well and in good spirits. I mean to hear some of the course, but lectures are not much to my taste, whatever the lecturer may be. If *read*, they are dismal flat, and you can't think why you are brought together to hear a man read his works which you could read so much better at leisure yourself; if delivered extempore, I am always in pain lest the gift of utterance should suddenly fail the orator in the middle, as it did me at the dinner given in honour of me at the London Tavern. 'Gentlemen,' said I, and there I stoppt, – the rest my feelings were under the necessity of supplying. Mrs Wordsworth *will* go on, kindly haunting us with visions of seeing the lakes once more which never can be realized.

Between us there is a great gulf – not of inexplicable moral antipathies
and distances, I hope (as there seemd to be between me and that
Gentleman concern'd in the Stamp office that I so strangely coiled up
from at Haydons).[4] I think I had an instinct that he was the head of
an office. I hate all such people – Accountants, Deputy Accountants.
The dear abstract notion of the East India Company, as long as she is
unseen, is pretty, rather Poetical; but as SHE makes herself manifest
by the persons of such Beasts, I loathe and detest her as the Scarlet
what-do-you-call-her of Babylon. I thought, after abridging us of all
our red letter days, they had done their worst, but I was deceived in
the length to which Heads of offices, those true Liberty haters, can
go. They are the tyrants, not Ferdinand, nor Nero – by a decree past
this week, they have abridged us of the immemorially-observed
custom of going at one o'clock of a Saturday, the little shadow of a
holiday left us. Blast them. I speak it soberly. Dear W. W., be thankful for your Liberty.

We have spent two very pleasant Evenings lately with Mr Monkhouse.

38. TO DOROTHY WORDSWORTH

[P.M. 25 November 1819]

Dear Miss Wordsworth,

You will think me negligent, but I wanted to see more of Willy,[1]
before I ventured to express a prediction. Till yesterday I had barely
seen him – Virgilium Tantum Vidi[2] – but yesterday he gave us his small
company to a bullock's heart – and I can pronounce him a lad of
promise. He is no pedant nor bookworm, so far I can answer. Perhaps
he has hitherto paid too little attention to other men's inventions, pre-
ferring, like Lord Foppington,[3] the 'natural sprouts of his own.' But he
has observation, and seems thoroughly awake. I am ill at remembering
other people's bon mots, but the following are a few. Being taken over
Waterloo Bridge, he remarked that if we had no mountains, we had a
fine river at least, which was a Touch of the Comparative, but then he
added, in a strain which augured less for his future abilities as a Political
Economist, that he supposed they must take at least a pound a week
Toll. Like a curious naturalist he inquired if the tide did not come up a
little salty. This being satisfactorily answered, he put another question as
to the flux and reflux, which being rather cunningly evaded than artfully
solved by that she-Aristotle Mary, who muttered something about its

getting up an hour sooner and sooner every day, he sagely replied, 'Then it must come to the same thing at last,' which was a speech worthy of an infant Halley![4] The Lion in the 'Change by no means came up to his ideal standard. So impossible it is for Nature in any of her works to come up to the standard of a child's imagination. The whelps (Lionets) he was sorry to find were dead, and on particular enquiry his old friend the Ouran Outang had gone the way of all flesh also. The grand Tiger was also sick, and expected in no short time to exchange this transitory world for another – or none. But again, there was a Golden Eagle (I do not mean that of Charing) which did much arride and console him. William's genius, I take it, leans a little to the figurative, for being at play at Tricktrack (a kind of minor Billiard-table which we keep for smaller wights, and sometimes refresh our own mature fatigues with taking a hand at), not being able to hit a ball he had iterate aimed at, he cried out, 'I cannot hit that beast.' Now the balls are usually called men, but he felicitously hit upon a middle term, a term of approximation and imaginative reconciliation, a something where the two ends, of the brute matter (ivory) and their human and rather violent personification into *men*, might meet, as I take it, illustrative of that Excellent remark in a certain Preface[5] about Imagination, explaining 'like a sea-beast that had crawled forth to sun himself.' Not that I accuse William Minor of hereditary plagiary, or conceive the image to have come ex traduce.[6] Rather he seemeth to keep aloof from any source of imitation, and purposely to remain ignorant of what mighty poets have done in this kind before him. For being asked if his father had ever been on Westminster Bridge, he answer'd that he did not know.

It is hard to discern the Oak in the Acorn, or a Temple like St. Paul's in the first stone which is laid, nor can I quite prefigure what destination the genius of William Minor hath to take. Some few hints I have set down, to guide my future observations. He hath the power of calculation in no ordinary degree for a chit. He combineth figures, after the first boggle, rapidly. As in the Tricktrack board, where the hits are figured, at first he did not perceive that 15 and 7 made 22, but by a little use he could combine 8 with 25 – and 33 again with 16, which approacheth something in kind (far let me be from flattering him by saying in degree) to that of the famous American boy.[7] I am sometimes inclined to think I perceive the future satirist in him, for he hath a sub-sardonic smile which bursteth out upon occasion, as when he was asked if London were as big as Ambleside, and indeed no other answer was given, or proper to be given, to so ensnaring and provoking a question. In the contour of scull certainly I discern something paternal. But whether in all respects the future man shall transcend his father's fame, Time the trier of geniuses must decide. Be it pronounced peremptorily at present, that Willy is a well-mannerd child, and though no great student, hath yet a lively eye for things that lie before him. Given in haste from my desk at Leadenhall. Your's and yours' most sincerely

C. LAMB

39. TO JOSEPH COTTLE

May 26, 1820.

My dear Sir,

I am quite ashamed of not having acknowledg'd your second kind present[1] earlier. But that unknown something, which was never yet discover'd, though so often speculated upon, which stands in the way of Lazy folks' answering letters, has presented its usual obstacle. It is not forgetfulness, nor disrespect, nor incivility, but terribly like all these bad things —

I have been in my time a great Epistolary Scribbler but the passion (& with it the facility) at length wears out, & it must be pumped up again by the heavy machinery of Duty, or Gratitude, when it should run free —

I have read your Poems with as much pleasure (I cannot say more) as I did the first Messiah, first I mean in order of reading, though the larger book was not quite unknown to me, having read portions of it at a friend's house —

Your Cambrian Poem is what I shall be tempted to repeat oftenest, as Human Poems take me in a mood more frequently congenial, than Divine. The Character of Llewellyn pleased me more than any thing else perhaps, & then some of the Lyrical Pieces, which are fine varieties —

It was quite a mistake that I could dislike anything you should write against Lᵈ Byron, for I have a thorough aversion to his character, and a very moderate admiration of his genius — he is great in so little a way — To be a Poet is to be The Man, the whole Man — not a petty portion of occasional low passion worked up into a permanent form of Humanity. Shakspeare has thrust such rubbishly feelings into a corner, the dark dusty heart of Don John in the much Ado. The fact is I have not yet seen your poem to him. It did not come with the rest, nor was I aware till your question, that it was out — I shall enquire & get it forth with —

Southey is in Town, whom I have seen slightly, Wordsw^th, expected, whom I hope to see much of –

Your neighbor Mich^l Castles, Morgan's friend, is also in Town, whom I shall trouble with this, if I do not get a Frank – I write with accelerated motion, for I have two or three bothering Clerks & Brokers about me, who always press in proportion as you seem to be doing something that is not business. I could exclaim a little profanely – but I think you do not like swearing – I conclude begging you to consider that I feel myself much obliged by your repeated kindness, & shall be most happy at any & all times to hear from you, Dear Sir. Yours truly

C. LAMB.

40. TO SAMUEL TAYLOR COLERIDGE

March 9th, 1822.

Dear C.,

It gives me great satisfaction to hear that the pig turned out so well – they are interesting creatures at a certain age – what a pity such buds should blow out into the maturity of rank bacon! You had all some of the crackling – and brain sauce – did you remember to rub it with butter, and gently dredge it a little, just before the crisis? Did the eyes come away kindly with no Œdipean avulsion? Was the crackling the colour of the ripe pomegranate? Had you no complement of boiled neck of mutton before it, to blunt the edge of delicate desire? Did you flesh maiden teeth in it? Not that I sent the pig, or can form the remotest guess what part Owen [1] could play in the business. I never knew him give anything away in my life. He would not begin with strangers. I suspect the pig, after all, was meant for me; but at the unlucky juncture of time being absent, the present somehow went round to Highgate. To confess an honest truth, a pig is one of those things I could never think of sending away. Teals, wigeons, snipes, barn-door fowl, ducks, geese – your tame villatic things – Welsh mutton, collars of brawn, sturgeon, fresh or pickled, your potted char, Swiss cheeses, French pies, early grapes, muscadines, I impart as freely unto my friends as to myself. They are but self-extended; but pardon me if I stop somewhere – where the fine feeling of benevolence giveth a higher smack than the sensual rarity – there my friends (or any good man) may command me; but pigs are pigs, and I myself therein am nearest to myself. Nay, I should think it an affront, an undervaluing done to Nature who bestowed such a boon upon me, if in a churlish mood I parted with the precious gift. One of the bitterest pangs of remorse I ever felt was when a child – when my kind old aunt had strained her pocket-strings to bestow a sixpenny whole plum-cake upon me. In my way home through the Borough, I met a venerable old man, not a mendicant, but thereabouts – a look-beggar, not a verbal petitionist; and in the coxcombry of taught-charity I gave away the cake to him. I walked on a little in all the pride of an Evangelical peacock, when of a sudden my old aunt's kindness crossed me – the sum it was to her – the pleasure she had a right to expect that I – not the old impostor – should take in eating her cake – the cursed ingratitude by which, under the colour of a Christian virtue, I had frustrated her cherished purpose. I sobbed, wept, and took it to heart so grievously, that I think I never suffered the like – and I was right. It was a piece of unfeeling hypocrisy, and proved a lesson to me ever after. The cake has long been masticated, consigned to the dunghill with the ashes of that unseasonable pauper.

But when Providence, who is better to us all than our aunts, gives me a pig, remembering my temptation and my fall, I shall endeavour to act towards it more in the spirit of the donor's purpose.

Yours (short of pig) to command in everything,

C. L.

41. TO WILLIAM WORDSWORTH

20th March, 1822.

My Dear Wordsworth,

A letter from you is very grateful, I have not seen a Kendal postmark so long! We are pretty well save colds and rheumatics, and a certain deadness to every thing, which I think I may date from poor John's Loss,[1] and another accident or two at the same time, that has made me almost bury myself at Dalston, where yet I see more faces than I could wish. Deaths over-set one and put one out long after the recent grief. Two or three have died within this last two twelvemths., and so many parts of me have been numbed. One sees a picture, reads an anecdote, starts a casual fancy, and thinks to tell of it to this person in preference to every other – the person is gone whom it would have peculiarly suited. It won't do for *another*. Every departure destroys a class of sympathies. There's Capt. Burney gone! – what fun has whist now? what matters it what you lead, if you can no longer fancy him looking over you? One never hears any thing, but the image of the particular person occurs with whom alone almost you would care to share the intelligence. Thus one distributes oneself about – and now for so many parts of me I have lost the market. Common natures do not suffice me. Good people, as they are called, won't serve. I want individuals. I am made up of queer points and I want so many answering needles. The going away of friends does not make the remainder more precious. It takes so much from them as there was a common link. A. B. and C. make a party. A. dies. B. not only loses A. but all A.'s part in C. C. loses A.'s part in B., and so the alphabet sickens by subtraction of interchangeables. I express myself muddily, capite dolente.[2] I have a dulling cold. My theory is to enjoy life, but the practice is against it. I grow ominously tired of official confinement. Thirty years have I served the Philistines, and my neck is not subdued to the yoke. You don't know how wearisome it is to breathe the air of four pent walls without relief day after day, all the golden hours of the day between 10 and 4 without ease or interposition. Tædet me harum quotidianarum formarum,[3] these pestilential clerk faces always in one's dish. O for a few years between the grave and the desk! they are the same, save that at the latter you are outside the machine. The foul enchanter – letters four do form his name – Busirane is his name in hell – that has curtailed you of some domestic comforts, hath laid a heavier hand on me, not in present infliction, but in taking away the hope of enfranchisement.[4] I dare not whisper to myself a Pension on this side of absolute incapacitation and infirmity, till years have sucked me dry. Otium cum indignitate.[5] I had thought in a green old age (O green thought!) to have retired to Ponder's End – emblematic name how beautiful! in the Ware road, there to have made up my accounts with Heaven and the Company, toddling about between it and Cheshunt, anon stretching on some fine Izaac Walton morning to Hoddesdon or Amwell, careless as a Beggar, but walking, walking ever, till I fairly walkd myself off my legs, dying walking!

The hope is gone. I sit like Philomel all day (but not singing) with my breast against this thorn of a Desk, with the only hope that some Pulmonary affliction may relieve me. Vide Lord Palmerston's report of the Clerks in the war office (Debates, this morning's Times) by which it appears in 20 years, as many Clerks have been coughd and catarrhd out of it into their freer graves.[6]

Thank you for asking about the Pictures. Milton hangs over my fire side in Covt. Gard. (when I am there), the rest have been sold for an old song, wanting the eloquent tongue that should have set them off!

You have gratifyd me with liking my meeting with Dodd. For the Malvolio story[7] – the thing is become in verity a sad task and I eke it out with any thing. If I could slip out of it I sh^d be happy, but our chief reputed assistants have forsaken us. The opium eater crossed us once with a dazzling path, and hath as suddenly left us darkling; and in short I shall go on from dull to worse, because I cannot resist the Bookseller's importunity – the old plea you know of authors, but I believe on my part sincere.

Hartley[8] I do not so often see, but I never see him in unwelcome hour. I thoroughly love and honor him.

I send you a frozen Epistle, but it is winter and dead time of the year with me. May heaven keep something like spring and summer up with you, strengthen your eyes and make mine a little lighter to encounter with them, as I hope they shall yet and again, before all are closed.

Yours, with every kind rem^be.   C. L.

I had almost forgot to say, I think you thoroughly right about presentation copies. I should like to see you print a book I should grudge to purchase for its size. D—n me, but I would have it though!

42. TO JOHN CLARE

India House, 31 Aug., 1822.

Dear Clare,

I thank you heartily for your present.[1] I am an inveterate old Londoner, but while I am among your choice collections, I seem to be native to them, and free of the country. The quantity of your observation has astonished me. What have most pleased me have been Recollections after a Ramble, and those Grongar Hill kind of pieces in eight syllable lines, my favourite measure, such as Cowper Hill and Solitude. In some of your story-telling Ballads the provincial phrases sometimes startle me. I think you are too profuse with them. In poetry *slang* of every kind is to be avoided. There is a rustick Cockneyism, as little pleasing as ours of London. Transplant Arcadia to Helpstone. The true rustic style, the Arcadian English, I think is to be found in Shenstone.[2] Would his Schoolmistress, the prettiest of poems, have been better, if he had used quite the Goody's own language? Now and then a home rusticism is fresh and startling, but where nothing is gained in expression, it is out of tenor. It may make folks smile and stare, but the ungenial coalition of barbarous with refined phrases will prevent you in the end from being so generally tasted, as you deserve to be. Excuse my freedom, and take the same liberty with my *puns*.

I send you two little volumes of my spare hours. They are of all sorts, there is a methodist hymn for Sundays, and a farce for Saturday night. Pray give them a place on your shelf. Pray accept a little volume,[3] of which I have [a] duplicate, that I may return in equal number to your welcome presents.

I think I am indebted to you for a sonnet in the London for August.

Since I saw you I have been in France,[4] and have eaten frogs. The nicest little rabbity things you ever tasted. Do look about for them. Make Mrs Clare pick off the hind quarters, boil them plain, with parsley and butter. The fore quarters are not so good. She may let them hop off by themselves.

> Yours sincerely,
> CHAS. LAMB.

43. TO WALTER WILSON

E. I. H. 16 dec. 22.

Dear Wilson

Lightening I was going to call you –

You must have thought me negligent in not answering your letter sooner. But I have a habit of never writing letters, but at the office – 'tis so much time cribbed out of the Company – and I am but just got out of the thick of a Tea Sale, in which most of the Entry of Notes, deposits &c. usually falls to my share. Dodwell is willing, but alas! slow. To compare a pile of my notes with his little hillock (which has been as long a building), what is it but to compare Olympus with a mole-hill. Then Wadd[1] is a sad shuffler. –

I have nothing of Defoe's[2] but two or three Novels, and the Plague History. I can give you no information about him. As a slight general character of what I remember of them (for I have not look'd into them latterly) I would say that 'in the appearance of *truth* in all the incidents and conversations that occur in them they exceed any works of fiction I am acquainted with. It is perfect illusion. The *Author* never appears in these self-narratives (for so they ought to be called or rather Autobiographies) but the *narrator* chains us down to an implicit belief in every thing he says. There is all the minute detail of a log-book in it. Dates are painfully pressed upon the memory. Facts are repeated over and over in varying phrases, till you cannot chuse but believe them. It is like reading

Evidence given in a Court of Justice. So anxious the story-teller seems, that the truth should be clearly comprehended, that when he has told us a matter of fact, or a motive, in a line or two farther down he *repeats* it with his favorite figure of speech, "I say" so and so, – though he had made it abundantly plain before. This is in imitation of the common people's way of speaking, or rather of the way in which they are addressed by a master or mistress, who wishes to impress something upon their memories; and has a wonderful effect upon matter-of-fact readers. Indeed it is to such principally that he writes. His style is elsewhere beautiful, but plain & *homely.* Robinson Crusoe is delightful to all ranks and classes, but it is easy to see that it is written in phraseology peculiarly adapted to the lower conditions of readers: hence it is an especial favorite with seafaring men, poor boys, servant maids &c. His novels are capital kitchen-reading, while they are worthy from their deep interest to find a shelf in the Libraries of the wealthiest, and the most learned. His passion for *matter of fact narrative* sometimes betrayed him into a long relation of common incidents which might happen to any man, and have no interest but the intense appearance of truth in them, to recommend them. The whole latter half, or two thirds, of Colonel Jack is of this description. The beginning of Colonel Jack is the most affecting natural picture of a young thief that was ever drawn. His losing the stolen money in the hollow of a tree, and finding it again when he was in despair, and then being in equal distress at not knowing how to dispose of it, and several similar touches in the early history of the Colonel, evince a deep knowledge of human nature; and, putting out of question the superior *romantic* interest of the latter, in my mind very much exceed Crusoe. Roxana (1st Edition) is the next in Interest, though he left out the best part of it [in] subsequent Editions from a foolish hypercriticism of his friend, Southerne. But Moll Flanders, the account of the Plague &c. &c. are all of one family, and have the same stamp of character.' –

[*At the top of the first page is added:*]
    Omitted at the end . . . believe me with friendly recollections, *Brother* (as I used to call you) Yours

C. LAMB.

[*Below the 'Dear Wilson' is added in smaller writing:*]
    The review was not mine, nor have I seen it.

44. TO BERNARD BARTON

9 Jan., 1823.

'Throw yourself on the world without any rational plan of support, beyond what the chance employ of Booksellers would afford you'!!!

Throw yourself rather, my dear Sir, from the steep Tarpeian rock,[1] slap-dash headlong upon iron spikes. If you had but five consolatory minutes between the desk and the bed, make much of them, and live a century in them, rather than turn slave to the Booksellers. They are Turks and Tartars, when they have poor Authors at their beck. Hitherto you have been at arm's length from them. Come not within their grasp. I have known many authors for bread, some repining, others envying the blessed security of a Counting House, all agreeing they had rather have been Taylors, Weavers, what not? rather than the things they were. I have known some starved, some to go mad, one dear friend literally dying in a workhouse. You know not what a rapacious, dishonest set these booksellers are. Ask even Southey who (a single case almost) has made a fortune by book drudgery, what he has found them. O you know not, may you never know! the miseries of subsisting by authorship. 'Tis a pretty appendage to a situation like yours or mine, but a slavery worse than all slavery to be a bookseller's dependent, to drudge your brains for pots of ale and breasts of mutton, to change your free thoughts and voluntary numbers for ungracious TASK-WORK. Those fellows hate *us*. The reason I take to be, that, contrary to other trades, in which the Master gets all the credit (a Jeweller or Silversmith for instance), and the Journeyman, who really does the fine work, is in the background: in *our* work the world gives all the credit to Us, whom *they* consider as *their* Journeymen, and therefore do they hate us, and cheat us, and oppress us, and would wring the blood of us out, to put another sixpence in their mechanic pouches. I contend, that a Bookseller has a *relative honesty* towards Authors, not like his honesty to the rest of the world. B[aldwin],[2] who first engag'd me as Elia, has not paid me up yet (nor any of us without repeated mortifying applials), yet how the Knave fawned while I was of service to him! Yet I dare say the fellow is punctual in settling his milk-score, &c. Keep to your Bank, and the Bank will keep you. Trust not to the Public, you may hang, starve, drown yourself, for anything that worthy *Personage* cares. I bless every star, that Providence, not seeing good to make me independent, has seen it next good to settle me upon the stable foundation of Leadenhall. Sit down, good B. B., in the Banking Office; what, is there not from six to Eleven P.M. 6 days in the week, and is there not all Sunday? Fie, what a superfluity of man's time if you could think so! Enough for relaxation, mirth, converse, poetry, good thoughts, quiet thoughts. Of the corroding torturing tormenting thoughts, that disturb the Brain of the unlucky wight, who must draw upon it for daily sustenance. Henceforth I retract all my fond complaints of mercantile employment, look upon them as Lovers' quarrels. I was but half in earnest. Welcome, dead timber of a desk, that makes me live. A little grumbling is a wholesome medicine for the spleen, but in my inner heart do I approve and embrace this our close but unharassing way of life. I am quite serious. If you can send me Fox, I will not keep it six *weeks*, and will return it, with warm thanks to yourself and friend, without blot or dog's ear. You much oblige me by this kindness.

Yours truly,   C. LAMB.

Please to direct to me at India Ho. in future. [? I am] not always at Russell St.

45. TO BERNARD BARTON

[Dated at end: 2 September (1823)]

Dear B. B.,

What will you say to my not writing? You cannot say I do not write now. Hessey[1] has not used your kind sonnet, nor have I seen it. Pray send me a Copy. Neither have I heard any more of your Friend's MS., which I will reclaim, whenever you please. When you come Londonward you will find me no longer in Cov^t Gard. I have a Cottage, in Colebrook row, Islington. A cottage, for it is detach'd; a white house, with 6 good rooms; the New River (rather elderly by this time) runs (if a moderate walking pace can be so termed) close to the foot of the house; and behind is a spacious garden, with vines (I assure you), pears, strawberries, parsnips, leeks, carrots, cabbages, to delight the heart of old Alcinous.[2] You enter without passage into a cheerful dining room, all studded over and rough with old Books, and above is a lightsome Drawing room, 3 windows, full of choice prints. I feel like a great Lord, never having had a house before.

The London I fear falls off. – I linger among its creaking rafters, like the last rat. It will topple down, if they don't get some Buttresses. They have pull'd down three, W. Hazlitt, Proctor,[3] and their best stay, kind light hearted Wainwright[4] – their Janus. The best is, neither of our fortunes is concern'd in it.

I heard of you from Mr Pulham[5] this morning, and that gave a fillip to my Laziness, which has been intolerable. But I am so taken up with pruning and gardening, quite a new sort of occupation to me. I have gather'd my Jargonels, but my Windsor Pears are backward. The former were of exquisite raciness. I do now sit under my own vine, and contemplate the growth of vegetable nature. I can now understand in what sense they speak of FATHER ADAM. I recognise the paternity, while I watch my tulips. I almost FELL with him, for the first day I turned a drunken gard'ner (as he let in the serpent) into my Eden, and he laid about him, lopping off some choice boughs, etc., which hung over from a neighbor's garden, and in his blind zeal laid waste a shade, which had sheltered their window from the gaze of passers by. The old gentlewoman (fury made her not handsome) could scarcely be reconciled by all my fine words. There was no buttering her parsnips. She talk'd of the Law. What a lapse to commit on the first day of my happy 'garden-state.'

I hope you transmitted the Fox-Journal to its Owner with suitable thanks.

Mr Cary,[6] the Dante-man, dines with me to-day. He is a model of a country Parson, lean (as a Curate ought to be), modest, sensible, no obtruder of church dogmas, quite a different man from Southey, you would like him.

Pray accept this for a Letter, and believe me with sincere regards

Yours

C. L.

2 Sept.

46. TO BERNARD BARTON

[9 January 1824]

Dear B. B.,

Do you know what it is to succumb under an insurmountable day mare – a whoreson lethargy, Falstaff calls it – an indisposition to do any thing, or to be any thing – a total deadness and distaste – a suspension of vitality – an indifference to locality – a numb soporifical goodfornothingness – an ossification all over – an oyster-like insensibility to the passing events – a mind-stupor, – a brawny defiance to the needles of a thrusting-in conscience – did you ever have a very bad cold with a total irresolution to submit to water gruel processes? – this has been for many weeks my lot, and my excuse – my fingers drag heavily over this paper, and to my thinking it is three and twenty furlongs from here to the end of this demi-sheet – I have not a thing to say – nothing is of more importance than another – I am flatter than a denial or a pancake – emptier than Judge Park's [1] wig when the head is in it – duller than a country stage when the actors are off it – a cypher – an O – I acknowledge life at all, only by an occasional convulsional cough, and a permanent phlegmatic pain in the chest – I am weary of the world – Life is weary of me – My day is gone into Twilight and I don't think it worth the expence of candles – my wick hath a thief in it, but I can't muster courage to snuff it – I inhale suffocation – I can't distinguish veal from mutton – nothing interests me – tis 12 o'clock and Thurtell [1] is just now coming out upon the New Drop – Jack Ketch [1] alertly tucking up his greasy sleeves to do the last office of mortality, yet cannot I elicit a groan or a moral reflection – if you told me the world will be at end tomorrow, I should just say, 'will it?' – I have not volition enough to dot my i's – much less to comb my EYEBROWS – my eyes are set in my head – my brains are gone out to see a poor relation in Moorfields, and they did not say when they'd come back again – my scull is a Grub street Attic, to let – not so much as a joint stool or a crackd jordan left in it – my hand writes, not I, from habit, as chickens run about a little when their heads are off – O for a vigorous fit of gout, cholic, tooth ache – an earwig in my auditory, a fly in my visual organs – pain is life – the sharper, the more evidence of life – but this apathy, this death – did you ever have an obstinate cold, a six or seven weeks' unintermitting chill and suspension of hope, fear, conscience, and every thing – yet do I try all I can to cure it, I try wine, and spirits, and smoking, and snuff in unsparing quantities, but they all only seem to make me worse, instead of better – I sleep in a damp room, but it does me no good; I come home late o' nights, but do not find any visible amendment.

Who shall deliver me from the body of this death?

It is just 15 minutes after 12. Thurtell is by this time a good way on his journey, baiting at Scorpion [2] perhaps, Ketch is bargaining for his cast coat and waistcoat, the Jew demurs at first at three half crowns, but on consideration that he may get somewhat by showing 'em in the Town, finally closes. –

C. L.

47. TO BERNARD BARTON

[P.M. 25 February 1824]

My Dear Sir,

Your title of Poetic Vigils [1] arrides me much more than A Volume of
Verse, which is no meaning. The motto says nothing, but I cannot
suggest a better. I do not like mottoes but where they are singularly
felicitous; there is foppery in them. They are unplain, un-Quakerish.
They are good only where they flow from the Title, and are a kind of
justification of it. There is nothing about watchings or lucubrations in
the one you suggest, no commentary on Vigils. By the way, a wag
would recommend you to the Line of Pope

> Sleepless himself – to give his readers sleep –

I by no means wish it. But it may explain what I mean, that a neat
motto is child of the Title. I think Poetic Vigils, as short and sweet as
can be desired, only have an eye on the Proof, that the Printer do not
substitute Virgils, which would ill accord with modesty or meaning.
Your suggested motto is antique enough in spelling, and modern enough
in phrases; a good modern antique: but the matter of it is germane to
the purpose only supposing the title proposed a vindication of yourself
from the presumption of authorship. The 1st title was liable to this
objection, that if you were disposed to enlarge it, and the bookseller
insisted on its appearance in Two Tomes, how oddly it would sound –

> A Volume of Verse
> in Two Volumes
> 2d edition &c –

You see thro' my wicked intention of curtailing this Epistolet by the
above device of large margin. But in truth the idea of letterising has
been oppressive to me of late above your candour to give me credit for.
There is Southey, whom I ought to have thank'd a fortnight ago for a
present of the Church Book. I have never had courage to buckle myself
in earnest even to acknowledge it by six words. And yet I am accounted
by some people a good man. How cheap that character is acquired! Pay
your debts, don't borrow money, nor twist your kittens neck off, or
disturb a congregation, &c. – your business is done. I know things
(thoughts or things – thoughts are things) of myself which would make
every friend I have fly me as a plague patient. I once***, and set a dog

upon a crab's leg that was shoved out under a moss of sea weeds, a pretty little feeler. – Oh! pah! how sick I am of that; and a lie, a mean one, I once told! –

I stink in the midst of respect.

I am much hypt; the fact is, my head is heavy, but there is hope, or if not, I am better than a poor shell fish – not morally when I set the whelp upon it, but have more blood and spirits; things may turn up, and I may creep again into a decent opinion of myself. Vanity will return with sunshine. Till when, pardon my neglects and impute it to the wintry solstice.

C. LAMB.

48. TO BERNARD BARTON

[(Early spring), 1824]

I am sure I cannot fill a letter, though I should disfurnish my scull to fill it. But you expect something, and shall have a Note-let. Is Sunday, not divinely speaking, but humanly and holydaysically, a blessing? Without its institution, would our rugged taskmasters have given us a leisure day, so often, think you, as once in a month? – or, if it had not been instituted, might they not have given us every 6th day? Solve me this problem. If we are to go 3 times a day to church, why has Sunday slipped into the notion of a *Holli*day? A Holyday I grant it. The puritans, I have read in Southey's Book,[1] knew the distinction. They made people observe Sunday rigorously, would not let a nursery maid walk out in the fields with children for recreation on that day. But *then* – they gave the people a holliday from all sorts of work every second Tuesday. This was giving to the Two Cæsars that which was *his* respective. Wise, beautiful, thoughtful, generous Legislators! Would Wilberforce[2] give us our Tuesdays? No, d—n him. He would turn the six days into sevenths,

> And those 3 smiling seasons of the year
> Into a Russian winter.

Old Play.

I am sitting opposite a person who is making strange distortions with the gout, which is not unpleasant – to me at least. What is the reason we do not sympathise with pain, short of some terrible Surgical operation? Hazlitt, who boldly says all he feels, avows that not only he does not pity sick people, but he hates them. I obscurely recognise his meaning. Pain is probably too selfish a consideration, too simply a consideration of self-attention. We pity poverty, loss of friends etc. more complex things, in which the Sufferers feelings are associated with others. This is a rough thought suggested by the presence of gout; I want head to extricate it and plane it. What is all this to your Letter? I felt it to be a good one, but my turn, when I write at all, is perversely to travel out of the record, so that my letters are any thing but answers. So you still want a motto? You must not take my ironical one, because your book, I take it, is too serious for it. Bickerstaff might have used it for *his* lucubrations. What do you think of (for a Title)

RELIGIO TREMULI
OR TREMEBUNDI[3]

There is Religio-Medici and Laici. — But perhaps the volume is not quite Quakerish enough or exclusively for it — but your own VIGILS is perhaps the Best. While I have space, let me congratulate with you the return of Spring, what a Summery Spring too! all those qualms about the dog and cray-fish melt before it. I am going to be happy and *vain* again.

A hasty farewell

C. LAMB.

49. TO BERNARD BARTON

May 15, 1824.

Dear B. B.,

I am oppressed with business all day, and Company all night. But I will snatch a quarter of an hour. Your recent acquisitions of the Picture and the Letter are greatly to be congratulated. I too have a picture of my father and the copy of his first love verses; but they have been mine long. Blake is a real name, I assure you, and a most extraordinary man, if he be still living. He is the Robert [William] Blake, whose wild designs accompany a splendid folio edition of the 'Night Thoughts,' which you may have seen, in one of which he pictures the parting of soul and body by a solid mass of human form floating off, God knows how, from a lumpish mass (fac Simile to itself) left behind on the dying bed. He paints in water colours marvellous strange pictures, visions of his brain, which he asserts that he has seen. They have great merit. He has *seen* the old Welsh bards on Snowdon — he had seen the Beautifullest, the strongest, and the Ugliest Man, left alone from the Massacre of the Britons by the Romans, and has painted them from memory (I have seen his paintings), and asserts them to be as good as the figures of Raphael and Angelo, but not better, as they had precisely the same retro-visions and prophetic visions with themself [himself]. The painters in oil (which he will have it that neither of them practised) he affirms to have been the ruin of art, and affirms that all the while he was engaged in his Water paintings, Titian was disturbing him, Titian the Ill Genius of Oil Painting. His Pictures — one in particular, the Canterbury Pilgrims (far above Stothard's) — have great merit, but hard, dry, yet with grace. He has written a Catalogue of them with a most spirited criticism on Chaucer, but mystical and full of Vision. His poems have been sold hitherto only in Manuscript. I never read them; but a friend at my desire procured the 'Sweep Song.' There is one to a tiger, which I have heard recited, beginning:

> Tiger, Tiger, burning bright,
> Thro' the desarts of the night,

which is glorious, but, alas! I have not the book; for the man is flown, wither I know not — to Hades or a Mad House. But I must look on him as one of the most extraordinary persons of the age. Montgomery's book[1] I have not much hope from. The Society, with the affected name,[2] has been labouring at it for these 20 years, and made few converts. I think it was injudicious to mix stories avowedly colour'd by fiction with the sad true statements from the parliamentary records, etc., but I wish the little Negroes all the good that can come from it. I batter'd my brains (not butter'd them — but it is a bad *a*) for a few verses for them, but I could make nothing of it. You have been luckier. But Blake's are the flower of the set, you will, I am sure, agree, tho' some of Montgomery's at the end are pretty; but the Dream awkwardly paraphras'd from B.[3]

With the exception of an Epilogue for a Private Theatrical, I have written nothing now for near 6 months. It is in vain to spur me on. I must wait. I cannot write without a genial impulse, and I have none. 'Tis barren all and dearth. No matter; life is something without scribbling. I have got rid of my bad spirits, and hold up pretty well this rain-damn'd May.

So we have lost another Poet.[4] I never much relished his Lordship's mind, and shall be sorry if the Greeks have cause to miss him. He was to me offensive, and I never can make out his great *power*, which his admirers talk of. Why, a line of Wordsworth's is a lever to lift the immortal spirit! Byron can only move the Spleen. He was at best a Satyrist, – in any other way he was mean enough. I dare say I do him injustice; but I cannot love him, nor squeeze a tear to his memory. He did not like the world, and he has left it, as Alderman Curtis advised the Radicals, 'If they don't like their country, damn 'em, let 'em leave it,' they possessing no rood of ground in England, and he 10,000 acres. Byron was better than many Curtises.

Farewell, and accept this apology for a letter from one who owes you so much in that kind.

Yours ever truly,   C. L.

50. TO THOMAS MANNING

[Not dated: *?* 26 January 1825]

My dear M.,

You might have come inopportunely a week since, when we had an inmate. At present and for as long as *ever* you like, our castle is at your service. I saw Tuthill [1] yesternight, who has done for me what may

> To all my nights and days to come,
> Give solely sovran sway and masterdom. [2]

But I dare not hope, for fear of disappointment. I cannot be more explicit at present. But I have it under his own hand, that I am *non*-capacitated (I cannot write it *in*-) for business. O joyous imbecility! Not a susurration of this to *anybody!*

Mary's love.   C. LAMB.

51. TO WILLIAM WORDSWORTH

Colebrook Cottage,
6 April, 1825.

Dear Wordsworth,

I have been several times meditating a letter to you concerning the good thing which has befallen me, but the thought of poor Monkhouse [1] came across me. He was one that I had exulted in the prospect of congratulating me. He and you were to have been the first participators, for indeed it has been ten weeks since the first motion of it.

Here I am then after 33 years slavery, sitting in my own room at 11

o'Clock this finest of all April mornings a freed man, with £441 a year
for the remainder of my life, live I as long as John Dennis, who outlived
his annuity and starved at 90. £441, i.e. £450, with a deduction of £9
for a provision secured to my sister, she being survivor, the Pension
guaranteed by Act Georgii Tertii, &c.

I came home for ever on Tuesday in last week. The incom-
prehensibleness of my condition overwhelm'd me. It was like passing from life into Eternity. Every year to be as long as three, i.e. to have
three times as much real time, time that is my own, in it! I wandered
about thinking I was happy, but feeling I was not. But that tumultu-
ousness is passing off, and I begin to understand the nature of the gift.
Holydays, even the annual month, were always uneasy joys: their conscious fugitiveness – the craving after making the most of them. Now,
when all is holyday, they are no holydays. I can sit at home in rain or
shine without a restless impulse for walkings. I am daily steadying, and
shall soon find it as natural to me to be my own master, as it has been
irksome to have had a master. Mary wakes every morning with an
obscure feeling that some good has happened to us.

Leigh Hunt and Montgomery[2] after their releasements describe the
shock of their emancipation much as I feel mine. But it hurt their
frames. I eat, drink, and sleep sound as ever. I lay no anxious schemes
for going hither and thither, but take things as they occur. Yesterday I
excursioned 20 miles, to day I write a few letters. Pleasuring was for
fugitive play days, mine are fugitive only in the sense that life is fugitive.
Freedom and life co-existent.

At the foot of such a call upon you for gratulation, I am ashamd to
advert to that melancholy event. Monkhouse was a character I learned to
love slowly, but it grew upon me, yearly, monthly, daily. What a
chasm has it made in our pleasant parties! His noble friendly face was
always coming before me, till this hurrying event in my life came, and
for the time has absorpt all interests. In fact it has shaken me a little. My
old desk companions with whom I have had such merry hours seem to
reproach me for removing my lot from among them. They were pleasant creatures, but to the anxieties of business, and a weight of possible
worse ever impending, I was not equal. Tuthill and Gilman gave me
my certificates. I laughed at the friendly lie implied in them, but my
sister shook her head and said it was all true. Indeed this last winter I was
jaded out, winters were always worse than other parts of the year,
because the spirits are worse, and I had no daylight. In summer I had
daylight evenings. The relief was hinted to me from a superior power,

when I poor slave had not a hope but that I must wait another 7 years with Jacob – and lo! the Rachel which I coveted is bro^t. to me –

Have you read the noble dedication of Irving's [3] 'Missionary Orations' to S. T. C. Who shall call this man a Quack hereafter? What the Kirk will think of it neither I nor Irving care. When somebody suggested to him that it would not be likely to do him good, videlicet [4] among his own people, 'That is a reason for doing it' was his noble answer.

That Irving thinks he has profited mainly by S. T. C., I have no doubt. The very style of the Ded. shows it.

Communicate my news to Southey, and beg his pardon for my being so long acknowledging his kind present of the 'Church,' which circumstances I do not wish to explain, but having no reference to himself, prevented at the time. Assure him of my deep respect and friendliest feelings.

Divide the same, or rather each take the whole to you, I mean you and all yours. To Miss Hutchinson I must write separate. What's her address? I want to know about Mrs M.

Farewell! and end at last, long selfish Letter!

C. LAMB.

52. TO SAMUEL TAYLOR COLERIDGE

[P.M. 2 July 1825]

Dear C.,

We are going off to Enfield, to Allsop's,[1] for a day or 2, with some intention of succeeding them in their lodging for a time, for this damn'd nervous Fever (vide Lond. Mag. for July)[2] indisposes me for seeing any friends, and never any poor devil was so befriended as I am. Do you know any poor solitary human that wants that cordial to life – a true friend? I can spare him twenty, he shall have 'em good cheap. I have gallipots of 'em – genuine balm of cares – a going – a going – a going. Little plagues plague me a 1000 times more than ever. I am like a disembodied soul – in this my eternity. I feel every thing entirely, all in all and all in etc. This price I pay for liberty, but am richly content to pay it. The Odes are 4-5^ths done by Hood,[3] a silentish young man you met at Islinton one day, an invalid. The rest are Reynolds's, whose sister H. has recently married. I have not had a broken finger in them.

They are hearty good-natured things, and I would put my name to 'em chearfully, if I could as honestly. I complimented them in a Newspaper, with an abatement for those puns you laud so. They are generally an excess. A Pun is a thing of too much consequence to be thrown in as a makeweight. You shall read one of the addresses over, and miss the puns, and it shall be quite as good and better than when you discover 'em. A Pun is a Noble Thing per se: O never lug it in as an accessory. A Pun is a sole object for reflection (vide *my* aids to that recessment from a savage state) — it is entire, it fills the mind: it is perfect as a Sonnet, better. It limps asham'd in the train and retinue of Humour: it knows it should have an establishment of its own. The one, for instance, I made the other day, I forget what it was.

Hood will be gratify'd, as much as I am, by your mistake. I liked 'Grimaldi' the best; it is true painting, of abstract Clownery, and that precious concrete of a Clown; and the rich succession of images, and words almost such, in the first half of the Mag. Ignotum.[4] Your picture of the Camel, that would not or could not thread your nice needle-eye of Subtilisms, was confirm'd by Elton, who perfectly appreciated his abrupt departure. Elton borrowed the 'Aids' from Hessey (by the way what is your Enigma about Cupid?[5] I am Cytherea's son, if I understand a tittle of it), and returned it next day saying that 20 years ago, when he was pure, he *thought* as you do now, but that he now thinks as you did 20 years ago. But E. seems a very honest fellow. Hood has just come in; his sick eyes sparkled into health when he read your approbation. They had meditated a copy for you, but postponed it till a neater 2d Edition, which is at hand.

Have you heard *the Creature* at the Opera House — Signor Non-vir sed VELUTI Vir?[6]

Like Orpheus, he is said to draw stocks &c. *after* him. A picked raisin for a sweet banquet of sounds; but I affect not these exotics. Nos DURUM genus,[7] as mellifluous Ovid hath it.

Fanny Holcroft is just come in, with her paternal severity of aspect. She has frozen a bright thought which should have follow'd. She makes us marble, with too little conceiving.'Twas respecting the Signor, whom I honour on this side idolatry. Well, more of this anon.

We are setting out to walk to Enfield after our Beans and Bacon, which are just smoking.

Kindest remembrances to the G.'s ever.
From Islinton,
2d day, 3d month of my Hegira
or Flight from Leadenhall.   C. L. Olim Clericus.[8]

53. TO BERNARD BARTON

[P.M. 10 August 1825]

Dear B. B.,

You must excuse my not writing before, when I tell you we are on a visit at Enfield, where I do not feel it natural to sit down to a Letter. It is at all times an exertion. I had rather talk with you, and Ann Knight,[1] quietly at Colebrook Lodge, over the matter of your last. You mistake me when you express misgivings about my relishing a series of scriptural poems. I wrote confusedly. What I meant to say was, that one or two consolatory poems on deaths would have had a more condensed effect than many. Scriptural – devotional topics – admit of infinite variety. So far from poetry tiring me because religious, I can read, and I say it seriously, the homely old version of the Psalms in our Prayerbooks for an hour or two together sometimes without sense of weariness.

I did not express myself clearly about what I think a false topic insisted on so frequently in consolatory addresses on the death of Infants. I know something like it is in Scripture, but I think humanly spoken. It is a natural thought, a sweet fallacy to the Survivors – but still a fallacy. If it stands on the doctrines of this being a probationary state, it is liable to this dilemma. Omniscience, to whom possibility must be clear as act, must know of the child, what it would hereafter turn out: if good, then the topic is false to say it is secured from falling into future wilfulness, vice, &c. If bad, I do not see how its exemption from certain future overt acts by being snatched away at all tells in its favor. You stop the arm of a murderer, or arrest the finger of a pickpurse, but is not the guilt incurred as much by the intent as if never so much acted? Why children are hurried off, and old reprobates of a hundred left, whose trial humanly we may think was complete at fifty, is among the obscurities of providence. The very notion of a state of probation has darkness in it. The all-knower has no need of satisfying his eyes by seeing what we will do, when he knows before what we will do. Methinks we might be condemn'd before commission. In these things we grope and flounder, and if we can pick up a little human comfort that the child taken is snatch'd from vice (no great compliment to it, by the bye), let us take it. And as to where an untried child goes, whether to join the assembly of its elders who have borne the heat of the day – fire-purified martyrs, and torment-sifted confessors — what know we? We promise heaven methinks too cheaply, and assign large revenues to minors, incompetent to manage them. Epitaphs run upon this topic of consolation, till the very frequency induces a cheapness. Tickets for admission into Paradise are sculptured out at a penny a letter, two-pence a syllable, &c. It is all a mystery; and the more I try to express my meaning (having none that is clear) the more I founder. Finally, write what your own conscience, which to you is the unerring judge, seems best, and be careless about the whimsies of such a half-baked notionist as I am. We are here in a most pleasant country, full of walks, and idle to our hearts' desire. Taylor has dropt the London.[2] It was indeed a dead weight. It has got in the Slough of Despond. I shuffle off my part of the pack, and stand like Xtian with light and merry shoulders. It had got silly, indecorous, pert, and every thing that is bad. Both our kind *rememb^ces* to Mrs K. and yourself, and stranger's-greeting to Lucy[3] – is it Lucy or Ruth? – that gathers wise sayings in a Book.

C. LAMB.

54. TO BERNARD BARTON

[P.M. 16 May 1826]

Dear B. B.,

I have had no spirits lately to begin a letter to you, though I am under obligations to you (how many!) for your neat little poem. 'Tis just what it professes to be, a simple tribute in chaste verse, serious and sincere. I do not know how Friends will relish it, but we out-lyers, Honorary Friends, like it very well. I have had my head and ears stuff'd up with the East winds. A continual ringing in my brain of bells jangled, or The Spheres touchd by some raw Angel. It is not George 3 trying the 100th psalm?[1] I get my music for nothing. But the weather seems to be softening, and will thaw my stunnings. Coleridge writing to me a week or two since begins his note – 'Summer has set in with its usual Severity.' A cold Summer is all I know of disagreeable in cold. I do not mind the utmost rigour of real Winter, but these smiling hypocrites of Mays wither me to death. My head has been a ringing Chaos, like the day the winds were made, before they submitted to the discipline of a weath-ercock, before the Quarters were made. In the street, with the blended noises of life about me, I hear, and my head is lightened, but in a room the hubbub comes back, and I am deaf as a Sinner. Did I tell you of a pleasant sketch Hood has done, which he calls *Very Deaf Indeed?* It is of a good naturd stupid looking old gentleman, whom a footpad has stopt, but for his extreme deafness cannot make him understand what he wants; the unconscious old gentleman is extending his ear-trumpet very complacently, and the fellow is firing pistol into it to make him hear, but the ball will pierce his skull sooner than the report reach his sensorium. I chuse a very little bit of paper, for my ear hisses when I bend down to write. I can hardly read a book, for I miss that small soft voice which the idea of articulated words raises (almost imperceptibly to you) in a silent reader. I seem too deaf to see what I read. But with a touch or two of returning Zephyr my head will melt. What Lyes you Poets tell about the May! It is the most ungenial part of the Year, cold crocuses, cold primroses, you take your blossoms in Ice, a painted Sun –

> Unmeaning joy around appears,
> And Nature smiles as if she sneers.

It is ill with me when I begin to look which way the wind sits. Ten years ago I literally did not know the point from the broad end of the Vane, which it was the [? that] indicated the Quarter. I hope these ill winds have blowd *over* you, as they do thro' me. Kindest rememb^ces to you and yours.

C. L.

55. TO JOHN BATES DIBDIN

Friday, some day in June, 1826. [P.M. 30 June 1826]
Dear D.,[1]

My first impulse upon opening your letter was pleasure at seeing your old neat hand, nine parts gentlemanly, with a modest dash of the clerical: my second a Thought, natural enough this hot weather, Am I to answer all this? why 'tis as long as those to the Ephesians and Galatians put together – I have counted the words for curiosity. But then Paul has nothing like the fun which is ebullient over yours. I don't remember a good thing (good like yours) from the 1st Romans to the last of the Hebrews. I remember but one Pun in all the Evangely, and that was made by his and our master: Thou art Peter (that is Doctor Rock) and upon this rock will I build &c.; which sanctifies Punning with me against all gainsayers. I never knew an enemy to puns, who was not an ill-natured man. Your fair critic in the coach reminds me of a Scotchman who assured me that he did not see much in Shakspeare. I replied, I dare say *not*. He felt the equivoke, lookd awkward, and reddish, but soon returnd to the attack, by saying that he thought Burns was as good as Shakspeare: I said that I had no doubt he was – to a *Scotchman*. We exchangd no more words that day. – Your account of the fierce faces in the Hanging, with the presumed interlocution of the Eagle and the Tyger, amused us greatly. You cannot be so very bad, while you can pick mirth off from rotten walls. But let me hear you have escaped out of your oven. May the Form of the Fourth Person who clapt invisible wet blankets about the shoulders of Shadrach Meshach and Abednego, be with you in the fiery Trial. But get out of the frying pan. Your business, I take it, is bathing, not baking.

Let me hear that you have clamber'd up to Lover's Seat; it is as fine in that neighbourhood as Juan Fernandez, as lonely too, when the Fishing boats are not out; I have sat for hours, staring upon a shipless sea. The salt sea is never so grand as when it is left to itself. One cock-boat spoils it. A sea-mew or two improves it. And go to the little church,[2] which is a very protestant Loretto, and seems dropt by some angel for the use of a hermit, who was at once parishioner and a whole parish. It is not too big. Go in the night, bring it away in your portmanteau, and I will plant it in my garden. It must have been erected in the very infancy of British Christianity, for the two or three first converts; yet hath it all the appertenances of a church of the first magnitude, its pulpit, its pews, its baptismal font; a cathedral in a nutshell. Seven people would crowd it like a Caledonian Chapel. The minister that divides the word there, must give lumping pennyworths. It is built to the text of two or three assembled in my name. It reminds me of the grain of mustard seed. If the glebe land is proportionate, it may yield two potatoes. Tythes out of it could be no more split than a hair. Its First fruits must be its Last, for 'twould never produce a couple. It is truly the strait and narrow way, and few there be (of London visitants) that find it. The still small voice is surely to be found there, if any where. A sounding board is merely there for ceremony. It is secure from earthquakes, not more from sanctity than size, for 'twould feel a mountain thrown upon it no more than a taper-worm would. Go and see, but not without your spectacles. By the way, there's a capital farm house two thirds of the way to the Lover's Seat, with incomparable plum cake, ginger beer, etc.

Mary bids me warn you not to read the Anatomy of Melancholy in your present *low way*. You'll fancy yourself a pipkin, or a headless bear, as Burton speaks of. You'll be lost in a maze of remedies for a labyrinth of diseasements, a plethora of cures. Read Fletcher; above all the Spanish Curate, the Thief or Little Nightwalker, the Wit Without Money, and the Lover's Pilgrimage. Laugh and come home fat. Neither do we think Sir T. Browne quite the thing for you just at present. Fletcher is as light as Soda water. Browne and Burton are too strong potions for an Invalid. And don't thumb or dirt the books. Take care of the bindings. Lay a leaf of silver paper under 'em, as you read them. And don't smoke tobacco over 'em, the leaves will fall in and burn or dirty their name-sakes. If you find any dusty atoms of the Indian Weed crumbled up in the Beaum^t and Fletcher, they are *mine*. But then, you know, so is the Folio also. A pipe and a comedy of Fletcher's the last thing of a night is the best recipe for light dreams and to scatter away Nightmares. Pro-batum est.[3] But do as you like about the former. Only cut the Baker's. You will come home else all crust; Rankings must chip you before you can appear in his counting house. And my dear Peter Fin Junr.,[4] do contrive to see the sea at least once before you return. You'll be ask'd about it in the Old Jewry. It will appear singular not to have seen it. And rub up your Muse, the family Muse, and send us a rhyme or so. Don't waste your wit upon that damn'd Dry Salter. I never knew but one Dry Salter, who could relish those mellow effusions, and he broke. You knew Tommy Hill,[5] the wettest of dry salters. Dry Salters, what a word for this thirsty weather! I must drink after it. Here's to thee, my dear Dibdin, and to our having you again snug and well at Colebrooke. But our nearest hopes are to hear again from you shortly. An epistle only a quarter as agreeable as your last, would be a treat.

Yours most truly
C. Lamb.

Timothy B. Dibdin, Esq., No. 9, Blucher Row, Priory, Hastings.

56. TO PETER GEORGE PATMORE

Mrs Leishman's, Chace, Enfield,
[No date: June 1827]

Dear Patmore,[1]

Excuse my anxiety – but how is Dash?[2] (I should have asked if Mrs Patmore kept her rules, and was improving – but Dash came uppermost. The order of our thoughts should be the order of our writing.) Goes he muzzled, or *aperto ore?*[3] Are his intellects sound, or does he wander a little in *his* conversation? You cannot be too careful to watch the first symptoms of incoherence. The first illogical snarl he makes, to St. Luke's with him! All the dogs here are going mad, if you believe the overseers; but I protest they seem to me very rational and collected. But nothing is so deceitful as mad people to those who are not used to them. Try him with hot water. If he won't lick it up, it is a sign he does not like it. Does his tail wag horizontally or perpendicularly? That has decided the fate of many dogs in Enfield. Is his general deportment cheerful? I mean when he is pleased – for otherwise there is no judging. You can't be too careful. Has he bit any of the children yet? If he has, have them shot, and keep *him* for curiosity, to see if it was the hydrophobia. They say all our army in India had it at one time – but that was in *Hyder*-Ally's time. Do you get paunch for him? Take care the sheep was sane. You might pull out his teeth (if he would let you), and then you need not mind if he were as mad as a Bedlamite. It would be rather fun to see his odd ways. It might amuse Mrs Patmore and the children. They'd have more sense than he! He'd be like a Fool kept in the family, to keep the household in good humour with their own understanding. You might teach him the mad dance set to the mad howl. *Madge Owl-et* would be nothing to him. 'My, how he capers!' [*In the margin is written:*] One of the children speaks this.

[*Three lines here are erased.*] What I scratch out is a German quotation from Lessing on the bite of rabid animals; but, I remember, you don't read German. But Mrs Patmore may, so I wish I had let it stand. The meaning in English is – 'Avoid to approach an animal suspected of madness, as you would avoid fire or a precipice:' – which I think is a sensible observation. The Germans are certainly profounder than we.

If the slightest suspicion arises in your breast, that all is not right with him (Dash), muzzle him, and lead him in a string (common pack-thread will do; he don't care for twist) to Hood's, his quondam master, and he'll take him in at any time. You may mention your suspicion or not, as you like, or as you think it may wound or not Mr H.'s feelings. Hood, I know, will wink at a few follies in Dash, in consideration of his former sense. Besides, Hood is deaf, and if you hinted anything, ten to one he would not hear you. Besides, you will have discharged your conscience, and laid the child at the right door, as they say.

We are dawdling our time away very idly and pleasantly, at a Mrs Leishman's, Chace, Enfield, where, if you come a-hunting, we can give you cold meat and a tankard. Her husband is a tailor; but that, you know, does not make her one. I knew a jailor (which rhymes), but his wife was a fine lady.

Let us hear from you respecting Mrs Patmore's regimen. I send my love in a — to Dash.

C. LAMB.

[*On the outside of the letter was written:*]

Seriously, I wish you would call upon Hood when you are that way. He's a capital fellow. I sent him a couple of poems – one ordered by his wife, and written to order; and 'tis a week since, and I've not heard from him. I fear something is the matter.

Omitted within
Our kindest remembrance to Mrs P.

57. TO MRS BASIL MONTAGU

[No date: Summer 1827]

Dear Madam,[1]

I return your List with my name. I should be sorry that any respect should be going on towards [Clarkson,][2] and I be left out of the conspiracy. Otherwise I frankly own that to pillarize a man's good feelings in his lifetime is not to my taste. Monuments, to goodness, even after death, are equivocal. I turn away from Howard's,[3] I scarce know why. Goodness blows no trumpet, nor desires to have it blown. We should be modest for a modest man – as he is for himself. The vanities of Life – Art, Poetry, Skill military, are subjects for trophies; not the silent thoughts arising in a good man's mind in lonely places. Was I C[larkson,] I should never be able to walk or ride near [Wade Mill][4] again. Instead of bread, we are giving him a stone. Instead of the locality recalling the noblest moment of his existence, it is a place at which his friends (that is, himself) blow to the world, 'What a good man is he!' I sat down upon a hillock at Forty Hill yesternight – a fine contemplative evening, – with a thousand good speculations about mankind. How I yearned with cheap benevolence! I shall go and inquire of the stone-cutter, that cuts the tombstones here, what a stone with a short inscription will cost; just to say – 'Here C. Lamb loved his brethren of mankind.' Everybody will come there to love. As I can't well put my own name, I shall put about a subscription:

	s.	d.	
Mrs —	5	0	
Procter	2	6	
G. Dyer	1	0	
Mr Godwin ..	0	0	
Mrs Godwin ..	0	0	
Mr Irving.. ..			a watch–chain
Mr —..			the proceeds of —
			first edition.*

	8	6

I scribble in haste from here, where we shall be some time. Pray request Mr M[ontagu] to advance the guinea for me, which shall faithfully be forthcoming; and pardon me that I don't see the proposal in quite the light that he may. The kindness of his motives, and his power of appreciating the noble passage, I thoroughly agree in.

With most kind regards to him, I conclude,

> Dear Madam,
> Yours truly,
> C. LAMB.

From Mrs Leishman's, Chase, Enfield.

58. TO BARRON FIELD

Oct. 4th, 1827.

I am not in humour to return a fit reply to your pleasant letter. We are fairly housed at Enfield, and an angel shall not persuade me to wicked London again. We have now six sabbath days in a week for – *none!* The change has worked on my sister's mind, to make her ill; and I must wait a tedious time before we can hope to enjoy this place in unison. Enjoy it, when she recovers, I know we shall. I see no shadow, but in her illness, for repenting the step! For Mathews – I know my own utter unfitness for such a task.[1] I am no hand at describing costumes, a great requisite in an account of mannered pictures. I have not the slightest acquaintance with pictorial language even. An imitator of me, or rather pretender to be *me*, in his Rejected Articles, has made me minutely describe the dresses of the poissardes at Calais![2] – I could as

* A capital book, by the bye, but not over saleable. – C. L.

soon resolve Euclid. I have no eye for forms and fashions. I substitute
analysis, and get rid of the phenomenon by slurring in for it its impression. I am sure you must have observed this defect, or peculiarity, in my
writings; else the delight would be incalculable in doing such a thing for
Mathews, whom I greatly like – and Mrs Mathews, whom I almost
greatlier like. What a feast 'twould be to be sitting at the pictures
painting 'em into words; but I could almost as soon make words into
pictures. I speak this deliberately, and not out of modesty. I pretty well
know what I can't do.

My sister's verses are homely, but just what they should be; I send
them, not for the poetry, but the good sense and good-will of them. I
was beginning to transcribe; but Emma[3] is sadly jealous of its getting
into more hands, and I won't spoil it in her eyes by divulging it. Come
to Enfield, and *read it.* As my poor cousin, the bookbinder, now with
God, told me, most sentimentally, that having purchased a picture of
fish at a dead man's sale, his heart ached to see how the widow grieved
to part with it, being her dear husband's favourite; and he almost apolo-
gised for his generosity by saying he could not help telling the widow
she was 'welcome to come and look at it' – e.g. at *his house* – 'as often as
she pleased.' There was the germ of generosity in an uneducated mind.
He had just *reading* enough from the backs of books for the '*nec sinit esse
feros*'[4] – had he read inside, the same impulse would have led him to
give back the two-guinea thing – with a request to see it, now and then,
at *her* house. We are parroted into delicacy. – Thus you have a tale for a
Sonnet.

Adieu! with (imagine both) our loves.   C. LAMB.

59. TO BERNARD BARTON

[P.M. 11 October 1828]

A splendid edition of Bunyan's Pilgrim[1] – why, the thought is enough
to turn one's moral stomach. His cockle hat and staff transformed to a
smart cockd beaver and a jemmy cane, his amice gray to the last Regent
Street cut, and his painful Palmer's pace to the modern swagger. Stop
thy friend's sacriligious hand. Nothing can be done for B. but to reprint
the old cuts in as homely but good a style as possible. The Vanity Fair,
and the pilgrims there – the silly soothness in his setting out countenance
– the Christian idiocy (in a good sense) of his admiration of the Shepherds on the Delectable Mountains, the Lions so truly Allegorical and

remote from any similitude to Pidcock's.[2] The great head (the author's) capacious of dreams and similitudes dreaming in the dungeon. Perhaps you don't know *my* edition, what I had when a child: if you do, can you bear new designs from Martin, enameld into copper or silver plate by Heath, accompanied with verses from Mrs Heman's pen – O how unlike his own –

> Wouldst thou divert thyself from melancholy?
> Wouldst thou be pleasant, yet be far from folly?
> Wouldst thou read riddles and their explanation?
> Or else be drowned in thy contemplation?
> Dost thou love picking meat? or wouldst thou see
> A man i' th' clouds, and hear him speak to thee?
> Wouldst thou be in a dream, and yet not sleep?
> Or wouldst thou in a moment laugh and weep?
> Or wouldst thou lose thyself, and catch no harm,
> And find thyself again without a charm?
> Wouldst read *thyself*, and read thou knowst not what,
> And yet know whether thou art blest or not
> By reading the same lines? O then come hither,
> And lay my book, thy head and heart together.

JOHN BUNYAN

Shew me such poetry in any of the 15 forthcoming combinations of show and emptiness, yclept Annuals. Let me whisper in your ear that wholesome sacramental bread is not more nutritious than papistical wafer stuff, than these (to head and heart) exceed the visual frippery of Mitford's Salamander God,[3] baking himself up to the work of creation in a solar oven, not yet by the terms of the context itself existing. Blake's ravings made genteel. So there's verses for thy verses; and now let me tell you that the sight of your hand gladdend me.

I have been daily trying to write to you, but paralysed. You have spurd me on this tiny effort, and at intervals I hope to hear from and talk to you. But my spirits have been in a deprest way for a long long time, and they are things which must be to you of faith, for who can explain depression? Yes I am hooked into the Gem,[4] but only for some lines written on a dead infant of the Editor's, which being as it were his property, I could not refuse their appearing, but I hate the paper, the type, the gloss, the dandy plates, the names of contributors poked up into your eyes on 1st page, and whistled thro' all the covers of magazines, the barefaced sort of emulation, the unmodest candidateship, bro[t] into so little space – in those old Londons a signature was lost in the wood of matter – the paper coarse (till latterly, which spoil'd them) – in short I detest to appear in an Annual.

What a fertile genius (an[d] a d quiet good soul withal) is Hood. He has 50 things in hand, fares to supply the Adelphi for the season, a comedy for one of the great theatres, just ready, a whole entertainment by himself for Mathews and Yates[5] to figure in, a meditated Comic Annual for next year, to be nearly done by himself. – You'd like him very much. Wordsworth I see has a good many pieces announced in one of em, not our Gem. W. Scott has distributed himself like a bribe haunch[6] among 'em. Of all the poets, Cary has had the good sense to keep quite clear of 'em, with Clergy-gentle-manly right notions. Don't think I set up for being proud in this point, I like a bit of flattery tickling my vanity as well as any one. But these pompous masquerades without masks (naked names or faces) I hate. So there's a bit of my mind. Besides they infallibly cheat you, I mean the booksellers. If I get but a copy, I only expect it from Hood's being my friend. Coleridge has lately been here. He too is deep among the Prophets – the Year-servers – the mob of Gentleman Annuals. But they'll cheat him, I know.

And now, dear B. B., the Sun shining out merrily, and the dirty clouds we had yesterday having washd their own faces clean with their own rain, tempts me to wander up Winchmore Hill, or into some of the delightful vicinages of Enfield, which I hope to show you at some time when you can get a few days up to the great Town. Believe me it would give both of us great pleasure to show you all three (we can lodge you) our pleasant farms and villages. –

We both join in kindest loves to you and yours. –

Saturday.   CH. LAMB REDIVIVUS.

60. TO BRYAN WALLER PROCTER

[? 29 January 1829]

When Miss Ouldcroft (who is now Mrs Beddome, and Bed— dom'd to her!) was at Enfield, which she was in summertime, and owed her health to its sun and genial influences, she wisited (with young lady-like impertinence) a poor man's cottage that had a pretty baby (O the yearnling!), and gave it fine caps and sweetmeats. On a day, broke into the parlour our two maids uproarious. 'O ma'am, who do you think Miss Ouldcroft (they pronounce it Holcroft) has been working a cap for?' 'A child,' answered Mary, in true Shandean female simplicity. 'It's the man's child as was taken up for sheep-stealing.' Miss Ouldcroft was staggered, and would have cut the connection; but by main force I made her go and take her leave of her protégée (which I only spell with a g because I can't make a pretty j). I thought, if she went no more, the Abactor [1] or Abactor's wife (vide Ainsworth) [2] would suppose she had heard something; and I have delicacy for a sheep-stealer. The overseers actually overhauled a mutton-pie at the baker's (his first, last, and only hope of mutton-pie), which he never came to eat, and thence inferred his guilt. *Per occasionem cujus* [3] I framed the sonnet; observe its elaborate construction. I was four days about it.

THE GYPSY'S MALISON

Suck, baby, suck, Mother's love grows by giving,
    Drain the sweet founts that only thrive by wasting;
Black Manhood comes, when riotous guilty living
    Hands thee the cup that shall be death in tasting.
Kiss, baby, kiss, Mother's lips shine by kisses,
    Choke the warm breath that else would fall in blessings;
Black Manhood comes, when turbulent guilty blisses
    Tend thee the kiss that poisons 'mid caressings.
Hang, baby, hang, mother's love loves such forces,
    Choke the fond neck that bends still to thy clinging;
Black Manhood comes, when violent lawless courses
    Leave thee a spectacle in rude air swinging.

So sang a wither'd Sibyl energetical,
And bann'd the ungiving door with lips prophetical.

Barry, study that sonnet. It is curiously and perversely elaborate. 'Tis a choking subject, and therefore the reader is directed to the structure of it. See you! and was this a fourteener to be rejected by a trumpery annual? forsooth, 'twould shock all mothers; and may all mothers, who would so be shocked, bed dom'd! as if mothers were such sort of logicians as to infer the future hanging of *their* child from the theoretical hangibility (or capacity of being hanged, if the judge pleases) of every infant born with a neck on. Oh B. C., my whole heart is faint, and my whole head is sick (how is it?) at this damned, canting, unmasculine unbxwdy (I had almost said) age! Don't show this to your child's mother or I shall be Orpheusized, scattered into Hebrus. Damn the King, lords, commons, and *specially* (as I said on Muswell Hill on a

Sunday when I could get no beer a quarter before one) all Bishops, Priests, and Curates. Vale.

[P.M. 27 February 1829]

Dear R.,

Expectation was alert on the receit of your strange-shaped present,[1] while yet undisclosed from its fusc envelope. Some said, 'tis a viol da Gamba, others pronounced it a fiddle. I myself hoped it a Liquer case pregnant with Eau di Vie and such odd Nectar. When midwifed into daylight, the gossips were at loss to pronounce upon its species. Most took it for a marrow spoon, an apple scoop, a banker's guinea shovel. At length its true scope appeared, its drift – to save the backbone of my sister stooping to scuttles. A philanthropic intent, borrowed no doubt from some of the Colliers. You save people's backs one way, and break 'em again by loads of obligation. The spectacles are delicate and Vulcanian. No lighter texture than their steel did the cuckoldy blacksmith frame to catch Mrs Vulcan and the Captain in. For ungalled forehead, as for back unbursten, you have Mary's thanks. Marry, for my own peculium of obligation, 'twas supererogatory. A second part of Pamela was enough in conscience. Two Pamelas in a house is too much without two Mr B.'s[2] to reward 'em.

Mary, who is handselling her new aerial perspectives upon a pair of old worsted stockings trod out in Cheshunt lanes, sends love. I, great good liking. Bid us a personal farewell before you see the Vactican.

CHAS. LAMB, Enfield.

[P.M. 10 April 1829]

Dear Robinson,

We are afraid you will slip from us from England without again seeing us. It would be charity to come and see me. I have these three days been laid up with strong rheumatic pains, in loins, back, shoulders. I shriek sometimes from the violence of them. I get scarce any sleep, and the consequence is, I am restless, and want to change sides as I lie, and I cannot turn without resting on my hands, and so turning all my body all at once like a log with a lever. While this rainy weather lasts, I have no hope of alleviation. I have tried flannels and embrocation in vain. Just at the hip joint the pangs sometimes are so excruciating, that I cry out. It is as violent as the cramp, and far more continuous. I am ashamed to whine about these complaints to you, who can ill enter into them. But indeed they are sharp. You go about, in rain or fine at all hours without discommodity. I envy you your immunity at a time of life not much removed from my own. But you owe your exemption to temperance, which it is too late for me to pursue. I in my life time have had my good things. Hence my frame is brittle – yours strong as brass. I never knew any ailment you had. You can go out at night in all weathers, sit up all hours. Well, I don't want to moralise. I only wish to say that if you are inclined to a game of Doubly Dumby,[1] I would try and bolster up myself in a chair for a rubber or so. My days are tedious, but less so and less painful than my nights. May you never know the pain and difficulty I have in writing so much. Mary, who is most kind, joins in the wish.

C. LAMB.

63. TO HENRY CRABB ROBINSON

[P.M. 17 April 1829]

I do not confess to mischief. It was the subtlest diabolical piece of malice, heart of man has contrived. I have no more rheumatism than that poker. Never was freer from all pains and aches. Every joint sound, to the tip of the ear from the extremity of the lesser toe. The report of thy torments[1] was blown circuitously here from Bury. I could not resist the jeer. I conceived you writhing, when you should just receive my congratulations. How mad you'd be. Well, it is not in my method to inflict pangs. I leave that to heaven. But in the existing pangs of a friend, I have a share. His disquietude crowns my exemption. I imagine you howling, and pace across

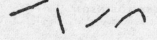

the room, shooting out my free arms legs &c. this way and that way, with an assurance of not kindling a spark of pain from them. I deny that Nature meant us to sympathise with agonies. Those face-contortions, retortions, distortions, have the merriness of antics. Nature meant them for farce – not so pleasant to the actor indeed, but Grimaldi[2] cries when we laugh, and 'tis but one that suffers to make thousands rejoyce.

You say that Shampooing is ineffectual. But *per se* it is good, to show the introv[ol]utions, extravolutions, of which the animal frame is capable. To show what the creature is receptible of, short of dissolution.

You are worst of nights, a'nt you?

Twill be as good as a Sermon to you to lie abed all this night, and meditate the subject of the day. 'Tis Good Friday. How appropriate!

Think when but your little finger pains you, what endured to white-wash you and the rest of us.

Nobody will be the more justified for your endurance. You won't save the soul of a mouse. 'Tis a pure selfish pleasure.

You never was rack'd, was you? I should like an authentic map of those feelings.

You seem to have the flying gout.

You can scarcely scrue a smile out of your face – can you? I sit at immunity, and sneer *ad libitum*.[3]

'Tis now the time for you to make good resolutions. I may go on breaking 'em, for any thing the worse I find myself.

Your Doctor seems to keep you on the long cure. Precipitate healings are never good.

Don't come while you are so bad. I shan't be able to attend to your throes and the dumbee at once.

I should like to know how slowly the pain goes off. But don't write, unless the motion will be likely to make your sensibility more exquisite.

Your affectionate and truly healthy friend   C. LAMB.

Mary thought a Letter from me might amuse you in your torment –

64. TO BERNARD BARTON

Enfield Chase Side
Saturday 25 July A.D. 1829. – 11 A.M.

There – a fuller plumper juiceier date never dropt from Idumean palm.[1] Am I in the dateive case now? if not, a fig for dates, which is more than a date is worth. I never stood much affected to these limitary specialities. Least of all since the date of my superannuation.

What have I with Time to do? ⎫ Dear B. B. – Your hand writing has
Slaves of desks, twas meant for you. ⎰ conveyed much pleasure to me

in the report of Lucy's restoration. Would I could send you as good news of my poor Lucy.[2] But some wearisome weeks I must remain lonely yet. I have had the loneliest time near 10 weeks, broken by a short apparition of Emma [3] for her holydays, whose departure only deepend the returning solitude, and by 10 days I have past in Town. But Town, with all my native hankering after it, is not what it was. The streets, the shops are left, but all old friends are gone. And in London I was frightfully convinced of this as I past houses and places – empty caskets now. I have ceased to care almost about any body. The bodies I cared for are in graves, or dispersed. My old Clubs, that lived so long and flourish'd so steadily, are crumbled away. When I took leave of our adopted young friend at Charing Cross, 'twas heavy unfeeling rain, and I had no where to go. Home have I none – and not a sympathising house to turn to in the great city. Never did the waters of the heaven pour down on a forlorner head. Yet I tried 10 days at a sort of a friend's house, but it was large and straggling – one of the individuals of my old long knot of friends, card players, pleasant companions – that have tumbled to pieces into dust and other things – and I got home on Thursday, convinced that I was better to get home to my hole at Enfield, and hide like a sick cat in my corner.

Less than a month I hope will bring home Mary. She is at Fulham, looking better in her health than ever, but sadly rambling, and scarce showing any pleasure in seeing me, or curiosity when I should come again. But the old feelings will come back again, and we shall drown old sorrows over a game at Picquet again. But 'tis a tedious cut out of a life of sixty four, to lose twelve or thirteen weeks every year or two. And to make me more alone, our illtemperd maid is gone, who with all her airs, was yet a home piece of furniture, a record of better days; the young thing that has succeeded her is good and attentive, but she is nothing – and I have no one here to talk over old matters with. Scolding and quarreling have something of familiarity and a community of inter-est – they imply acquaintance – they are of resentment, which is of the family of dearness. I can neither scold nor quarrel at this insignificant implement of household services; she is less than a cat, and just better than a deal Dresser. What I can do, and do overdo, is to walk, but deadly long are the days – these summer all-day days, with but a half hour's candlelight and no firelight. I do not write, tell your kind in-quisitive Eliza,[4] and can hardly read.

In the ensuing Blackwood will be an old rejected farce [5] of mine, which may be new to you, if you see that same dull Medley. What things are all the Magazines now! I contrive studiously not to see them. The popular New Monthly is perfect trash. Poor Hessey, I suppose you see, has failed. Hunt and Clarke too. Your 'Vulgar truths' will be a good name – and I think your prose must please – me at least – but 'tis useless to write poetry with no purchasers. 'Tis cold work Authorship without something to puff one into fashion. Could you not write something on Quakerism – for Quakers to read – but nominally addrest to Non Quakers? explaining your dogmas – waiting on the Spirit – by the analogy of human calmness and patient waiting on the judgment? I scarcely know what I mean, but to make Non Quakers reconciled to your doctrines, by shewing something like them in mere human operations – but I hardly understand myself, so let it pass for nothing.

I pity you for over-work, but I assure you no-work is worse. The mind preys on itself, the most unwholesome food. I brag'd formerly that I could not have too much time. I have a surfeit. With few years to come, the days are wearisome. But weariness is not eternal. Something will shine out to take the load off, that flags me, which is at present intolerable. I have killed an hour or two in this poor scrawl. I am a sanguinary murderer of time, and would kill him inchmeal just now. But the snake is vital. Well, I shall write merrier anon. – 'Tis the present copy of my countenance I send – and to complain is a little to alleviate. – May you enjoy yourself as far as the wicked wood will let you – and think that you are not quite alone, as I am. Health to Lucia and to Anna and kind rememb^ces.

Yours forlorn.   C. L.

65. TO JAMES GILLMAN

30 Nov., 1829.

Dear G.,

The excursionists reached home, and the good town of Enfield a little after four, without slip or dislocation. Little has transpired concerning the events of the back-journey, save that on passing the house of 'Squire Mellish,[1] situate a stone-bow's cast from the hamlet, Father Westwood, with good-natured wonderment, exclaimed, 'I cannot think what is gone of Mr Mellish's rooks. I fancy they have taken flight somewhere; but I have missed them two or three years past.' All this while, according to his fellow-traveller's report, the rookery was darkening the air above with undiminished population, and deafening all ears but his with their cawings. But nature has been gently withdrawing such phenomena from the notice of Thomas Westwood's[2] senses, from the time he began to miss the rooks. T. Westwood has passed a retired life in this hamlet of thirty or forty years, living upon the minimum which is consistent with gentility, yet a star among the minor gentry, receiving the bows of the tradespeople and courtesies of the alms' women daily. Children venerate him not less for his external show of gentry, than they wonder at him for a gentle rising endorsation of the person, not amounting to a hump, or if a hump, innocuous as the hump of the buffalo, and coronative of as mild qualities. 'Tis a throne on which patience seems to sit – the proud perch of a self-respecting humility, stooping with condescension. Thereupon the cares of life have sate, and rid him easily. For he has thrid the *augustiæ domûs*[3] with dexterity. Life opened upon him with comparative brilliancy. He set out as a rider or traveller for a wholesale house, in which capacity he tells of many hair-breadth escapes that befell him; one especially, how he rode a mad horse into the town of Devizes; how horse and rider arrived in a foam, and to the utter consternation of the expostulating hostlers, innkeepers, &c. It seems it was sultry weather, piping hot; the steed tormented into frenzy with gad-flies, long past being roadworthy; but safety and the interest of the house he rode for were incompatible things; a fall in serge cloth was expected; and a mad entrance they made of it. Whether the exploit was purely voluntary, or partially; or whether a certain personal defiguration in the man part of this extraordinary centaur (non-assistive to partition of natures) might not enforce the conjunction, I stand not to inquire. I look not with 'skew eyes into the deeds of heroes. The hosier that was burnt with his shop, in Field-lane, on Tuesday night, shall have past to heaven for me like a Marian Martyr, provided always, that he consecrated the fortuitous incremation with a short ejaculation in the exit, as much as if he had taken his state degrees of martyrdom *in formâ*[4] in the market vicinage. There is adoptive as well as acquisitive sacrifice. Be the animus what it might, the fact is indisputable, that this composition was seen flying all abroad, and mine host of Daintry may yet remember its passing through his town, if his scores are not more faithful than his memory. After this exploit (enough for one man), Thomas Westwood seems to have subsided into a less hazardous occupation; and in the twenty-fifth year of his age we find him a haberdasher in Bow Lane: yet still retentive of his early riding (though leaving it to rawer stomachs), and Christmasly at night sithence to this last, and shall to his latest Christmas, hath he, doth he, and shall he, tell after supper the story of the insane steed and the desperate rider. Save for Bedlam or Luke's no eye could have guessed that melting day what house he rid for. But he reposes on his bridles, and after the ups and downs (metaphoric only) of a life behind the counter – hard riding sometimes, I fear, for poor T. W. – with the scrapings together of the shop, and *one anecdote*, he hath finally settled at Enfield; by hard economising, gardening, building for himself, hath reared a mansion, married a daughter, qualified a son for a counting-house, gotten the respect of high and low, served for self or substitute the greater parish offices: hath a special voice at vestries; and, domiciliating us, hath reflected a portion of his house-keeping respectability upon your humble servants. We are greater, being his lodgers, than when we were substantial renters. His name is a passport to take off the sneers of the native Enfielders against obnoxious foreigners. We are endenizened. Thus much of T. Westwood have I thought fit to acquaint you, that you may see the exemplary reliance upon Providence with which I entrusted so dear a charge as my own sister to the guidance of a man that rode the mad horse into Devizes. To come from his heroic character, all the amiable qualities of domestic life concentre in this tamed Bellerophon.[5] He is excellent over a glass of grog; just as pleasant without it; laughs when he hears a joke, and when (which is much oftener) he hears it not; sings glorious old sea songs on festival nights; and but upon a slight acquaintance of two years, Coleridge, is as dear a deaf old man to us, as old Norris, rest his soul! was after fifty. To him and his scanty literature (what there is of it, *sound*) have we flown from the metropolis and its cursed annualists, reviewers, authors, and the whole muddy ink press of that stagnant pool.

Now, Gillman again, you do not know the treasure of the Fullers. I calculate on having massy reading till Christmas. All I want here, is books of the true sort, not those things in boards that moderns mistake for books – what they club for at book clubs.

I did not mean to cheat you with a blank side; but my eye smarts, for which I am taking medicine, and abstain, this day at least, from any aliments but milk-porridge, the innocent taste of which I am anxious to renew after a half-century's disacquaintance. If a blot fall here like a tear, it is not pathos, but an angry eye.

Farewell, while my *specilla*[6] are sound.

Yours and yours,

                                                      C. LAMB.

66. TO MARY SHELLEY

[No date: *c.* 18 January 1830]

Dear Mrs Shelly,[1]

If you ever run away, which is problematical, don't run to a country village, which has been a market town, but is such no longer. Enfield, where we are, is seated most indifferently upon the borders of Middlesex, Essex, and Hertfordshire, partaking of the quiet dulness of the first, & the total want of interest pervading the two latter Counties. You stray into the Church yard, hoping to find a Cathedral. You think, I will go and look at the Print shops, and there is only one, where they sell Valentines. The chief Bookseller deals in prose versions of Melodrama, with plates of Ghosts and Murders, and other Subterranean passages. The tarts in the only Pastry-cook-looking shop are baked stale. The Macaroons are perennial, kept torpid in glass cases, excepting when Mrs **** gives a card party. There is no jewellers, but there's a place where brass knobs are sold. You cast your dreary eyes about, up Baker Street, and it gets worse. There was something like a tape and thread shop at that end, but here – is two apples stuck between a farthings worth of ginger bread, & the children too poor to break stock.

The week days would be intolerable, but for the superior invention which they show here in making Sundays worse. Clowns stand about what was the Market place, and spit minute-ly to relieve ennui. Clowns, to whom Enfield trades-people are gentle people. Inland Clowns, Clods, and things below cows. They assemble to infect the air with dulness from Waltham marshes. They clear off o' the Monday mornings, like other fogs. It is ice, but nobody slides, nobody tumbles down, nobody dies as I can see, or nobody cares if they do, the Doctors seem to have no Patients, there is no Accidents nor Offences, a good thief would be something in this well-governed Hamlet. We have for indoors amusement a Library without books, and the middle of the week hopes of a Sunday newspaper to link us by filmy associations to a world we are dead to. Regent Street was, and it is by difficult induction we infer that Charing Cross still is. There may be Plays. But nobody here seems to have heard of such contingencies.

You go out with a dog, and the dog comes home with you, and the difference is, he does not mind dirty stockings.

67. TO WILLIAM WORDSWORTH

[P.M. 22 January 1830]

And is it a year since we parted from you at the steps of Edmonton Stage? There are not now the years that there used to be. The tale of the dwindled age of men, reported of successional mankind, is true of the same man only. We do not live a year in a year now. 'Tis a punctum stans.[1] The seasons pass us with indifference. Spring cheers not, nor winter heightens our gloom, Autumn hath foregone its moralities, they are hey-pass re-pass [as] in a show-box. Yet as far as last year occurs back, for they scarce shew a reflex now, they make no memory as heretofore – 'twas sufficiently gloomy. Let the sullen nothing pass.

Suffice it that after sad spirits prolonged thro' many of its months, as it called them, we have cast our skins, have taken a farewell of the pompous troublesome trifle calld housekeeping, and are settled down into poor boarders and lodgers at next door with an old couple, the Baucis and Baucida of dull Enfield. Here we have nothing to do with our victuals but to eat them, with the garden but to see it grow, with the tax gatherer but to hear him knock, with the maid but to hear her scolded. Scot and lot, butcher, baker, are things unknown to us save as spectators of the pageant. We are fed we know not how, quietists, confiding ravens. We have the otium pro dignitate,[2] a respectable insignificance. Yet in the self condemned obliviousness, in the stagnation, some molesting yearnings of life, not quite kill'd, rise, prompting me that there was a London, and that I was of that old Jerusalem.

In dreams I am in Fleetmarket, but I wake and cry to sleep again. I die hard, a stubborn Eloisa in this detestable Paraclete.[3] What have I gained by health? intolerable dulness. What by early hours and moderate meals? – a total blank. O never let the lying poets be believed, who 'tice men from the chearful haunts of streets – or think they mean it not of a country village. In the ruins of Palmyra I could gird myself up to solitude, or use to the snorings of the Seven Sleepers, but to have a little teazing image of a town about one, country folks that do not look like country folks, shops two yards square, half a dozen apples and two penn'orth of overlookd gingerbread for the lofty fruiterers of Oxford Street – and, for the immortal book and print stalls, a circulating library that stands still, where the shew-picture is a last year's Valentine, and whither the fame of the last ten Scotch novels has not yet travel'd (marry, they just begin to be conscious of the Red Gauntlet),[4] to have a new plasterd flat church, and to be wishing that it was but a Cathedral.

The very blackguards here are degenerate. The topping gentry, stock brokers. The passengers too many to ensure your quiet, or let you go about whistling, or gaping – too few to be the fine indifferent pageants of Fleet Street. Confining, room-keeping, thickest winter is yet more bearable here than the gaudy months. Among one's books at one's fire by candle one is soothed into an oblivion that one is not in the country, but with the light the green fields return, till I gaze, and in a calenture[5] can plunge myself into Saint Giles's. O let no native Londoner imagine that health, and rest, and innocent occupation, interchange of converse sweet and recreative study, can make the country any thing better than altogether odious and detestable. A garden was the primitive prison till man with promethean felicity and boldness luckily sinn'd himself out of it. Thence followd Babylon, Nineveh, Venice, London, haberdashers, goldsmiths, taverns, playhouses, satires, epigrams, puns – these all came in on the town part, and the thither side of innocence. Man found out inventions.

From my den I return you condolence for your decaying sight, not for any thing there is to see in the country, but for the miss of the pleasure of reading a London newspaper. The poets are as well to listen to, any thing high may, nay must, be read out – you read it to yourself with an imaginary auditor – but the light paragraphs must be glid over by the proper eye, mouthing mumbles their gossamery substance. 'Tis these trifles I should mourn in fading sight. A newspaper is the single gleam of comfort I receive here, it comes from rich Cathay with tidings of mankind. Yet I could not attend to it read out by the most beloved voice. But your eyes do not get worse, I gather. O for the collyrium of Tobias[6] inclosed in a whiting's liver to send you with no apocryphal good wishes! The last long time I heard from you, you had knock'd your head against something. Do not do so. For your head (I do not flatter) is not a nob, or the top of a brass nail, or the end of a nine pin – unless a Vulcanian hammer could fairly batter a Recluse out of it, then would I bid the smirch'd god knock and knock lustily, the two-handed skinker.

What a nice long letter Dorothy has written! Mary must squeeze out a line propriâ manu,[7] but indeed her fingers have been incorrigibly nervous to letter writing for a long interval. 'Twill please you all to hear that, tho' I fret like a lion in a net, her present health and spirits are better than they have been for some time past: she is absolutely three years and half younger, as I tell her, since we have adopted this boarding plan.

Our providers are an honest pair, dame Westwood and her husband

– he, when the light of prosperity shined on them, a moderately thriving haberdasher within Bow Bells, retired since with something under a competence, writes himself parcel gentleman, hath borne parish offices, sings fine old sea songs at threescore and ten, sighs only now and then when he thinks that he has a son on his hands about 15, whom he finds a difficulty in getting out into the world, and then checks a sigh with muttering, as I once heard him prettily, not meaning to be heard, 'I have married my daughter however,' – takes the weather as it comes, outsides it to town in severest season, and a' winter nights tells old stories not tending to literature, how comfortable to author-rid folks! and has *one anecdote*, upon which and about forty pounds a year he seems to have retired in green old age. It was how he was a *rider* in his youth, travelling for shops, and once (not to baulk his employer's bargain) on a sweltering day in August, rode foaming into Dunstable upon a *mad horse* to the dismay and expostulary wonderment of inn-keepers, hostlers &c. who declared they would not have bestrid the beast to win the Darby. Understand the creature gall'd to death and desperation by gad flies, cormorants winged, worse than beset Inachus' daughter.

This he tells, this he brindles and burnishes on a' winter's eves, 'tis his star of set glory, his rejuvenescence to descant upon. Far from me be it (dii avertant) [8] to look a gift story in the mouth, or cruelly to surmise (as those who doubt the plunge of Curtius) [9] that the inseparate conjuncture of man and beast, the centaur-phenomenon that staggered all Dunstable, might have been the effect of unromantic necessity, that the horse-part carried the reasoning, willy nilly, that needs must when such a devil drove, that certain spiral configurations in the frame of Thomas Westwood unfriendly to alighting, made the alliance more forcible than voluntary. Let him enjoy his fame for me, nor let me hint a whisper that shall dismount Bellerophon. Put case he was an involuntary martyr, yet if in the fiery conflict he buckled the soul of a constant haberdasher to him, and adopted his flames, let Accident and He share the glory! You would all like Thomas Westwood.

How weak is painting to describe a man! Say that he stands four feet and a nail high by his own yard measure, which like the Sceptre of

Agamemnon[10] shall never sprout again, still you have no adequate idea, nor when I tell you that his dear hump, which I have favord in the picture, seems to me of the buffalo — indicative and repository of mild qualities, a budget of kindnesses, still you have not the man. Knew you old Norris of the Temple, 60 years ours and our father's friend, he was not more natural to us than this old W. the acquaintance of scarce more weeks. Under his roof now ought I to take my rest, but that back-looking ambition tells me I might yet be a Londoner.

Well, if we ever do move, we have encumbrances the less to impede us: all our furniture has faded under the auctioneer's hammer, going for nothing like the tarnishd frippery of the prodigal, and we have only a spoon or two left to bless us. Clothed we came into Enfield, and naked we must go out of it. I would live in London shirtless, bookless.

Henry Crabb is at Rome, advices to that effect have reach'd Bury. But by solemn legacy he bequeath'd at parting (whether he should live or die) a Turkey of Suffolk to be sent every succeeding Xmas to us and divers other friends. What a genuine old Bachelor's action! I fear he will find the air of Italy too classic. His station is in the Hartz forest, his soul is *Begoethed*.[11] Miss Kelly we never see; Talfourd not this half-year; the latter flourishes, but the exact number of his children, God forgive me, I have utterly forgotten, we single people are often out in our count there. Shall I say two? One darling I know they have lost within a twelvemonth, but scarce known to me by sight, and that was a second child lost.

We see scarce anybody. We have just now Emma with us for her holydays; you remember her playing at brag with Mr Quillinan at poor Monkhouse's! She is grown an agreeable young woman; she sees what I write, so you may understand me with limitations. She was our inmate for a twelvemonth, grew natural to us, and then they told us it was best for her to go out as a Governess, and so she went out, and we were only two of us, and our pleasant house-mate is changed to an occasional visitor. If they want my sister to go out (as they call it) there will be only one of us. Heaven keep us all from this acceding to Unity!

Can I cram loves enough to you all in this little O? Excuse particularizing. C. L.

68. TO DR J. VALE ASBURY

[? April 1830]

Dear Sir,[1]

It is an observation of a wise man that 'moderation is best in all things.' I cannot agree with him 'in liquor.' There is a smoothness and oiliness in wine that makes it go down by a natural channel, which I am positive was made for that descending. Else, why does not wine choke us? could Nature have made that sloping lane, not to facilitate the down-going? She does nothing in vain. You know that better than I. You know how often she has helped you at a dead lift, and how much better entitled she is to a fee than yourself sometimes, when you carry off the credit. Still there is something due to manners and customs, and I should apologise to you and Mrs. Asbury for being absolutely carried home upon a man's shoulders thro' Silver Street, up Parson's Lane, by the Chapels (which might have taught me better), and then to be deposited like a dead log at Gaffar Westwood's, who it seems does not 'insure' against intoxication. Not that the mode of conveyance is objectionable. On the contrary, it is more easy than a one-horse chaise. Ariel in the 'Tempest' says

> On a Bat's back do I fly,
> After sunset merrily.

Now I take it that Ariel must sometimes have stayed out late of nights. Indeed, he pretends that 'where the bee sucks, there lurks he,' as much as to say that his suction is as innocent as that little innocent (but damnably stinging when he is provok'd) winged creature. But I take it, that Ariel was fond of metheglin,[2] of which the Bees are notorious Brewers. But then you will say: What a shocking sight to see a middle-aged gentle-man-and-a-half riding a Gentleman's back up Parson's Lane at midnight. Exactly the time for that sort of conveyance, when nobody can see him, nobody but Heaven and his own conscience; now Heaven makes fools, and don't expect much from her own creation; and as for conscience, She and I have long since come to a compromise. I have given up false modesty, and she allows me to abate a little of the true. I like to be liked, but I don't care about being respected. I don't respect myself. But, as I was saying, I thought he would have let me down just as we got to Lieutenant Barker's Coal-shed (or emporium) but by a cunning jerk I eased myself, and righted my posture. I protest, I thought myself in a palanquin;[3] and never felt myself so grandly carried. It was a slave under me. There was I, all but my reason. And what is reason? and what is the loss of it? and how often in a day do we do without it, just as well? Reason is only counting, two and two makes four. And if on my passage home, I thought it made five, what matter? Two and two will just make four, as it always did, before I took the finishing glass that did my business. My sister has begged me to write an apology to Mrs A. and you for disgracing your party; now it does seem to me, that I rather honoured your party, for every one that was not drunk (and one or two of the ladies, I am sure, were not) must have been set off greatly in the contrast to me. I was the scapegoat. The soberer they seemed. By the way is magnesia good on these occasions?

   iii pol: [? pil:] med:sum:ante noct:in rub:can:.[4] I am no licentiate, but know enough of simples to beg you to send me a draught after this model. But still you'll say (or the men and maids at your house will say) that it is not a seemly sight for an old gentleman to go home pick-a-back. Well, may be it is not. But I have never studied grace. I take it to be a mere superficial accomplishment. I regard more the internal acquisitions. The great object after supper is to get home, and whether that is obtained in a horizontal posture or perpendicular (as foolish men and apes affect for dignity) I think is little to the purpose. The end is always greater than the means. Here I am, able to compose a sensible rational apology, and what signifies how I got here? I have just sense enough to remember I was very happy last night, and to thank our kind host and hostess, and that's sense enough, I hope

CHARLES LAMB.

N.B. – What is good for a desperate head-ache? Why, Patience, and a determination not to mind being miserable all day long. And that I have made my mind up to.

So, here goes. It is better than not being alive at all, which I might have been, had your man toppled me down at Lieut. Barker's Coal-shed. My sister sends her sober compliments to Mrs A. She is not much the worse.

Yours truly,
C. LAMB.

69. TO BASIL MONTAGU

[P.M. *13 July 1830*]

Dear Montagu,[1]
  I cannot pass over the disgraceful circumstance of my leaving No. 25

Bedford Square in liquor. But *then*, are not those kind friends, who for 4 years have been dissuading me from a country life, in part participation?

I seem to me in a confused manner to remember something about your putting up (a low phrase) for Woodstock.[2] Now don't think me impertinent in saying that for my own part I wish you unsuccessful. You have had thro' life, what few can claim, a character. It has been that of perfect independence and individuality. You have been, & long may you be, Basil Montagu. Your individualism must be lost in a place where all is Party. What was Horne Tooke? What is Erskine?[3] No Single Thoughted man of self-impulse can be in his place in the House of *Commons*. Having said so much, the impertinence of which you may impute to last night's fumes, I will only add that if you persist for Woodstock, I am your man for any electioneering ballads, squibs, or dirty interference whatever, & most heartily wish you success.

Mayn't I come again some day. I never tipsify twice running in the same house.

Basil Montagu Esqr, 25 Bedford Square.   C. L.

70. TO GEORGE DYER

Dec. 20, 1830.

Dear Dyer,

I would have written before to thank you for your kind letter, written with your own hand. It glads us to see your writing. It will give you pleasure to hear that, after so much illness, we are in tolerable health and spirits once more. Miss Isola intended to call upon you after her night's lodging at Miss Buffam's, but found she was too late for the stage. If she comes to town before she goes home, she will not miss paying her respects to Mrs. Dyer and you, to whom she desires best love. Poor Enfield, that has been so peaceable hitherto, has caught the inflammatory fever,[1] the tokens are upon her! and a great fire was blazing last night in the barns and haystacks of a farmer, about half a mile from us. Where will these things end? There is no doubt of its being the work of some ill-disposed rustic; but how is he to be discovered? They go to work in the dark with strange chemical preparations unknown to our forefathers. There is not even a dark lantern to have a chance of detecting these Guy Fauxes. We are past the iron age, and are got into the fiery age, undream'd of by Ovid. You are lucky in

Clifford's Inn where, I think, you have few ricks or stacks worth the burning. Pray keep as little corn by you as you can, for fear of the worst.

It was never good times in England since the poor began to speculate upon their condition. Formerly, they jogged on with as little reflection as horses: the whistling ploughman went cheek by jowl with his brother that neighed. Now the biped carries a box of phosphorus in his leather-breeches; and in the dead of night the half-illuminated beast steals his magic potion into a cleft in a barn, and half a country is grinning with new fires. Farmer Graystock said something to the touchy rustic that he did not relish, and he writes his distaste in flames. What a power to intoxicate his crude brains, just muddlingly awake, to perceive that something is wrong in the social system! – what a hellish faculty above gunpowder!

Now the rich and poor are fairly pitted; we shall see who can hang or burn fastest. It is not always revenge that stimulates these kindlings. There is a love of exerting mischief. Think of a disrespected clod that was trod into earth, that was nothing, on a sudden by damned arts refined into an exterminating angel, devouring the fruits of the earth and their growers in a mass of fire! What a new existence! – what a temptation above Lucifer's! Would clod be any thing but a clod, if he could resist it? Why, here was a spectacle last night for a whole country! – a Bonfire visible to London, alarming her guilty towers, and shaking the Monument with an ague fit – all done by a little vial of phosphor in a Clown's fob! How he must grin, and shake his empty noddle in clouds, the Vulcanian Epicure! Can we ring the bells backward? Can we unlearn the arts that pretend to civilize, and then burn the world? There is a march of Science; but who shall beat the drums for its retreat? Who shall persuade the boor that phosphor will not ignite?

Seven goodly stacks of hay, with corn-barns proportionable, lie smoking ashes and chaff, which man and beast would sputter out and reject like those apples of Asphaltes and bitumen.[2] The food for the inhabitants of earth will quickly disappear. Hot rolls may say: 'Fuimus panes, fuit quartern-loaf, et ingens gloria Apple-pasty-orum.'[3] That the good old munching system may last thy time and mine, good un-incendiary George, is the devout prayer of thine,

To the last crust,   CH. LAMB

71. TO THOMAS ALLSOP[1]

[P.M. 2 June 1832]

At midsummer or soon after (I will let you know the previous day), I will take a day with you in the purlieus of my old haunts. No offence has been taken, any more than meant. My house is full at present, but empty of its chief pride. She is dead to me for many months. But when I see you, then I will say, Come and see me. With undiminished friendship to you both,

Your faithful but queer   C. LAMB.

How you frighted me! Never write again, 'Coleridge is dead,' at the end of a line, and tamely come in with
'to his friends' at the beginning of another. Love is quicker, and fear from love, than the transition ocular from Line to Line.

72. TO MARIA FRYER[1]

Feb. 14, 1834.

Dear Miss Fryer,

Your letter found me just returned from keeping my birthday (pretty innocent!) at Dover-street. I see them pretty often. I have since had letters of business to write, or should have replied earlier. In one word, be less uneasy about me; I bear my privations very well; I am not in the depths of desolation, as heretofore. Your admonitions are not lost upon me. Your kindness has sunk into my heart. Have faith in me! It is no new thing for me to be left to my sister. When she is not violent her rambling chat is better to me than the sense and sanity of this world. Her heart is obscured, not buried; it breaks out occasionally; and one can discern a strong mind struggling with the billows that have gone over it. I could be nowhere happier than under the same roof with her. Her memory is unnaturally strong; and from ages past, if we may so call the earliest records of our poor life, she fetches thousands of names and things that never would have dawned upon me again, and thousands from the ten years she lived before me. What took place from early girlhood to her coming of age principally lives again (every important thing and every trifle) in her brain with the vividness of real presence. For twelve hours incessantly she will pour out without intermission all her past life, forgetting nothing, pouring out name after name to the Waldens[2] as a dream; sense and nonsense; truths and errors huddled together; a medley between inspiration and possession. What things we are! I know you will bear with me, talking of these things. It seems to ease me; for I have nobody to tell these things to now. Emma, I see, has got a harp! and is learning to play. She has framed her three Walton pictures, and pretty they look. That is a book you should read;[3] such sweet religion in it – next to Woolman's![4] though the subject be baits and hooks, and worms, and fishes. She has my copy at present to do two more from.

Very, very tired, I began this epistle, having been epistolising all the morning, and very kindly would I end it, could I find adequate expressions to your kindness. We did set our minds on seeing you in spring. One of us will indubitably. But I am not skilled in almanac learning, to know when spring precisely begins and ends. Pardon my blots; I am glad you like your book. I wish it had been half as worthy of your acceptance as 'John Woolman.' But 'tis a good-natured book.

73. TO HENRY FRANCIS CARY[1]

[April 1834]

I protest I know not in what words to invest my sense of the shameful violation of hospitality, which I was guilty of on that fatal Wednesday. Let it be blotted from the calendar. Had it been committed at a layman's house, say a merchant's or manufacturer's, a cheesemonger's or greengrocer's, or, to go higher, a barrister's, a member of Parliament's, a rich banker's, I should have felt alleviation, a drop of self-pity. But to be seen deliberately to go out of the house of a clergyman drunk! a clergyman of the Church of England too! not that alone, but of an expounder of that dark Italian Hierophant, an exposition little short of *his* who dared unfold the Apocalypse: divine riddles both and (without supernal grace vouchsafed) Arks not to be fingered without present blasting to the touchers. And, then, from what house! Not a common glebe or vicarage (which yet had been shameful), but from a kingly repository of sciences, human and divine, with the primate of England for its guardian, arrayed in public majesty, from which the profane vulgar are bid fly. Could all those volumes have taught me nothing better!

With feverish eyes on the succeeding dawn I opened upon the faint light, enough to distinguish, in a strange chamber not immediately to be recognised, garters, hose, waistcoat, neckerchief, arranged in dreadful order and proportion, which I knew was not mine own. 'Tis the common symptom, on awaking, I judge my last night's condition from. A tolerable scattering on the floor I hail as being too probably my own, and if the candlestick be not removed, I assoil myself. But this finical arrangement, this finding everything in the morning in exact diametrical rectitude, torments me. By whom was I divested? Burning blushes! not by the fair hands of nymphs, the Buffam Graces?[2] Remote whispers suggested that I *coached* it home in triumph – far be that from working pride in me, for I was unconscious of the locomotion; that a young Mentor accompanied a reprobate old Telemachus; that, the Trojan like, he bore his charge upon his shoulders, while the wretched incubus, in glimmering sense, hiccuped drunken snatches of flying on the bat's wings after sunset. An aged servitor was also hinted at, to make disgrace more complete: one, to whom my ignominy may offer further occasions of revolt (to which he was before too fondly inclining) from the true faith; for, at a sight of my helplessness, what more was needed to drive him to the advocacy of independency?

Occasion led me through Great Russell Street yesterday. I gazed at the great knocker. My feeble hands in vain essayed to lift it. I dreaded that Argus Portitor,[3] who doubtless lanterned me out on that prodigious night. I called the Elginian marbles. They were cold to my suit. I shall never again, I said, on the wide gates unfolding, say without fear of thrusting back, in a light but a peremptory air, 'I am going to Mr Cary's.' I passed by the walls of Balclutha.[4] I had imaged to myself a zodiac of third Wednesdays irradiating by glimpses the Edmonton dulness. I dreamed of Highmore! I am de-vited to come on Wednesdays.

Villanous old age that, with second childhood, brings linked hand in hand her inseparable twin, new inexperience, which knows not effects of liquor. Where I was to have sate for a sober, middle-aged-and-a-half gentleman, literary too, the neat-fingered artist can educe no notions but of a dissolute Silenus, lecturing natural philosophy to a jeering Chromius or a Mnasilus.[5] Pudet.[6] From the context gather the lost name of —.

THE PARTY AT HAYDON'S

In December Wordsworth was in town, and as Keats wished to know him I made up a party to dinner of Charles Lamb, Wordsworth, Keats and Monkhouse, his friend, and a very pleasant party we had.

I wrote to Lamb, and told him the address was '22 Lisson Grove, North, at Rossi's, half way up, right hand corner.' I received his characteristic reply.

'My dear Haydon,
'I will come with pleasure to 22. Lisson Grove, North, at Rossi's, half way up, right hand side, if I can find it.

'Yours,
'C. LAMB.

'20. Russel Court,
Covent Garden East,
half way up, next the corner,
left hand side.'

On December 28th the immortal dinner came off in my painting-room, with Jerusalem towering up behind us as a background. Wordsworth was a fine cue, and we had a glorious set-to, – on Homer, Shakespeare, Milton and Virgil. Lamb got exceedingly merry and exquisitely witty; and his fun in the midst of Wordsworth's solemn intonations of oratory was like the sarcasm and wit of the fool in the intervals of Lear's passion. He made a speech and voted me absent, and made them drink my health. 'Now,' said Lamb, 'you old lake poet, you rascally poet, why do you call Voltaire dull?' We all defended Wordsworth, and affirmed there was a state of mind when Voltaire would be dull. 'Well,' said Lamb, 'here's Voltaire – the Messiah of the French nation, and a very proper one too.'

He then, in a strain of humour beyond description, abused me for putting Newton's head into my picture, – 'a fellow,' said he, 'who believed nothing unless it was as clear as the three sides of a triangle.' And then he and Keats agreed he had destroyed all the poetry of the rainbow by reducing it to the prismatic colours. It was impossible to resist him, and we all drank 'Newton's health, and confusion to mathematics'. It was delightful to see the good-humour of Wordsworth in giving in to all our frolics without affectation and laughing as heartily as the best of us.

By this time other friends joined, amongst them poor Ritchie who was going to penetrate by Fezzan to Timbuctoo. I introduced him to all as 'a gentleman going to Africa'. Lamb seemed to take no notice; but all of a sudden he roared out, 'Which is the gentleman we are going to lose?' We then drank the victim's health, in which Ritchie joined.

In the morning of this delightful day, a gentleman, a perfect stranger, had called on me. He said he knew my friends, had an enthusiasm for Wordsworth and begged I would procure him the happiness of an introduction. He told me he was a comptroller of stamps, and often had correspondence with the poet. I thought it a liberty; but still, as he seemed a gentleman, I told him he might come.

When we retired to tea we found the comptroller. In introducing him to Wordsworth I forgot to say who he was. After a little time the comptroller looked down, looked up and said to Wordsworth, 'Don't you think, sir, Milton was a great genius?' Keats looked at me, Wordsworth looked at the comptroller. Lamb who was dozing by the fire turned round and said, 'Pray, sir, did you say Milton was a great genius?' 'No, sir; I asked Mr. Wordsworth if he were not.' 'Oh,' said Lamb, 'then you are a silly fellow.' 'Charles! my dear Charles!' said Wordsworth; but Lamb, perfectly innocent of the confusion he had created, was off again by the fire.

After an awful pause the comptroller said, 'Don't you think Newton a great genius?' I could not stand it any longer. Keats put his head into my books. Ritchie squeezed in a laugh. Wordsworth seemed asking himself, 'Who is this?' Lamb got up, and taking a candle, said, 'Sir, will you allow me to look at your phrenological development?' He then turned his back on the poor man, and at every question of the comptroller he chaunted –

> Diddle diddle dumpling, my son John
> Went to bed with his breeches on.

The man in office, finding Wordsworth did not know who he was, said in a spasmodic and half-chuckling anticipation of assured victory, 'I have had the honour of some correspondence with you, Mr. Wordsworth.' 'With me, sir?' said Wordsworth, 'not that I remember.' 'Don't you, sir? I am a comptroller of stamps.' There was a dead silence; – the comptroller evidently thinking that was enough. While we were waiting for Wordsworth's reply, Lamb sung out

> Hey diddle diddle,
> The cat and the fiddle.

'My dear Charles!' said Wordsworth, —

> Diddle diddle dumpling, my son John,

chaunted Lamb, and then rising, exclaimed, 'Do let me have another look at that gentleman's organs.' Keats and I hurried Lamb into the painting-room, shut the door and gave way to inextinguishable laughter. Monkhouse followed and tried to get Lamb away. We went back but the comptroller was irreconcilable. We soothed and smiled and asked him to supper. He stayed though his dignity was sorely affected. However, being a good-natured man, we parted all in good-humour, and no ill effects followed.

All the while, until Monkhouse succeeded, we could hear Lamb struggling in the painting-room and calling at intervals, 'Who is that fellow? Allow me to see his organs once more.'

It was indeed an immortal evening. Wordsworth's fine intonation as he quoted Milton and Virgil, Keats' eager inspired look, Lamb's quaint sparkle of lambent humour, so speeded the stream of conversation, that in my life I never passed a more delightful time. All our fun was within bounds. Not a word passed that an apostle might not have listened to. It was a night worthy of the Elizabethan age, and my solemn Jerusalem flashing up by the flame of the fire, with Christ hanging over us like a vision, all made up a picture which will long glow upon —

> that inward eye
> Which is the bliss of solitude.

Keats made Ritchie promise he would carry his Endymion to the great desert of Sahara and fling it in the midst.

Poor Ritchie went to Africa, and died, as Lamb foresaw, in 1819. Keats died in 1821, at Rome. C. Lamb is gone, joking to the last. Monkhouse is dead, and Wordsworth and I are the only two now living (1841) of that glorious party.

[From the Autobiography of Benjamin Robert Haydon]

APPENDIX TWO

A SELECTION OF LAMB'S NOTES
FROM *SPECIMENS OF THE ENGLISH DRAMATIC POETS* (1808)

NOTE ON *The Case Is Altered*,
A COMEDY, BY BEN JOHNSON.

The passion for wealth has worn out much of its grossness by tract of time.
Our ancestors certainly conceived of money as able to confer a distinct
gratification in itself, not alone considered simply as a symbol of wealth.
The oldest poets, when they introduce a miser, constantly make him
address his gold as his mistress; as something to be seen, felt, and hugged; as
capable of satisfying two of the senses at least. The substitution of a thin
unsatisfying medium for the good old tangible gold, has made avarice
quite a Platonic affection in comparison with the seeing, touching, and
handling pleasures of the old Chrysophilites. A bank-note can no more
satisfy the touch of a true sensualist in this passion, than Creusa could return
her husband's embrace in the shades. See the Cave of Mammon in Spenser;
Barabas's contemplation of his wealth in the Jew of Malta; Luke's raptures
in the City Madam, &c. Above all, hear Guzman, in that excellent old
Spanish novel, The Rogue, expatiate on the 'ruddy cheeks of your golden
Ruddocks, your Spanish Pistolets, your plump and full-faced Portuguese,
and your clear-skinned pieces of eight of Castile,' which he and his fellows
the beggars kept secret to themselves, and did 'privately enjoy in a plentiful
manner.' 'For to have them, for to pay them away, is not to enjoy them; to
enjoy them is to have them lying by us, having no other need of them than
to use them for the clearing of the eye-sight, and the comforting of our
senses. These we did carry about with us, sewing them in some patches of
our doublets near unto the heart, and as close to the skin as we could
handsomely quilt them in, holding them to be restorative.'

NOTE ON *A New Wonder: a Woman Never Vext*,
A COMEDY BY ROWLEY.

The old play-writers are distinguished by an honest boldness of exhibition; they show every thing without being ashamed. If a reverse in

fortune be the thing to be personified, they fairly bring us to the prison-grate and the alms-basket. A poor man on our stage is always a gentleman; he may be known by a peculiar neatness of apparel, and by wearing black. Our delicacy, in fact, forbids the dramatizing of distress at all. It is never shown in its essential properties;[1] it appears but as the adjunct to some virtue, as something which is to be relieved, from the approbation of which relief the spectators are to derive a certain soothing of self-referred satisfaction. We turn away from the real essences of things to hunt after their relative shadows, moral duties: whereas, if the truth of things were fairly represented, the relative duties might be safely trusted to themselves, and moral philosophy lose the name of a science.

[1] Guzman de Alfarache, in that good old book 'The Spanish Rogue,' has summed up a few of the properties of poverty: – 'That poverty, which is not the daughter of the spirit, is but the mother of shame and reproach; it is a disreputation that drowns all the other good parts that are in man; it is a disposition to all kind of evil; it is man's most foe; it is a leprosy full of anguish; it is a way that leads unto hell; it is a sea wherein our patience is overwhelmed, our honour is consumed, our lives are ended, and our souls are utterly lost and cast away for ever. The poor man is a kind of money that is not current; the subject of every idle housewife's chat; the offscum of the people; the dust of the street, first trampled under foot and then thrown on the dunghill; in conclusion, the poor man is the rich man's ass; he dineth with the last, fareth of the worst, and payeth dearest: his sixpence will not go so far as a rich man's threepence; his opinion is ignorance; his discretion, foolishness; his suffrage, scorn; his stock upon the common, abused by many and abhorred of all. If he come in company, he is not heard; if any chance to meet him, they seek to shun him; if he advise, though never so wisely, they grudge and murmur at him; if he work miracles, they say he is a witch; if virtuous, that he goeth about to deceive; his venial sin is a blasphemy; his thought is made treason; his cause, be it never so just, it is not regarded; and, to have his wrongs righted, he must appeal to that other life. All men crush him; no man favoureth him; there is no man that will relieve his wants; no man that will comfort him in his miseries; nor no man that will bear him company, when he is all alone, and oppressed with grief. None help him; all hinder him; none give him, all take from him; he is debtor to none, and yet must make payment to all. O, the unfortunate and poor condition of him that is poor, to whom even the very hours are sold, which the clock striketh, and pays custom for the sunshine in August!'

NOTE ON *A Fair Quarrel*,
A COMEDY, BY MIDDLETON AND ROWLEY.

The insipid levelling morality to which the modern stage is tied down would not admit of such admirable passions as these scenes are filled with. A puritanical obtuseness of sentiment, a stupid infantile goodness, is creeping among us, instead of the vigorous passions, and virtues clad in flesh and blood, with which the old dramatists present us. Those noble and liberal casuists could discern in the differences, the quarrels, the animosities of man, a beauty and truth of moral feeling, no less than in the iterately inculcated duties of forgiveness and atonement. With us all is hypocritical meekness. A reconciliation scene (let the occasion be never so absurd or unnatural) is always sure of applause. Our audiences come to the theatre to be complimented on their goodness. They compare notes with the amiable characters in the play, and find a wonderful similarity of disposition between them. We have a common stock of dramatic morality out of which a writer may be supplied without the trouble of copying it from originals within his own breast. To know the boundaries of honour, to be judiciously valiant, to have a temperance which shall beget a smoothness in the angry swellings of youth, to esteem life as nothing when the sacred reputation of a parent is to be defended, yet to shake and tremble under a pious cowardice when that ark of an honest confidence is found to be frail and tottering, to feel the true blows of a real disgrace blunting that sword which the imaginary strokes of a supposed false imputation had put so keen an edge upon but lately; to do, or to imagine this done in a feigned story, asks something more of a moral sense, somewhat a greater delicacy of perception in questions of right and wrong, than goes to the writing of two or three hackneyed sentences about the laws of honour as opposed to the laws of the land, or a common-place against duelling. Yet such things would stand a writer nowadays in far better stead than Captain Ager and his concientious honour; and he would be considered as a far better teacher of morality than old Rowley or Middleton if they were living.

NOTE ON *The Rich Jew of Malta, A Tragedy,*
BY MARLOWE.

Marlow's Jew does not approach so near to Shakspeare's, as his Edward II. does to Richard II. Shylock in the midst of his savage purpose is a man. His motives, feelings, resentments, have something human in them. 'If you wrong us, shall we not revenge?' Barbaras is a mere monster brought in with a large painted nose to please the rabble. He kills in sport, poisons whole nunneries, invents infernal machines. He is just such an exhibition as a century or two earlier might have been played before the Londoners, *by the Royal Command*, when a general pillage and massacre of the Hebrews had been previously resolved on in the cabinet. It is curious to see a superstition wearing out. The idea of a Jew (which our pious ancestors contemplated with such horror) has nothing in it now revolting. We have tamed the claws of the beast, and pared its nails, and now we take it to our arms, fondle it, write plays to flatter it: it is visited by princes, affects a taste, patronizes the arts, and is the only liberal and gentlemanlike thing in Christendom.

BIOGRAPHICAL INDEX OF CORRESPONDENTS AND CONTEMPORARIES

Barton, Bernard (1784–1849): Quaker poet. He began working in a shop, became a coal and corn merchant, a private tutor in Liverpool and, finally (in 1809), a clerk in the private bank of Dykes and Alexander in Suffolk. He was a contributor to the *London Magazine*, through which he met Lamb in 1822.

Burney, Admiral James (1750–1821): sailor. Son of Charles Burney, the music historian, and brother of Fanny Burney, the novelist. He first met Lamb at Rickman's house in 1803 and was friendly with several of Lamb's circle of friends, including Hazlitt and Crabb Robinson.

Burney, Martin Charles (1788–1852): barrister, son of Admiral Burney. Thomas Westwood described him as 'the ugliest of men, hugest of eaters, honestest of friends'. Lamb dedicated the second volume of his works (1818) to Martin Burney.

Chambers, Charles (died *c.* 1857): surgeon, educated at Christ's Hospital later than Lamb. His brother John was a colleague of Lamb's at the East India House.

Cottle, Joseph (1770–1835): author and publisher in Bristol. He issued the early work of Coleridge, Southey and Charles Lloyd, including, in 1798, the *Lyrical Ballads*.

Dyer, George (1755–1841): poet, scholar and journalist. He was educated at Christ's Hospital, leaving (before Lamb's arrival) in 1774 and going to Emmanuel College, Cambridge.

Field, Barron (1786–1846): barrister, whose father was apothecary to Christ's Hospital and whose brother, Francis John Field, was a fellow clerk of Lamb's at East India House. He was drama critic for *The Times* and contributed to the *Reflector*, *Quarterly Review* and the *London Magazine*. He was a close friend of Lamb, Crabb Robinson and Leigh Hunt.

Gillman, Dr James (1792–1839): a surgeon living in Highgate, with whom Coleridge lived from 1816 until his death in 1834. He was one of the co-signatories in the medical report of 1825 that enabled Lamb to retire from the East India Company.

Godwin, William (1756–1836): philosopher, political theorist and novelist. His most well-known work of reform was the *Inquiry Concerning Political Justice* (1793). Lamb wrote the epilogue to Godwin's tragedy, *Antonio* (1800), and a prologue for his tragedy *Faulkener* (1807). In 1805, Godwin and his wife founded the Juvenile Library that published Charles and Mary Lamb's works for children (1805–11). Lamb referred to Godwin as The Professor, and is reported to have said that Godwin had read more books that were not worth reading than any man in England.

Hunt, James Henry Leigh (1784–1859): editor, essayist and poet. Educated at Christ's Hospital later than Lamb, they were close friends by 1812 when Hunt was imprisoned for libelling the Prince Regent, and Lamb was one of his frequent visitors. Hunt edited his brother's magazine, the *Examiner*, from 1808, to which Lamb contributed. Hunt's most interesting writing about Lamb is a review of Lamb's Works (*Examiner*, March 1819), a description of Lamb's library in the essay 'My Books' (*Literary Examiner*, 5/12 July 1823), and various references in his *Autobiography* (1850).

Kelly, Frances Maria (Fanny) (1790–1882): actress and singer, whose career Lamb had followed and written about admiringly between 1813 and 1825. They met probably in 1816; in July 1819, Lamb proposed to her and was turned down (see note 2 to Letter 37, p. 429).

Lloyd, Charles (junior) (1775–1839): poet, eldest son of Charles Lloyd the Birmingham banker and philanthropist. As a young man he was a close friend of Lamb and Coleridge: in 1796 he lived with Coleridge in Bristol, and in 1797 he visited Lamb. It was Charles Lloyd who first introduced Lamb to Manning in December 1799, when he and his brother Robert were studying with Manning at Cambridge.

Lloyd, Robert (1778–1811): third son of Charles Lloyd, senior, the Quaker banker. After differences with his father in 1799, Lloyd went to London and lived for a time with Lamb, whom he had first met in 1797. In 1809 his father bought him a partnership in a Birmingham bookselling and printing firm. For further details of the Lloyds, see *Charles Lamb and the Lloyds* by E. V. Lucas (London, 1898).

Manning, Thomas (1772–1840): mathematician and linguist. He first met Lamb at Cambridge in 1799 and became, despite Manning's elaborate and protracted travels in Europe and China, one of Lamb's closest friends. The son of a Norfolk rector, Manning was one of the first European scholars of Chinese, and the first Englishman to enter Lhasa in Tibet.

Morgan, John James (died 1820): a lawyer, who became a businessman and eventually a bankrupt. He was educated at Christ's Hospital and was a friend of Coleridge and Lamb.

Procter, Bryan Waller (1787–1874): poet who wrote under the name of Barry Cornwall. Educated at Harrow, he became a solicitor and barrister and, in 1832, was appointed Metropolitan Commissioner of Lunacy. He met Lamb at Leigh Hunt's, probably in 1817, and was a frequent contributor to the *London Magazine* between 1820 and 1825. Procter's *Charles Lamb: A Memoir* was published by Edward Moxon & Co. in 1866.

Rickman, John (1771–1840): parliamentary official and statistician. The son of a clergyman, he was educated at Guildford Grammar School and Oxford. A close friend of Southey's, Rickman was introduced to Lamb by George Dyer in 1800. Rickman supplied Southey with material for articles in the *Edinburgh Review* and the *Annual Register*, and wrote an article on the Poor Laws entitled 'The Means of Improving the People' (*Quarterly Review*, April 1818). His most important work was improving national census-taking procedures.

Robinson, Henry Crabb (1775–1867): barrister and diarist. His diary, written between 1811 and 1867, has a large number of references to Lamb.

Southey, Robert (1774–1843): poet and voluminous writer of books and articles, mostly for the *Quarterly Review*. Educated at Westminster School and Oxford, Southey was an early friend of Coleridge's, with whom he planned the utopian scheme of Pantisocracy (see note 7 to Letter 7, p. 421), and was also his brother-in-law. He first met Lamb in 1795 and they remained friends throughout their lives. Southey was made Poet Laureate in 1813.

Talfourd, Sir Thomas Noon (1795–1854): judge and dramatist. Talfourd met Lamb in 1815, and he was executor and trustee in both of Lamb's wills. He was also Lamb's first biographer, publishing in 1837 *The Letters of Charles Lamb, with a Sketch of his Life*. Dickens dedicated *The Pickwick Papers* to him.

NOTES

1. *On the Genius and Character of Hogarth*

1. (p. 27) *an old-fashioned house in —shire*: the house was Blakesware in Hertfordshire, where Lamb's maternal grandmother, Mary Field, was housekeeper and which he visited as a child.

2. (p. 30) *Ferdinand Count Fathom*: the hero of Smollett's novel *Adventures of Ferdinand Count Fathom* (1754).

3. (p. 33) *somewhere in his lectures*: the passage referred to is in the fourteenth of the *Discourses on Painting*.

4. (p. 34) 'Honest Whore': 1604, a play by Thomas Dekker (1572–1632).

5. (p. 35) *Bunbury*: William Henry Bunbury (1750–1811), an artist and caricaturist of private means and social prominence.

6. (p. 36) *the late Mr Barry*: the painter James Barry (1741–1806), who was a Royal Academician and professor of painting.

7. (p. 37) *the Foots, the Kenricks*: Samuel Foote (1720–77) and William Kenrick (1725?–79) were both popular dramatists of that period.

8. (p. 38) *Mr Burke*: Edmund Burke (1728–97), politician and political and aesthetic theorist.

9. (p. 41) *Tom Jones . . . Blifil*: characters in Fielding's *Tom Jones* (1749).

10. (p. 41) *Strap . . . Random*: characters in Smollett's *Roderick Random*.

11. (p. 41) *Parson Adams*: a character in Fielding's *Joseph Andrewes*.

12. (p. 44) *Uncle Toby and Mr Shandy*: characters in Sterne's novel *Tristram Shandy*.

13. (p. 44) *tædium . . . formarum*: 'the tedium of everyday things'.

2. *On the Tragedies of Shakspeare*

1. (p. 46) *Mr K.*: John Philip Kemble (1757–1823). He first appeared as Hamlet on 30 September 1783, at Drury Lane.

2. (p. 46) *Mrs S.*: Mrs Siddons (1755–1831), John Kemble's sister.

3. (p. 49) *Banks or Lillo*: John Banks was a Restoration melodramatist; George Lillo (1693–1739) was the author of *George Barnwell – The London Merchant or The History of George Barnwell* (1731), mentioned later in the essay. The story, from Percy's *Reliques*, tells how the apprentice, George, robs his master and kills his uncle, incited by the ambitious and attractive Millwood. For nearly a century the play was performed at Christmas and Easter holidays as an instructive moral lesson for apprentices.

4. (p. 54) *Tate and Cibber*: Nahum Tate (1652–1715), dramatist and poet, and Colley Cibber (1671–1757). Lamb ironically called them Shakspeare's Improvers in an essay of that title (*Spectator*, 22 November 1828), for their re-writing of some of Shakespeare's plays.

5. (p. 54) *Mr C.'s exertions in that part*: George Frederick Cooke (1756–1811). Lamb reviewed Cooke's Richard III in the *Morning Post* of 8 January 1802.

6. (p. 55) *Glenalvon*: a character in Home's tragedy *Douglas* (1757). Lamb wrote an early poem on the play and, during his six weeks in the asylum at Hoxton, in 1795, he imagined himself to be Norval, the young ill-starred hero of *Douglas*.

7. (p. 58) *by chandelier light*: in 1811, when Lamb was writing this, the stage was lit by chandeliers.

8. (p. 59) *the Orrery Lecturer at the Haymarket*: named after Charles Boyle, Earl of Orrery, the Orrery was a mechanism designed to represent the motions of the planets around the sun by means of clockwork.

9. (p. 60) *Webb*: a theatrical robe-maker at Chancery Lane.

3. Edax on Appetite

1. (p. 61) *the Editor of the Reflector*: James Henry Leigh Hunt (1784–1859).

2. (p. 61) *quibus hunc . . . partem*: 'with these things you can alleviate the pain and rid yourself of most of this disease'.

3. (p. 61) *piacula*: ways of making expiation or atonement.

4. (p. 62) *Ventri natus . . . mensæ*: the phrases can be translated respectively, 'glutton born', 'gluttony dedicated', 'insane appetite', 'abyss of edibles', 'indulger in feasts', 'no restrainer of appetite', 'hunter of the sumptuous'.

5. (p. 63) *old Baucis*: the wife of Philemon, a good old countryman in Greek mythology. Zeus and Hermes came to earth to test men's piety and were refused hospitality by everyone except Philemon and Baucis.

6. (p. 63) *Heliogabalus*: often referred to by Lamb, Heliogabalus was a Roman Emperor (AD 218–22) famous for his beauty and the elaborate ceremonials over which he presided. The shameless extravagance of his life shocked even the Roman public. He was described as 'insulting the intelligence of the community by horseplay of the wildest description and by childish practical joking'.

7. (p. 63) *Curii and Dentati*: Curii was a famous Roman general. The pun is an allusion to Lucius Scippius Dentatus, the 'Roman Achilles', who was a legendary embodiment of the civic and military virtues of the plebeians in their struggles against both the patricians and external enemies.

8. (p. 64) *Mandeville . . . Fable of the Bees*: Bernard Mandeville (1670?–1733), whose *Fable of the Bees* (1714) was one of Lamb's favourite books.

9. (p. 64) *lusus naturae*: 'sport of nature'.

10. (p. 65) *in petto*: Italian for 'undisclosed'.

4. *Hospita on the Immoderate Indulgence of the Pleasures of the Palate*

1. (p. 69) *Anthropophagism*: cannibalism.

2. (p. 70) *Mr Malthus's Thoughts . . . Population*: Thomas Robert Malthus (1766–1834), whose very influential *Essay on the Principle of Population* was published in 1798. Malthus's theory was that population increased geometrically while food supply increased only arithmetically. If economic prosperity led to an increase in population, the ultimate cost would be a food crisis which would then reduce the population to a level compatible with subsistence. This seemed to be a 'natural' limit to progress.

5. *The Good Clerk, A Character*

1. (p. 73) *the dexter ear*: the right ear.

2. (p. 73) *the George Barnwells of the day*: see note 3 to 'The Tragedies of Shakspeare' (p. 403).

3. (p. 73) *Drayton*: Michael Drayton (1563–1631), poet.

4. (p. 73) *'The Complete English Tradesman'*: published in 1727.

5. (p. 74) *The Fable of the Bees*: see note 7 to 'Edax on Appetite' (p. 404).

6. (p. 75) *as Solomon says*: Proverbs 22:7.

6. *Wordsworth's 'Excursion'*

1. (p. 77) *to be called the Recluse*: this poem was never completed by Wordsworth.

2. (p. 78) *the caravan which Thompson so feelingly describes*: in 'Winter' (ll. 799–809), part of James Thomson's *The Seasons*, which appeared in its first complete edition in 1730.

3. (p. 79) *Walton's Complete Angler*: one of Lamb's favourite books, by Izaak Walton (1593–1683), published in 1653.

4. (p. 80) *Dodona*: Zeus's sanctuary.

5. (p. 80) *Fairfax's Translation*: the quotation is from Edward Fairfax's translation (1600) of Tasso's *Gerusalemme Liberata*, XVI, 13. 'Leden' means 'language'.

FROM *Essays of Elia* (1823) AND *Last Essays of Elia* (1833)

7. *The Two Races of Men*

1. (p. 95) *Alcibiades . . . our late incomparable Brinsley*: Alcibiades is one of the characters in Plato's *Symposium*; and Brinsley is Richard Brinsley Sheridan, the extravagant dramatist.

2. (p. 95) *meum and tuum*: 'my' and 'your'.

3. (p. 95) *beyond Tooke*: an allusion to the philological theories in *The Diversions of Purley* by John Horne Tooke (1736–1812).

4. (p. 95) *obolary*: possessing only small coins, poor; a nonce-word coined by Lamb.

5. (p. 95) *lene tormentum*: 'gentle torment'.

6. (p. 96) *the Albion*: In 1801, Lamb worked briefly on the *Albion*.

7. (p. 96) *periegesis*: description of a place.

8. (p. 97) *cana fides*: 'distinguished grey'.

9. (p. 97) *mumping visnomy*: begging face.

10. (p. 97) *Comberbatch*: in December 1793, while still at Cambridge, Coleridge left the university and enlisted in the 15th Light Dragoons under the name of Silas Tomkyn Comberbache.

11. (p. 98) *deodands*: things given to God.

12. (p. 98) *spiteful K.*: James Kenney (1780–1849), Irish dramatist. Lamb wrote an Epilogue to Kenney's farce *Debtor and Creditor* in 1814.

13. (p. 99) *tripling their value*: on one page of Lamb's Beaumont and Fletcher folio Coleridge wrote two notes, adding at the bottom of the page 'NB – I shall not be long here, Charles! – I gone, you will not mind my having spoiled a book in order to leave a Relic.'

8. *A Quakers' Meeting*

1. (p. 100) *Boreas, and Cesias, and Argestes loud*: Greek wind-gods.

2. (p. 101) *Master Zimmerman*: Johann Georg Zimmerman (1728–95), Swiss philosophical writer and physician who wrote on nervous disorders and whose books were translated into every European language. He was also private physician to George III and Frederick the Great. His character was an eccentric combination of sentimentalism, melancholy and enthusiasm, which is doubtless why he appealed to Lamb.

3. (p. 102) *Fox and Dewesbury*: George Fox (1624–91) founded the Society of Friends. William Dewesbury was one of Fox's first colleagues and a famous preacher.

4. (p. 103) *Jocos Risus-que*: 'a laughable joke'.

5. (p. 103) *Trophonius*: 'the Feeder', a Boeotian oracular god. Pausanius, the Greek traveller and geographer, describes in his *Guide to Greece* the elaborate preliminary ritual after which the inquirer is snatched away underground and given direct revelation.

9. *The Old and the New Schoolmaster*

1. (p. 105) *old Ortelius . . . Arrowsmith*: Abraham Ortellius (1527–98), Dutch geographer and author of *Theatrum Orbis Terrae* (1570). Aaron Arrowsmith (1750–1823) was a famous contemporary cartographer.

2. (p. 105) *My friend M.*: Thomas Manning, see Biographical Index (p. 400).

3. (p. 107) *the Lilys, and the Linacres*: William Lily (1468–1522), English scholar; Thomas Linacre (1460–1524), English humanist and physician.

4. (p. 108) *Flori- . . . Spici-legia*: 'flower-' and 'spice-laws', i.e. folklore.

5. (p. 109) *cum multis aliis*: 'along with many other things'.

6. (p. 109) *the famous Tractate . . . Hartlib*: Milton's *Tractate on Education*, published in 1644.

7. (p. 109) *mollia tempora fandi*: 'at the most intimate moments'.

8. (p. 109) *the Panorama . . . the Panopticon*: the Panorama was a place in London where a picture of a landscape, or a map, was arranged on the inside of a cylindrical surface (the walls of the room) around the spectator. George Bartley (1782–1858), the comedian, lectured on astronomy and poetry at the Lyceum during Lent; for an orrery see note 8 to 'On the Tragedies of Shakspeare' (p. 404). The Panopticon was a telescope.

10. *Imperfect Sympathies*

1. (p. 113) *Imperfect Sympathies*: The original title in the *London Magazine* was 'Jews, Quakers, Scotchmen, and other Imperfect Sympathies'.

2. (p. 113) *the author of the Religio Medici*: Sir Thomas Browne (1605–82).

3. (p. 115) *John Buncle*: *The Life of John Buncle, Esq.* (part I published in 1756, part II in 1766) was by Thomas Amory (1691?–1788).

4. (p. 115) *I have a print . . . pretensions*: the print was the Virgin of the Rocks. Crabb Robinson's diary tells us that the Scotsman was a friend of Godwin's called Smith, and records his reply to Lamb's remark as: 'Why, Sir, from all I have heard of you as well as from what I have myself seen, I certainly entertain a very high opinion of your abilities, but I confess that I have not formed any opinion concerning your personal pretensions.'

5. (p. 116) *Thomson*: James Thomson (1700–1748), born in Roxburghshire, author of *The Seasons*.

6. (p. 116) *Rory*: Rory was Roderick Random's schoolboy name in Smol-

lett's novel of that name (Smollett himself came from a Dumbartonshire family).

7. (p. 116) *the story of Hugh of Lincoln*: at the age of ten, so the story goes, Hugh was found dead in a Jew's house, having been scourged and crucified in imitation of the death of Christ. In the general indignation several Jews were hanged.

8. (p. 117) *congeeing*: bowing.

9. (p. 117) *keck*: retch.

10. (p. 117) *B—*: John Braham (1774?–1856), the great tenor.

11. (p. 117) *Kemble*: John Philip Kemble (1757–1823), the actor.

12. (p. 119) *Penn*: William Penn (1644–1718), English Quaker and founder of Pennsylvania.

11. *Witches, and Other Night-Fears*

1. (p. 121) *indigent eld*: people in the old days.

2. (p. 122) *the History of the Bible . . . never seen*: the *New History of the Holy Bible from the Beginning of the World to the Establishment of Christianity*, by Thomas Stackhouse (1677–1752), was published in 1737. Lamb makes two other references to this picture, once in a draft of his play *John Woodvil* (1802) and once in his story *The Witch Hunt* (1808).

3. (p. 124) *Dear little T. H.*: Thornton Hunt, Leigh Hunt's eldest son.

4. (p. 125) *the noble Dream of this poet*: the reference is to 'A Dream', a poem in Barry Cornwall's *Dramatic Scenes* (1819). Barry Cornwall was the pen-name of Bryan Waller Procter (1787–1874).

5. (p. 126) *Ino Leucothea*: 'white goddess' or 'runner on the foam', a sea-goddess identified with Ino, daughter of Cadmus. See *Odyssey* 5, 333–5.

12. *Grace before Meat*

1. (p. 127) *manducation*: chewing or eating (often used in a theological context, as in communion).

2. (p. 128) *a rarus hospes*: 'an infrequent guest'.

3. (p. 128) *Jeshurun*: see Isaiah 44.

4. (p. 129) *Heliogabalus*: see note 6 to 'Edax On Appetite' (p. 404).

5. (p. 131) *C—*: Coleridge.

6. (p. 131) *the author of the 'Rambler'*: Samuel Johnson.

7. (p. 131) *Dagon*: the fish-god worshipped by the Philistines; see Judges 16:23, and Samuel 5.

8. (p. 132) *C.V.L.*: Charles Valentine le Grice (1773–1858), friend of Lamb and Coleridge, who became a clergyman.

9. (p. 132) *Non tunc . . . locus*: that was not the place (for such a thing).

10. (p. 132) *good creatures*: The Grace Before Meat at Christ's Hospital in Lamb's time was: 'Give us thankful hearts, O Lord God, for the Table which

thou has spread for us. Bless thy good Creatures to our use, and us to their service, for Jesus Christ his sake. Amen.'

11. (p. 132) *horresco referens*: 'I shudder to think of it'.

13. *My First Play*

1. (p. 133) *Garrick's Drury*: Garrick's Drury Lane was condemned in 1791, the new theatre being built in 1794.

2. (p. 133) *my godfather F.*: Francis Fielde (died 1809).

3. (p. 134) *orders*: tickets.

4. (p. 135) *Artaxerxes*: an opera by Thomas Arne (1710–78). The date of this performance was probably 1 December 1780. It is not incidental that the reference just before to 'the maternal lap' is one of only two references in Lamb's work to his mother.

5. (p. 135) *Harlequin's Invasion*: a pantomime by Garrick (1759).

6. (p. 135) *Lun's Ghost . . . Rich*: *Lun's Ghost* was produced on 3 January 1782. Lun was the character which John Rich (1682?–1761), the pantomimist and theatrical manager, played in pantomime.

7. (p. 135) *the Way of the World*: a play by Congreve.

8. (p. 136) *Isabella*: Garrick's version of *The Fatal Marriage* (1694) by Thomas Southerne (1660–1746).

14. *Distant Correspondents*

1. (p. 137) *B. F.*: Barron Field (1786–1846), barrister.

2. (p. 137) *parasangs*: a Persian measure of length between 3 and 3½ miles.

3. (p. 137) *P. . . . in the Bench*: P. is unidentifiable; the Bench is the King's Bench Prison.

4. (p. 138) *Munden*: Joseph Shepherd Munden (1758–1832), English comedian and friend of Lamb. Lamb wrote twice on Munden, once in the *Examiner* (November 1819) and once in the *Athenaeum* (February 1832). He also wrote a skit-autobiography of him for the *London Magazine* (February 1825).

5. (p. 138) *flam*: a lie or trick.

6. (p. 139) *the late Lord C.*: Thomas Pitt, second Baron Camelford (1775–1804), killed in a duel in Kensington.

7. (p. 140) *melior lutus*: 'the better mud'.

8. (p. 140) *sol pater*: 'the sun-father'.

9. (p. 141) *Do you bleach*: Lamb is referring here to the idea that illegitimacy wears out in the third generation, letting a natural son's descendant resume the ancient coat of arms.

10. (p. 141) *Sally W—r*: Miss Winter, an acquaintance of Lamb's.

11. (p. 141) *J. W.*: James White (1775–1820), a friend of Lamb's from his school-days.

15. On the Artificial Comedy of the Last Century

1. (p. 143) *Alsatia*: controversial territory between France and Germany. In the seventeenth century the district of Whitefriars, between the Thames and Fleet Street, was known as Alsatia because it afforded sanctuary to debtors and criminals.

2. (p. 143) *the Catos of the pit*: a reference to the Roman politician Marcus Porcius, renowned for his legal ability and his stern, censorious commitment to traditional morality.

3. (p. 143) *The Fainalls . . . Lady Touchwoods*: Fainall in Congreve's *Way of the World*; Mirabel in Farquhar's *Inconstant*; Dorimant in Etheredge's *Man of Mode*; Lady Touchstone in Congreve's *Double Dealer*.

4. (p. 144) *Angelica*: in *Love for Love*.

5. (p. 144) *the impertinent Goshen*: a happy place of light and abundance; see Exodus 10:23.

6. (p. 145) *Sir Simon . . . Sir Paul Pliant's children*: all these characters are in Wycherley's *Love in a Wood*.

7. (p. 146) *Carrington Bowles*: five members of the Bowles family had the same names. Lamb's friend probably lived from 1763 to 1830 and was a print seller and publisher.

8. (p. 146) *old Teazle King*: Thomas King (1730–1805), manager of Drury Lane, was the original Sir Peter Teazle in the first night of *The School for Scandal*, 8 May 1777.

9. (p. 147) *crim-con*: criminal conversation.

10. (p. 147) *amphisbænas*: a legendary serpent with a head at each end.

11. (p. 147) *this manager's comedy*: Sheridan was manager of Drury Lane when *The School for Scandal* was first produced.

16. Detached Thoughts on Books and Reading

1. (p. 149) *the Relapse*: a play by Sir John Vanbrugh (1664–1726).

2. (p. 149) *Shaftesbury . . . Jonathan Wild*: Anthony Ashley Cooper (1671–1713), third Earl of Shaftesbury and author of *Characteristicks of Men, Manners, Opinions, Times* (1711); *Jonathan Wild the Great* (1743), a novel by Fielding.

3. (p. 149) *Adam Smith*: (1723–90), political economist and author of *The Wealth of Nations* (1776).

4. (p. 149) *Anglicanas or Metropolitanas*: the *Encyclopaedia Metropolitana* began appearing in 1817, giving 'sciences and systematic arts entire and in their natural sequence'; Coleridge contributed to it. Anglicana is an invention of Lamb's and probably an allusion to the Britannica, first published 1768–71.

5. (p. 150) *Paracelsus . . . Raymund Lully*: Theophrastus Von Hohenheim (1493–1541), German-Swiss physician and theosophist, author of several medical and mystical treatises. Ramon Lull (c. 1235–1315) was a Catalan author, mystic, Franciscan missionary and martyr, with a reputation of being an alchemist. In

his diary, Crabb Robinson notes that Lamb had 'the finest collection of shabby books' he had seen: 'such a number of first-rate works in very bad condition is, I think, nowhere to be found'.

6. (p. 150) *Russia backs*: book-spines made of Russian leather.

7. (p. 150) *by his Duchess*: Margaret Cavendish, first Duchess of Newcastle, prolific author.

8. (p. 151) *The wretched Malone*: Edmond Malone (1741–1812), a scholar and critic, whose edition of Shakespeare was published in 1790. The bust was actually painted white, not whitewashed, in 1793.

9. (p. 152) *pro bono publico*: 'for the general good'.

10. (p. 152) *Nando's*: a contraction for Ferdinando's, a coffee-house in Fleet Street.

11. (p. 152) *Poor Tobin*: James Webbe Tobin (1767–1814), a friend of Coleridge, Lamb and Godwin.

12. (p. 153) *Cythera*: Aphrodite's sacred Greek island.

13. (p. 153) *a volume of Lardner*: Nathaniel Lardner (1684–1768), Unitarian theologian.

14. (p. 153) *Martin B——* : Martin Burney.

15. (p. 153) *a quaint poetess of our day*: Mary Lamb.

17. *Confessions of a Drunkard*

1. (p. 155) This paper has troubled some of the more devoted 'lovers of Elia' and was risky for Lamb to publish: clerks could easily lose their jobs if it was known that they drank excessively, as Lamb clearly did intermittently. Its publishing history is of interest in the light of this. It was first printed, with a number of editorial changes, in the *Philanthropist* (No. IX, 1813); reprinted in Basil Montagu's book *Some Enquiries into the Effects of Fermented Liquors* in 1814, and then again published as an essay of Elia in the *London Magazine* for August 1822. Lamb apparently reprinted it for two reasons; for the first and only time in his life he was abroad, in France, and could not supply a new essay. Also, a reviewer in the *Quarterly* had written that he was convinced the 'Confessions', as published in Montagu, were genuine confessions of Lamb's. So Lamb added the following note to the full text of the essay published in the *London Magazine*:

We have been induced, in the first instance, to re-print a Thing, which he [Elia] put forth in a friend's volume some years since, entitled the Confessions of a Drunkard, seeing that Messieurs the Quarterly Reviewers have chosen to embellish their last dry pages with fruitful quotations therefrom; adding, from their peculiar brains, the gratuitous affirmation, that they have reason to believe that the describer (in his delineations of a drunkard forsooth!) partly sate for his own picture. The truth is, that our friend had been reading among the Essays of a contemporary, who has perversely been confounded with him, a paper in which *Edax* (or the *Great Eater*) humorously complaineth of an inordinate appetite; and it struck him, that a better paper – of deeper interest, and wider usefulness – might be made out of the imagined experiences of a *Great Drinker*. Accordingly he set to work, and with that mock fervor, and counterfeit earnestness, with which he is too apt to over-realise his descriptions, has given us – a frightful picture indeed – but no more resembling the man *Elia*, than the fictitious *Edax* may be supposed to identify itself with Mr L., its author. It is indeed a compound extracted out of his long observations of the effect of drinking upon all the world about him; and this accumulated mass of misery he hath centered (as the custom is with judicious essayists) in a single figure. We deny not that a portion of his own experiences may have passed into the picture (as who, that is not a washy fellow, but must at some times have felt the after-operation of a too generous cup?) – but then how heightened! how exaggerated! – how little within the sense of the Review, where a part, in their slanderous usage, must be understood to stand for the whole! – but it is useless to expostulate with this Quarterly slime, brood of Nilus, watery heads with hearts of jelly, spawned under the sign of Aquarius, incapable of Bacchus, and therefore cold, washy, spiteful, bloodless. – Elia shall string them up one day, and show their colours – or rather how colourless and vapid the whole fry – when he putteth forth his long promised, but unaccountably hitherto delayed, Confessions of a Water-drinker.

2. (p. 155) *Dehortations*: dissuasions.

3. (p. 158) *Tartarus*: an abyss in Homer, as far below Hades as earth is below heaven.

4. (p. 158) *Piscatoribus Sacrum*: the special room belonging to Piscator.

5. (p. 159) *a Sybaritic effeminacy*: a Sybarite was an inhabitant of Sybaris, a Greek city in Ancient Italy famed for its luxury.

18. *A Dissertation upon Roast Pig*

1. (p. 162) *my friend M.*: Thomas Manning; see Biographical Index (p. 400).

2. (p. 165) *mundus edibilis ... princeps obsoniorum*: 'the edible world' ... 'the best of those things usually eaten with bread'.

3. (p. 165) *amor immunditiae*: 'love of filth'.

4. (p. 165) *praeludium*: 'prelude'.

5. (p. 166) *sapors*: tastes or savours.

6. (p. 167) *intenerating*: tenderizing.

7. (p. 167) *St Omer's*: a French Jesuit college, which of course Lamb never attended.

19. *A Bachelor's Complaint of the Behaviour of Married People*

1. (p. 170) *usufruct*: 'Use, enjoyment, or profitable possession (of something)' – *O.E.D.* This is the first recorded usage.

20. *A Character of the Late Elia*

1. (p. 175) *A character . . . Elia*: this is the original essay, published in the *London Magazine*, that was cut to serve as the Preface to the *Last Essays of Elia*.

2. (p. 175) *his friends T. and H.*: the publishers Taylor and Hessey.

3. (p. 175) *P—r . . . Allan C—*: see note 8 to the Letter of Elia to Robert Southey (p. 417).

4. (p. 175) *manes*: 'soul of the dead'.

5. (p. 175) *a Tale of Lyddalcross*: Cunningham contributed six stories of a proposed series for the *London Magazine* called *Twelve Tales of Lyddalcross*. They were published between January and June 1822.

6. (p. 177) *a statist*: a statesman.

7. (p. 177) *The toga virilis*: the man's toga.

21. *The Old Margate Hoy*

1. (p. 179) *thou old Margate Hoy*: this famous old boat was replaced in 1815 by a steam-boat, the *Thames*, the first proper steam-boat used on the river. The poet Cowper, in a letter of July 1779 to the Revd William Unwin, wrote that 'The [Margate] hoy went to London every week, loaded with mackerel and herrings, and returned loaded with company.'

2. (p. 179) *parching up Scamander*: see Iliad 20, 21. The river Scamander rose to destroy Achilles, but Hephaestus, the fire-god, was sent by Zeus to turn back the waters with fire.

3. (p. 180) *additaments*: a legal term meaning additions.

4. (p. 180) *Genius Loci*: 'genius of the place'.

5. (p. 181) *the Reculvers*: two western towers of the church of Reculver, near Herne Bay – important landmarks.

6. (p. 183) *the mighty Plate, or Orellana*: the rivers Plate and Amazon. Also an allusion to Thomson's *Seasons*, 'Summer', ll. 840, 843. The following quotation is from the same poem, ll. 1002–3.

7. (p. 183) *Juan Fernandez*: Robinson Crusoe's island.

8. (p. 183) *Is this the mighty ocean . . .*: v. 129 from 'Gebir' (1798), by Walter Savage Landor (1775–1864).

9. (p. 184) *Amphitrites*: Amphitrite, wife of Poseidon.

10. (p. 184) *Meschek*: see Psalm 120:5.

22. *The Superannuated Man*

1. (p. 186) *Sera . . . Libertas*: 'freedom that turned and looked on me, albeit late,' from Virgil, *Eclogues* 1, 27.

2. (p. 186) *A Clerk I was . . .*: Not actually by the farce writer John O'Keefe (1747–1833), but from *Inkle and Yarico* (1787) by George Colman the younger (1762–1836).

3. (p. 188) *This noble benefit*: See note 1 to 'The Convalescent' (below). On the day of Lamb's retirement the Court of Directors drew up this minute: 'Resolved that the resignation of Mr Charles Lamb, of the Accountant General's office, on account of certified ill-health, be accepted, and it appearing that he has served the Company faithfully for thirty-three years, and is now in receipt of an income of £730 per annum, he be allowed a pension of £450 . . . to commence from this day.'

4. (p. 188) *Esto perpetua*: 'may you last forever'.

5. (p. 189) *a Tragedy, by Sir Robert Howard*: *The Vestal Virgin, or the Roman Ladies* (1665).

6. (p. 190) *a Gresham or a Whittington*: Sir Richard Gresham (1485?–1549), Lord Mayor of London. Richard Whittington (died 1423), three times Mayor of London and hero of the nursery tale.

7. (p. 191) *washed the Ethiop white*: see Jeremiah 13:23.

8. (p. 191) *Black Monday*: the first schoolday after a vacation.

9. (p. 191) *cantle*: portion.

10. (p. 191) *Lucretian pleasure*: a reference to a passage in Lucretius (2, 1) which describes the pleasure we can feel seeing a ship labouring at sea from the safe vantage of the land.

11. (p. 192) *cum dignitate*: 'with dignity'.

12. (p. 192) *Opus operatum est*: 'the work is finished'.

23. *The Convalescent*

1. (p. 193) *The Convalescent*: in March 1825 Lamb retired from East India House, after thirty-three years, with a pension of £450 a year. He was seriously ill during the spring and summer of that year.

2. (p. 193) *tergiversation*: a pun on the literal meaning of turning one's back on something.

3. (p. 193) *Mare Clausum*: a 'closed sea', that part of a sea over which a country has sovereign rights.

4. (p. 194) *thin douceur*: bank-note.

5. (p. 196) *terra firma*: 'solid ground'.

6. (p. 196) *In Articulo Mortis*: 'at the point of death'.

7. (p. 196) *Tityus*: a giant killed by Zeus and thrown into Tartarus, where two vultures or snakes devoured his liver. His body covered nine acres.

24. *Stage Illusion*

1. (p. 197) *Jack Bannister's cowards*: John 'Jack' Bannister (1760–1836), actor and comedian.

2. (p. 198) *Gatty*: Henry Gattie (1774–1844), actor famous for playing old people.

3. (p. 198) *Mr Emery*: John Emery (1777–1822), apparently the 'best impersonator of countrymen of his day'.

4. (p. 199) *Mr Wrench*: Benjamin Wrench (1778–1843), a famous comedian.

25. Sanity of True Genius

1. (p. 200) *did Nature ... sea below*: from 'On the death of Mr William Harvey' by Abraham Cowley (1618–67).

2. (p. 201) *Wither*: George Wither (1588–1667). 'Maddest fits' is from *The Sheperds Hunting*, Eclogue 4, 409.

3. (p. 201) *Lane's novels*: novels published around 1800 by William Lane (1738–1814) of the Minerva Press, Leadenhall Street. The name became proverbial for bad novels.

4. (p. 201) *fantasques*: fancies or whims.

5. (p. 202) *the cave of Mammon*: Spenser's *The Faerie Queene* 2, 7. The stanzas referred to are 49 ('Ambition'), 54 ('Hesperian Fruit'), 57–60 ('Tantalus'), 61 ('Pilate').

26. Barrenness of the Imaginative Faculty in the Productions of Modern Art

1. (p. 204) *Somerset House*: in the Strand, where the Royal Academy exhibitions were held from 1780 to 1837.

2. (p. 204) *a justly admired neoteric*: the word 'neoteric' means a modern painter. This is a reference to Turner's 'Garden of the Hesperides' which was exhibited at the British Institution in 1806.

3. (p. 204) *custos*: 'guard, custodian'.

4. (p. 205) *Hercules aut Diabolus*: 'Hercules of the Devil'.

5. (p. 205) *Ab extra*: 'from outside'.

6. (p. 205) *Daughters three ... golden tree*: from Milton's *Comus*, ll. 982–3.

7. (p. 205) *a modern artist*: John Martin (1787–1854).

8. (p. 205) *the late King*: George IV (1762–1830), Prince Regent 1811–20.

9. (p. 206) *Mr Farley*: Charles Farley (1771?–1859), manager of the Covent Garden pantomimes.

10. (p. 206) *Eliphaz ... the servants*: see Job 4:13–15.

11. (p. 206) *the words of Daniel*: see Daniel 5.

12. (p. 208) *the swallowing up of Pompeii*: by the eruption of Vesuvius in AD 79. Systematic excavations of Pompeii began in 1763.

13. (p. 208) *Sun ... Ajalon*: see Joshua 10:12.

14. (p. 208) *the great picture at Angerstein's*: the picture is by Sebastian del Piombo (1485–1577). The merchant and philanthropist John Julius Angerstein (1735–1832) donated at his death his collection of pictures, which formed the nucleus of the National Gallery.

15. (p. 209) *Cornuto*: see Coleridge's *Biographia Literaria* (1817) ch. 21. A *cornuto* is a horned man, a cuckold.

16. (p. 210) *the solitary but sufficient Three*: Shem, Ham and Japhet, who were sufficient to repopulate the earth.

17. (p. 210) *a Demiurgus*: the creator of the world who, in Gnostic philosophy, is subordinate to the supreme God.

18. (p. 210) *Vulcanian Three ... Pyracmon*: the first two were Cyclopses; Pyracmon worked at Vulcan's forge under Etna. Mongibello was the Sicilian name for Etna, used by Spenser and Dante.

19. (p. 211) *Guzman de Alfarache*: published by Mateo Aleman in 1599. An English translation by James Mabbe was published in 1623, entitled *The Spanish Rogue*.

ESSAYS AND SKETCHES (1821–7)

27. *Review of the First Volume of Hazlitt's* Table-Talk, *1821 (unpublished)*

1. (p. 215) *Captain Steele ... Isaac Bickerstaff ... Nestor Ironside*: Sir Richard Steele (1672–1729), playwright and essayist, editor of the *Tatler* and co-editor with Addison of the *Spectator*; Bickerstaff and Ironside were the invented characters through which Steele wrote his essays.

2. (p. 216) *Lucubrations*: meditations, studies.

3. (p. 216) *Vision of Mirza*: Addison's 'Vision of Mirzah' was published in the *Spectator* on 1 September 1711 (see *Selections From The Tatler and The Spectator*, Penguin, 1982, p. 467).

4. (p. 217) *thin consistencies*: Paradise Lost 2, 1, 941.

5. (p. 223) *too respective eyes*: King John I, i, 188.

6. (p. 223) *anatomize Regan*: King Lear III, vi, 74.

7. (p. 223) *familiar faces*: a reference to Lamb's poem 'The Old Familiar Faces'.

8. (p. 225) *without o'erflowing full*: from 'Cooper's Hill' by Sir John Denham (1615–69) l. 192.

9. (p. 226) *the last infirmity of common minds*: from Milton's 'Lycidas' l. 71.

10. (p. 226) *look a little ... skin taken off*: from Swift's *A Tale of a Tub* (1704).

28. *Letter of Elia to Robert Southey, Esquire*

1. (p. 228) *an unfriendly office*: Lamb's essay 'Witches, And Other Night-Fears' made a reference to Leigh Hunt's son Thornton: 'Dear little T.H., who of all children has been brought up with the most scrupulous exclusion of every taint of superstition.' As Lamb pointed out, Thornton still suffered from night-terrors. Southey took this essay as an opportunity to attack the radical Hunt in an article in the *Quarterly Review* (January 1823) entitled the 'Progress of In-

fidelity'. Southey's point can be illustrated by the following passage from the article: 'Unbelievers have not always been honest enough . . . to express their real feelings; but this we know concerning them, that when they have renounced their birthright of hope, they have not been able to divest themselves of fear.'

2. (p. 228) *encomium*: panegyric.

3. (p. 228) *an exile at Genoa*: in 1821, at the invitation of Byron and Shelley, the Hunts moved to Italy. They arrived in 1822 just before Shelley was drowned.

4. (p. 229) *a given king in bliss*: a reference to Southey's 'Vision of Judgement' (1820) in which, among other things, George III is received into heaven.

5. (p. 230) *a noble Lord*: Byron, whose 'Vision of Judgement' (1821) ridiculing Southey's poem, begins 'Saint Peter sat by the celestial gate/His keys were rusty, and the lock was dull'.

6. (p. 230) *The Methodists . . . their founder*: Southey's *Life of Wesley* was published in 1820.

7. (p. 231) *Castle Angelo*: a prison in Rome that is Hadrian's tomb.

8. (p. 231) *the article of friendships*: the initialled friends are respectively Randal Norris, Thomas Noon Talfourd, Thomas Griffiths Wainewright, Henry Francis Cary, Allan Cunningham, Bryan Waller Proctor, Thomas Allsop, James Gillman, William Wordsworth, Thomas Monkhouse, Henry Crabb Robinson, Thomas Clarkson, George Dyer, Colonel Phillips, William Ayrton; see the Biographical Index.

9. (p. 231) *Pantisocracy*: see note 7 to Letter 7 (p. 421).

10. (p. 232) *the authors of Rimini and of the Table-Talk*: Leigh Hunt and Hazlitt.

11. (p. 233) *per saltum*: 'with a leap' (of the imagination).

12. (p. 234) *an ill-judged subject*: Hunt's Story of Rimini was scathingly reviewed in *Blackwood* (November 1817) under the heading 'The Cockney School of Poetry', the review stressing that the poem seemed to be 'about' incest.

13. (p. 235) *the Political Justice*: William Godwin's *Inquiry Concerning Political Justice* (1793).

14. (p. 235) *C.*: Coleridge.

15. (p. 236) *Mr Belsham's Lectures*: Thomas Belsham (1750–1829) had been a Professor of Divinity at the Dissenting Academy at Daventry. He then became a Unitarian minister, succeeding Joseph Priestly in Hackney in 1794.

29. *Readers Against the Grain*

1. (p. 240) *the arrack*: a strong fermented palm juice used to make punch.

2. (p. 241) *trap-ball*: an old bat-and-ball game.

3. (p. 241) *that Apocryphal dragon*: a reference to Daniel 7.

4. (p. 242) *Longmans . . . Cadell*: contemporary publishers.

30. A Vision of Horns

1. (p. 245) *cockades*: rosettes, worn as a badge in the hat.

2. (p. 247) *wittols*: men who know of their wives' infidelity and accept it.

3. (p. 247) *dehonestate*: dishonour or disparage.

31. The Illustrious Defunct

1. (p. 248) *the object . . . moribund*: the last State Lottery in England was held on 18 October 1826.

2. (p. 248) *epicedium*: a funeral ode.

3. (p. 248) *multis . . . occidit*: 'it killed with kindness'.

4. (p. 249) *Alnaschar*: a beggar who inherited a hundred pieces of silver and invested them in a basket of glassware. Dreaming of future riches, he imagined he had married the daughter of the chief Vizier and in the dream he spurned her with his foot and so actually kicked over the basket, smashing all the glass (see 'The Barber's Fifth Brother' in *The Arabian Nights*).

5. (p. 249) *the blue-coat boy*: a boy from Christ's Hospital drew the tickets from the wheels in Coopers' Hall.

6. (p. 250) *the Alchemist*: play by Ben Jonson.

7. (p. 251) *an Ignis fatuus*: a will-o'-the wisp.

8. (p. 251) *Crede . . . habes*: 'you get what you believe'.

9. (p. 252) *crim-cons*: criminal conversations.

32. Many Friends

1. (p. 254) *dear Variorum*: various readers. The 'Lepus' papers, as they were known, appeared in the *New Times* during 1825 in a series called 'Variorum'.

2. (p. 254) *Taedet . . . formarum*: 'I find these everyday things wearisome'.

3. (p. 255) *Seven Sleepers*: the heroes of a legend translated from the Syriac by Gregory of Tours, A D250/251. Seven Christian youths, fleeing from persecution by the Emperor Decius, took refuge in a cave. The cave was walled up with the intention of starving them to death but they fell into a miraculous sleep, waking up many years after the persecution.

4. (p. 256) *Lepus*: 'the hare'.

33. Dog Days

1. (p. 257) *The Every-Day Book*: the *Every-Day Book* appeared serially in 1825 and 1826, edited by William Hone (1780–1842), who eventually dedicated it to Lamb.

34. *A Character*

1. (p. 259) *Egomet*: 'I myself', an emphatic Latin form of *ego*.

2. (p. 259) *Jack-Ketchery*: Jack Ketch was a famous hangman.

3. (p. 260) *nimium vicini*: 'far too near'. An allusion to Virgil's *Eclogues* 9, 28: 'Mantua vae miserae nimium vicina Cremonae' – 'Mantua, alas, too near to ill-starred Cremona' (therefore sharing the fate of Cremona which had rebelled against Augustus and so been confiscated).

4. (p. 260) *his fane of Diana*: his temple of Diana.

5. (p. 260) *a Pagod*: an idol or image of a deity in the East.

35. *Charles Lamb's Autobiography*

1. (p. 261) *Lamb's Autobiography*: this was written by Lamb in the *Autograph Book* of William Upcott (1779–1845), who was an assistant librarian at the London Institution. The piece was intended for a proposed second edition of the *Biographical Dictionary*, but was eventually used by John Forster for an article in the *New Monthly Magazine* in 1853, after Lamb's death.

2. (p. 261) *teste suâ manu*: 'with your hand as a witness', on oath.

3. (p. 261) *Leadenhall Street*: where East India House was.

Letters

1. *To Samuel Taylor Coleridge*

1. (p. 265) *May*: William May was the landlord of the Salutation and Cat in Newgate Street where Coleridge and Lamb used to meet from 1794 to 5; on this occasion, Coleridge seems to have left unable to pay his bill.

2. (p. 265) *Allen*: Robert Allen (1772–1805) was a contemporary of Coleridge and Lamb's at Christ's Hospital, and was training to be a surgeon at the Westminster Hospital. He first introduced Coleridge to Southey.

3. (p. 265) *your Watchman*: between March and May of 1796 Coleridge published, at eight-day intervals, ten issues of a miscellany called *The Watchman*.

4. (p. 265) *Le Grice*: Charles Valentine Le Grice (1773–1858) was another contemporary of Coleridge and Lamb's at Christ's Hospital. One of the few documents referring to Lamb's period of 'madness' is a rough draft by Valentine Le Grice:

I am not certain as to dates, but I think about the year 1795, poor Lamb suffered a temporary derangement of his intellects, and confinement under medical care was necessary. I remember it from this circumstance. I received a very long letter from Lamb – very well written – the main purpose of which was to advise me to [?read] Hartley on Man, one expression in it I perfectly remember. 'Hartley appears to me to have had as clear an insight into all the [secrets] of the human mind as I have into the items of a Ledger – as an Accountant has – a good counting-Housical Simile you'll say, and appropos from a clerk in the India House'. The very next day I received a letter from his mother to say that the supposed [letter] that I among other friends had received [had been written in a state of madness] – that she was sorry to say that a temporary confinement was necessary, and that she desired that I would make no reply to it.

5. (p. 266) *White . . . Vortigern*: James White (1775–1820) was a friend and exact contemporary of Lamb's at Christ's Hospital. He was the author (probably helped by Lamb) of *Original Letters, &c. of Sir John Falstaff and His Friends* (1796). William Henry Ireland's pseudo-Shakespearian *Vortigern and Rowena* had been unsuccessfully produced at Drury Lane in April 1796.

6. (p. 266) *your conciones ad populum*: Coleridge's *Conciones ad Populum; or Addresses to the People* had been published in Bristol in November 1795.

3. *To Samuel Taylor Coleridge*

1. (p. 269) *Sam Le Grice*: younger brother of Charles (see note 4, Letter 1, above), also at Christ's Hospital with Coleridge and Lamb.

2. (p. 270) *£130 or £120 a year*: Lamb's salary throughout his life was as follows: for the first three years at the East India House, beginning 5 April 1792, he received no official wages, but an annual gratuity of £30. After this probationary period he was given £40 for 1795–6, raised to £70 in 1796; this could be increased by extra work, and he received a small holiday grant. In 1797 his income was £80, in 1799 £90, and from then until 1814 it rose by £10 every second year.

3. (p. 270) *a necessarian*: the doctrine that the will is not free but subject to causes beyond it.

4. (p. 271) *Sara*: Sara Fricker (died 1845) was Southey's sister-in-law and married Coleridge in 1795.

5. *To Samuel Taylor Coleridge*

1. (p. 274) *little one*: David Hartley Coleridge (1796–1849), first child of the Coleridges, was born on 19 September.

6. *To Samuel Taylor Coleridge*

1. (p. 274) *a* caput mortuum, *not a* cor vivens: a 'dead head', not a 'living heart'.

2. (p. 274) *Thy Watchman's . . . verses*: at Easter the bellman, or watchman, would leave verses at the houses on his beat as a reminder of his importance.

3. (p. 274) *Rowland . . . Olivers*: Trading a Rowland for an Oliver is exchanging one extravagance for another.

4. (p. 276) *Hannah More*: (1745–1833), a prolix dramatist, novelist, and religious writer.

5. (p. 276) *Nature and Art*: a romance by Mrs Inchbald (1753–1821), published in 1796.

7. *To Samuel Taylor Coleridge*

1. (p. 277) *that second strophe*: the criticism in the first paragraph is of Coleridge's 'Ode on the Departing Year'.

2. (p. 277) *a dull gambogium*: gamboge is a yellow gum-resin.

3. (p. 278) *did the wand of Merlin wave*: from Coleridge's version of Lamb's sonnet 'Was it some sweet device of Faery'.

4. (p. 278) *Mr Merlin*: John Joseph Merlin (1735–1803) was a conjurer, and a watch, clock, engine and musical instrument maker, who came to London in 1760.

5. (p. 278) *inter se*: 'between themselves'.

6. (p. 278) *quoad famam*: 'with respect to reputation'.

7. (p. 279) *Susquehanah scheme*: Coleridge, Southey and Timothy Allen devised a scheme, in 1794, to found a kind of utopian society called a pantisocracy, on land owned by the theologian and scientist Joseph Priestley (1733–1804) on the banks of the Susquehanah, in Pennsylvania in the United States.

8. (p. 280) *a Berkleyan*: a believer in the idealism of the Irish philosopher George Berkeley (1685–1753).

9. (p. 280) *Woe . . . Kedar*: See Psalms 120:5.

10. (p. 280) *Ecquid . . . virtutem*: '(do you arouse in him) anything like ancient virtue?' (*Aeneid* 3, 342–3).

9. *To Samuel Taylor Coleridge*

1. (p. 283) *Theses Quædam Theologicæ*: 'Certain Theological Propositions'. A protracted disagreement between Lloyd, Coleridge and Lamb prompted this and the previous letter, after which Lamb broke off his correspondence with

Coleridge for nearly two years (for details of this, see Marrs, vol. 1, p. 129). After blaming Lamb for taking sides with Lloyd against him, Coleridge wrote to Lloyd: 'Poor Lamb . . . if he wants only knowledge, he may apply to me.' Lloyd showed this to Lamb, who responded with these Certain Theological Propositions.

2. (p. 283) *Virtutes . . . participes*: 'the less shining virtues redolent of earth and man'.

3. (p. 284) *vide Poems*: an allusion to Coleridge's 'To the Author of "The Robbers"', l. 12.

10. To Thomas Manning

1. (p. 284) *the Falstaff's Letters*: see Letter 1, note 5 (p. 420).

2. (p. 284) *Potosi*: a Bolivian city that was at this time a rich silver-mining centre.

3. (p. 284) *Bread, and Beer, and Coals*: Lamb is referring here to the cries of 'Bread, Peace and No Pitt' that people shouted at George III on his way to open parliament in October 1795. The war with France, and Pitt (Prime Minister and Chancellor of the Exchequer) introducing an income tax and perpetuating the land tax, meant that England was in the throes of financial panic.

4. (p. 284) *the Abbe Sieyes*: Abbé Emmanuel-Joseph Sieyes (1748–1836) was one of the influential theorists of the French Revolution.

5. (p. 284) *Burnet's Own Times*: Bishop Gilbert Burnet (1643–1715) wrote a *History of His Own Time* (1723–4).

11. To Samuel Taylor Coleridge

1. (p. 285) *Miss Wesley*: Sarah Wesley (1760–1828), daughter of Charles Wesley.

2. (p. 285) *jorum*: a large drinking bowl, or large drink.

3. (p. 286) *D'Israeli*: Isaac D'Israeli (1766–1848), author and father of Benjamin D'Israeli.

4. (p. 287) *Woodfall*: George Woodfall (1756–1836) and his father, Sampson, were the printers of Coleridge's translation of Wallenstein.

13. To Robert Lloyd

1. (p. 289) *Bishop Taylor*: Jeremy Taylor (1613–67), Bishop of Down and Connor and author of various religious works of which Lamb was consistently fond.

2. (p. 289) *Sophia's being brought to bed*: Lloyd's wife, Sophia, gave birth to a son, Charles, later that year.

14. To Samuel Taylor Coleridge

1. (p. 290) *the Post*: the *Morning Post*, which Coleridge wrote for in 1798.

2. (p. 290) *phlebotomising*: blood-letting. *The Anatomy of Melancholy* by Sir Robert Burton (1577–1640) was another of Lamb's favourite books.

3. (p. 290) *Lambe*: this was the spelling used by the *Anti-Jacobin* in 1798 when it attacked Coleridge, Southey, Lloyd and Lamb (among others) for being radicals.

4. (p. 290) *the Anthology*: the second volume of the *Annual Anthology*, edited by Southey, in which Coleridge's 'Lewti' was reprinted.

5. (p. 291) *don't make me ridiculous . . . verses*: in lines 28, 68 and 75 of Coleridge's poem 'This Lime-Tree Bower My Prison', Lamb is referred to as 'gentle-hearted Charles'.

6. (p. 291) *fate 'and wisest Stewart' say No*: an adaptation of l. 149 of Milton's 'On The Morning of Christ's Nativity'; Stewart is Daniel Stuart (1766–1846), editor of the *Morning Post* and the *Courier*.

7. (p. 291) *cum . . . caeteris*: 'with many books and things'.

16. To Samuel Taylor Coleridge

1. (p. 293) *your satire upon me*: Coleridge's poem 'This Lime-Tree Bower My Prison'.

2. (p. 293) *that scandalous piece . . . Devonshire*: a reference to Coleridge's poem 'Ode to Georgiana, Duchess of Devonshire'.

3. (p. 294) *Pauper . . . est*: [Cinna] wants to seem poor and poor he is' (Martial's *Epigrams*, VIII, l. 19).

4. (p. 294) *Mors, Febris, Pallor*: Roman deifications of death, sickness or torment, and fear.

17. To Thomas Manning

1. (p. 296) *the Tower Militia*: the part of the building that Lamb worked in was known as 'The Tower'.

2. (p. 297) *The Farmer's Boy*: a poem by Robert Bloomfield, an agricultural labourer from Suffolk, published in March 1800.

18. To Thomas Manning

1. (p. 297) *Ecquid . . . Archimedes*: 'what does Archimedes have in mind'.

2. (p. 297) *impedimenta viarum*: 'obstructions on the way'.

3. (p. 297) *racemi . . . pendentes*: 'branches hanging too high'.

4. (p. 297) *Mr Crisp*: Manning's landlord, and a barber by profession.

5. (p. 298) *Greek with Porson . . . Thelwall*: Richard Porson (1759–1808) was an editor of Euripides and, from 1792, Regius Professor of Greek at Cambridge. John Thelwall (1764–1834) was a friend of Coleridge's, and a Jacobin reformer.

6. (p. 298) *sapit hominem*: '[whatever] smacks of men' (Martial, X, 4).

7. (p. 298) *Kemble*: John Philip Kemble (1757–1823), the actor who was also a manager of Drury Lane. The play Lamb refers to is *Pride's Cure*.

19. To Thomas Manning

1. (p. 300) *beautiful Quakers of Pentonville*: probably a reference to Hester Savory (1777–1803), whom Lamb loved (but did not declare his love to) between 1800 and 1803 when he was living in Pentonville. She is commemorated in a poem of 1803, 'Hester'.

20. To Thomas Manning

1. (p. 301) *the other Professor*: William Godwin.

2. (p. 301) *Lawsuits . . . fire cause*: a reference to Godwin's *Enquiry Concerning the Principles of Political Justice* (Book 2, chapter 2). Godwin imagines that his mother, the Archbishop of Cambrai Fénelon and a chambermaid were caught in a fire in the Archbishop's Palace and debates which one should be saved if only one of them could be.

3. (p. 301) *Deo . . . nolente*: 'God willing and the devil not willing'.

4. (p. 302) *ortolans*: a kind of bunting.

21. To William Wordsworth

1. (p. 302) Probably the second volume of the second (1800) edition of *Lyrical Ballads*.

2. (p. 303) *St Leons*: a novel by William Godwin, published in 1799.

3. (p. 305) *Barbara Lewthwaite*: a reference to Wordsworth's poem 'The Pet Lamb: A Pastoral'.

4. (p. 305) *my Play*: *John Woodvill: a Tragedy* (1800).

22. To Robert Lloyd

1. (p. 305) *Walton*: Izaak Walton (1593–1683), author of *The Compleat Angler*.

2. (p. 305) *Holy Living . . . Thomas à Kempis*: Lamb is referring to Jeremy Taylor's *The Rule and Exercises of Holy Living* and Thomas à Kempis's *De Imitatione Christi*.

3. (p. 305) *Priscilla*: the Lloyds' sister (1782–1815) who married Christopher Wordsworth, the poet's brother.

4. (p. 305) *like a bribed haunch*: an allusion to Falstaff's remark to Mistress Ford (*The Merry Wives of Windsor* V, v), 'Divide me like a bribe buck, each a haunch'.

23. *To Thomas Manning*

1. (p. 307) *two quotations*: respectively, ll. 339–43 of 'Michael: a Pastoral', and ll. 98–9 of 'The Brothers'.

2. (p. 309) *that thing to Colman*: probably Lamb's play *John Woodvill*. The dramatist George Colman (1762–1836) was manager of the Haymarket theatre from 1789 to 1813.

3. (p. 309) *a Play on a Persian story*: William Godwin's play *Abbas, King of Persia*.

24. *To Thomas Manning*

1. (p. 310) *Elijah's widow*: the cruse would always pour oil (Kings 1:17. 12–16).

2. (p. 310) *pipkin*: an earthenware container for oil.

25. *To Robert Lloyd*

1. (p. 311) *Cooke*: George Frederick Cooke (1756–1811), actor.

2. (p. 312) *Overreach*: Sir Giles Overreach in Massinger's play *A New Way to Pay Old Debts*, which Lamb quotes below (V, i, 363–4).

3. (p. 312) *Pierre and Jaffier . . . Young's* Revenge: the references in this paragraph are as follows: Pierre, Jaffier and Belvidera are characters in *Venice Preserv'd*; Monimia in Otway's *The Orphan*; Calista in Nicholas Rowe's *The Fair Penitent*; and Alexander in Nathaniel Lee's *The Rival Queens*. The quotation is from Drayton's 'To My Most Dearly-loved Friend Henry Reynolds Esquire, of Poets and Poesie'. *All For Love* is by Dryden, and *The Revenge* by Edward Young.

4. (p. 312) *Plumstead*: one of the Lloyd brothers.

27. *To Robert Lloyd*

1. (p. 314) *benevolent . . . Brewer*: possibly Plumstead Lloyd.

28. *To Thomas Manning*

1. (p. 315) *I am his word-banker*: Manning had asked Lamb to keep his letters from abroad.

2. (p. 315) *Rumfordizing*: Sir Benjamin Thompson, Count von Rumford, was the founder of the Royal Institution, inventor of the Rumford stove and a relentless scientific and philosophical experimenter.

3. (p. 316) *Smelfungus*: Sterne refers to Smollet in *A Sentimental Journey* as 'the lamented smelfungus'.

4. (p. 316) *Stuart*: Daniel Stuart (1766–1846), proprietor of the *Morning Post*.

5. (p. 316) *Ludisti . . . abire est*: 'You have played enough, it is time to leave' (Horace, *Epistles* 2, 2, 214–15).

6. (p. 316) *The Professor's Rib*: in December 1801 Godwin had married Mrs Mary Jane Clairmont.

7. (p. 316) *Libera . . . amicis*: 'Free us writers from our friends'.

8. (p. 316) *The Londoner*: published in the *Morning Post*, 1 February 1802. Manning wrote to Lamb (6 April 1802): 'I like your Londoner very much, there is a deal of happy fancy in it, but it is not strong enough to be seen by the generality of readers. Yet if you would write a volume of Essays in the same stile you might be sure of its succeeding.'

9. (p. 318) *Mrs Shandy . . . Yorick*: from *Tristram Shandy*.

29. *To Thomas Manning*

1. (p. 319) *Stoddart*: Sir John Stoddart (1773–1856), a barrister of Lincoln's Inn, brother of Hazlitt's first wife, Sarah.

2. (p. 320) *the Clarksons*: Thomas Clarkson (1760–1846) was a reformer and anti-slavery agitator, becoming Vice-President of the Anti-Slavery Society. His wife, Catherine, was a childhood friend of Crabb Robinson and introduced him to Lamb, Coleridge and Wordsworth.

3. (p. 321) *St Gothard*: the pass in the Alps through which Manning had just walked.

4. (p. 321) *Fenwick*: John Fenwick (died 1820), author and editor. He owned and edited the *Albion*, which Lamb worked for briefly in 1801.

5. (p. 321) *nam . . . repono*: 'here I give up my gloves and the game [of boxing]' *Aenid* V, 484.

6. (p. 321) *Marshall*: Godwin's amanuensis and literary agent.

7. (p. 321) *Holcroft*: Thomas Holcroft (1745–1809), dramatist, novelist and translator, imprisoned for high treason in 1794.

30. *To Thomas Manning*

1. (p. 322) *Prester John*: an extraordinary Christian potentate who, according to legend (and various travel books, including Mandeville's), ruled remote regions of Asia and Africa in the twelfth century. Manning was about to sail for China.

2. (p. 322) *Hartley's method*: David Hartley (1705–57), English philosopher, physician and psychologist.

3. (p. 322) *foolish stories . . . brass*: a reference to Chaucer's *Squire's Tale*.

4. (p. 322) *Hellebore*: an ancient remedy for mental illness.

5. (p. 323) *the reverse of fishes . . . meat*: an allusion to Marvell's poem 'The Character of Holland', ll. 29–30: 'The fish ofttimes the burgher dispossessed/And sat not as a meat but as a guest.'

31. *To Thomas Manning*

1. (p. 324) *As Wordsworth sings . . . your love*: an allusion to Wordsworth's poem 'Poet's Epitaph'.

32. *To Thomas Manning*

1. (p. 325) *a sequel to 'Mrs Leicester'*: in 1809 Charles and Mary Lamb published *Poetry for Children*, and second editions of *Mrs Leicester's School* and *Tales from Shakespeare*.

2. (p. 325) *Hazlitt . . . life of Holcroft*: Hazlitt continued, so to speak, *The Memoirs of Thomas Holcroft*, which were published in 1816.

33. *To William Wordsworth*

1. (p. 329) *Alsager*: Thomas Alsager (1779–1846), musical and financial writer for *The Times*. It was after reading Alsager's copy of the folio of Chapman's *Homer* that Keats composed his famous sonnet.

2. (p. 329) *Heautontimorumenos:The Self-Tormentor*, a comedy by Terence.

3. (p. 329) *a curious letter . . . Habeas Corpus*: Capell Lofft (1751–1824), lawyer and philanthropist, wrote to the *Morning Chronicle* in August 1815. Lucas gives an account of his argument in one of the letters: 'Bonaparte, with the concurrence of the admiralty, is within the limits of British local allegiance. He is a temporary, considered as private, though not a natural born subject, and as such within the limits of 31 Car. II, the Habeas Corpus Act.'

4. (p. 330) *3 volumes . . . Drama*: *A course of Lectures on Dramatic Art and Literature* (1815) by von Schlegel, translated by Black.

5. (p. 330) *Did you ever read . . . Pilgrim*: *De la Sagess* (1601) by the French philosopher Pierre Charron, and *The Parable of the Pilgrim* (1664) by Simon Patrick, Bishop of Chichester and Ely.

34. *To William Wordsworth*

1. (p. 330) *the Revise of the Poems and letter*: the proofs of Wordsworth's 'Letter to a Friend of Burns', and his *Thanksgiving Ode with Other Short Pieces* (1816).

2. (p. 331) *mild Arcadians ever blooming*: from Pope's 'Song by a Person of Quality', l. 5.

3. (p. 331) *Gilman*: James Gillman (1782–1839), the doctor Coleridge went to stay with in April 1816. He planned to be there for a month and stayed for the rest of his life.

4. (p. 332) *Pleasure of Hope . . . Petition*: 'The Pleasure of Hope' (1799) by Thomas Campbell, and Thomas Moss's 'The Beggars Petition', were included in Lamb's *Poems on Several Occasions* (1769).

5. (p. 332) *a taking*: a passion.

35. *To William Wordsworth*

1. (p. 333) *Have you read . . . Examiner*: an unsigned review by Hazlitt in the *Examiner*, 8 September 1816.

2. (p. 333) *the fate of Cinna the Poet*: the poet of whom one of the mob in *Julius Caesar* shouts 'Tear him for his bad verses' (III, iii, 31).

3. (p. 333) *after all . . . abuse them*: this is Lamb's mis-remembering of a sentence from Francis Jeffrey's review of *The Excursion* in the *Edinburgh Review* of November 1814, which read: 'But the truth is, that Mr Wordsworth, with all his perversities, is a person of great powers.'

4. (p. 333) *agnomen or agni-nomen*: 'fourth name' or 'lamb-name'.

5. (p. 333) *H—*: Hazlitt.

6. (p. 334) *M. would have had 'em . . . Crispin did for me*: William Gifford (1756–1826), of the *Quarterly Review*, seems to have persuaded the publisher John Murray to reject an offer Barron Field had made to Murray to publish two volumes of Lamb's essays.

36. *To Charles Chambers*

1. (p. 335) *on account of Quin*: the actor James Quin (1693–1766). Portrayed as Jeremy Midford in Smollett's *Humphrey Clinker*, he had wanted to send for the head of the cook who 'had committed felony, on the person of that John Dory, which is mangled in a cruel manner, and even presented without sauce – O Tempora! O Mores!'

2. (p. 335) *Apicius and Heliogabalus*: see note 6 to 'Edax on Appetite' (p. 404).

3. (p. 336) *a fine story about Truss*: this is Lamb's story. William Henry Truss was appointed as an extra clerk in the East India House in 1800.

4. (p. 336) *Dr Parr . . . dead*: Dr Samuel Parr (1747–1825) was not two months dead until 6 May 1825.

37. *To Mrs William Wordsworth*

1. (p. 337) *Miss Burrell*: Fanny Burrell (born 1795), actress and singer.

2. (p. 337) *Fanny Kelly*: Francis Maria Kelly (1790–1882), actress and singer, to whom Lamb proposed in July 1819. She refused him – apparently, though Lamb may not have known this, for fear of what she took to be the taint of insanity in the family.

3. (p. 337) *Lalla Rooks*: 'Lalla Rooke' (1817), a poem by Thomas Moore (1779–1852).

4. (p. 340) *as there seemd to be . . . Haydons*: see Appendix One (p. 392).

38. *To Dorothy Wordsworth*

1. (p. 340) *Willy*: this letter refers to the visit of Wordsworth's son William, then nine years old, to the Lambs.

2. (p. 340) *Virgilium Tantum Vidi*: 'I saw a man as great as Virgil' (Ovid, 'Tristia', 4, 10, 51).

3. (p. 340) *Lord Foppington*: a character in Vanbrugh's play *The Relapse*.

4. (p. 341) *Halley*: (1656–1742) second Astronomer Royal, who successfully predicted the re-run of the comet that bears his name.

5. (p. 341) *a certain Preface*: Wordsworth's preface to the 1815 edition of his poems.

6. (p. 341) *ex traduce*: 'by tradition'.

7. (p. 341) *the famous American boy*: Zerah Colburn, who was a mathematical prodigy. He was born in Vermont in 1804, and exhibited by his father in America and Europe.

39. *To Joseph Cottle*

1. (p. 342) *your second kind present*: a copy of Cottle's poem 'Fall of Cambria'. In 1820, Cottle had published an 'Expostulatory Epistle to Lord Byron', who had ridiculed Cottle's brother in 'English Bards and Scotch Reviewers'.

40. *To Samuel Taylor Coleridge*

1. (p. 343) *Owen*: Lamb's landlord in Russell Street.

41. *To William Wordsworth*

1. (p. 344) *poor John's Loss*: John Lamb (1763–1821), Charles's elder brother, died in October 1821.

2. (p. 345) *capite dolente*: 'sorrowful head'.

3. (p. 345) *Tædet me . . . formarum*: 'I am tired of these everyday forms' (Terence, 'Eunuchus' 2, 3, 6).

4. (p. 345) *The foul enchanter . . . enfranchisement*: Busirane is the 'foul enchanter' from whom Britomart rescues Amoret in Spenser's *Faerie Queene* 3, 11; *letters four do form his name* is Coleridge's reference to Pitt in 'Fire, Famine and Slaughter': here they refer to Joseph Hume, M.P. (1777–1855), who had successfully attacked 'abuses' in the East India Company, revised the system of collecting revenue (affecting Wordsworth as distributor of stamps) and opposed a scheme for reducing pension charges.

5. (p. 345) *Otium cum indignitate*: 'Freedom with indignity'.

6. (p. 345) *Lord Palmerston's report . . . graves*: the report in *The Times* of 21 March had said, among other things, that 'since 1810 not fewer than 26 clerks had died of pulmonary complaints, and disorders arising from sedentary habits'.

7. (p. 346) *the Malvolio story*: a reference to Lamb's essay 'On Some of the Old Actors', *London Magazine*, February 1822.

8. (p. 346) *Hartley*: Coleridge's son Hartley, who was twenty-five and living in London.

42. *To John Clare*

1. (p. 346) *your present*: Clare, who had met Lamb, possibly, the previous year, had sent him his *Poems, Descriptive of Rural Life and Scenery* (1820), and *The Village Minstrel and Other Poems* (1821).

2. (p. 346) *Shenstone*: William Shenstone (1714–63).

3. (p. 347) *a little volume*: *Tracts* by Sir Thomas Browne.

4. (p. 347) *I have been in France*: in August 1822 Lamb and Mary went to France. It was his only trip abroad.

43. *To Walter Wilson*

1. (p. 347) *Dodwell . . . Wadd*: two East India House clerks, old colleagues of Wilson's.

2. (p. 347) *I have nothing of Defoe's*: Wilson was beginning to write his *Memoirs of the Life and Times of Daniel Defoe*, published in 1830.

44. *To Bernard Barton*

1. (p. 349) *the steep Tarpeian rock*: a cliff overhanging the Roman forum from which murderers and traitors were thrown.

2. (p. 349) *Baldwin*: Robert Baldwin was the senior partner in the publishing firm of Baldwin, Cradock and Joy who, on 1 January 1820, started the *London Magazine*. He sold it to Taylor and Hessey in 1821 after the death of John Scott, the editor.

45. *To Bernard Barton*

1. (p. 350) *Hessey*: James Augustus Hessey (1785–1875), publisher and partner in the firm of Taylor and Hessey, who published the *London Magazine* from 1821 to 5.

2. (p. 350) *old Alcinous*: king Alcinous in the Odyssey, father of Nausicaa. He owned a large orchard of fruit trees.

3. (p. 350) *Proctor*: see Biographical Index (p. 400).

4. (p. 351) *Wainwright*: Thomas Griffiths Wainewright (1794–1847), painter and prose writer, who contributed to the *London Magazine* from the first issue until early in 1823; one of his pseudonyms was Janus Weathercock.

5. (p. 351) *Mr Pulham*: a clerk in the East India House who in 1825 made a famous etching of Lamb talking to his colleagues at work.

6. (p. 351) *Mr Cary*: Henry Francis Cary (1772–1844) published a famous translation of *The Divine Comedy* in 1814. From 1826 to 1837 (roughly the period of his friendship with Lamb) he was Assistant Keeper of Printed Books at the British Museum.

46. *To Bernard Barton*

1. (p. 352) *Judge Park ... Thurtell ... Jack Ketch*: on 6–7 January 1824, in a famous murder trial, Thurtell was convicted of the murder of William Weare of Lyon's Inn. The presiding judge was Sir James Alan Park, and Thurtell was hanged at Hertford on 9 January, on a gallows of his own design. Ketch was the proverbial name for the hangman, who was always allowed the dead man's clothes.

2. (p. 352) *baiting at Scorpion*: the sign of the zodiac passed on the way to the next world.

47. *To Bernard Barton*

1. (p. 353) *Poetic Vigils*: Barton's fourth book of verse, published in 1824.

48. *To Bernard Barton*

1. (p. 354) *Southey's Book*: The Book of the Church.

2. (p. 354) *Wilberforce*: William Wilberforce (1759–1833), abolitionist, parliamentarian and one of the leading Puritans of the time.

3. (p. 355) *RELIGIO ... TREMEBUNDI*: 'the religion of a trembling man or of trembling piety'.

49. To Bernard Barton

1. (p. 356) *Montgomery's book*: James Montgomery (1771–1854), poet and editor who compiled an *Album* in 1824 to be sold in aid of child chimney-sweeps, for which Lamb sent him a copy of Blake's 'The Chimney Sweeper'.

2. (p. 356) *The Society, with the affected name*: The Society for Ameliorating the Condition of Infant Chimney Sweepers.

3. (p. 356) *the Dream . . . from B.*: the Album ended with three 'Climbing-Boys Soliloquys' by Montgomery, the second of which used the dream in Blake's Song.

4. (p. 356) *we have lost another Poet*: Byron had died, 19 April 1824.

50. To Thomas Manning

1. (p. 357) *Tuthill*: Sir George Leman Tuthill (1772–1835), the physician. In 1825, he was co-signatory with James Gillman for the medical report which enabled Lamb to retire on 29 March 1825.

2. (p. 357) *To all my nights . . . masterdom*: from Macbeth I, v, 67–8.

51. To William Wordsworth

1. (p. 357) *poor Monkhouse*: Thomas Monkhouse (1783–1825), a London merchant. Cousin of the Hutchinsons' and related, by marriage, to Wordsworth.

2. (p. 358) *Leigh Hunt and Montgomery*: both editors and poets imprisoned for political libels.

3. (p. 359) *Irving*: Edward Irving (1792–1834), Scottish minister and schoolmaster who founded the Catholic Apostolic Church.

4. (p. 359) *videlicet*: 'evidently'.

52. To Samuel Taylor Coleridge

1. (p. 359) *Allsop's*: Thomas Allsop (1795–1880), silk-merchant and stockbroker; a friend of Coleridge and Lamb, he sent them presents of game. He was one of the executors of Lamb's will of 1823.

2. (p. 359) *vide Lond. Mag . . . July*: Lamb is referring to his essay 'The Convalescent'.

3. (p. 359) *Hood*: Thomas Hood (1799–1845), writer. His *Odes and Addresses to Great People*, written in collaboration with J. H. Reynolds, was published in 1825.

4. (p. 360) *Mag. Ignotum*: the 'Ode to the Great Unknown', the author of the Scotch novels.

5. (p. 360) *your Enigma about Cupid*: a reference to Coleridge's *Aids to Reflection* (1825): 'And most noteable it is, that soon after the promulgation and spread of the Gospel had awakened the moral sense, and had opened the eyes even of its wiser Enemies to the necessity of providing some solution to this great problem of the Moral World, the beautiful Parable of Cupid and Psyche was brought forward as a rival (in italics) FALL OF MAN: and the fact of a moral corruption connatural with the human race was again recognised.'

6. (p. 360) *Signor Non-vir sed VELUTI Vir*: the Italian castrato, Giovanni Battista Velluti (1781–1861), who first appeared in England in 1825.

7. (p. 360) *Nos DURUM genus*: 'we are a hard race [who know what work is]'; from Ovid's *Metamorphoses* l. 414.

8. (p. 360) *Olim Clericus*: 'once a clerk'.

53. *To Bernard Barton*

1. (p. 361) *Ann Knight*: a Quaker who kept a school at Woodbridge, where Barton was staying at the time.

2. (p. 362) *Taylor has dropt the London*: Henry Southern took over the *London Magazine* in September 1825.

3. (p. 362) *Lucy*: Barton's daughter.

54. *To Bernard Barton*

1. (p. 362) *George 3 trying the 100th psalm*: a reference to the end of Byron's 'Vision of Judgement'; 'All I saw farther, in the last confusion,/Was, that King George slipp'd into heaven for one;/And when the tumult dwindled to a calm,/I left him practising the hundredth psalm.'

55. *To John Bates Dibdin*

1. (p. 363) *D.*: John Bates Dibdin (*c.* 1799–1829) was a clerk with a London shipping office, Rankings, who met Lamb at East India House. He had gone to Hastings to recover his health and seems to have been living above a baker's.

2. (p. 364) *the little church*: Hollington Rural Church.

3. (p. 365) *Probatum est*: 'it is proven'.

4. (p. 365) *Peter Fin Junr.*: a character in Richard Jones's play of 1822, *Peter Finn's Trip to Brighton*.

5. (p. 365) *Tommy Hill*: Thomas Hill (1760–1840). Drysalter, book-collector, bon vivant, dilettante and gossip who gave dinners for the literary.

56. To Peter George Patmore

1. (p. 365) *Patmore*: Peter George Patmore (1786–1855), author and editor. A friend of Hazlitt's, who introduced him to Lamb in 1826.

2. (p. 365) *Dash*: Thomas Hood's large dog, which had stayed with the Lambs at Enfield.

3. (p. 365) *aperto ore*: 'with mouth uncovered'.

57. To Mrs Basil Montagu

1. (p. 367) *Dear Madam*: see note 1 to Letter 69 (p. 437).

2. (p. 367) *Clarkson*: see note 2 to Letter 29 (p. 426).

3. (p. 367) *Howard's*: John Howard (the philanthropist) and Dr Johnson were the first statues erected in St Paul's.

4. (p. 367) *Wade Mill*: where Clarkson's memorial stands, in Hertfordshire.

58. To Barron Field

1. (p. 368) *For Mathews ... such a task*: Charles James Mathews (1803–78), actor and dramatist. He suggested, through Field, that Lamb should write the descriptions for the catalogue of Mathews's collection of theatrical portraits.

2. (p. 368) *an imitator of me ... Calais*: P. G. Patmore, in his *Rejected Articles*, published in 1826.

3. (p. 369) *Emma*: Emma Isola (1809–91), who first met the Lambs at Cambridge in 1820. By 1821 she was visiting the Lambs regularly and was virtually adopted by them, as she was an orphan. Wordsworth had been taught at Cambridge by her grandfather. She married Edward Moxon, the publisher, in 1833.

4. (p. 369) *nec sinit esse feros*: from Ovid (Ep. ex Ponto, II, 9, 47): 'Ingenuas didicisse fideliter artes/Emollit mores, nec sinit esse feros'; 'A careful study of the arts refines the manners, stops their becoming crude'.

59. To Bernard Barton

1. (p. 369) *a splendid ... Bunyan's Pilgrim*: published by John Murray in 1830, with a *Life of Bunyan* by Southey and illustrations by John Martin and W. Harvey.

2. (p. 370) *Pidcock's*: Pidcock showed his lions at Bartholomew Fair.

3. (p. 370) *Mitford's Salamander God*: possibly a reference to something in the collection of Revd John R. Mitford (1781–1859), a writer, scholar and book-collector that Lamb knew.

4. (p. 370) *the Gem*: a magazine edited by Thomas Hood.

5. (p. 371) *Mathews and Yates*: joint managers of the Adelphi Theatre.

6. (p. 371) *W. Scott . . . bribe haunch*: Sir Walter Scott (1771–1832). For 'a bribe haunch', see note 4 to Letter 22 (p. 425).

60. *To Bryan Waller Procter*

1. (p. 372) *the Abactor*: cattle-thief.
2. (p. 372) *vide Ainsworth*: a reference to Robert Ainsworth's *Thesaurus* (1736), which gives only 'abactus – driven away by force'.
3. (p. 372) *Per occasionem cujus*: 'instigated by this (occasion)'.

61. *To Henry Crabb Robinson*

1. (p. 373) *your strange shaped present*: on setting off for Rome, Crabb Robinson had sent Lamb a copy of Richardson's *Pamela*, thinking that he had borrowed one.
2. (p. 373) *two Mr B.'s*: in Richardson's novel, Pamela marries and reforms the young squire B.

62. *To Henry Crabb Robinson*

1. (p. 374) *Doubly Dumby*: a form of whist in which two 'hands' are exposed, so that each of the two players manages two 'hands'.

63. *To Henry Crabb Robinson*

1. (p. 374) *the report of thy torments*: Crabb Robinson had gone to have a course of Turkish baths at Brighton to treat a sudden attack of acute rheumatism.
2. (p. 374) *Grimaldi*: Joseph Grimaldi, the clown.
3. (p. 375) *ad libitum*: for pleasure.

64. *To Bernard Barton*

1. (p. 375) *Idumean palm*: a reference to Virgil, *Georgics* 3, 12.
2. (p. 375) *Lucy*: see note 3 to Letter 53 (p. 433).
3. (p. 376) *Emma*: see note 3 to Letter 58 (p. 434).
4. (p. 376) *Eliza*: Barton's sister.
5. (p. 376) *an old rejected farce*: *The Pawnbroker's Daughter*, which was printed in *Blackwood*, January 1830.

65. *To James Gillman*

1. (p. 377) *Squire Mellish*: William Mellish, at that time MP for Middlesex.

2. (p. 377) *Thomas Westwood*: Westwood had been a haberdasher, and after his retirement was an agent for an insurance company. In 1827, the Westwoods were next-door neighbours of the Lambs at Enfield, and in October 1829 the Lambs gave up their house and lodged with the Westwoods until 1833.

3. (p. 378) *augustiæ domûs*: 'straitened means at home', a reference to Juvenal's *Satires* 3, 165 and 6, 357.

4. (p. 378) *in formâ*: 'in shape'.

5. (p. 379) *Bellerophon*: a Corinthian of remarkable beauty and courage.

6. (p. 379) *specilla*: here meaning 'glasses'.

66. *To Mary Shelley*

1. (p. 380) *Mrs Shelley*: Mary Shelley (1797–1851), author of *Frankenstein* and other novels, Shelley's second wife and the daughter of William Godwin and his first wife, Mary Wollstonecraft.

67. *To William Wordsworth*

1. (p. 381) *punctum stans*: 'a small point in time'.

2. (p. 381) *otium pro dignitate*: 'leisure for the sake of dignity'.

3. (p. 381) *Eloisa . . . Paraclete*: Abelard's monastic school was later occupied by Eloisa.

4. (p. 381) *the Red Gauntlet*: by Walter Scott, published in 1824.

5. (p. 382) *a calenture*: a fever or delirium that usually occurs aboard ship in tropical climates.

6. (p. 382) *the collyrium of Tobias*: a collyrium is an eye-salve or poultice.

7. (p. 382) *propriâ manu*: 'with her own hand'.

8. (p. 383) *dii avertant*: 'let the gods avert it'.

9. (p. 383) *the plunge of Curtius*: there was a story that a chasm once opened in the forum in Rome which could be closed up only if Rome's greatest treasure was thrown into it. At this point the brave Curtius, fully mounted and armed, leapt in: all that remained was a dried-up pool, called Lacus Curtius.

10. (p. 384) *the Sceptre of Agamemnon*: see the *Iliad* 1, 234.

11. (p. 384) *his soul is Begoethed*: Crabb Robinson, a friend of Goethe's, had recently visited Goethe in Weimar, who told him that he admired Lamb's sonnet 'The Family Name'.

68. *To Dr J. Vale Asbury*

1. (p. 385) *Dear Sir*: Dr J. Vale Asbury (1792–1871) was a doctor at Enfield who treated Emma Isola in 1830.

2. (p. 385) *metheglin*: a Welsh fermented liquor made from honey.

3. (p. 385) *a palanquin*: a litter for one person, consisting of a box on poles carried on men's shoulders.

4. (p. 386) *iii pol . . . can*: an invented prescription suggesting three medium pills to be taken at night, but with what else is not clear.

69. *To Basil Montagu*

1. (p. 386) *Montagu*: Basil Montagu (1770–1851), barrister, author, humanitarian and early friend of Wordsworth and Coleridge's.

2. (p. 387) *putting up . . . Woodstock*: Montagu was considering standing as MP for Woodstock.

3. (p. 387) *Horne Tooke . . . Erskine*: John Horne Tooke (1736–1812), politician and philologist. In May 1794 Hardy, Thelwall and Tooke, among others, were tried for treason and acquitted due largely to the defence of the Whig lawyer, Erskine.

70. *To George Dyer*

1. (p. 387) *the inflammatory fever*: Lamb is referring to the incendiarism by agricultural workers at this time, who were reacting to poor wages and the competition of new machinery.

2. (p. 388) *those apples of Asphaltes and bitumen*: see Milton's *Paradise Lost*, 10, 564–7.

3. (p. 388) *Fuimus panes . . . Apple-pasty-orum*: 'we loaves have had our day', from *Aeneid* 2, 325: 'Fuimus Troes, fuit Ilium et ingens/ Gloria Teucrorum': 'no longer are we Trojans; Ilium and the great glory of the Teucrians has gone'.

71. *To Thomas Allsop*

1. (p. 389) *Thomas Allsop*: see note 1 to Letter 52 (p. 432).

72. *To Maria Fryer*

1. (p. 389) *Maria Fryer* (died *c.* 1848) was a friend and school-fellow of Emma Isola.

2. (p. 389) *the Waldens*: the Waldens let lodgings in their Edmonton house to mental patients, as Mr Walden had previously worked in an asylum. Mary Lamb stayed there when she couldn't remain at home. In 1833, Lamb thought she should be there permanently; he moved in with her, living there until he died.

3. (p. 390) *That is a book you should read*: Izaak Walton's *Compleat Angler*.

4. (p. 390) *Woolman's*: John Woolman (1720–72) was an American Quaker minister and writer who moved to England; his *Journal* was one of Lamb's favourite books.

73. *To Henry Francis Cary*

1. (p. 390) *Henry Francis Cary*: see note 6 to Letter 45 (p. 431). This letter is undated and Lucas gives it as 1834.

2. (p. 391) *the Buffam Graces*: Lamb's landladies at Southampton Buildings. The Lambs lived there in 1809 and 1830, and usually stayed there whenever they went to London.

3. (p. 391) *that Argus Portitor*: the gate-keeper who seemed, like Argus guarding Io, to have a hundred eyes.

4. (p. 391) *I passed by the walls of Balclutha*: a line from Ossian. The poet James Macpherson (1736–96) published *Fragments of Ancient Poetry Collected in the Highlands* (1760) and *Fingal* (1762), an epic poem supposed to have been translated from the original of Ossian, a Gaelic bard.

5. (p. 391) *Silenus . . . Chromius . . . Mnasilus*: in Book 6 of Virgil's *Eclogues*, Chromis appears with Mnasilus as a friend of Silenus.

6. (p. 391) *pudet*: 'he is ashamed'.

Penguin Classics

SIR THOMAS BROWNE

THE MAJOR WORKS

Edited by C. A. Patrides

'Men that look upon my outside, perusing only my condition, and fortunes, do erre in my altitude; for I am above Atlas his shoulders.'

The highly modulated rhythms of Sir Thomas Browne's prose encompass a tonal range unique by any standards. His interests included theology as much as embryology, and philology no less than cartography. Of his six major works, all brilliant examples of his art, five are here made available in full: *Religio Medici*, *Hydriotaphia*, *The Garden of Cyrus*, *A Letter to a Friend* and *Christian Morals*. In addition there are substantial selections from *Pseudodoxia Epidemica*, his colossal exploration of 'vulgar errors'.

This volume also contains Dr Samuel Johnson's 'Life of Sir Thomas Browne', while the fully explanatory notes incorporate Coleridge's perceptive comments as well as textual variants. The editor's introduction and extensive bibliography will be of the greatest use to student and general reader alike.

CHRISTOPHER MARLOWE

THE COMPLETE PLAYS

Edited by J. B. Steane

In recent years there has been a widening of opinion about Marlowe; at one extreme he is considered an atheist rebel and at the other a Christian traditionalist. There is as much divergence in Marlowe's seven plays and, as J. B. Steane says in his introduction, that a man's work should encompass the extremes of *Tamburlaine* and *Edward the Second* is one of the most absorbingly interesting facts of literature; the range of Marlowe's small body of work covers such amazingly unlike pieces as *Doctor Faustus* and *The Jew of Malta*. Controlled and purposeful, these plays contain a poetry which enchants and lodges in the mind.

Penguin Classics

HENRY FIELDING

TOM JONES

Edited by R. P. C. Mutter

'I am shocked to hear you quote from so vicious a book. I am sorry to hear you have read it . . .' So said Dr Johnson of *Tom Jones*, and there were those who held it responsible for the two earthquake shocks which hit London shortly after its publication in 1749. Few readers will nowadays subscribe to such a view. For most readers this is one of the great comic novels in the English language, a vivid Hogarthian panorama of eighteenth-century life, with a plot which Coleridge described as one of the three most perfect ever planned. In addition *Tom Jones* possesses an underlying seriousness and all the rich and generous humanity of its author.

SAMUEL RICHARDSON

PAMELA

Introduction by Margaret A. Doody
Edited by Peter Sabor

When *Pamela, or Virtue Rewarded* appeared in two volumes in November 1740 it was an immediate bestseller, the first example of that phenomenon in the history of English fiction. Told in a series of letters to her parents, it is the story of a serving maid, Pamela Andrews, who, on the death of her mistress, is relentlessly pursued by the lady's son, Mr B. In Richardson's words, he tries 'by all manner of temptation to seduce her' but she indignantly repels him with 'many innocent stratagems to escape the snares laid for her virginity'.

The publication of the novel was followed by a 'Pamela' rage – motifs appeared on teacups and fans, Richardson produced a two-volume sequel in 1741, and Fielding wrote the famous parodies *Shamela* and *Joseph Andrews*. Many praised the novel enthusiastically for both its liveliness and its morality, but some condemned it as undignified and low, seeing in the servant girl's story a pernicious 'levelling' tendency. It is certainly a revolutionary book: it changed the life of the novel as a literary genre. This edition of the first part of *Pamela*, based on the 1801 text and incorporating corrections made in 1810, makes Richardson's final version of the original two-volume novel generally available for the first time.

Penguin Poetry

WILLIAM WORDSWORTH

THE PRELUDE

A Parallel Text edited by J. C. Maxwell

Wordsworth's great autobiographical poem, subtitled *Growth of a Poet's Mind*, was completed in 1805–6. During the rest of his life his interest in the work persisted, and the poem was several times revised, to be published soon after his death in 1850. Originally intended as the first part of a massive three-part poem, *The Prelude* contains some of the greatest poetry Wordsworth wrote on those events and feelings of his youth which lie behind so much of his most powerful work.

Critics and readers have differed over the relative merits of the 1805–6 and 1850 versions of the poem. The two versions are here presented in parallel for the first time in a paperback edition, and the edition has been so designed as to enable the reader to follow either version without interruption, or to compare the versions should he so wish. The manuscripts have been re-examined and many errors in both texts corrected from manuscript evidence. The editor's introduction and notes comment on the manuscript history of the poem and deal with points of difficulty.

SAMUEL TAYLOR COLERIDGE

POEMS AND PROSE

A Selection by Kathleen Raine

'His genius . . .' wrote William Hazlitt, 'had angelic wings and fed on manna. He talked on for ever; and you wished him to talk on for ever . . .'

Like no other poet Coleridge was, in five short years, 'visited by the Muse'. The flowering of his poetry happened, above all, in the single year from the summer of 1797 when he first became friends with Dorothy and William Wordsworth. That was the year in which he wrote *The Ancient Mariner*, the first part of *Christabel*, *Kubla Khan* and other poems that were, as Kathleen Raine writes, 'the works not of his talent but of his genius'.

As well as Coleridge's finest poems, this Penguin Poetry Library edition contains selections from his letters and his main critical writings, including extracts from *Biographia Literaria* and several of his revolutionary essays on Shakespeare.

Penguin Classics

WILLIAM MAKEPEACE THACKERAY

VANITY FAIR

Edited by J. I. M. Stewart

In *Vanity Fair* there is, to quote Thackeray, 'a great quantity of eating and drinking, making love and jilting, laughing and the contrary, smoking, cheating, fighting, dancing and fiddling: there are bullies pushing about, bucks ogling the women, knaves picking pockets, policemen on the look-out, quacks bawling in front of their booths, and yokels looking up at the tinselled dancers and poor old rouged tumblers.'

Through this free-wheeling mêlée of brilliant improvisations sail Becky Sharp, one of literature's most resourceful, engaging and amoral characters, and Amelia Sedley, her less lustrous but more ambiguous foil. Their story is, in J. I. M. Stewart's words, 'a land-mark in the history of English fiction'.

HENRY JAMES

THE GOLDEN BOWL

Introduction by Gore Vidal
Notes by Patricia Crick

'*The Golden Bowl* is a work unique among all his novels: it is James's only novel in which things come out right for his characters ... He had finally resolved the questions, curious and passionate, that had kept him at his desk in his inquiries into the process of living. He could now make his peace with America – and he could now collect and unify the work of a lifetime' – Leon Edel in *The Life of Henry James*

'When he died one felt there was no one to ask about anything. Up to then one felt someone knew' – Ezra Pound

Penguin Classics

HERMAN MELVILLE

MOBY DICK

Edited by Harold Beaver

'It is of the horrible texture of a fabric that should be woven of ships' cables and hawsers. A Polar wind blows through it, and birds of prey hover over it.'

So wrote Melville about his masterpiece; and into his tale of Captain Ahab's insane quest of the white whale he poured all of his own youthful experience and a minute study of the literature of whales and whaling; but into it also went other experiences, other reading, other insights ... into the 'power of blackness' and the deepest dreams and obsessions of mankind.

WILLIAM JAMES

VARIETIES OF RELIGIOUS EXPERIENCE

Edited by Martin E. Marty

In this classic work William James explores the psychology of religion, applying the scientific method to a field that had previously been treated as theoretical, abstract philosophy. James believed that individual religious experiences, rather than the precepts of organized religions, were the backbone of the world's religious life. His discussions of conversion, repentance, mysticism and saintliness, and his observations on actual, personal religious experiences all support this thesis.

In his Introduction, Martin E. Marty discusses how James's pluralistic view of religion led to his remarkable tolerance for extreme forms of religious behaviour, a willingness to take risks in formulating his own theories, and a welcome lack of pretentiousness in his observations on how an individual stands in relation to the divine.

Penguin Fiction

SAUL BELLOW
MR SAMMLER'S PLANET

To escape the European horror Mr Sammler was obliged to crawl from his own grave – and to kill. There seems to be no escaping the continuing American horror. Everyone, it appears, suffers from a mania for explaining everything and understanding nothing.

With accurate but reluctant frequency, Mr Sammler divines the sickness of the present and recalls the madness of the past. His global sensitivity (he knows what might be happening everywhere) seems to be his own disease. He is assured by Dr Lal that a perfect society is attainable – on the moon. Meanwhile, on Mr Sammler's planet, so recognizably our own, there seems to be little chance of getting it. Unless we all learn to suffer from Mr Sammler's disease.

ISAAC BASHEVIS SINGER
ENEMIES: A LOVE STORY

Herman Broder is his own worst enemy. A survivor of the Nazi holocaust, he has arrived in New York an embittered, soulless man. Three women love him – his wife, his mistress, and Tamara, who he believed had been shot in Poland. In the circumstances of his extraordinary dilemma, there is no room for further complications. But Herman loves all three women, and hates himself. So, as they say, with friends like that, who needs enemies?

'Recognizably the creation of the greatest living novelist' – Dame Rebecca West in the *Sunday Telegraph*

Pelican Books

SIGMUND FREUD

THE INTERPRETATION OF DREAMS

The Interpretation of Dreams is generally agreed to be Freud's major and most original work. By a detailed investigation of these universal phenomena he discovered a way of exploring the unconscious, recognized that dreams, like neurotic symptoms, are products of a conflict and compromise between conscious and unconscious impulses and was able to classify the differences between the primary and secondary processes of thought – between the modes of functioning in the unconscious and conscious regions of the mind. In addition Freud was led to revise his methods of treatment for neurotic patients by introducing the valuable technical adjunct of dream-interpretation and to develop, largely based on this remarkable work, his revolutionary theories of the Oedipus complex and of the profound importance of infantile life and sexuality for the development of adults.

Although depressed by its initially cool reception, Freud wrote in the Preface to the third English edition: 'It contains, even according to my present-day judgement, the most valuable of all the discoveries it has been my good fortune to make. Insight such as this falls to one's lot but once in a lifetime.'

D. W. WINNICOTT

PLAYING AND REALITY

Dreaming, playing, creativity, cultural experience and the often hidden rivalry between a male and a female element in the individual are among the apparently random topics discussed by Dr Winnicott in this study. The connection, however, lies in what are termed 'transitional objects' and phenomena – the rags, dolls and teddy-bears which provide a child's first 'not-me' experience.

With its case-histories, its comments on the motivation of artists and its tentative and attractive manner of thinking aloud, Dr Winnicott's last book makes a fitting epilogue to his famous books on childhood. It exposes the roots of that *joie de vivre* he frequently awakened in others – children and adults alike.

ENGLISH AND AMERICAN
LITERATURE IN PENGUINS

☐ *Main Street* **Sinclair Lewis** £4.95

The novel that added an immortal chapter to the literature of America's Mid-West, *Main Street* contains the comic essence of Main Streets everywhere.

☐ *The Compleat Angler* **Izaak Walton** £2.50

A celebration of the countryside, and the superiority of those in 1653, as now, who love *quietnesse, vertue* and, above all, *Angling*. 'No fish, however coarse, could wish for a doughtier champion than Izaak Walton' – Lord Home

☐ *The Portrait of a Lady* **Henry James** £2.50

'One of the two most brilliant novels in the language', according to F. R. Leavis, James's masterpiece tells the story of a young American heiress, prey to fortune-hunters but not without a will of her own.

☐ *Hangover Square* **Patrick Hamilton** £3.95

Part love story, part thriller, and set in the publands of London's Earls Court, this novel caught the conversational tone of a whole generation in the uneasy months before the Second World War.

☐ *The Rainbow* **D. H. Lawrence** £2.50

Written between *Sons and Lovers* and *Women in Love, The Rainbow* covers three generations of Brangwens, a yeoman family living on the borders of Nottinghamshire.

☐ *Vindication of the Rights of Woman*
Mary Wollstonecraft £2.95

Although Walpole once called her 'a hyena in petticoats', Mary Wollstonecraft's vision was such that modern feminists continue to go back and debate the arguments so powerfully set down here.

B446